RURAL LAND TAKINGS LAW IN MODERN CHINA

One of the most pressing issues in contemporary China is the massive rural land takings that have taken place at a scale unprecedented in human history. Expropriation of land has dispossessed and displaced millions for several decades, despite the protection of property rights in the Chinese Constitution. Combining meticulous doctrinal analysis with in-depth historical investigation, Chun Peng tracks the origin and evolution of China's rural land takings law over the twentieth century and demonstrates an enduring tradition of land takings for state-led social transformation, under which the takings law is designed to be power-confirming. With changed sociopolitical circumstances and a new rights-respecting constitutional agenda, a rebalance of the law is now underway, but only within existing parameters. Peng provides a piercing analysis of how land has been used by the largest developing country in the world to develop itself, at what costs and where the future might be.

Chun Peng is Assistant Professor at Peking University Law School. He received his doctorate and master's degree in law from the University of Oxford and holds a double degree in law and economics from Peking University. He has published widely on Chinese constitutional law, administrative law and comparative law in English and Chinese. Besides scholarly work, he writes op-eds on China and the world at *The Diplomat*, *China Daily* and *Caixin*. He also provides consultancy to the Ministry of Land and Natural Resources and local governments on legal reforms in China.

RURAL LAND TAKINGS LAW IN MODERN CHINA

Origin and Evolution

CHUN PENG
Peking University

CAMBRIDGE
UNIVERSITY PRESS

CAMBRIDGE
UNIVERSITY PRESS

University Printing House, Cambridge CB2 8BS, United Kingdom

One Liberty Plaza, 20th Floor, New York, NY 10006, USA

477 Williamstown Road, Port Melbourne, VIC 3207, Australia

314–321, 3rd Floor, Plot 3, Splendor Forum, Jasola District Centre, New Delhi – 110025, India

79 Anson Road, #06–04/06, Singapore 079906

Cambridge University Press is part of the University of Cambridge.

It furthers the University's mission by disseminating knowledge in the pursuit of education, learning, and research at the highest international levels of excellence.

www.cambridge.org
Information on this title: www.cambridge.org/9781107190931
DOI: 10.1017/9781108120395

First published 2018

Printed in the United Kingdom by Clays, St Ives plc

A catalogue record for this publication is available from the British Library.

Library of Congress Cataloging-in-Publication Data
Names: Peng, Chun, (Law teacher), author.
Title: Rural land takings law in modern China : origin and evolution / Chun Peng, Peking University, Beijing.
Description: New York, NY : Cambridge University Press, 2018. | Includes index.
Identifiers: LCCN 2017050591 | ISBN 9781107190931
Subjects: LCSH: Eminent domain – China. | Land tenure – Law and legislation – China. | Land tenure – Government policy – China. | Authoritarianism – China. | Land reform – China.
Classification: LCC KNQ2820 .P46 2017 | DDC 343.51/0252–dc23
LC record available at https://lccn.loc.gov/2017050591

ISBN 978-1-107-19093-1 Hardback

For my parents, Peng Zhonghao and Wang Shuming

CONTENTS

FIGURES

TABLES

ACKNOWLEDGMENTS

This book grew out of my trips as a student to three countries over the last decade. It all started when I came across the Chongqing Nail House incident during my exchange at the National University of Singapore in my junior year in college. Startled by the picture of a single house standing alone in a deep pit, I started to explore why land expropriation has generated so many conflicts and tragedies in my country, first with a course paper in Singapore and later in a graduation thesis at Peking University and a doctoral dissertation at Oxford.

Along the way, I have accumulated debts to many individuals and institutions. First and foremost, I would like to express my sincere gratitude to my tutors at Oxford. Professor Paul Craig kindly took me in eight years ago and has always been a tremendous source of guidance, encouragement and support, even after I finished my doctoral studies. I am extremely grateful for his patience, wisdom and kindness, which inspire me to become the best possible scholar and teacher that I can be. My cosupervisor, Dr. Patricia Thornton, has also devoted much time and energy to reading and commenting on earlier drafts of this book. I have benefited from her insights on politics and society in China, and our discussions are always stimulating. Moreover, it has been both relaxing and exhilarating to talk with Professor Reza Hasmath about research and other things of mutual interest, such as basketball.

I am very fortunate to have a group of mentors at Peking University Law School, which is my alma mater and the institution I am now working for. Professor Wang Xixin has been a tremendous inspiration not only with his academic expertise in Chinese public law and political development, but also with his commitment to promoting the rule of law in China in a pragmatic and constructive manner. Professor Zhang Qianfan has offered me many opportunities to work for and learn from him, and Professor Shen Kui encouraged me to pursue a career in academia after supervising my college graduation paper. Dean Zhang Shouwen, Professors Jiang Ming'an, Chen Duanhong, Zhan Zhongle,

Wang Lei, Jiang Shigong and Dr. Li Yuanyuan have also graced me with their kindness and trust. They are the finest teachers and colleagues one can hope for.

Outside Oxford and Peking University, Professor John S. Baker has been a mentor and friend to me for almost a decade, and his support and advice are invaluable. Dr. Suzanne Yang and Dr. Stephen Reid organized extremely interesting training programs and hosted most enjoyable tea parties and luncheons at their house, which will always be fond memories.

Furthermore, I want to say thanks to many friends who have supported and motivated me over the years, including Liao Kezhong, Wang Xiangping, Wang Jianbin, Li Kunrui, Guo Yicong, Liu Shuichang, Li Zi, Tao Yu, Ge Cheng, Zhang Zichen, Liang Kun, Liu Yifan, Wu Yimin, Yan Tian, Liu Han, Rogier Creemers, Ewan Smith, Nicole Stremlau and Iginio Gagliardone. In particular, I want to thank Sunny Chiang, who helped me so much in times of need. I would also like to thank the colleagues and friends at Oxford Continuing Education Department, including Professor Alan Hudson, Professor Jonathan Michie, Annette Lord, Patrick Tilbury, Isabel Finch, Caroline Airey, Jim Campbell, Alison Boulton and James Boulton, who have made Oxford my second home.

In 2011, I had a brief stint conducting empirical research back in my hometown – the city of Changde in Hunan Province – and received warm hospitality from Mr. Liu Jianyao and Mrs. Yin Fangming, the directors of the city land administration bureau. In particular, I accompanied Mr. Zhong Guowen and his "demolition team" when they went to talk to the peasants who were to be expropriated. They broke the stereotype portrayed in the mass media by showing incredible patience and sympathy. Their work is most difficult and undervalued.

I also want to express my gratitude to the China Oxford Scholarship Fund (especially Mr. Timothy Beardson and Ms. Susan Yu), St. Catherine's College, Oxford Law Faculty, the China Scholarship Council, the Great Britain China Center (particularly Mr. Richard Pascoe) and the Peking University–Lincoln Institute Center for Urban Development and Land Policy (Professor Liu Zhi and Professor He Canfei specifically) for generously providing me with financial support at different points over the past ten years.

This book has its origin in my doctoral dissertation at Oxford. I am indebted to the examiners of my transfer, confirmation and viva tests for their constructive suggestions: Professors Denis Galligan and Nick Barber at Oxford, as well as Dr. Zhu Sanzhu from School of Oriental and

African Studies, University of London, and Dr. Eva Pils from King's College London. At the publication stage, I am extremely grateful to Mr. Joe Ng for his support of the project and his considerable patience with the tight schedule of a junior academic. My thanks also go to the three anonymous readers for their helpful comments and criticisms. Miss Cai Peiru kindly offered her assistance in finalizing the footnotes, which is greatly appreciated.

Parts of this book were previously published as journal articles and have been revised and updated before being reproduced here. Chapter 2 is based on "Chinese Rural Land Expropriation Law: Problems, Prescriptions and Obstacles," *China-EU Law Journal* (Vol. 4, Iss. 2, 2015). Chapter 5 is a revised version of "Theoretical Foundations of Land Takings Powers in China: Competing Traditions and Common Legacy," *Peking University Law Journal* (Vol. 3, Iss. 1, 2015). A small part of Chapter 7 first appeared in "Decision-Making and Scrutiny of Rural Land Expropriation in China: Conventional Wisdom and Beyond," *Hong Kong Law Journal* (Vol. 45, Part 2, 2015). My thanks are due to these journals for their kind permission for me to reuse these printed materials.

Last, and above all, this book is for the loving memory of my uncle Wang Yafei and for the good health of my maternal grandmother Deng Yunhua. Most importantly, my parents, who never went to college, sacrificed so much to bestow upon me the greatest thing any parents can give to their children – an education. I hope to make up a bit for those Spring Festivals spent oceans apart with this humble book, which is dedicated to them.

ABBREVIATIONS

ALL	Administrative Litigation Law
ALUP	Annual Land Use Plan
ARL	Administrative Reconsideration Law
CAC	Constitutional Amending Committee
CCP	Chinese Communist Party
CPPCC	Chinese People's Political Consultative Committee
GDP	Gross Domestic Product
KMT	Kuo Min Tang
IWLO	ideal Western legal order
LAL	Land Administration Law
LALIR	Land Administration Law Implementation Regulation
LUMP	Land Use Master Plan
MLR	Ministry of Land and Natural Resources
MLRSC	Measures on Land Requisition for State-led Construction
NPC	National People's Congress
NPCSC	National People's Congress Standing Committee
PAL	Prime Agricultural Land
PRC	People's Republic of China
RECHSL	Regulation on Expropriation and Compensation of Houses above State-owned Land
RLRSC	Regulation on Land Requisition for State-led Construction
SCP	Short-term Construction Plan
SOE	State-owned Enterprise
SPC	Supreme People's Court
SPR	Small Property Rights
TP	Transition Paradigm
TVE	Township and Village Enterprise
UREAL	Urban Real Estate Administration Law
URP	Urban Rural Plan
URPL	Urban and Rural Planning Law
USSR	Union of Soviet Socialist Republics
VAT	Value Added Tax

1

Introduction

In March 2007, the photo on the cover of this book went viral online: a two-story brick building perched over a huge 17-meter deep excavated pit, like an isolated island in the ocean. The house, located in Chongqing, the mega-metropolis in southwestern China, belonged to a couple, Wu Ping and Yang Wu, who refused to make way for the local government's decision to expropriate the property. Until then, they had held out for more than two years while the other 280 households in the same area had all given up, moved out and made room for a commercial development project supported by the local government. Regarded by millions of netizens as a symbol of grassroots courage and perseverance, the house was widely applauded as the "toughest nail house in history."[1]

The reason that the house was called a "nail house" is not difficult to understand: it endured against the government order of expropriation just like a nail against a hammer. The picture soon attracted extensive media coverage and stirred up a heated public outcry. In defense of their house, Wu and Yang put up two banners around their building. One reads that "citizens' lawful private property must not be violated" and the other "the state respects and protects human rights," both of which are excerpts from the 2004 amendment to the 1982 PRC Constitution. To millions of Chinese, the toughest nail house effectively becomes a public test case as to whether in China the "fundamental law of the country" really holds "supreme legal authority," and whether the first-of-its-kind *Property Law* (*wuquan fa*) that had recently been passed would make any difference in reality.

In China today, incidents such as the nail house in Chongqing are common occurrences.[2] Most notably, in Wukan Village in Guangdong

[1] Jeremy Goldkorn, "Property Rights: the Coolest Nail House in History," March 22, 2007, available at www.danwei.org/bbs/property_rights_the_coolest_na.php.

[2] For an incomplete list of the nail house incidents in China over the years, see "Cases of the Toughest Nail House in Various Localities (盘点各地最牛钉子户)," November 23, 2012, available at bbs.tianya.cn/post-worldlook-621557–1.shtml.

Province in 2011, a scandalous land-taking deal escalated into a full-blown standoff between villagers and the local government which dragged on for three months.[3] In the end, the provincial government stepped in with a rather reconciliatory approach, which diffused the situation through negotiation and was applauded as an innovative model of governance in an authoritarian state.[4] Similarly, the nail house in Chongqing was ultimately pulled out after the local authority conceded a satisfactory compensation package to the family.[5] Nevertheless, these incidents, with their relatively peaceful endings, seem to be the exception rather than the rule. What have frequented the headlines over the years are stories of confrontation and conflicts, destruction and even death in land takings all over the country. In 2005, six farmers were killed and more than 100 others were seriously injured in Dingzhou in the Hebei province, when they were brutally attacked by dozens of armed men hired by the local authority to drive them away and seize their land.[6] In 2009, Tang Fuzhen from Chengdu died from self-immolation after she pleaded, to no avail, with the local government to stop demolishing her house.[7] In July 2016, the body of Gong Xuehui, a 60-year-old villager from the Yuelu District of Changsha city in Hunan, was found buried in the debris of her own house. Initially thought to be missing, she was found 21 days after her property was bulldozed without prior notice. Until then, she had insisted on staying and refused to accept the compensation and resettlement arrangements on offer. Early one morning in June, a group of black-uniformed men entered Gong's house by surprise and dragged her family out.[8] The process was messy and chaotic, and Ms. Gong was somehow left behind. She became

[3] For a detailed analysis, see Hualing Fu, "What Does Wukan Offer? Land-Taking, Law, and Dispute Resolution," in Fu Hualing and John Gillespie (eds.), *Resolving Land Disputes in East Asia: Exploring the Limit of Law* (Cambridge: Cambridge University Press, 2014).

[4] Tie Zhang, "What Does the Wukan Transition Tell Us (乌坎转机"提示我们什么)," December 22, 2011, available at opinion.people.com.cn/GB/16677909.html; Rahul Jacob and Jamil Anderlini, "Wukan Offers Democratic Model for China," January 31, 2012, available at www.ft.com/content/989564ac-4b10-11e1-88a3-00144feabdc0?mhq5j=e3.

[5] "Nail House in Chongqing Demolished," *China Daily*, April 3, 2007, available at www.chinadaily.com.cn/china/2007-04/03/content_842221.htm.

[6] Philip Pan, "Chinese Peasants Attacked in Land Dispute," *Washington Post*, June 15, 2005, available at www.washingtonpost.com/wp-dyn/content/article/2005/06/14/AR2005061401542.html.

[7] Roger Cohen, "A Woman Burns," *New York Times*, January 25, 2010, available at www.nytimes.com/2010/01/26/opinion/26iht-edcohen.html?_r=0.

[8] Hui Xiao and Liangzi Sun, "Missing for 21 days, a Property Owner Died in Debris after Forceful Demolition (失踪21天，长沙一业主殒命强拆废墟)," July 8, 2016, available at guancha.gmw.cn/2016-07/08/content_20882304.htm.

yet another name to be added to the long list of casualties in conflict-ridden land takings in China.

The Wu and Yang family, residents in Dingzhou and Wukan, Tang Fuzhen and Gong Xuehui, along with millions of other Chinese citizens, all live in an era when land takings are happening at a scale unprecedented in human history. Some have compared what is going on in socialist China today to the historical episode in capitalist England hundreds of years ago, suggesting that the People's Republic is experiencing a "new enclosure movement."[9] Although it might be disputed whether or not such an analogy stands in its finer details, it is hardly deniable that land taking features prominently in the social and political landscape of contemporary China. It therefore constitutes a key to unlock the secret behind the transformation and challenges of the largest and fastest-growing developing country in the world. This book is an inquiry into this phenomenon from a legal perspective. What, then, does land taking mean in China?

1.1 Defining Land Taking in China

More than a couple of Chinese words have so far been used to denote compulsory acquisition of land by public authorities. This is because since the late nineteenth century, as will be demonstrated in this book, the idea of compulsory acquisition of land has been taken up by major political forces in China to fulfill distinct strategic objectives, and in different ways. "Land taking," literally translated as *zhengdi*, is the most broadly conceived term to express the idea. Although the term itself is never actually adopted in any statutory texts, it will be deployed as the umbrella concept to cover all kinds of mandatory public acquisition of land described and analyzed in this book. We start by looking at how land taking is defined in extant Chinese law.

Under Article 10 in the current PRC Constitution enacted in 1982,[10] only two types of public land ownership exist in post-reform socialist China: state-owned urban land and collective-owned rural land. While

9 Qinglian He, *Traps of Modernization: Contemporary China's Economic and Social Problems* (现代化的陷阱：当代中国的经济社会问题) (Beijing: Today's China Press, 1998), chapter 2.

10 The People's Republic of China has in total four written Constitutions to date, which were passed in 1954, 1975, 1978 and 1982. The 1982 Constitution is the one in effect today and has been subject to four amendments, in 1988, 1993, 1999 and 2004. Without specification, the Constitution means the 1982 Constitution as amended in 2004.

land should not be privately owned, aboveground structures such as buildings can be privately owned, which means that publicly owned land can be privately used. Against such a backdrop, there are two types of land takings in Chinese law. One is the transfer of use-rights for state-owned land from private holders back to the state, which is called the state power to withdraw (*shouhui*) land. Its statutory basis currently lies in Article 58 of the 2004 *Land Administration Law* (LAL).[11] When privately used state-owned land is withdrawn, privately owned property above the withdrawn land is concurrently expropriated by the state, with a different legal underpinning found in Article 13 of the Constitution, "The state may, for the public interest and in accordance with law, expropriate or requisition private property and make compensation for the private property expropriated or requisitioned." The second type of land taking under present Chinese law is the power of the state to compulsorily transfer ownership of rural land from collectives to itself, which is enshrined in the third paragraph of Article 10 in the Constitution and is called the power of expropriation (*zhengshou*), which reads, "The state may, in the public interest, expropriate or requisition land and make compensation in accordance with law."[12] Similar to the urban context, expropriation of rural collective land also involves the expropriation of private property, such as buildings and plants, thereon. This means that as a Chinese legal term "expropriation" refers to the state's permanent taking of the ownership of any nonstate (communal and private) property on land or otherwise, as prescribed by Article 13 of the Constitution. Hence, in existing Chinese law, land taking can mean

[11] It reads, "Under any of the following circumstances, the land administration department of the people's government concerned may, with the approval of the people's government that has originally approved the use of land or that possesses the approval authority, withdraw the right to the use of the state-owned land: (1) The land is needed for public interest; (2) The use of the land needs to be readjusted for renovating the old urban area according to urban planning; (3) At the expiration of land transfer contract, the land user has not applied for extending the period or, if he has applied for such extension, the application is not approved; (4) The use of the originally allocated state-owned land is terminated because, among other things, the organization that used the land is dissolved or moved away; or (5) Highways, railways, airports or ore fields become abandoned with approval. The user granted with the land-use right shall be compensated appropriately when its right to the use of state-owned land is withdrawn according to the provisions of sub-paragraphs (1) and (2) in the preceding paragraph." N.B. The PRC Land Administration Law was initially enacted in 1986 and subsequently revised in 1988, 1998 and 2004. The term first appeared in Article 19 of the 1986 and 1988 versions of the legislation and then in Article 58 of the 1998 version.

[12] The Chinese text is "国家为了公共利益的需要，可以依照法律规定对土地实行征收或者征用并给予补偿."

either the state withdrawal of use-rights of urban land it owns (and the expropriation of the private property thereon) or state expropriation of the ownership of rural collective land (as well as the private property thereon).

It is worth noting that in daily language it is demolition and relocation (*chaiqian*) that is most frequently used to refer to land takings, capturing rather bluntly the essence of the incident described. In the legal sense, "demolition and relocation" was once a statutory term used in the 1991 and 2001 *Regulation on the Management of Urban House Demolition and Relocation*, standing for the withdrawal of use-rights of state-owned urban land and the attendant expropriation of any private property above the land. This was officially changed by the 2011 *Regulation on Expropriation and Compensation of Houses above State-owned Land* (RECHSL), which replaces demolition and relocation with expropriation to refer to the taking of private property on state-owned land. Also worth noting is that land takings can be either permanent or temporary. Different terms have been used at different times over the last century to connote permanent land takings, including both requisition (*zhengyong*) and expropriation (*zhengshou*). The 2004 constitutional amendment eventually stipulates that expropriation means the permanent compensatory transfer of ownership to the state, while requisition refers to the temporary compensatory transfer of use-rights to the state.[13] For the sake of reflecting the terminological change in history, both words will be used in their original form, with *zhengyong* translated as "requisition" and *zhengshou* as "expropriation," although attention should be paid to the changed meaning of these terms over time.

This book focuses on permanent rural land takings, which is only part of China's current land-taking regime. It should be admitted that before the 1982 Constitution was enacted to give shape to the present land-taking system there was no formal statutory distinction between rural and urban land, particularly in regards to legal title/ownership. Nonetheless, over the last century, the divide between rural and urban land has been ever present, and rural land continues to assume critical strategic importance in a predominantly agrarian country such as China, as evidenced by the Chinese Communist Party's (CCP's) distinctive rural land policies during both the revolutionary years and the PRC period. Against this background,

[13] Zhaoguo Wang, "Explanatory Report on the Draft Constitutional Amendment at the Second Session of the Tenth National People's Congress (关于中华人民共和国宪法修正案草案的说明)," March 8, 2004, available at www.people.com.cn/GB/shizheng/8198/31983/32185/2380223.html.

as will be demonstrated in this book, rural land takings have had a much longer and richer history in modern China than its urban analogue. Only with a better grasp of such a history, which has unfortunately been overlooked by previous research, are we able to arrive at a more contextualized understanding of the theories and praxes of compulsory public acquisition of private property in China. Moreover, as China is still urbanizing and industrializing, large-scale conversion of rural to urban land will continue for quite some time to come. As will be shown by this book, rural land taking plays a crucial role in this process. In this situation, besides providing a longer historical perspective, concentrating on rural land taking offers us an opportunity to look into the future.

1.2 Massive Rural Land Expropriation in Contemporary China

Over the years, stories such as those of the Wu and Yang family, Tang Fuzhen and Gong Xuehui, as frequently as they hit the headlines, are but a fraction of a large number of incidents of rural land takings across the country. According to statistical yearbooks published by China's Ministry of Land and Natural Resources (MLR), the total amount of rural land expropriated between 2004 and 2014 was 4,279,633.51 hectares – i.e. almost 10.58 million acres.[14]

As to the magnitude of rural land expropriation prior to the 2000s, a research team led by Chen Xiwen, a high-ranking Chinese official in charge of agricultural matters, concluded in 2008 that between 1978 and 2001, 28342500 *mu* or 4.67 million acres of rural land was expropriated.[15] Apparently, there has been a huge spike in the scale of rural land expropriation in China since the turn of this century. Putting these two figures together, we have at least 15.28 million acres, or 61,512.2 km^2, of

[14] Calculated from data recorded in MLR (ed.), *China Land Resource Statistical Yearbook 2011* (中国国土资源统计年鉴2011) (Beijing: Dizhi Press), p. 89; MLR (ed.), *China Land Resource Statistical Yearbook 2012* (中国国土资源统计年鉴2012) (Beijing: Dizhi Press), p. 77; MLR (ed.), *China Land Resource Statistical Yearbook 2015* (中国国土资源统计年鉴2015) (Beijing: Dizhi Press), p. 89. The MLR first started to publish official statistics on the scale of rural land expropriation annually from 2004.

[15] Chen Xiwen, Zhao Yang and Luo Dan, *Review and Outlook of 30-Year Reform in Rural China* (中国农村改革三十年回顾与展望) (Beijing: Renmin Press, 2008), p. 192. The famed Chinese sociologist Yu Jianrong came up with an even higher figure that, between 1990 and 2002, 47.36 million *mu* or 7.8 million acres of cultivated land were taken for non-agricultural construction. See Jianrong Yu, "Land Loss and Job Loss by the Peasants is a Serious Political Problem (农民失地失业是一个严重的政治问题)" (2004) 1 *Exploration and Free Views* (探索与争鸣) 10.

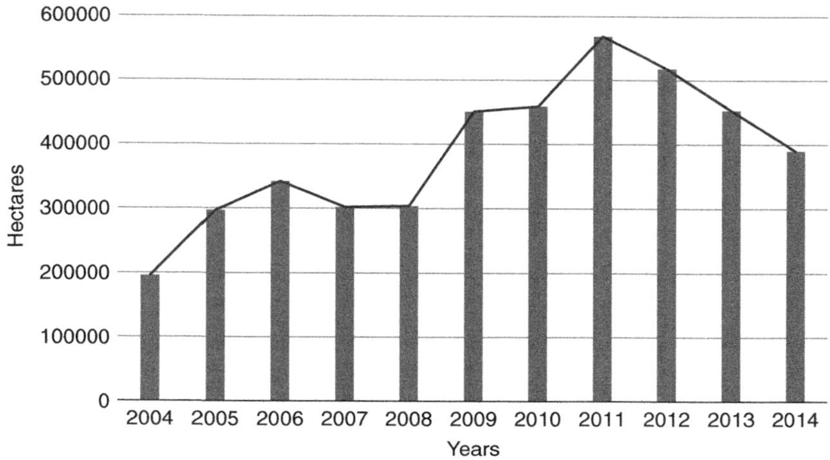

Figure 1.1 Massive and accelerating rural land expropriation in contemporary China

rural land taken in less than four decades – an area twice the size of Belgium. It is no exaggeration to say that rural land taking in contemporary China is unprecedented in human history.

Understandably, land takings of such enormous speed and scale have had a huge impact upon a huge number of China's rural residents, who are consequently dubbed the "land-losing peasants" (*shidi nongmin*). Over the years, based on divergent calculating methods, leading Party newspapers[16] and top-level officials[17] have supplied different numbers of

[16] In 2001, a People's Daily report revealed that from 1997 to 2000 nearly 20 million peasants had experienced land expropriation and were in need of relocation and settlement. See Jun Xia, "No More One-off Compensation for Land Acquisition (土地征用不再实行一次性补偿)," *People's Daily*, October 25, 2001, available at www.china.com.cn/zhuanti2005/txt/2001-10/25/content_5070170.htm. In 2004, another People's Daily report suggested that there were 40 million land-losing peasants and the annual increase was two million. See Yong Gao, "How do Land-losing Peasants Live: Theoretical Discussion about the Problem of Land-losing Peasants (失去土地的农民如何生活: 关于失地农民问题的理论探讨)," *People's Daily*, February 2, 2004, available at www.people.com.cn/GB/guandian/1034/2314535.html. In 2012, a third report on People's Daily claimed that there were 40–50 million land-losing peasants at the time. See Yongping Zhao, "Land Acquisition and Demolition and Relocation: Why in a Hurry (征地拆迁何太急)," *People's Daily*, July 15, 2012, available at society.people.com.cn/n/2012/0715/c1008-18518505.html.

[17] In 2011, a member of the national Chinese People's Political Consultative Committee (CPPCC) suggested that the total number of land-losing peasants in China was no less than 40 million. See "Committee Member Zhang Yuanfu: According to Expert Estimate, Land-losing Peasants in China at the Moment are no less than 40 Million (张富员委员:

land-losing peasants, increasing from 20 million between 1997 and 2001 to 40 million in 2004 and then to 40–50 million in 2012. Meanwhile, the media and academia have also put forward estimates that vary greatly, ranging from 20 million up to 2004,[18] 47 million between 1987 and 2001,[19] 40–50 million up to 2011,[20] 40.82 million between 1997 and 2009,[21] 50.93–55.25 million between 1987 and 2001,[22] 66.3 million until 2002,[23] 80 million until 2003,[24] 120 million until 2011[25] and 200 million as of 2010.[26] There are also numerous predicted figures, ranging from 70 million by 2021[27] to 100 million by 2020.[28] It should be readily apparent that on this front there is thus far no consensus data, except that in 2012 the MLR eventually acknowledged that more than 25 million Chinese peasants had gone through land expropriation between 2008

据专家测算目前中国失地农民累积不少于4000万人)," March 9, 2011, available at 2011lianghui.people.com.cn/GB/214392/14099239.html.

18 Rujiang Ge, Haiping Pan and Xinya Wang, "Who Produces 20 Million Land-Losing Peasants: Investigation of the New Disadvantaged Group in the Waves of Urbanization (谁制造了两千万失地农民：城市化浪潮中的新弱势群体调查)" (2004) 1 *China Reform (Rural Edition)* (中国改革：农村版) 12.

19 Haibo Zhang and Xing Tong, "The Adaptability to Urban Context and Self-identity in Acquired Modernity of Groups Forced to be Urbanized (被动城市化群体城市适应性与现代性获得中的自我认同)" (2006) 2 *Journal of Sociological Research* (社会学研究), 86.

20 China Academy of Social Sciences (ed.), *Annual Report on Urban Development of China 2011* (中国城市发展报告2011) (Beijing: China Social Science Academic Press, 2011).

21 Yaping Li, "Research on the Problem of Land-Losing Peasants in China's Urbanization Process (我国城市化进程中失地农民问题研究)," Master Thesis, Shandong University (2011), p. 21.

22 "Scholar's Count of China's Landless and Land-Losing Peasants to be Over 1.8 Billion (学者推算我国无地失地农民总数在1.8亿以上)" (2004) 4 *Information for Leader's Policy-making* (领导决策信息) 29.

23 Yu, "Land Loss and Job Loss by the Peasants is a Serious Political Problem," 10.

24 Xiaowo Ying, "Worries about Land in China (中国土地忧思录)," September 3, 2003, available at www.southcn.com/finance/picture/200309030072.htm.

25 Qinglian He, "How Many Land-losing Peasants are there in China? (中国失地农民知多少)," January 9, 2011, available at www.voafanti.com/gate/big5/www.voachinese.com/articleprintview/776030.html.

26 Lihua Tong, "Land-losing Peasants across the Country should be over 100 Million at Present (当前全国失地农民应当超过一亿人)," October 20, 2010, available at blog.legaldaily.com.cn/blog/html/20/2443320-9538.html.

27 Hui Wang and Ran Tao, "How to Achieve a Systematic Breakthrough in the Reform of Land Acquisition System: Recommendations to the Draft Amendments to Land Administration Law (如何实现征地制度改革的系统性突破 – 兼论对土地管理法修改草案的建议)" (2009) 6 *Southeast Research* (东南学术) 10.

28 "Democratic and Progressive Party Center: Number of Land-Losing Peasants over 100 Million by 2020 (民进中央: 2020年失地农民数量将超过一亿)," March 14, 2009, available at news.163.com/09/0314/05/54BHBOPP000136K8.html.

and 2011.[29] Since this figure accounts for a mere four-year period and massive rural land takings have been underway in China for decades, the true size of the rural population affected could easily be multiple times larger.

Given the enormity of the area and the vast numbers of people affected, rural land expropriation has long been considered a thorny problem with a series of critical consequences. To start with, as it is usually followed by land use conversion, large-scale rural land expropriation has resulted in loss of agricultural land (cultivated land in particular) to residential, industrial and commercial development on a worryingly scale and at a rapid pace,[30] causing widespread concerns about food security and ecological integrity in a country that feeds 20 percent of the world's population with only 7 percent of the world's farmland and that is facing an increasingly severe environmental crisis.[31] Furthermore, by displacing or even dispossessing millions, rural land expropriation has also led to frequent occurrences of what is called "domicide" across the country,[32] characterized by appalling deprivation, dislocation and destitution of those expropriated.[33] This issue has therefore become a breeding ground for contention, resistance and protests in contemporary Chinese society, posing a serious threat to the much-valued social stability and harmony.[34] What happened in Wukan and Dingzhou are but the most infamous examples in this regard.

Against this backdrop, land expropriation evokes much dissatisfaction, frustration and indignation in China. As well as petitions and

[29] "Ministry of Land Resources: Compensation for Land Expropriation in 3.5 Trillion in Four Years (国土资源部:征地拆迁补偿4年支出3.5万亿)," December 26, 2012, available at news.xinhuanet.com/fortune/2012-12/26/c_124148072.htm.

[30] Samuel Ho and George Lin, "Non-Agricultural Land Use in Post-Reform China" (2004) 179 *The China Quarterly* 758.

[31] Erik Lichtenberg and Chengri Ding, "Land Use Efficiency, Food Security, and Farmland Preservation in China" (2006) 18 *Land Lines* 2.

[32] John Porteous and Sandra Smith, *Domicide: The Global Destruction of Home* (Montreal and Kingston: McGill-Queen's University Press, 2001). The Chinese manifestation of domicide in Shanghai is documented by Qin Shao, *Shanghai Gone: Domicide and Defiance in a Chinese Megacity* (Lanham: Rowman & Littlefield Publishers, 2013).

[33] You-tien Hsing, *The Great Urban Transformation: Politics of Land and Property in China* (New York: Oxford University Press, 2010), chapter 7.

[34] The oft-cited finding in Yu Jianrong's survey concludes that 65 percent of rural "mass incidents" (euphemism for protests) were triggered by local governments' forceful and violent land expropriation. See Yu, "Land Loss and Job Loss by the Peasants is a Serious Political Problem," p. 10.

protests,[35] bitter satire is also used to give voice and vent to the social agony surrounding land takings. Released in January 2009, the American sci-fi blockbuster *Avatar* quickly captivated the Chinese audience, as it did around the globe.[36] Notwithstanding its popularity, after less than one month it was pulled from screens by China's film authority. The reason behind this was never publicly explained, but widespread speculation suggested that this Hollywood fantasy set on an imaginary alien planet had cut across the political fault-lines in China.[37] Parallels had then been drawn between indigenous inhabitants on Planet Na'vi facing earthly colonialism and the Chinese citizens facing government land takings. Many Chinese netizens mockingly commented that the only reason the Na'vi tribes could successfully hold out against invaders from earth was that the all-powerful Chinese state machinery was not summoned. As satirical, if not cynical, as that may be, it reflects the solemn reality that ordinary people in China generally feel vulnerable and helpless in land takings, with their last resort oftentimes reduced to violent or suicidal protests, as epitomized by the case of Tang Fuzhen later that same year.[38]

This sense of powerlessness was tapped into and smartly twisted when a game called *Nail Household vs. Demolition Team* became an instant favorite among Chinese online gamers in 2010. The ingenuity of it did not lie in its originality, as it was essentially a copy of the international hit *Plants vs. Zombies*. But in changing the two opposing sides to a Chinese family in an isolated house like the one shown on the book cover and demolition crew, it was played 1.8 million times within two weeks[39] and

[35] In 2013, the deputy director of China's National Bureau of Letters and Visits admitted at a press conference that petitions through the letters and visits system are mostly due to rural and urban land takings. "National Bureau of Letters and Visits: Most Reported Issues from the People's Letters and Visits are about Expropriation and Demolition (信访局:群众来信来访反映突出在征地拆迁等问题)," November 28, 2013, available at www.chinanews.com/gn/2013/11-28/5557433.shtml.

[36] In fact, *Avatar* became the highest grossing film in the Chinese domestic market, until finally being overtaken by the Chinese film *Monster Hunt* (捉妖记) in 2015.

[37] Ben Child, "Avatar Smashes Chinese All-time Box-office Record," January 19, 2010, available at www.theguardian.com/film/2010/jan/19/avatar-smashes-chinese-record.

[38] For a critical analysis of expropriation violence in China, see Sally Sargeson, "Violence as Development: Land Expropriation and China's Urbanization" (2013) 40 *Journal of Peasant Studies* 1065.

[39] Tania Branigan, "China Embraces Web Game Depicting Family's Fight with Demolition Crew," September 16, 2010, available at theguardian.com/world/2010/sep/16/china-game-family-fight-demolition.

shot up to rank as the third most-played game in that month in China.[40] By comparing the expropriation team to bloodthirsty zombies, and, more importantly, by equipping the entire nail household (even the baby boy) with such weapons as rocks, knives and firearms that they would never have had in reality, the game offered millions of players a safe and fun sanctuary to express their deep and long-held discontent.

There is perhaps no better satirical epitome of the era marked by massive rural land takings than the word "China" itself. Split into "*Chi*" and "*Na*," the country's English name has been reinterpreted into its Chinese homonym, which literally means "what to demolish" or "tear that down."[41] Rather provocatively, this reveals the significant place land taking holds in contemporary Chinese society. In this way, land taking opens up a window into the successes and struggles experienced by one of the fastest changing countries in the world over decades.

1.3 Making Sense of China's Rural Land Expropriation Law

For more than a decade, a huge amount of ink has been spilled on documenting and explaining the phenomenon of massive rural land expropriation in China and the resultant social tensions, controversy and conflicts. The blaming fingers have usually been pointed at the failure of the Chinese rural land takings law to effectively regulate and restrain the Chinese government's power to expropriate. The point of departure of relevant legal analyses is invariably the third paragraph of Article 10 in the Constitution, which authorizes the state to expropriate land for public interest and make compensation in accordance with the law. This is the Chinese constitutional takings clause.[42]

There are obviously three key components in China's existing constitutional takings clause – "public interest," "compensation" and "in accordance with law." Article 42 of the 2007 *Property Law* provides that

[40] Qingshu Zhou, "The Game Nail Household v. Demolition Team Gone Viral on the Internet (钉子户大战拆迁队游戏爆红网络)," September 15, 2010, available at news.17173.com/content/2010-09-15/20100915093022315,1.shtml.

[41] Ni Tao, "Ugly Urban Buzzword Chai Na, Tear it Down," August 16, 2010, available at www.shanghaidaily.com/Opinion/chinese-perspectives/Ugly-urban-buzzword-chai-na-tear-it-down/shdaily.shtml.

[42] Article 13 of the current Constitution, as mentioned, deals more broadly with state taking of any private property, including private structure and crops on public land. Therefore, strictly speaking, the Chinese takings clause includes both paragraph three of Article 10 and Article 13. In the process of land takings both will be implicated. For the sake of analysis, however, this book focuses on the part specifically concerning land takings.

rural land expropriation shall be carried out "in accordance with legally determined authority and procedures." Accordingly, "in accordance with law" is typically regarded as the overarching requirement of legality, in both substantive and procedural terms, over expropriation decision-making and compensation. In this light, the state power of land expropriation in China seems to be placed under constitutional constraints not so different to those found in other countries, most notably the United States.

The Fifth Amendment to the 1787 American Constitution reads, "Nor shall private property be taken for public use, without just compensation." Despite differences in the exact wording, the similarity between these two constitutional takings clauses is hard to overlook. Present in both are the prerequisite of some public purpose ("public interest" in China and "public use" in America) and the requirement of compensation ("compensation" in China and "just compensation" in America). In this light, juxtaposing the Chinese land takings law against its American counterpart becomes a prevalent approach in the existing literature, with the aim of identifying, explaining and criticizing the former's failure. In other words, the third paragraph of Article 10 in the 1982 Constitution has been regarded as China's own Fifth Amendment, the core function of which is to protect land rights of rural collectives and residents from the expropriation power of the state, a task largely unaccomplished in practice. This leads to prevalence of Sino–US comparative studies in interpreting and critiquing the Chinese law on rural land expropriation.

To be sure, this is not to say that the United States is the only comparator. Comparisons with other countries have also been carried out.[43] A recent example can be found in *The Constitutional Protection of Private Property in China*, which is a systematic comparative survey of

43 See e.g. Li Zhang, "The Scrutiny Mechanism of Public Purpose in Land Expropriation in France and the Lessons for China (法国土地征收公益性审查机制及其对中国的启示)" (2009) 1 *Administrative Law Studies* (行政法学研究) 135; Zhijie Yuan, "Public Interest in Land Expropriation in Germany (德国土地征收中的公共利益)" (2010) 2 *Administrative Law Studies* (行政法学研究) 119. More recently, in addition to those developed Western countries, China's takings law has also been juxtaposed with its counterpart in another large developing country – India. Yet by adopting virtually the same evaluative criteria, the conclusion is unsurprisingly that the current Chinese takings law is not only "far from the common standards of Western countries, but it is also far behind that of India, a comparable big developing economy." See Chuanhui Wang, *The Constitutional Protection of Private Property in China: Historical Evolution and Comparative Research* (Cambridge: Cambridge University Press, 2016), p. 307.

the takings laws in China, the United States, Germany and India to reveal "the unfairness, unjustness and insufficiency in China's application of three constitutional doctrines – public use, just compensation and due process or procedure."[44] Nor does it mean that every piece of work on this topic assumes a comparative stance.[45] But to a considerable degree the present thinking about China's rural land expropriation law is animated and shaped by comparison with the American takings law. For instance, just by skimming the titles of research in Chinese on this issue, one will find that most works translate *zhengshou* or *zhengdi* as "eminent domain," a term used mainly in the United States. In contrast, the phrase used in continental Europe is "expropriation," and in the United Kingdom "compulsory purchase." This is more than a mere matter of translation. On a deeper level, it reveals a conceptual association shared within the academic community between *zhengdi* in China and eminent domain in the United States. Besides such scholarly acknowledgment, official recognition is also showcased by the MLR organizing a conference in 2008 to invite top policy-makers and senior legal academics in China to sit down with government officials, judges and scholars from the United States to learn about the American experience of eminent domain law. That is the only international conference on reforming China's land takings law held at such a high official level so far.[46]

The fascination with American takings jurisprudence in China can be attributed to a set of factors. To begin with, it certainly helps that English is the most widely learned foreign language in China. The global impact of America and its legal system may also be conducive.[47] Another contributing factor is the active involvement in the Chinese legal reforms by a variety of American actors from the government to research institutions, to which the 2008 MLR conference is one of many testimonies. While all the above factors are somewhat exogenous, the following are endogenous and highly instrumental. To begin with, as already demonstrated, the textual resemblance between the two countries'

[44] Wang, *The Constitutional Protection of Private Property in China*, title page.

[45] More discussion on the implicit rather than explicit dominance of the Sino–US comparison on previous research will appear in the next section.

[46] For a synopsis of the conference, see Jing Wang, "A Synopsis of the Conference on Eminent Domain and Land Dispute Resolution Mechanism in China and America (中美土地征收和土地纠纷解决机制研讨会综述)" (2008) 4 *Administrative Law Review* (行政法论丛) 132.

[47] For an opposite account of the global influence of the US constitution, see David S. Law and Mila Versteeg, "The Declining Influence of the United States Constitution" (2012) 87 (3) *New York University Law Review* 762.

constitutional takings clauses is generally treated as a reliable ground, if not a urgent call, for those concerned with the failure of China's takings law to look beyond the Pacific for inspiration. Second, and more significantly, no other developed country in the world has witnessed as much controversy and debate about land takings as the United States,[48] a situation highly reminiscent of what has been happening in China. In the meantime, however, eminent domain disputes in the United States are nowhere near those in China because in America takings-related conflicts are basically settled in the courts instead of the streets. Hence, to Chinese observers, the extensive eminent domain jurisprudence generated in America is both a fertile territory for comparative investigation and a rich source from which lessons can be drawn to improve China's own takings law.

It is against this background that China's rural land expropriation law has been exposited and critiqued over the past decade. The central question addressed in this line of inquiry is: Why do these two similar constitutional takings clauses play out differently in practice? Put another way: Why is the Chinese rural land expropriation law substantially less effective than its American analogue in checking takings power and upholding land rights, when it should have done the same job? The overall finding is that the promise made by the Chinese constitutional takings clause is not honored since the subordinate laws and regulations on rural land expropriation are underdeveloped, in a number of ways, in comparison to the American counterpart. China's own Fifth Amendment is therefore not yet duly implemented. The diagnoses and prescriptions advanced along these lines will be examined more fully in the next chapter. However, it is apposite at this juncture to introduce the Transition Paradigm that has thus far dominated existing research in this area.

1.4 Transition Paradigm

"Transition Paradigm" (TP) as an academic term was first coined by Thomas Carothers in 2002.[49] Originally, it referred to the analytic model or framework adopted by the development-assistance community to understand, and indeed predict, democratization around the world

48 Rachelle Alterman (ed.), *Takings International: A Comparative Perspective on Land Use Regulation and Compensation Rights* (Chicago: American Bar Association, 2010), p. 5.

49 Thomas Carothers, "The End of the Transition Paradigm" (2001) 13 *Journal of Democracy* 5.

since the coming of the "third wave" of democracy in the 1970s.[50] It represents the widely held belief at the time that democratization was underway in countries moving away from dictatorial rule. Under the original TP, democracy is defined by regularized national elections, which are regarded as the endpoint of social and political transition. The transition to democratization is conceptualized basically as a natural and inevitable process. The only remaining question is when and how to trigger and accomplish the transition.

Before explaining what the TP means in our context, and why it has shaped the present understanding of China's rural land takings law, I hasten to add two caveats. First, differences among the adherents to the TP, which will become clear in the next chapter, are neither dismissed nor ignored. As a matter of fact, past research on this topic contains abundant nuances and variations in approaches, perspectives and viewpoints. To identify a paradigm therein hence does not intend to be, and indeed cannot be, an all-encompassing summary of all relevant discussion. Rather, what the TP does is to encapsulate four core assumptions on which previous works, regardless of their differences, are based. Second, not all those committed to (or, more accurately, falling prey to) the TP do so in a conscious, explicit or wholesale way. More often than not, those four assumptions underpin the existing literature without surfacing to become openly and systematically stated propositions. This does not reduce, but in fact enhances the tightness of the grip these premises have on the extant scholarship. The TP is therefore a reconstructed abstraction aiming to lay bare those hitherto unspoken and unexamined beliefs so that they can be scrutinized, tested and ultimately refuted.

Overall, the TP in this book refers to the conviction widely shared in previous research that China's law on rural land expropriation should be and actually is in a transitional state, and moving toward a more advanced stage epitomized by the American eminent domain law – a process only to be hindered by an entrenched feature of the Chinese fiscal system known as "land finance" (*tudi caizheng*). Once that barrier is cleared out, the expected and indeed desired transition will be underway. Specifically, the TP includes the following four core assumptions.

First and foremost, the *teleological assumption*. Much existing research holds the view that in terms of the takings law, America's today should and will be China's tomorrow. To be clear, this is not to say that it is

[50] This idea first appeared in Samuel P. Huntington, *The Third Wave: Democratization in the Late Twentieth Century* (Norman: University of Oklahoma Press, 1991).

universally claimed that the Chinese takings law ought to and is going to duplicate the US law. A closer look at the American jurisprudence of eminent domain reveals that it is anything but a monolithic and static model that can be readily exported in a wholesale fashion to China. For instance, the judicial interpretations of the "public use" provision in the Fifth Amendment have changed to a considerable degree over time.[51] The determination of "fair market value" as the just compensation standard, and whether that adequately indemnifies the condemnees, are by no means immune to debate.[52] There is also no uniform practice regarding the "due process of law" in eminent domain, either on the federal level or among the states.[53] Last but not least, even the seemingly simple term "taking" has substantively expanded in terms of its coverage over the course of last century.[54]

Nevertheless, for all the inconsistencies and controversies, the American takings law is still believed by many to have offered a model worthy of emulation to China due to the following reasons. First, as will be demonstrated in more detail in the next chapter, the public interest requirement in the Chinese constitutional takings clause has been plagued by triple challenges that in effect makes it toothless to restrain the government in land takings. Consequently, it has been widely agreed that expropriation decisions in China shall be, like in America, subject to both ex ante and ex post checks by way of enhanced legislative scrutiny and public participation, as well as judicial review. Equally, if not more important is that rural land in China shall be permitted to become convertible to urban construction land through the market instead of expropriation. It is suggested that only in this way can the presently extensive scope of expropriation in China be narrowed down to fulfill the public interest prerequisite. Furthermore, the conventional wisdom

[51] Chenglin Liu, "The Chinese Takings Law from a Comparative Perspective" (2008) 26 *Washington University Journal of Law & Policy* 325–32.

[52] Christopher Serkin, "The Meaning of Value: Assessing Just Compensation for Regulatory Takings" (2005) 99 *Northwestern University Law Review* 677; Ann E. Gergen, "Why Fair Market Value Fails as Just Compensation" (1993) 14 *Hamline Journal of Public Law and Policy* 239; Laura H. Burney, "Just Compensation and the Condemnation of Future Interests: Empirical Evidence of the Failure of Fair Market Value" (1989) *Brigham Young Law Review* 789.

[53] David Zachary Hudson, "Eminent Domain Due Process" (2010) 119 *Yale Law Journal* 1280. Worth noting is that today there are 21 states which do not require any pre-condemnation notice or hearing in legislation, and not all their state courts have filled the gap through case law.

[54] William Michael Treanor, "The Original Understanding of the Takings Clause and the Political Process" (1995) 95 *Columbia Law Review* 782.

goes that the current Chinese expropriation compensation standards, based on original use of the expropriated land, ought to be replaced by the fair market value standard adopted under American law in order to become just and fair. And the expropriatees in China shall be given, as their American counterparts, the opportunity to negotiate and challenge the compensation arrangements, which have been decided almost unilaterally by the government.

On a deeper level, the above teleological projection is founded on the understanding that the constitutional takings clauses of these two countries are functionally equivalent to each other. Particularly emblematic in this regard is the popularity of the following quote in China over recent years: "A man's house is his castle, which the wind may blow through, the rain may fall in but the king may not enter."[55] Extensively quoted by both the popular press and academic research, this medieval England-rooted motto has been widely considered as the very value foundation Chinese takings law should rest upon; as one Chinese scholar once emphatically lamented, "In China, a man's house has never been, nor is it now, his castle."[56] To be clear, this has less to do with whatever libertarian bent the Chinese society entertains than with the general recognition that the Chinese takings law has failed to perform its proper duty. Understandably, it is the avid hope of people such as the Wu and Yang family, Tang Fuzhen and Gong Xuehui that their houses may one day, like in America, become safe and impenetrable castles.

Second, the *developmental assumption*. For more than a decade, the above teleological position has gained considerable traction in China. Yet, as will be shown in the next chapter, despite a few spots of light here and there, the past decade actually saw very little substantive progress that brings the Chinese takings law closer to the American model. However, that is not thought to detract from the validity of the teleological assumption. The reason is that Chinese local governments are known to be financially motivated to carry out rural land expropriation extensively since the late 1980s and particularly since 1994, when the tax-sharing reform put them under fiscal pressure. "Land finance" is the term to describe the fact that Chinese local governments rely heavily on land expropriation and subsequent land transfer (*tudi churang*) for such financial benefits as sources of funding and borrowing. The lack of

[55] In Chinese "风能进，雨能进，国王不能进." For the original quote and its history, see Joseph William Singer, "The Ownership Society and Takings of Property: Castles, Investments, and Just Obligations" (2006) 30 *Harvard Environmental Law Review* 309.

[56] Wang, *The Constitutional Protection of Private Property in China*, p. 2.

incentive or even resistance of the local governments under land finance is therefore held accountable as the biggest obstacle to the much anticipated and desired reform of China's takings law. In stark contrast, such strong financial incentive to exercise eminent domain is almost nonexistent among American subnational governments. For many, this explains the absence of pervasive land takings in the United States. The controversial *Kelo* case of 2005 serves as a somber reminder that American local authorities act similarly when they too feel the pressure to promote local economic growth and generate revenue.[57] In this way, the nonactualization of transition actually reinforces instead of undermines the teleological projection. And there is this increasing realization that an overhaul of China's central-local fiscal system is required to overcome land finance so that the expected transition can finally be set in motion. In essence, the idea is that once local governments in China do not expropriate land for financial benefits they will stop expropriating extensively and be willing to increase compensation. This then opens up the room for more systematic reforms of China's takings law.

Third, the *temporal assumption*. Under the TP, rural land expropriation is framed mainly as a problem of the post-reform era since pervasive takings have only taken place after the marketization of urban land use-right in the late 1980s, especially after the 1994 tax-sharing reform due to land finance. This is surely not to say that rural land expropriation did not happen before. It did. But land taking in the pre-reform era is not problematized because at that time local governments were not financially incentivized to expropriate and the scale of expropriation had not picked up.

From a legal standpoint, as mentioned earlier, previous analyses invariably start from the third clause of Article 10 in the current Constitution, which was passed in the post-reform period. Although references had been made to pre-reform constitutional takings clauses such as Article 13 of the 1954 Constitution, Article 6 of the 1975 Constitution and Article 6 of the 1978 Constitution,[58] none of them

[57] In the *Kelo* case, private land was taken and originally intended for the pharmaceutical giant Pfizer to boost the local economy and improve employment. See *Kelo* v. *City of New London*, 545 U.S. 469 (2005).

[58] See Lekun Feng, "On the Purpose of Land Expropriation (土地征用目的之研讨)" (2005) 24 *Journal of Lanzhou Jiaotong University* (兰州交通大学学报) 68; Chuanhao Tian, Hong Yang and Jia Zhou, "Land Acquisition System in China: Historical Evolution, Current Problems and Reform Directions (中国征地制度：历史演变、现实问题与改革方向)," 2009, available at wenku.baidu.com/view/f0f48e8102d276a200292ec2.html.

has received any serious scholarly treatment. On the one hand, the 1975 and 1978 takings clauses were perhaps neglected because of their origins during the tumultuous Cultural Revolution, a period officially labeled as a major setback in China's legal and political development.[59] Moreover, both clauses read: "The state may compulsorily purchase, requisition or nationalize urban and rural land as well as other means of production under the conditions prescribed by law." The noticeable absence of the public interest requirement distances them from the present constitutional takings clause. On the other hand, even though in 1982 the constitutional amendment committee admitted that the 1954 Constitution, rather than the two Cultural Revolution constitutions, was the model for the 1982 Constitution,[60] and despite the fact that the present constitutional takings clause does bear striking resemblance to the 1954 clause, it has never been suggested that the original takings clause might shed any light on the existing law. In this circumstance, in tandem with the inclination to see the social and political problem of rural land takings as emerging only after the opening and reform era, the relevant legal and constitutional issues are conceptualized in temporal terms as post-reform, too.

Fourth, and lastly, the *conceptual assumption*. This means a particular conception of the takings power shared by past research, which is largely unarticulated but can be teased out by reviewing what have been cited as components of the Chinese takings law over the last century. For instance, regarded as the first piece of legislation in this area promulgated by the communist government, the 1939 *Land Regulation of Shan'ganning Border Region* provided that, for roads, military use or public buildings, the government could expropriate people's land and pay land price.[61] That was followed by the 1944 *Land Rights Regulation of Shan'ganning Border Region*, stipulating that for national defense

[59] Resolution on Certain Questions in the History of Our Party Since the Founding of the People's Republic of China (关于建国以来党的若干历史问题的决议), promulgated by CCP Central Committee on June 27, 1981, available at cpc.people.com.cn/GB/64162/71380/71387/71588/4854598.html.

[60] Peng Zhen, "Report on the Draft Amendment of the PRC Constitution (关于中华人民共和国宪法修改草案的报告) (originally published in 1982)," in *Selected Works of Peng Zhen* (彭真文选) (Beijing: Renmin Press, 1991).

[61] Arts. 18 and 19, *Land Regulation of Shan'ganning Border Region* (陕甘宁边区土地条例), promulgated by Shan'ganning Border Region Government on April 4, 1939, in Shanxi Archival Institute and Shanxi Academy of Social Science (ed.), *Selected Government Documents of Shan'ganning Border Region* (陕甘宁边区政府文件选编) (Beijing: Dang'an Press, 1986), vol. 1, p. 226.

facilities, public roads, urban renewal and other undertakings in the public interest, the government could expropriate land owned by individuals or social groups.[62] Moving into the PRC era, the 1953 *Measures on Land Requisition for State-led Construction* (1953 MLRSC) prescribed in Articles 2–3 that the state might requisition land needed for national defense facilities, factories, mines, railways, public transportation, water conservancy and irrigation projects, and municipal works, as well as other economic and cultural developments, as long as the vital interests of local people are respected and appropriate settlement provided for those affected. The 1958 *Measures on Land Requisition for State-led Construction* (1958 MLRSC) followed suit (Articles 2–3). The 1982 *Regulation on Land Requisition for State-led Construction* (1982 RLRSC) authorized the state to requisition with compensation rural collective-owned land for the construction of economic, cultural, military and social public undertakings (Articles 2 and 9). Apparently, despite difference in terminology, these stipulations, which are regarded as parts of the Chinese takings law, all ascribe two essential elements to the power of land takings: (1) some kind of public works as the purpose and (2) the requirement of compensation. With this, the Sino–US comparison is not only possible, but virtually necessary because both are understood to deal with the same public power.

The above four assumptions are internally consistent with and mutually supportive of one another. While the conceptual assumption establishes the case for Sino–US comparison and the teleological assumption points out the normatively desirable destination, the temporal and developmental assumptions explain, in practical terms, what prevents the anticipated and desired transition from happening. Therefore, under the TP, the land takings clause in the 1982 Constitution is seen to have made a promise similar to the Fifth Amendment to the American Constitution. With this as the departure point, much of the existing analyses revolve around exposing and critiquing the deficiencies of the Chinese law on rural land expropriation, which is regarded to have betrayed the promise

[62] Art. 13, *Land Rights Regulation of Shan'ganning Border Region* (陕甘宁边区地权条例), promulgated by Shan'ganning Border Region Government in December 1944, in Division of Legal History at Northwestern Academy of Politics and Law (ed.), *Selected Materials of Modern Chinese Legal History 1840-1949* (中国近代法制史选集1840-1949) (Beijing: Division of Legal History at Northwestern Academy of Politics and Law, 1985), vol. 1, p. 586. Note that the 1939 draft of this 1944 Regulation stipulates in Article 25 that for the same purposes the government may requisition the needed land for a price (备价征用). This means that requisition in the 1944 Regulation does require the payment of land price.

of China's own Fifth Amendment in failing to properly constrain the takings power and protecting property rights. As a result, a consensus has now been reached that the goal of reform in this field is to honor this broken constitutional promise by triggering the transition toward the American model, which has so far been impeded by land finance and will be realized once that obstacle is removed.

It is worth noting at this point that due to its primary focus on the black-letter law of rural land expropriation, especially how it has broken the constitutional promise, the TP naturally bears a doctrinal bent in contrast to the more sociological approach that examines how the law actually operates in reality. But that does not negate the validity and influence of the TP because to a large extent the sociological approach too is under its spell, as exemplified by all three sociologically oriented book-length treatments currently available in the English language on this topic.[63] For instance, You-tien Hsing explored the complex and complicated state–society interaction in land expropriation and demonstrated the variegated spatial strategies adopted by the Chinese government at different levels, vertically organized functional state agencies (dubbed as the "socialist land masters"), private developers, as well as the expropriatees. Situated in the discipline of human geography, Hsing's research centered on the concept of "territoriality," meaning the strategization by various stakeholders to define and defend the occupation and control of a place. Coming from a different disciplinary background, the historian Qin Shao examined in detail a plethora of legal, extra-legal and illegal tactics deployed by local residents to resist government expropriation. Using "domicide" and "defiance" as primary analytical prisms, Shao offered a vivid ethnography about how government land grabs were responded to on the ground in China's megacity Shanghai during the last decade. More recently, Hualing Fu and John Gillespie co-edited a volume looking at resolution of land disputes, including those caused by land expropriation, in East Asia. Out of all seven chapters on China in that volume, only one chapter by Lei Chen is dedicated to the doctrinal and institutional aspects of the Chinese takings law. The six other chapters are devoted to documenting and analyzing how the written legal texts are interpreted, deployed and distorted in expropriation-based disputes by various actors, including the local governments and expropriatees, covering such topics as contending conceptions of property rights upheld

[63] Hsing, *The Great Urban Transformation*; Shao, *Shanghai Gone*; Fu and Gillespie, *Resolving Land Disputes in East Asia*.

by different parties[64] and the use of mediation and court proceedings to diffuse social tension or highlight grievances.[65]

A common theme running through all these studies is their concern for the law in action instead of the law on paper, which is for good reasons. As will be shown in this book, the existing rural land expropriation law in China does face enormous enforcement difficulties, manifested by, among other things, rampant unauthorized expropriation, an enormous amount of small property housing[66] and embezzlement of compensation by officials and rural collective leaders. Yet what is missing from the sociologically minded research is, quite unavoidably, the interest in and consequently an inquiry into what the legal texts really mean and how they have been formulated in the first place. For instance, Hsing observed that,

> Although collective land requisitions need to be based on the "public interest," the lack of definition of "public interest" has been taken not as a constraint, but as an excuse of land grabs. In the name of the public interest, urban governments are able to expropriate farmland to build commercial housing complexes, industrial zones, wholesale and retail markets, golf courses, and amusement parks.[67]

In a similar critical tone, Shao remarked that "laws, much like traffic signs, are treated as something optional in China. Their enforcement is essentially pragmatic, to serve the interest of the enforcers themselves – the local governments in most cases."[68] In their introductory chapter, Fu and Gillespie spelled out the central puzzle addressed by their book: "From a legal perspective, the proliferation of land disputes is puzzling, because it is occurring at the same time as governments in China and Vietnam are clarifying property rights and improving formal dispute resolution institutions." The answer suggested in their volume is that there is a marked gap between the written rules and on-the-ground operation of such rules, frustrating to a large degree any well-meaning intentions embedded in or any improvements on the Chinese law of

[64] Eva Pils, "Contending Conceptions of Ownership in Urbanizing China," in Fu and Gillespie, *Resolving Land Disputes in East Asia.*

[65] Susan H. Whiting and Hua Shao, "Courts and Political Stability: Mediating Rural Land Disputes," in Fu and Gillespie, *Resolving Land Disputes in East Asia*; Xin He, "Protest-supported Housing Demolition Litigation and Social Change in China," in Fu and Gillespie, *Resolving Land Disputes in East Asia.*

[66] The phenomenon of small property housing in China and its relationship with rural land expropriation law will be discussed in more depth in Chapter 8.

[67] Hsing, *The Great Urban Transformation*, p. 95.

[68] Shao, *Shanghai Gone*, p. 18.

property rights and expropriation. For example, in comparing China and America through the *Kelo* case, Frank Upham issued a damning verdict on the former: "Eminent domain abuse in the United States, at least, has the virtue of being legal; in other words, it is an abuse only in the sense that the acquiring government is using its legal power when it should not be doing so, either for moral or political reasons."[69] This is another way of saying that in the PRC abusive land takings are enacted outside the legal realm, with the written constitutional mandate completely neglected and sidelined.

There is of course nothing wrong with pinpointing the fact that Chinese takings law has often denigrated into excuses for local governments to justify their unjustifiable exercises of the takings power. But to think that such abuses are happening *in spite of* the law is, on a deeper level, not so different from the conventional doctrinal analyses, which find that such abuses occur *because of* the law and its deficiencies. Both positions share the underlying premise that the central function of the Chinese takings law is to constrain the takings power and protect private property, just like its American analogue. According to Upham, "The only issue was whether the taking of plaintiffs' property was for a 'public use,' as required by the federal constitution, a test functionally equivalent to the provisions of the Vietnamese and Chinese constitutions."[70] Given that the public interest provision in the Chinese constitutional takings clause and the public use requirement in the American Fifth Amendment are functionally equivalent to one another, in lacking any definition on what public interest means, the Chinese rural land expropriation law can be seen both as constituting a pretext for abusive land grabs (as Hsing does following the sociological approach) and as suffering from one serious defect (as the conventional doctrinal literature maintains). In this sense, both perspectives converge in their subscription to the core component of the TP – the teleological assumption. They come up with distinctive explanations as to why the Chinese Fifth Amendment does not work in practice: the doctrinal camp points the finger of blame at the inadequacies of the written law whilst the sociological camp holds the sluggish enforcement of the legal texts culpable. Insofar as their normative and prescriptive outlook is concerned, however, they are bedfellows resting upon the same foundation.

[69] Fu and Gillespie, *Resolving Land Disputes in East Asia*, p. 49. [70] Ibid., p. 44.

1.5 Theme, Thesis and Structure of the Book

This book aims to challenge the foundation on which the conventional wisdom is placed. The TP will be called into question and its core assumptions refuted. Since the TP amounts to an internally coherent account, in descriptive, normative and prescriptive terms, of the current Chinese rural land takings law, and the four mutually supportive assumptions form an analytically indissoluble complex, the only way to overcome the TP is to reshape its problematique and reorient the line of inquiry. Specifically, instead of asking why the Chinese rural land takings law has failed to honor China's own Fifth Amendment and what can be done as remedy, this book investigates how it has become what it is today. Its overarching theme is to explore the origin and evolution of China's rural land takings law over time, for which a historical approach is adopted.

However, that is not to discount the value of the doctrinal and sociological approaches, which have generated much insight into the relevant law. But lacking a historical understanding, we are unable to come to terms with what exactly gives rise to this less-than-ideal situation where the takings law in China seems both defective and ineffective. Does the Chinese legislator consciously and purposefully neglect the constitutional promise when drafting and implementing subordinate statutes and regulations regarding rural land expropriation? Or is it an unintended consequence due to innocently erroneous reading of the constitutional mandate? Or is the takings clause itself effectively an example of a "sham constitution" that is never designed for actual enforcement?[71] Without considering these questions, the existing doctrinal and sociological studies are incapable of explaining how the law has originated and evolved up to the present day. That can only be addressed through an in-depth examination of the historical context that has shaped the law. An *internal* and *sympathetic* understanding of the law is therefore the objective here.

An internal understanding is defined by its contrast to an external reading that sees the Chinese rural land takings law primarily through a comparative prism, manifested by the Sino–US comparison mentioned before. The risk associated therein has been well articulated by Donald Clarke, a seasoned American commentator on Chinese law. He took issue with what he called the "ideal western legal order" (IWLO) framework that analyzes Chinese law by treating it explicitly or implicitly

[71] David S. Law and Mila Versteeg, "Sham Constitutions" (2013) 101 *California Law Review* 863.

as an imperfect realization of the Western legal system. This way of thinking, as argued by Clarke, is questionable since the ideal against which the Chinese legal system is measured is oftentimes unstated and unjustified. Even when a particular version of the IWLO is stated and justified, to analyze Chinese law through such evaluative comparison is still likely to fall short of telling us something significant and interesting about it. This is because while demonstrating to what extent the Chinese law measures up to some sort of external standard, such a comparative approach is hardly illuminating as to its internal structures, values and dynamics. Worse still, since a comparative perspective necessarily entails identifying the comparable, i.e. determining what is there to be compared, it tends to assume certain functional and conceptual equivalence between Chinese and foreign legal phenomena. It typically starts from what is understood as the salient features of a foreign (and supposedly universal) legal system, and then uses that as the guiding light to depict Chinese law. As a consequence, the comparative approach is likely to blind us to those legal experiences that are unique to China, which hardly have any analogue in non-Chinese contexts and cannot be observed or comprehended through comparison. The lenses we employ to look at the world not only enlighten us, but also impose limitations upon what we can discover.

In the meantime, given the idealized nature of the comparator, IWLO analysis usually, though not necessarily, takes a critical stance toward Chinese law and spots shortcomings here and there. One extreme manifestation is the so-called ethnocentric *Legal Orientalism*, which, as explained by Teemu Ruskola, considers China to be a nonlegal nonsubject lacking the universal and desirable values that are only found in the West, epitomized by the USA.[72] This is the opposite to the sympathetic understanding this book endeavors to achieve, which practices ethics of Orientalism recommended by Ruskola by allowing the subject of Chinese rural land takings law, both in the ordinary sense (as an area of scholarly inquiry) and in the sense of subjectification (recognizing it as a subject capable of agency), to emerge from its own historical conditions. To put it differently, a sympathetic reading of Chinese law requires us to analyze it following its own logic and in its own terms, rather than in light of its performance in realizing certain pregiven functions.[73] If such advice is

[72] Teemu Ruskola, *Legal Orientalism: China, the United States and Modern Law* (Cambridge, MA: Harvard University Press, 2013), pp. 42, 55.

[73] Ibid., pp. 54–55.

followed, as sensibly pointed out by Donald Clarke, a riddle previously identified in China's legal system from a critical standpoint may simply be a mistake. Errors and aberrations detected before may turn out to be no more than normal and expected phenomena.[74] However, it should be cautioned that the point here is emphatically not isolating Chinese law from criticism. Nor is it to claim that it is in any sense equal or superior to Western law. Rather, it is that the descriptive and the physiological must come before the prescriptive and the pathological. One is of course entitled to pass judgment upon and recommend improvement measures for a particular branch of Chinese law. But that had better be done based on a sympathetic understanding so that the criticism can be immanent and grounded in the sense that it uses the law's own premises, principles and functions to identify tensions and difficulties within it.

Against this background, the core aim of book is to offer a contextualized description and immanent critique of China's rural land takings law, based on an internal and sympathetic understanding of its origin and evolution. The principal substantive argument advanced here is that the Chinese rural land takings law is by nature sui generis, meaning that it is shaped by the distinctive intellectual, political and social conditions in modern China, and as a result cannot be understood through comparison or conflation with the American law of eminent domain.

To begin with, for more than a century in China, the concept "taking" has had a much more expansive connotation than the conventional meaning of compensatory expropriation for specific public works. Most notably, it included compensationless land nationalization initiated by the communist party-state. In marked contrast to the USA, where the takings power is the *last resort* used only diffusely and occasionally to solve such problems as holdouts that cannot solved by voluntary market mechanism, in modern China the takings power has been conceptualized and deployed as the *first resort* to systematically carry out macro social transformation programs, be it revolutionary campaigns or economic development. There is a long-standing tradition of land takings for state-led social transformation characterized by expansive, nonparticipatory and unchallengeable takings power, which predates the opening and reform era since the late 1970s. Massive rural land taking is not just a contemporary issue, but has a longer historical lineage. It is therefore

[74] Donald C. Clarke, "Puzzling Observations in Chinese Law: When Is a Riddle Just a Mistake?," in Stephen Hsu (ed.), *Understanding China's Legal System: Essays in Honor of Jerome A. Cohen* (New York: New York University Press, 2003).

necessary to extend the investigative horizon beyond the post-reform period to the late nineteenth century when the intellectual foundation of the Chinese takings law was laid. "Modern China" in the book title is shorthand for this time period, which is also generally recognized in the historiography of China. Crucially, the original Chinese constitutional takings clause in the 1954 Constitution had not been designed to perform an equivalent function as the Fifth Amendment to the American Constitution. Instead, it was intended to be power-confirming, rather than power-constraining and right-protecting. Such a constitutional agenda was very much inherited by the existing constitutional takings clause in the 1982 Constitution. Against this backdrop, from the 1950s to this day, the Chinese rural land expropriation law has exhibited amazingly strong path dependence with three enduring features: the presumption of state expropriation in nonagricultural use of rural collective land; expropriation decision-making through hierarchical review and approval according to state planning and a socialist principle that considers the state as the representative of public interest and expropriation as obligation rather than transaction or sacrifice. In this light, the existing rural land expropriation law in China is not, as the conventional wisdom holds, an unfortunate betrayal of the constitutional mandate, but a faithful reflection thereof. It is in this sense that the widely perceived aberration in China's rural land takings law should be seen as normal and expected.

That said, for more than a decade there has been mounting pressure for deeper reforms. Nonetheless, very little progress has been made in rolling out the popular reform proposals suggested by previous commentators, which in one way or another aim to bring the Chinese rural land takings law closer to its American counterpart. But that cannot be entirely blamed on land finance, as suggested by the received wisdom. The reason is that whereas land finance does provide incentives for local governments to expropriate more and resisting substantive reforms, it is by no means the root cause of the existing arrangements, which would have been the same and will not wither away even without land finance. This is not to suggest, however, that the current rural land expropriation law is without problems or is immune to further change. Quite the contrary – it faces criticism and challenges with regard to its effectiveness, efficiency, fairness and constitutionality because of the momentous changes that have occurred to the conditions that were once congenial. In particular, constitutional amendments since the late 1990s formally commit the Chinese party-state to respect the rule of law, human rights and private property. A rights-protecting agenda has been introduced into China's constitutional takings jurisprudence and a better balance between the competing power-confirming and power-constraining traditions is thus needed. Yet since a complete abandoning of the power-confirming tradition of rural land takings for social transformation is unlikely to happen anytime soon, the Chinese rural land expropriation law is by no means expecting imminent meltdown or transition to the American model. Instead, it will continue to evolve within the current broad parameters. In the foreseeable future, relevant reform will only be marginal and gradual, with the focus on strengthening public participation in the making of spatial plans and sharing more expropriation surplus to the expropriated.

The remainder of this book proceeds in seven chapters. The second and third chapters set the scene for readers by presenting the conventional wisdom in this field. Chapters 4–5 explore the origin of China's rural land takings law by analyzing the original takings clause of 1954 and examining the theoretical foundations of land takings laid down in the early twentieth century. Chapter 6 offers an in-depth analysis of the current constitutional takings clause enacted in 1982, and Chapter 7 exposes the continuity of the expropriation law from the pre-reform era to the reform period. The final chapter takes stock, presents an immanent critique of the existing law and discusses its future prospects.

2

A Broken Constitutional Promise

Diagnoses and Prescriptions

For more than a decade, rural land takings law has been one of the most researched topics in Chinese legal studies. As previewed in the previous chapter, under the TP, the conventional wisdom goes that China's constitutional takings clause is not implemented because the existing takings law is considerably underdeveloped compared with its American counterpart in constraining the takings power and protecting property rights. As mentioned, past analyses centered on the present constitutional takings clause, with a three-pronged structure: the public interest prerequisite, obligation to compensate and the general requirement of legality in expropriation decision-making and compensation. Against this background, diagnoses and prescriptions have been put forward on why constitutional protection of private property is ineffective in China and how that can be fixed.

This chapter presents the conventional wisdom in three sections. Section 2.1 discusses the triple challenge facing the public interest prerequisite. Section 2.2 explains the statutory compensation standard, which has long been criticized as both unjust and unfair, substantively and procedurally. Section 2.3 goes on to examine a set of reform recommendations suggested by previous studies that aim to make China's own Fifth Amendment work in practice.

2.1 Public Interest Prerequisite: Triple Challenge

2.1.1 The Definitional Challenge

As one would expect, the constitutionally embedded public interest requirement is central to justifying government decisions of expropriation. For example, in the United States, much ink has been spilled by judges and scholars on the appropriate remit of the public use clause in the Fifth Amendment to the federal constitution. At the state level, legislatures have also played an active role in delineating the four corners thereof.[1] Yet it is suggested that "although the doctrine of public interest is now entrenched in China's laws and constitution, its role in limiting the government taking power is still weak or nearly nonexistent."[2] Therefore, the public interest prerequisite in the Chinese constitutional takings clause is suggested to be "symbolized," meaning that it has no real impact in expropriation decision-making.[3]

The so-called symbolization of the public interest clause starts with the fact that its scope has never been demarcated. On the one hand, although it has a series of statutory analogues, including the 2007 *Property Law* (Article 42), 2009 *Urban Real Estate Administration Law* (UREAL, Article 6) and 2004 LAL (Article 2), its exact meaning has never been spelled out. Neither the national nor the local people's congress has ever defined what public interest means as far as expropriation is concerned.

Second, and perhaps more problematically, Chinese courts have so far remained silent on the public interest prerequisite. This is in direct contrast with the American situation, where both federal and state courts have been, for centuries, expounding and fine-tuning the boundary of the constitutional public use clause when reviewing individual takings decisions. Yet there is no interpretation from China's Supreme People's Court (SPC) or local courts on what public interest entails in land takings. That is because government decisions to expropriate rural land have long been considered nonjusticiable because they are regarded either as administrative decisions with finality (*xingzheng zhongju caijue*)[4] or abstract administrative acts (*chouxiang xingzheng xingwei*),[5] both of which are excluded from judicial review according to Article 12 of the 1989 *Administrative Litigation Law* (ALL).

1 For instance, after the contentious *Kelo* case in which the US Supreme Court ruled in favor of eminent domain for the sake of economic development, there was a widespread backlash among many state legislatures to amend the state law on eminent domain to provide a more stringent definition of public purpose of eminent domain. The Castle Coalition, "50 State Report Card: Tracking Eminent Domain Reform Since Kelo," 2009, available at www.castlecoalition.org/index.php?option=com_content&task=view&id=2412&Itemid=129.

2 Chuanhui Wang, *The Constitutional Protection of Private Property in China: Historical Evolution and Comparative Research* (Cambridge: Cambridge University Press, 2016), p. 165.

3 Ibid.

4 Jie Cheng, "Procedural Anomy and Reconstruction in Land Expropriation and Requisition (土地征收征用中的程序失范与重构)" (2006) 1 *Legal Studies* (法学研究) 72.

5 Eva Pils, "Peasants" Struggle for Land in China," in Yash Ghai and Jill Cottrell (eds.), *Marginalized Communities and Access to Justice* (London: Routledge, 2010), p. 142.

To be sure, it is almost impossible to pin down a concept as nebulous as public interest with absolute precision. Around the world, the legitimate scope of public purpose in land takings is usually highly contested. Nevertheless, it is not a logical necessity that an absence of judicial and statutory definition of public interest will open the floodgates for expansive or even abusive expropriation. The reason is that the open-texturedness of the term does not mean that it is not without any boundaries. While there are some borderline cases where it is difficult to tell whether certain takings are in the public interest, not every case is a hard case. It is reasonable to think that in many, if not most, instances there should be and will be a generally accepted line between public and nonpublic interest and that the government ought to refrain from expropriating for the latter.

Unfortunately, however, as already suggested, in contemporary China rural land expropriation has been carried out for almost all kinds of ends, many of which hardly qualify as public interest understood in any sensible way.[6] A 2003 MLR report admitted that between 2000 and 2001, in the 16 provinces surveyed, 21.9 percent of expropriated rural land was subsequently used for profit-making development such as golf courses, shopping malls, sports stadiums, commercial housing and so on.[7] How are local governments in China able to do so?

2.1.2 The Structural Challenge

There are many factors behind the nationwide fervor of rural land expropriation, the most crucial of which lies in a unique feature of the current land administration system in China. In most cases when rural land is put to nonagricultural purposes, it must first be converted into urban land through state expropriation. I call this the structural challenge

[6] Chenglin Liu, "The Chinese Takings Law from a Comparative Perspective" (2008) 26 *Washington University Journal of Law & Policy* 318; Chenglin Liu, "Informal Rules, Transaction Costs, and the Failure of the "Takings' Law in China" (2005) 29 *Hastings International and Comparative Law Review* 6; Jianlin Chen, "China's 'Ding Zi Hu', US's Kelo and Singapore's En-bloc Process: A New Model For Economic Development Eminent Domain From a Giving's Perspective" (2008) 24 *Journal of Land Use and Environmental Law* 115; Annette M. Kim, "Land Takings in the Private Interest: Comparisons of Urban Land Development Controversies in the United States, China, and Vietnam" (2009) 11 *Cityscape* 19.

[7] Xinshe Lu (ed.), *Studying the Problem of Land Expropriation, Exploring the Road of Reform* (研究征地问题探索改革之路) (Beijing: China Dadi Press, 2003), vol. 1, p. 46. The editor was then the deputy minister of the MLR.

to the constitutional public interest prerequisite, which is manifested in two ways: one is the "urbanization challenge," and the other the "de-agrarianization challenge."

Before we move on to explain these two challenges, "urbanization" and "de-agrarianization" need be defined. Urbanization is ordinarily understood as the socioeconomic transformation of human society, characterized by large-scale migration of people from the countryside to live and work in the cities. De-agrarianization is used in the developmental economics literature to describe social change involving economic activity reorientation, occupational adjustment and spatial realignment of human settlement.[8] In our context, however, these two terms have different connotations. First and foremost, they stand for the alteration in the legal categorization of land. Under existing law, land in China is classified in two ways: (1) urban and rural land depending on location and ownership; and (2) agricultural, construction and unused land according to use.[9] Each parcel of land is assigned a specific use, which cannot be converted without authorization. Against this backdrop, urbanization means the conversion of land legally classified as rural into land legally classified as urban. De-agrarianization means the conversion of land legally designated for agricultural uses into nonagricultural purposes – industrial, commercial, military, governmental, infrastructural and so on. Of course, such legal changes are usually driven by – and, in turn, drive – broader socioeconomic changes described by urbanization or de-agrarianization in the ordinary sense. But here these two terms stand for changes in land classification.

The urbanization challenge to the public interest requirement arises out of the land ownership regime in China. The first two paragraphs of Article 10 of the current Constitution prescribe that urban land is owned by the state and rural land belongs to the collectives. The fourth paragraph forbids sales of land. In the existing literature, these provisions are interpreted to mean that if land is to change hands from collectives to the state, it cannot be sold but must go through expropriation by the state, which is supposed to own all urban land in China. In this way, urbanization and expropriation are tied together.[10]

The de-agrarianization challenge exists because extant law places stringent use limitations upon rural collective-owned land. According

[8] Deborah Fahy Bryceson, "Deagrarianization and Rural Employment in Sub-Saharan Africa: a Sectoral Perspective" (1996) 24 *World Development* 99.

[9] 1982 Constitution, art. 10; 2004 LAL, art. 4.

[10] More detailed discussion of this point will appear in Chapter 6.

to Articles 43 and 63 of the 2004 LAL and Article 9 of the 2009 UREAL, the default position is that lawful usage of rural land is confined to agricultural purposes such as cultivation, pasture and so on. For nonagricultural uses, on the one hand, it cannot be transferred via the market to noncollective parties (including sales and leases) but must first be expropriated and converted into state-owned urban land. In particular, Article 9 of the UREAL stipulates that collective-owned land within planned urban areas (*chengshi guihua qu*) must be expropriated and turned into state-owned urban land before the use-rights thereof can be transferred. On the other hand, apart from a relatively small breakthrough that emerged recently,[11] rural collectives can use their land for nonagricultural purposes without expropriation under only five exceptional scenarios: (1) for peasant household residential plots (*zhaiji di*); (2) for local public utilities and social welfare facilities;[12] (3) for township and village enterprises (TVEs); (4) for joint ventures established by rural collectives with other parties using use-rights in rural land as in-kind contribution;[13] and (5) in case of bankruptcy or merger of the abovementioned TVEs and joint ventures that result in transfer of use-rights to noncollective entities, land may continue to be used for the original nonagricultural purpose.[14] The first two are categorized as nonprofit rural construction land (*gongyi xing jiti jianshe yongdi*), while the latter three are categorized as for-profit rural construction land (*jingying xing jiti jianshe yongdi*).[15] Even for these permissible construction uses, rural collectives still need to obtain government authorization.[16] Except for these five cases, nonagricultural use of rural land must go through expropriation and subsequent transfer of

[11] This will be discussed in Chapter 3.

[12] 2004 LAL, art. 43. Peasant household residential plots are the land allocated by the collectives to their member peasant households to build family houses on. This is a legacy of China's collectivization campaign, which started in the 1950s and was first enshrined in a 1962 Central Party document. In the post-reform era, it became formally recognized in law. See art. 21, *Revised Draft Regulation on the Work in the Rural People's Communes* (农村人民公社工作条例修正草案), promulgated by CCP Central Committee on September 27, 1962, available at www.moa.gov.cn/zwllm/zcfg/flfg/200601/t20060120_539367.htm. See also 2004 LAL, art. 8; 2007 Property Law, chapter 13.

[13] 2004 LAL, art. 60. [14] 2004 LAL, art. 63.

[15] This is an important distinction in understanding the most recent pilot land reforms in China. For more discussion, see Chapter 3.

[16] 2004 LAL, art. 44. For what it is worth, it is further stipulated in Article 41 of the 2007 Urban and Rural Planning Law (URPL) that rural collectives ought to obtain planning permission from the government when initiating permissible construction use of their agricultural land.

land use-rights. I call this the presumption of state expropriation in non-agricultural use of rural land.

The structural interlocking of expropriation and urbanization/de-agrarianization is of utmost importance to understanding the enormity of rural land takings in today's China. While the definitional challenge to the public interest prerequisite makes massive expropriation *possible*, the structural challenge effectively renders it *necessary*. Whenever rural land is needed to make way for urban expansion and nonagricultural development, it is done through expropriation. It is therefore no wonder that rapidly urbanizing and industrializing China has been experiencing large-scale rural land expropriation for decades.

But that rings alarm bells to those concerned with the written constitutional mandate of expropriation for public interest. For instance, more than a decade ago, the eminent Chinese economist Qiren Zhou suggested there was a "paradox of expropriation" embedded in China's rural land takings law.[17] His formulation is that if a private factory occupies a piece of rural land without expropriation, this is unlawful because it breaks the legal limitation over nonagricultural uses of rural land. To avoid this, the government then has to expropriate rural land for the private factory, which is nevertheless unconstitutional for violating the public interest prerequisite.[18] On a more general level, Professor Zhou's point is that since the post-expropriation land development cannot possibly be carried out by the state alone, it is inevitable that the expropriated land will be transferred by the state to private developers and end up generating profits for them. Expropriation of this kind is undeniably in the private rather than public interest.

While definitely right in pointing out the danger, if not the reality, of expropriation being deployed to benefit private parties, Professor Zhou went too far in implying that private interests should never be involved in the process of promoting public interest. To be clear, no government has

[17] Qiren Zhou, "Property Rights on Rural Land and the Land Acquisition System: A Critical Choice for China's Urbanization (农地产权与征地制度: 中国城市化面临的重大选择)" (2004) 4 *China Economic Quarterly* (经济学季刊) 193.

[18] It is logically sensible to say that without a legal definition of what constitutes public interest to begin with, it is not possible to determine whether or not an action is unconstitutional in the legal sense. Nevertheless, one can still meaningfully talk about the unconstitutionality of certain expropriation decisions that are not in the public interest as defined in any reasonable fashion. In this sense, the paradox here is not a legal one at the moment, but will become one once a reasonable definition of public interest is supplied.

monopoly over all undertakings that contribute to public interest. A case in point is that a market comprised of private participants oftentimes does a much better job than the state in growing the economy and raising living standards. It is both reasonable and legitimate for government to hand expropriated rural land out for private use and development when public interest can be better served thereby. Of course, this is not always justified. For example, it is morally indefensible to expropriate Peter's land and transfer it to Paul simply because Peter the peasant uses his land for agricultural production and Paul the industrialist will put such land to commercial uses that are more profitable. Rather, the point is that private use and development of expropriated land does not by definition defy the public interest prerequisite. There is a line – and sometimes a very fine one – to be drawn here. As discussed, in America it is ultimately for the judiciary to fulfill that task. But the Chinese courts have not performed any similar function. Lacking an impartial arbitrator to determine the public interestedness of expropriation decisions, the constitutional public interest prerequisite is rendered redundant.

2.1.3 *The Procedural Challenge*

Given that a definitive definition of public purpose in land takings is difficult to achieve, a procedural approach has been taken by many countries, including the United States, to demand democratic authorization of and public input into the decision-making of takings, exemplified by the due process doctrine entrenched in both the Fifth and Fourteenth Amendments to the US Constitution. In China, however, the expression of "in accordance with law" in the constitutional takings clause is criticized for imposing "no limits through its literal reading" upon ordering expropriation.[19] More critically, neither the legislature nor the expropriated is conferred in law any opportunity to scrutinize or take part in the decision-making process. The public interest prerequisite has thus not been procedurally operationalized, which further reduces the likelihood that expropriation decisions reflect the interests of the local community.[20] Instead, expropriation decision-making in China is confined within the government system through a top-down review and approval mechanism.

19 Wang, *The Constitutional Protection of Private Property in China*, p. 246.
20 Ibid., pp. 247–55.

The administrative hierarchy of China has five tiers: national, provincial, prefectural, county and township.[21] Under existing law, rural land expropriation is initiated by prefectural and county governments, which submit their expropriation application to the provincial or national government for authorization.[22] Once decisions are made by provincial or central government, the 2004 LAL and the current *Land Administration Law Implementation Regulation* (LALIR) stipulate that the condemnees will go through the so-called "two notifications and one registration" process, where they will be informed of the expropriation decision and the approved overall compensation plan, and asked to register for their property rights in land and aboveground structures so as to help determine the amount of compensation due to each household.[23] Throughout this process, local governments are not required either to consult the expropriated or to address their objection against the takings decisions per se. The condemnees are legally entitled to do nothing but accept approved expropriation.[24]

Overall, the constitutional public interest prerequisite has neither substantive nor procedural guarantee in existing Chinese law. As demonstrated, the decision to expropriate is essentially an administrative prerogative immune to legislative scrutiny, judicial checks and public participation. Hence, the relevant law is criticized as "undue because it does not fairly balance government power and private property rights."[25] In this situation, one can only hope that the other prong of the constitutional takings clause – the obligation to compensate – will provide some solace in forming an extra layer of constraint over the takings power. However, that is not the case.

2.2 Expropriation Compensation: Unjust and Unfair

2.2.1 Unjust Statutory Compensation Standard

To start with, compared with its American counterpart, the Chinese constitutional compensation requirement is considered to be defective

[21] Villages are considered self-governing organizations at the grassroots level by the Organic Law of Village Committee first enacted in 1988. Yet it is well known that Chinese villages are under great influence of the government and are far from truly autonomous.

[22] 2004 LAL, arts. 21, 44, 45.

[23] 2004 LAL, art. 46; 2011 LALIR, art. 25. Since 2004 there have been a series of policy changes on this front, which will be discussed in more detail in Chapter 3. But the statutory procedural arrangements remain unaltered.

[24] Wang, *The Constitutional Protection of Private Property in China*, p. 272.

[25] Ibid., p. 271.

for missing the adjective "just" before "compensation."[26] The concern here is more substantial than formal: without the qualifying prefix "being just," the government is conferred too broad a discretionary remit to establish whatever compensation standard it sees fit, which seems to be exactly what happens.

The national statutory compensation standard for rural land expropriation in China is set out in Article 47 of the 2004 LAL,[27] which can be broken down into three components: compensation for land (*tudi buchang fei*), compensation for resettling the expropriated (*anzhi buzhu fei*) and compensation for fixtures and standing crops above the expropriated land (*dishang fuzhuo wu ji qingmiao buchang fei*). As a matter of principle, the first two components are calculated based on the original use (*yuan yongtu*) of the expropriated land, meaning that compensation for land and resettlement is predicated on the current land value. For example, if a parcel of cultivated land gets expropriated, the statutory standard of land compensation is set at 6–10 times its "average annual output" (*pingjun nianchan zhi*) of agricultural products over the 3 years prior to expropriation. The resettlement compensation standard for each condemnee is 4–6 times of the average annual output, while the maximum resettlement compensation per hectare cannot exceed 15 times that value.[28] As to expropriation of other types of land, such as nonprofit and for-profit rural construction land, relevant compensation standards are not specified in the LAL. The power to formulate such standards is devolved to provincial governments, which should take into account the compensation standard for cultivated land prescribed in the LAL. This means that the average annual output of cultivated land serves as the benchmark for expropriation compensation for all sorts of rural land. For instance, most provincial rules prescribe that the compensation standard for expropriating rural construction land is the same as that for expropriation of adjacent cultivated land.[29] Similarly, compensation standards for fixtures and standing crops above land are also formulated at the provincial level. In practice, such power is typically delegated

[26] Ibid., p. 76. [27] It is echoed by Article 42 of the 2007 *Property Law*.

[28] Total resettlement fee per hectare = average annual output × 4–6 × number of people resettled per hectare. If 4–6 × number of people resettled per hectare >15, the resettlement compensation will still be 15 × average annual output.

[29] Maohui Qu and Zhifang Zhou, "A Study on Compensation Standards for Land Expropriation in China: An Analysis based on Local Legislative Texts (中国土地征收补偿标准研究：基于地方立法文本的分析)" (2009) 3 *Legal Studies* (法学研究) 169.

further down, to prefectural and county governments, and there is no uniform practice in this regard.

Overall, the national statutory compensation standard demands that if land compensation and resettlement compensation together is inadequate to maintain the "original living standards" (*yuanyou shenghuo shuiping*) of the expropriated, provincial governments may increase the amount of resettlement compensation. However, the sum is capped at 30 times the average annual output.[30] That said, it is also stipulated that the State Council may, considering the level of social and economic development and under special circumstances, raise compensation standards for land and resettlement.

Such a national statutory standard has been criticized as unjust mainly on three grounds. First, it is under fire for being too vague. As it only establishes the interval between minimum and maximum amount of compensation, it is up to local governments, especially the expropriation-initiating prefectural and county governments, to work out specific standards and decide on the exact amount of compensation to be paid in individual cases on the basis of the statutory formula of "average annual output × multiplier." However, without supplying any concrete guidelines, the national statutory standard has granted very wide discretion to local governments, which have often made arbitrary, inconsistent and unfair compensation decisions.[31] For example, since the local governments are responsible for assessing and determining the average annual output, it is not uncommon that they intentionally undervalue such output to suppress compensation. Moreover, they have also been able to manipulate the multiplier, which usually hinges on the future use of the expropriated land, resulting in adjacent parcels of land receiving very different compensation simply due to being expropriated for different purposes.[32]

Second, the statutory compensation standard is condemned for being unfairly low. The argument goes that being capped at 30 times the

[30] As the maximum land compensation fee is set at 10 times the average annual output, at most the provincial governments may increase the resettlement compensation from 15 times to 20 times the average annual output.

[31] Chengri Ding, "Policy and Praxis of Land Acquisition in China" (2007) 24 *Land Use Policy* 8.

[32] Empirical research has shown that the amount of compensation paid for land to be used for public purposes is significantly lower than land used by private investors. See Klaus Deininger and Songqing Jin, "Securing Property Rights in Transition: Lessons from Implementation of China's Rural Land Contracting Law" (2009) 70 *Journal of Economic Behavior and Organization* 22.

average agricultural output, it falls short in reflecting even the current value of rural land.[33] The reasoning is as follows. As the time limitation of peasants' tenure over rural cultivated land is currently prescribed in law to be 30 years,[34] one can assume that the total current value of 30-year land use-rights is the discounted income generated by using such land over 30 years, which may simply be set at 30 times the average annual agricultural output.[35] It is further suggested that the value of 30-year use-rights constitutes around 85 percent of the value of full ownership,[36] making the capitalization rate 2.8 percent.[37] Therefore, fair compensation for expropriating collective ownership of cultivated land in its current use should be 35 times the average annual agricultural output – higher than the upper limit of statutory standard at 30 times.[38] However, this method of valuation is erroneous for predicating the value of use-rights upon the gross income it generates, i.e. the average annual output over a 30-year period, rather than the net income with production costs deducted. In the Chinese agricultural sector, cost of production may be

33 Valerie Jaffee Washburn, "Regular Takings or Regulatory Takings: Land Expropriation in Rural China" (2011) 20 *Pacific Rim Law & Policy Journal* 86.

34 2002 Rural Land Contracting Law, art. 20. Note that the tenure terms for grassland and forestland are longer, at 30–50 years and 30–70 years respectively; "30-year term" is used for the sake of convenience in analysis.

35 Washburn, "Regular Takings or Regulatory Takings," 87. It generously assumes that the annual rate of growth of agricultural output will suffice to cancel out whatever the appropriate discount rate is, and that the 30-year term of the present use-rights holder is just beginning. It should be noted that in 2008, the central authority declared that the peasants" use-rights over cultivated land would "remain unchanged for a very long time," generally interpreted to have extended the term of such rights from 30 years to infinity. But this change does not affect the validity of calculating the ownership value through dividing annual net return by the capitalization rate. For the policy change, see The Decision on Major Issues on Promoting Rural Reform and Development (关于推进农村改革发展若干重大问题的决定), part 3, point 1, promulgated by CCP Central Committee on October 12, 2008, available at www.gov.cn/test/2008-10/31/content_1136796.htm; see also Opinions on Promoting Agricultural Development and Continuous Increase of Peasants' Income in 2009 (关于2009年促进农业稳定发展农民持续增收的若干意见)", point 17, " promulgated by CCP Central Committee and State Council on December 31, 2008, available at www.gov.cn/gongbao/content/2009/content_1220471.htm. For relevant analysis of this change, see Robin Dean and Tobias Damm-Luhr, "A Current Review of Chinese Land-Use Law and Policy: A "Breakthrough" in Rural Reform?" (2010) 19 *Pacific Rim Law & Policy Journal* 138.

36 Washburn, "Regular Takings or Regulatory Takings," 86–87.

37 Average annual output × 30 ÷ 85%=average annual output ÷ 2.8%.

38 If a local government chooses, in a fully lawful manner, the lowest ends of the scale, i.e. 6 times annual output for land compensation and 4 times for resettlement compensation, the total compensation stands at 10 times the average annual output, which is merely one-third or one-fourth of the supposedly fair value.

set quite generously at 50 percent of the gross income, making the annual net profit half of the annual income.[39] In this case, with a 2.8 percent capitalization rate, the value of rural agricultural land ownership is about 17.86 times the average annual output, lower than the 30-times statutory cap. The point here, however, is not accuracy of calculation. It is that the statutory compensation standard is not necessarily less than the discounted value of full ownership of agricultural land in its original use.[40]

That said, the present statutory compensation standard remains under heavy criticism for being unjust due to a third – and most important – reason. Being based on the original use of expropriated land, it effectively denies the expropriatees any share in the value increase when their land is expropriated and converted into state-owned urban land, which can then be used for much more profitable nonagricultural purposes. The government reaps most of the "expropriation surplus" without sharing it with the land-owning collectives and rural residents.[41] From a legal perspective, expropriation surplus refers to the additional rights brought about by the very process of expropriation that lifts all the land use restrictions over rural land mentioned earlier. Once collective-owned rural land is expropriated and turned into state-owned urban land, it is no longer constrained to agricultural purposes and a very limited set of construction uses, but can be put to all sorts of nonagricultural ends, be they commercial, industrial or residential. This is done through what is known as the primary land market (*yiji tudi shichang*), where local governments transfer, after expropriation, use-rights of the now state-owned urban land to private parties, including commercial developers, who can then exchange such use-rights on the secondary land market (*erji tudi shichang*). As the Chinese economy has been growing rapidly, conversion from nonmarketizable rural land into marketized urban land usually results in enormous land-value increase. This is the expropriation surplus in economic terms, which largely falls into the purse of local states. Numerous empirical studies have disclosed the wide gap between expropriation compensation and the revenue governments get from post-expropriation land transfer. One estimate was that only 5 percent

39 Chengri Ding, "Compensation for Land Expropriation in China: Economic Analysis and Policy Recommendation (中国征地补偿制度的经济分析及征地改革建议)" (2007) 21 *China Land Science* (中国土地科学) 5.

40 If the local governments choose the lowest ends of the compensation scale at 10 times the average annual output, it will be lower than the true value. But if compensation worth over 20 times the average annual output is paid, it is then higher than the true value.

41 Washburn, "Regular Takings or Regulatory Takings," 84–88.

of all revenue generated from converting rural agricultural land to urban construction land since 1979 had been paid as compensation.[42] A 17-province survey in 2006 showed that 65.5 percent of the peasants whose land had been taken were dissatisfied with the amount of compensation they received.[43] Hence, across the country there are petitions and protests by expropriatees who feel unfairly treated when they see the huge difference between their paltry compensation and the enormous gain accrued to governments and developers.[44] It is therefore suggested that the "use of annual output as the method for calculating compensation moves compensation away from the expropriated land's real market value," which is "the commonly accepted explanation of the constitutional compensation principle."[45]

2.2.2 Disputing Compensation: Limited Room

However dissatisfactory the compensation, under existing law, rural condemnees can only bring up their objection at the post-approval and post-implementation stages. As mentioned earlier, the expropriated will be notified of the expropriation decisions and approved overall compensation plan after expropriation initiatives are authorized. Within ten working days of receiving approval from the central or provincial government, the initiating prefectural/county government shall serve an expropriation notice, detailing the approving authority, scope and proposed use of the expropriated land as well as the approved compensation standards and resettlement plan. Upon notification, the potential condemnees should go to the county/prefectural land bureaus to register for compensation with proof of property rights in land and aboveground structures. Within 45 days of the expropriation notice, the county/prefectural land bureau shall formulate and publish a detailed compensation plan specifying who gets what. Only at this point can the expropriated lodge objections. This is called the "post-approval challenge." Specifically, the expropriated can request a public hearing within ten days

42 Ibid., 67.

43 Keliang Zhu, Roy Prosterman, Jianping Ye, Ping Li, Jeffrey Riedinger and Yiwen Ouyang, "The Rural Land Question in China: Analysis and Recommendations based on a 17-province Survey" (2006) 38 *NYU Journal of International Law and Politics* 782.

44 The famous Wukan protest in 2011 was an example in point. See Michael Bristow, "Wukan Unrest: Why do Chinese Farmers Riot?," December 15, 2011, available at www.bbc.co.uk/news/world-asia-china-16193089.

45 Wang, *The Constitutional Protection of Private Property in China*, pp. 230–31.

of publication of the detailed compensation plan. If requested, the relevant land bureau ought to hold a public hearing to collect objections and comments and submit an updated compensation plan that is supposed to take account of comments and objections to the expropriation-initiating local government for authorization.[46] However, the current legal mechanism for post-approval challenges suffers from two defects, which significantly reduces the possibility of success. First, failure to hold public hearings upon request may lead to internal disciplinary actions against responsible officials, but that does not affect the validity of detailed compensation plan.[47] Second, since local land bureaus are not required to provide any feedback after public consultation or hearing, there is no guarantee that objections from the expropriated are taken seriously. In fact, once the updated detailed compensation plan is authorized, it starts to be implemented along with the expropriation decision.

At the post-implementation stage, if there remains any dispute on compensation and resettlement arrangements, it should first be mediated by the initiating government, and then in case of impasse submitted to provincial government for adjudication.[48] Exhaustion of this

[46] Arts. 4–5,7–10,15, Measures of Notice of Land Expropriation (征用土地公告办法), promulgated by MLR on October 18, 2002, available at www.mlr.gov.cn/zwgk/zdzc/201508/t20150805_1362061.htm. See also 2004 LAL, arts. 45–48; 1998 LALIR, art. 25.

[47] Art. 34, Rules on Public Hearings of Land Resources (国土资源听证规定), promulgated by MLR on January 1, 2004, available at www.mlr.gov.cn/zwgk/flfg/gtzybl/200504/t20050426_637346.htm.

[48] It should be noted that there are competing interpretations of Article 25 of the 1998 LALIR, which stipulates that compensation disputes should be first be mediated by the initiating government and then adjudicated by the expropriation-approving government. The MLR holds that adjudication is an independent dispute resolution mechanism separate from administrative reconsideration. Therefore, it shall be carried out by the expropriation-approving government, i.e. the provincial or central government. See Notice on Accelerating the Establishment of the Mediation and Adjudication System for Disputes on Land Expropriation Compensation and Resettlement (关于加快推进征地补偿安置争议协调裁决制度的通知), promulgated by MLR on June 21, 2006, available at www.gov.cn/zwgk/2006-07/05/content_327489.htm. In contrast, the State Council Office of Legal Affairs is of the opinion that adjudication here actually means administrative reconsideration. The 1999 ARL prescribes in Article 13 that application for administrative reconsideration should be lodged with the government at the next level above the one making the administrative decisions. Since a compensation plan is considered a specific administrative act undertaken by the county or prefectural government, adjudication/administrative reconsideration should then be filed to the prefectural or provincial government at one level above, not the expropriation-approving governments. See Notice on Administrative Reconsideration on Disputes of Land Expropriation Compensation and Resettlement (关于依法做好征地补偿安置争议行政复议工作的通知), promulgated by Office of Legal Affairs of State Council on May 23, 2011, available at www.hffzb.gov.cn/11672/11678/201605/t20160527_1997541.html. In practice, most

mediation–adjudication process is a precondition for filing administrative reconsideration or litigation against detailed compensation and resettlement plans.[49] Four problems have been identified with this type of post-implementation challenge. First, as subnational governments are at the same time the initiating and approving authorities as well as the mediating and adjudicating bodies, the impartiality and effectiveness of this mediation–adjudication process are dubious.[50] Second, as detailed compensation plans could be and indeed had been formulated and published by some prefectural or county governments in the form of "red letterhead" documents (*hongtou wenjian*), local courts had in practice considered such plans as abstract administrative acts with a general binding effect and hence held them to be immune to judicial review.[51] Nevertheless, this is a misapplication of law because according to a judicial interpretation issued by the SPC, abstract administrative acts are "all documents of a normative character issued to address unspecified subjects and can be applied repeatedly."[52] Therefore, compensation plans in specific expropriation cases should have been treated as concrete administrative acts since they are certainly directed at specified subjects (the expropriatees) and will be applied only once (in that particular case of land expropriation).[53]

Third, even if the courts do apply the law correctly and review compensation decisions, it is still hardly any solace. The reason is that administrative litigation in China is limited in scope of review.

provinces have set adjudication by provincial government as the procedural precondition for further administrative reconsideration or litigation. See Office of Legislative Affairs of Anhui People's Government and Anhui Department of Land Resources, "Study on Land Expropriation Compensation and Resettlement Disputes Settlement and Adjudication System (征地补偿安置争议协调裁决制度研究)," March 13, 2013, available at www.ahfzb.gov.cn/content/detail/566a9281f3cd010f3e2085e9.html.

49 Art.10, Rules on Issues of Hearing Administrative Cases related to Rural Collective Land (关于审理涉及农村集体土地行政案件若干问题的规定), promulgated by SPC on August 7, 2011, available at www.law-lib.com/law/law_view.asp?id=359831.

50 Xiaohui Mo, "An Reassessment of the Land Expropriation Compensation Disputes Settlement and Adjudication System (征地补偿安置争议协调裁决制度的再审议)" (2011) 7 *Administrative Management Reform* (行政改革管理) 32.

51 Eva Pils, "Land Disputes, Rights Assertion and Social Unrest: A Case from Sichuan" (2006) 19 *Columbia Journal of Asian Law* 263.

52 Art. 2, Interpretation on Several Questions regarding the Implementation of the PRC (关于执行中华人民共和国行政诉讼法若干问题的解释), promulgated by SPC on March 8, 2000, available at www.law-lib.com/law/law_view.asp?id=33&page=2.

53 Pils, "Land Disputes, Rights Assertion and Social Unrest: A Case from Sichuan," 264; Jie Cheng, "Judicial Review Power in Land Expropriation Disputes (土地征用纠纷的司法审查权)" (2004) 2 *Legal Studies* (法学研究) 52.

According to Article 6 of the ALL amended most recently in 2015,[54] courts are only empowered to inquire into the legality, not the merits or appropriateness of government actions. This means that the courts can only examine whether or not specific compensation decisions in individual expropriation cases are in line with the compensation standards formulated in the form of generally applicable rules,[55] which until 2015 had been unreviewable abstract administrative acts. The newly amended ALL in Article 53 empowers citizens to request the court to review the legality of general compensation standards indirectly when they challenge the individual compensation decisions made accordingly. As already shown, however, given that the prefectural and county governments have wide discretion to formulate compensation standards within the four corners of the statutory standards that are framed very broadly, the courts' hands are in effect still tied when it comes to questioning the lawfulness of local compensation standards. Last but not least, Article 25 of the present LALIR prescribes that any pending dispute over the compensation and resettlement decisions should not affect the implementation of approved expropriation decisions. This means that the expropriated will not be able to delay the enforcement of expropriation by way of challenging compensation arrangements.

Overall, the foregoing discussion demonstrates that the expropriation compensation regime established under existing Chinese law is bedeviled by unjust standards and a lack of avenues for condemnees to seek remedy. To be sure, there are more problems than are covered here. For instance, a particularly vexing issue is payment of compensation. Article 25 of LALIR requires compensation to be paid in full within three months upon approval of the detailed compensation plan. Yet an official report conceded that between 1999 and 2004 local governments defaulted on, held back and misappropriated a total amount of 17.5 billion yuan of takings compensation across the country.[56] In response, starting from 2003, China's central authorities

54 Article 5 of the 1989 ALL had the same prescription.

55 Junfeng Yang, "Administrative Litigation or Civil Litigation: Resolution of Disputes on the Amount of Expropriation Compensation (行政诉讼还是民事诉讼：征收补偿数额争议之解决)" (2014) 1 *Global Law Review* (环球法律评论) 88.

56 Guanshi Qiu, "China Sorting out Payment Arrears of Land Compensation Fees to Expropriated Peasants (中国清理拖欠征用农民土地补偿费)," December 31, 2004, available at www.chinanews.com/news/2004/2004-12-31/26/523273.shtml.

have reiterated time and again that compensation must be paid on time and in full.[57] The State Council stated in 2004 that if compensation and resettlement plans are not duly delivered, the condemnees could refuse to turn in the expropriated land.[58] In 2010, the central government issued two rescripts within a month demanding timely and complement payment of compensation.[59] Unfortunately, however, these efforts all turned out to be less than effective as local governments are still withholding compensation.[60]

To summarize, as mentioned in the introductory chapter, the existing literature is dominated by the Sino–US comparative approach, with the line of inquiry focusing on why the similarly structured Chinese constitutional takings clause performs differently in practice. The main findings in this light were presented in the previous two sections. It is now widely agreed that in China the constitutional promise on public interest prerequisite and requirement of compensation has not been honored by existing rural land expropriation law. Against this background, over the last decade, a plethora of reform proposals have been advanced.

57 "State Council Vigorously Disciplines the Land Market (国务院大力治理土地市场)," September 28, 2003, available at news.sina.com.cn/c/2003-09-28/2249835092s.shtml; Urgent Notice on Further Regulating Land Market and Strictly Controlling Land Administration (关于深入开展土地市场治理整顿严格土地管理的紧急通知), promulgated by General Office of State Council on April 29, 2004, available at www.yuanlin.com/rules/Html/Detail/2006-4/628.html; points 8 and 11, Decision on Deepening Reform and Enhancing Land Administration (关于深化改革严格土地管理的决定), promulgated by State Council on October 21, 2004, available at www.mlr.gov.cn/zwgk/flfg/tdglflfg/200601/t20060112_642080.htm; 2004 LAL, art. 49; 2007 Property Law, art.42.

58 State Council, Decision on Deepening Reform and Enhancing Land Administration, point 15.

59 Point 2, Urgent Notice on Further Tightening the Administration of Expropriation and Demolition and Effectively Protecting Legal Rights and Interests of the People (关于进一步严格征地拆迁管理工作切实维护群众合法权益的紧急通知), promulgated by General Office of State Council on May 15, 2010, available at xxgk.fengxin.gov.cn/fxxgtj/zfxxgk_45007/fgwj_45020/gfxwj_45022/201709/t20170912_393932.html; point 3, Notice on Further Improving Administration of Expropriation (关于进一步做好征地管理工作的通知), promulgated by MLR on June 26, 2010, available at www.mlr.gov.cn/zwgk/zytz/201007/t20100713_154433.htm.

60 For example, in 2014, a violent dispute in Pingdu City of Shandong, which cost the life of a peasant, broke out because of delayed and incomplete payment of compensation. See Jieqi Luo and Xudong Qin, "Closer Look: How a Land Dispute Led to a Farmer Dying in an Arson Attack," 24 March 2014, available at english.caixin.com/2014-03-24/100655852.html.

2.3 Prescriptions: Toward the Chinese Fifth Amendment

2.3.1 *Giving Teeth to Public Interest Prerequisite*

As demonstrated earlier in this chapter, the public interest prerequisite in China's constitutional takings clause has been vaguely defined, structurally redundant and procedurally unoperationalized. Consequently, proposals have been put forth to overcome the triple challenge.

First of all, to tackle the definitional challenge, two approaches have been advanced: one is definition-based and the other capacity-based. The definition-based approach focuses on establishing a narrower and more refined statutory definition of public interest in expropriation. Numerous scholarly attempts have been made in this direction, which primarily take two forms. The analytical method focuses on linguistic/semantic analysis of the component words "public" and "interest"[61] or comparing public interest with such related concepts as "national interest," "social interests," "common interests" and "collective interests."[62] Still others try to list out the essential traits of public interest, such as being nonprofit, long-term and inclusive, and so on.[63]

The other form of the definition-based approach is the enumerative method that purports to formulate a definitive list of what qualifies as public interest in land expropriation, which can then be added to a series of below-constitution statutes that echo the constitutional public interest prerequisite. Even though it has been suggested that to come up with an exhaustive definition of a concept as elastic as public interest is virtually impossible,[64] references have been made to Germany, Japan, Taiwan and

[61] Jianmiao Hu and Yijing Xin, "An Investigation into the Concept of Public Interest (公共利益概念透析)" (2004) 10 *Legal Science Monthly* (法学) 1; Jingbin Wang, "On the Definition of Public Interest: A Jurisprudential Analysis of a Foundational Category in Public Law (论公共利益之界定:一个公法基石性范畴的法理学分析)" (2005) 1 *Rule of Law and Social Development* (法制与社会发展) 129; Jinguang Hu and Kai Wang, "The Definition of Public interest in Chinese Constitution (我国宪法上公共利益的界定)" (2005) 1 *China Legal Science* (中国法学) 18.

[62] Wang, "On the Definition of Public Interest"; Hu and Wang, "The Definition of Public interest in Chinese Constitution."

[63] Linhong Yang, "On Public Interest (试论公共利益)," in *Chinese Administrative Law after the Constitutional Amendment: Essays of the 2004 Annual Conference of Chinese Administrative Law Society* (修宪之后的中国行政法：中国法学会行政法学研究会2004年年会论文集) (Beijing: Chinese University of Political Science and Law Press, 2005), pp. 582–83; Feng Yang, "How to Define Public interest in Property Expropriation (财产征收中的公共利益如何界定)" (2005) 10 *Legal Science Monthly* (法学) *94*.

[64] Liming Wang, "On Implementation of Property Law and the Improvement on Expropriation and Requisition System (物权法的实施与征收征用的完善)" (2008) 4 *Law Science Magazine* (法学杂志) 17.

Hong Kong, where some kind of enumerative list or catalogue of public interest purposes in land takings is written into law.[65] Most famously, the eminent Chinese civil law scholar Huixing Liang proffered such a list in his draft version of the *Property Law*.[66] But that was not incorporated by the finalized act of 2007. It should be mentioned, though, that the 2011 RECHSL, which deals with state withdrawal of use-rights of state-owned urban land, does offer a list of specific items that are considered to be manifestations of public interest.[67] This brings up the possibility that a similar list can also be adopted with respect to rural land expropriation.[68] As a matter of fact, in 2011, officials from the MLR suggested that an enumerative catalogue of public interest would be included in the draft

[65] Jialong Liao, "On the Scope of Public interest (关于公共利益的范围)" (2006) 7 *People's Congress Research* (人大研究) 29.

[66] Huixing Liang (ed.), *Draft Property Law of China: Clauses, Commentaries, Rationales and Reference Legislative Models* (中国物权法草案建议稿: 条文、说明、理由与参考立法例) (Beijing: Shehui Kexue Wenxian Press, 2000), pp. 191–93.

[67] Article 8 reads, "Where, for public interest such as safeguarding the national security and promoting the national economic and social development, it is necessary to expropriate a building under any of the following circumstances, the people's government at the city or county level shall make a decision to expropriate the building:

(1) necessary for national defense and foreign affairs;

(2) necessary for the construction of energy, transportation, water and other infrastructures as organized and implemented by the government;

(3) necessary for a public cause such as science and technology, education, culture, health, sports, environment and resource protection, disaster prevention and mitigation, protection of cultural relics, social welfare or municipal utilities as organized and implemented by the government;

(4) necessary for the construction of a social housing project as organized and implemented by the government;

(5) necessary for the redevelopment of old cities where dilapidated buildings concentrate and infrastructure lags behind as organized and implemented by the government according to the relevant provisions of the Urban and Rural Planning Law; or

(6) necessary for any other public interest as prescribed by law or administrative regulation."

[68] Another possible candidate for a list of public interest purposes for land expropriation may be found in the 2001 Catalogue of Allocated Land Use (划拨用地目录), which listed a total of 19 kinds of use for which land may be allocated by the government to private users without charge, including government and military facilities; criminal system facilities including prisons and detention centers; infrastructure development such as railways, minefields, highways, harbors and airports; as well as non-profit educational, scientific research, sports, cultural, medical, and social housing development projects. However, in practice rural land expropriation has been used for purposes far wider than this.

amendment to the 2004 LAL then under deliberation.[69] Nevertheless, as the 2004 LAL is still yet to be comprehensively revised, that remains to be actualized.

Alternatively, the capacity-based approach to the definitional challenge is twofold. One aspect is rights-centered, aiming to enhance the capacity of the expropriated vis-à-vis state takings power by way of "propertization of property rights" and "fundamentalization of private property." In China's present Constitution, prescriptions on private property are not situated in the second chapter that enshrines citizens' basic rights, but in the first chapter, "General Principles" (*zonggang*), which lays out the basic political, social and economic structure of the state.[70] It is thus argued that private property should be included in the second chapter as one of citizens' basic rights through either moving the current private property clauses from the first to the second chapter in the Constitution or adding new clauses in the second chapter. This will then elevate private property to a higher constitutional status, which can at least focus society's attention on the protection of private property and may indirectly and informally restrain the government's ruthless expropriation activities.[71] This is what fundamentalization of private property means. In the meantime, since the first two paragraphs of Article 10 in the present Constitution only mention ownership rights in land and land use-right is not listed as an independent constitutional right, it is suggested that a new paragraph should be inserted to stipulate that such rights are also constitutional rights. This will then strengthen, as argued, the position of individual peasants who enjoy only nonownership use-rights over land.

The second tenet of the capacity-based approach deals with the definitional challenge from a different angle. It is power-centered in the sense that it tries to enhance the capacity of China's legislature and judiciary in controlling the government's takings power. First, at the highest level, it is proposed that a constitutional review body be established to conduct an abstract review of unconstitutional legislation and application of constitutional principles in individual expropriation cases.[72] At present,

69 See "The Process of Amending the Land Administration Law is Started but the Difficulty lies in Defining Public Interest in Land Expropriation (土地管理法修改启动 征地界定公共利益成难题)," April 20, 2011, available at news.sina.com.cn/c/2011-04-20/014722322126.shtml.

70 Reasons for this arrangement will be discussed in Chapter 4.

71 Wang, *The Constitutional Protection of Private Property in China*, pp. 311–12.

72 Ibid., p. 320.

Chinese courts are not allowed to apply the Constitution directly in litigation.[73] While the Standing Committee of the National People's Congress (NPCSC) is entrusted by Article 67 of the Constitution and Articles 97–99 of the 2015 *Legislation Law* with the task to review the constitutionality of regulation and rules issued by the government and local legislatures, such reviewing power has never been deployed publicly and does not cover legislation enacted by National People's Congress (NPC) and its standing committee.[74] Hence, the recommendation goes that a double-level review mechanism shall be instituted with one special committee under the NPCSC for the review of lower-level legislation by local legislators and the State Council and another special committee under the NPC for reviewing NPC/NPCSC legislation. It is further suggested that courts hearing individual takings cases should preferably be allowed to submit their request for constitutional review directly to the reviewing body.[75] In this way, the hope is that any statutes, regulations and rules regarding rural land expropriation that contradict the constitutional public interest prerequisite will be spotted more easily and invalidated more effectively.

Second, in respect to specific expropriation decisions, as mentioned earlier, such decisions are currently made inside the government hierarchy without external legislative or judicial supervision. Therefore, many have proposed opening the decision-making process to be reviewed by local people's congresses, which can, as certain a commentator has stated, play the role of a "public interest machine" in sanctioning or rejecting expropriation decisions within their respective jurisdiction.[76] In a similar vein, it is proposed that China's courts should

[73] Decision on Annulling the Relevant Judicial Interpretations Enacted Before the End of 2007 (the seventh Batch) (最高人民法院关于废止2007年底以前发布的有关司法解释(第七批)的决定), promulgated by SPC on December 28, 2008, available at www.npc.gov.cn/npc/xinwen/fztd/sfjs/2008-12/27/content_1465018.htm.

[74] For discussion of constitutional enforcement in China, see Thomas E. Kellogg, "Constitutionalism with Chinese Characteristics? Constitutional Development and Civil Litigation in China" (2009) 7 *International Journal of Constitutional Law* 215; Tom Ginsburg and Yan Lin, "Constitutional Interpretation in Law-Making: China's Invisible Constitutional Enforcement Mechanism" (2015) 63 *American Journal of Comparative Law* 467; Keith Hand, "Resolving Constitutional Disputes in Contemporary China" (2011) 7 *University of Pennsylvania Asia Law Review* 51; Qianfan Zhang, "A Constitution without Constitutionalism? The Paths of Constitutional Developments in China" (2010) 8 *International Journal of Constitutional Law* 950.

[75] Wang, *The Constitutional Protection of Private Property in China*, pp. 320–321.

[76] Qianfan Zhang, "What is Public Interest: A Definition from Social Utilitarianism and its Constitutional Limits (公共利益是什么社会功利主义的定义及其宪法上的局限性)"

also step in to dictate what public interest in expropriation means and to assess individual expropriation decisions accordingly. In other words, they should do what their American counterparts have been doing for a long time. This is of course not to suggest that China should copy and paste the manner in which American courts have interpreted the public use clause. Rather, the point is that at least judicial review of expropriation decisions per se should be permitted in law.[77] Nor is this calling for judicialization of the Constitution in China. The well-known nonjusticiability of China's written constitution is very unlikely to change in the near future. Yet since the constitutional public interest prerequisite has also appeared in the expropriation clause (Article 42) of the 2007 *Property Law*, courts' checking the public interestedness of expropriation decisions can be placed on this nonconstitutional statutory basis and thereby does not amount to judicialization of the written constitution. However, given the aforementioned fact that rural land expropriation decisions are still regarded as nonjusticiable, it does require broadening the scope of administrative litigation or reclassifying expropriation decisions as judicially reviewable, which is exactly what has been advocated.[78]

That being said, even if the definitional challenge gets removed through one or more of the recommendations presented above, the constitutional public interest prerequisite would continue to fail to place real limits upon rural land expropriation if the structural challenge persists. This is because as long as state expropriation remains the only lawful way to carry out urbanization and de-agrarianization, even when

(2005) 1 *Legal Forum* (法学论坛) 28; Qianfan Zhang, "The Plight and Solution of Public Interest: The Constitutional Interpretation of Public Use Clause in American Eminent Domain and its Implications to China (公共利益的困境与出路：美国公用征收条款的宪法解释及其对中国的启示)" (2005) 5 *China Legal Science* (中国法学) 58; Zhongmin Tang and Zebin Wen, "On Definitional Models of Public interest (关于公共利益的界定模式)" (2006) 5 *Modern Law Science* (现代法学) 95.

77 Zhang, "The Plight and Solution of Public Interest"; Zuolian Yao, "The Public interest Standard in Eminent Domain for Public Use: The Evolution of American Case Law (公用征收中的公共利益标准：美国判例的发展演变)" (2006) 1 *Global Law Review* (环球法律评论) 107; Xiangming Liu, "A Comparative Study of the Important Issues in Eminent Domain Systems in China and America (中美征收制度重要问题之比较)" (2007) 6 *China Legal Science* (中国法学) 33; Qinghua Wang, "Eminent Domain, Public Use and Fair Compensation: Comments On the Decision of Kelo v. City of New London (土地征收、公共使用与公平补偿 – 评Kelo v. City of New London一案判决)" (2007) 2 *Peking University Law Review* (北大法律评论) 479; Wang, *The Constitutional Protection of Private Property In China*, pp. 320–21.

78 Cheng, "Judicial Review Power in Land Expropriation Disputes." It is argued that decisions of expropriation are not abstract administrative acts but specific administrative acts that are judicially reviewable.

an individual expropriation decision is held to be outside of the public interest, it must proceed simply because there is no other way around.

Logically there are two solutions. One is to abandon the public interest clause entirely, and the other is to revamp China's land administration system so that state expropriation will not be required when rural land is converted into urban land for nonagricultural purposes. The first view is in the extreme minority.[79] It is seen as taking a step too far because countries around the world have legally or even constitutionally entrenched some sort of public purpose requirement for takings of private property. The second view keeps the public interest requirement but tries to decouple expropriation from urbanization/de-agrarianization so that the structural challenge can be eradicated. Strictly speaking, this is not about providing a narrower definition of public interest. Its central objective is to open up the space for voluntary transfer of rural land so that the scope of state expropriation can be reduced. First, it has been suggested that Article 10(1) in the Constitution, that "urban land is owned by the state," should be removed,[80] after which conversion of rural land into state-owned land is detached from expropriation. Second, another prevalent proposal holds that the draconian land use restrictions over collective land should be lifted. Recall that whereas rural collective land can only be used, without first being expropriated, for such nonagricultural purposes as local public utilities, peasant household residential plots, TVEs and collective joint ventures, urban state-owned land is immune from such limitations and can be developed and marketized more freely. For years this dual-track land system has been criticized as an anomaly signifying a partial reform where China is yet to finish its journey toward a true market economy under the rule of law.[81] Broadly speaking, there are four lines of argument in support of this point.

First is the thesis of "truncation of ownership." This phrase initially coined by the American economist Harold Demsetz was introduced to

79 Hongmei Zhao, "The Unnecessary Distinction between Public Interest and Non-public Interest: A New Model of Interactions between Government and Society in Land Expropriation (无需区分"公共利益"与"非公共利益" – 征地制度的政府、社会联动新模式构想)" (2006) 8 *China Land* (中国土地) 17.

80 Xueyang Cheng, "Chinese System of State Ownership of Land from a Public Law Perspective (公法视角下的中国国有土地制度)" (2011) 25 *China Land Science* (中国土地科学) 20.

81 Shitong Qiao, "The Politics of Chinese Land: Partial Reform, Vested Interests and Small Property" (2016) 29 (1) *Columbia Journal of Asia Law* 70.

the Chinese audience by Qiren Zhou in the mid-1990s.[82] The core idea is that a part of the complete bundle of ownership rights may be taken out because "the position for controlling and abolishing the restraints of private rights has been granted to the state or already assumed by the state." According to Article 71 of the 1986 *General Provisions of Civil Law*,[83] ownership (*suoyouquan*) in the private law context includes the rights to possess, use, benefit from and dispose of (including transfer) the property. Against this backdrop, an argument gaining much traction among economists and civil law scholars in China is that stringent use limitation imposed by the 2004 LAL effectively renders the constitutional protection of collective ownership of rural land partial and nominal. Rural land ownership is severely truncated in the sense that the right to use rural land for nonagricultural ends and the right to transfer it on the market are deprived.[84]

This situation gives rise to the second proposition denouncing China's bifurcated land system. Given the presumption of state expropriation in nonagricultural use of rural land, rural land is barred from being marketized for nonagricultural purposes. The primary land market is therefore monopolized by the state, which is criticized for having frustrated the realization of a complete market economy in China.[85] The third and fourth criticisms against China's dichotomous land regime are of a legal nature. On the one hand, the fact that state land ownership and collective land ownership receive differential treatments in terms of use limitation makes many contend that the latter is unjustifiably discriminated

[82] Harold Demsetz, *Ownership, Control and the Firm: The Organization of Economy Activity* (Oxford: Basil Blackwell, 1988), pp. 18–19, cited in Qiren Zhou, "Reform in China's Rural Areas: The Changes in the Relationship between the State and Land Ownership: A Retrospect on the Changes in Economic Institutions," in Zhenglai Deng (ed.), *China's Economy: Rural Reform and Agricultural Development* (Singapore: World Scientific Publishing Company, 2009), pp. 340–41. The Chinese version of this chapter was first published in 1995 at the journal *China Social Sciences Quarterly* based in Hong Kong.

[83] As China does not have a civil code yet, the general provisions remain to be the most comprehensive rules of civil law to date.

[84] This argument still holds much currency today. Searching "ownership truncation" (所有权/产权残缺) on China's main search engine *Baidu* yields a large number of results. The abovementioned paper by Qiren Zhou seems to be the first academic work that deploys the term to analyze collective land ownership in China.

[85] Shouying Liu, "The Dual Land Rights System and Truncation of Land Market in China (中国的二元土地权利制度和土地市场残缺)," 21 September 2008, available at www.chinathinktanks.org.cn/content/detail/id/2932712.

against[86] with unequal constitutional protection.[87] On the other hand, it is contended that use restrictions over collective land ownership established by the 2004 LAL are unconstitutional because they violate the principle of proportionality for imposing excessive limitations upon property rights of the rural collectives and peasants.[88]

Over the years, three types of reform proposals have been put forth to unify the dualist land system in China. First, it is argued that rural land shall be privatized and marketized so that individual peasants may transfer their land on the market for nonagricultural purposes without going through expropriation.[89] Second, the opposite standpoint has also been taken, namely that rural land shall be nationalized while individual peasants retain use-rights and are permitted to convert or transfer rural land for nonagricultural uses without expropriation.[90] Third, the middle-ground and most prevailing position maintains collective ownership of rural land, but asks for the lifting of existing use limitations to allow rural collectives and peasants to convert or transfer their land for nonagricultural uses without expropriation.[91] Underneath their apparent differences, all these reform recommendations purport to get rid of the built-in lockstep between expropriation and urbanization/de-agrarianization so that the constitutional public interest prerequisite will no longer be structurally redundant.

In addition to proposals targeting the definitional and structural challenges facing the constitutional public interest prerequisite, to resolve the procedural challenge a consensus has been reached in the existing literature that the expropriated should be granted the legal right to have some

[86] Xianjin Huang, "On Discrimination of Land Rights (论地权歧视)" (1996) 7 *Problems of Rural Economy* (农村经济问题) 16.

[87] Wang, *The Constitutional Protection of Private Property in China*, p. 303.

[88] Zhongxia Li, "Analysis of the Constitutionality of Transfer of Rural Land（农村土地流转的合宪性分析）" (2015) 4 *China Legal Science* (中国法学) 136.

[89] The most prominent spokesmen for land privatization in China are economists such as Yushi Mao, Hong Sheng, Zhiwu Chen and Guanzhong Wen.

[90] This is a minority view. See e.g. Fengzhang Li, "The Nature of Collective Land Ownership, "Against Rights" through "Hollow Rights" (通过"空权利"来"反权利"：集体土地所有权的本质及其变革)" (2010) 5 *Rule of Law and Social Development* (法制与社会发展) 16.

[91] Daoyuan Liu, Qunying Lin and Xiangkun Cao, "The Analysis of the Ownership of Collective Land of the Property Law: From the Perspective of Land Expropriation (《物权法》中集体土地权利析论 – 从土地征收视角的检视" (2007) 1 *Journal of Central South University of Forestry & Technology* (中南林业科技大学学报) 25; Wang, *The Constitutional Protection of Private Property in China*, p. 318.

say in the expropriation decision-making.[92] As mentioned, for the time being the condemnees are not legally entitled to raise objections to expropriation decisions. It has therefore been suggested that not only should they be consulted about the expropriation initiatives, they should also be given the opportunity to influence the review and approval process and ultimately to say no to expropriation initiatives.

2.3.2 *Increasing Compensation*

As mentioned, the conventional wisdom holds that the constitutional requirement of compensation is violated by an existing compensation regime that is unjust and unfair in both substantive and procedural terms. Specifically, the statutory standards are inequitably inadequate and there is only limited room for expropriatees to challenge compensation standards and individual compensation decisions.

For many years, the prevailing proposal points to importation of the fair market value standard practiced in many countries, including the United States.[93] In particular, this position is adopted by *China 2030*, a report jointly issued in 2013 by the World Bank and the Development Research Center of State Council, a top official think tank in China.[94] What, then, is "fair market value"? Simply put, it means the price "a willing seller would pay and a willing buyer would accept" at the time of

[92] Jiansheng Zhang, "On Administrative Procedure of Expropriation: Collective Land Expropriation as the Example (行政征收程序论 – 以集体土地征收为例)" (2009) 2 *Oriental Law* (东方法学) 22; Guoqian Liu, "Due Process Reform of Review and Approval of Land Expropriation (土地征收审批的正当程序改革)" (2012) 4 *Legal Studies* (法学研究) 126; Aihua Zou, "Basic Ideas and Concrete Solutions to Improve the Land Expropriation Examination and Approval System (完善土地征收审批制度的基本思路与具体对策)" (2011) 2 *Journal of National Academy of Administration* (国家行政学院学报) 95.

[93] Liu, "A Comparative Study of the Important Issues in Eminent Domain Systems in China and America"; Qianfan Zhang, "'Just Compensation' and Constitutional Check upon Eminent Domain (公正补偿与征收权的宪法限制)" (2005) 2 *Legal Studies* (法学研究) 25; Aihua Zou, "Rights to Compensation and Social Security of the Expropriated Peasants (被征地农民的补偿权与社会保障权)" (2009) *Tribune of Political Science and Law* (政法论坛) 100; Sara Davis, Jacques deLisle and Roy Prosterman, "Property Seizure in China: Politics, Law and Protest," Roundtable before the Congressional-Executive Commission on China, 2004, available at www.cecc.gov/events/roundtables/property-seizure-in-china-politics-law-and-protest.

[94] Development Research Center of State Council and World Bank, "China 2030: Building a Modern, Harmonious, and Creative Society," March 23, 2013, p. 136, available at documents.worldbank.org/curated/en/781101468239669951/China-2030-building-a-modern-harmonious-and-creative-society.

takings.[95] In reality, fair market value in compulsory land acquisition becomes ascertainable only through counterfactually simulating a market environment, a typical way of which is to examine the price of recent comparable sales.[96] To many, introduction of the fair market value standard to Chinese rural land expropriation can kill two birds with one stone. First, while the current standard is determined ex parte by the government which has the incentive to suppress compensation, fair market value is much more objective in trying to approximate the price "a willing seller would pay and a willing buyer would accept" at the time of takings. It can therefore reduce as much as possible the subjectivity and arbitrariness in the formation of the compensation standard. Second, and more crucially, it is generally believed that market-based compensation will enable the expropriated to obtain the expropriation surplus in economic terms. Although at this moment the rural collectives cannot transfer their land on the market for most nonagricultural ends and the fair market value standard is not immediately available given the absence of any comparable sales,[97] many have argued that the price at which local governments transfer the land after expropriation should be used as the benchmark to determine its market price, and the condemnees should be compensated based on the post-expropriation value of land rather than on its original use. Better still, if a unified land market gets established, the rural collectives and peasants will be allowed to transfer their land for nonagricultural purposes. In that case, not only can rural landowners reap the increased land value without undergoing expropriation, market prices for rural land will also gradually emerge, which can then be used to set compensation standards for rural land expropriation.

To be sure, transplanting the fair market value standard will not end disputes concerning compensation. An effective dispute resolution mechanism is also needed. However, as demonstrated earlier, in China the channel to challenge compensation standards and individual compensation decisions at both the post-approval and post-implementation stages is flawed at best and blocked at worst. In this situation, it has been

[95] See e.g. *United States* v. *Miller 317 US 369, 374 (1943).*

[96] Thomas W. Merrill, "Incomplete Compensation for Takings" (2002) 11 *NYU Environmental Law Journal* 116.

[97] Pils, "Land Disputes, Rights Assertion and Social Unrest: A Case from Sichuan" 250; Benjamin van Rooij, "The Return of the Landlord: Chinese Land Acquisition Conflicts as Illustrated by Peri-Urban Kunming" (2007) 39 *Journal of Legal Pluralism and Unofficial Law* 220; Washburn, "Regular Takings or Regulatory Takings: Land Expropriation in Rural China," 106.

suggested that the expropriated shall be granted the right to challenge the government over compensation decisions[98] and that they shall be permitted to petition the courts to scrutinize compensation standards more effectively.[99]

If ever put into practice, the aforementioned reform suggestions aiming at giving teeth to the public interest prerequisite and raising compensation will certainly transform Chinese rural land expropriation law and finally make China's own Fifth Amendment work. Nonetheless, in spite of a groundswell of support for a systematic overhaul of the law in this area for more than ten years, what has actually happened is that none of the above proposals has been adopted so far. Surely this is not to say that there is no change whatsoever. Quite the contrary – a series of reforms have been rolled out since the early 2000s. But they largely fall short of the prescriptions just presented. The next chapter will introduce these limited reforms and explain the conventional wisdom about the biggest barrier to deeper change in this field.

[98] Rooij, "The Return of the Landlord," 219.
[99] Cheng, "Judicial Review Power in Land Expropriation Disputes," 53–54.

3

Limited Reform

Symptoms and Causes

This chapter first documents reform measures adopted by the Chinese central authority since the turn of this century concerning both the public interest prerequisite and the requirement of compensation. It will be shown that most of the popular prescriptions introduced in the preceding chapter have yet to be implemented. The conventional explanation as to why that is the case is presented in the second section. The central idea is that the Chinese local governments have been financially reliant upon expropriating land, a phenomenon known as "land finance." This is widely regarded as the biggest obstacle to the long overdue reform of rural land expropriation law. More substantive reform will proceed after alternative sources of fiscal revenue become available.

At the outset, it is worth noting that all reform measures adopted so far have taken the form of central party or government policies, NPCSC decisions, ministerial rules (*bumen guizhang*) and other nonstatutory rules. There has been no formal revision to the LAL or UREAL, the governing laws in this field. This means that description of the formal law in the preceding chapter remains accurate, even though in practice new policies and rules have already been put in place. This is an example of "benign illegality" (*liangxing weifa*), a widely observed feature of legal reforms in contemporary China. It refers to a situation where certain reform measures are considered to be positive and necessary in a fast-changing society, even though their formal legality is questionable as their breach of the written law (including the Constitution) is not expressly acknowledged or justified.[1] This legitimacy problem was to

[1] This term was first introduced in Tiechuan Hao, "On Benign Violations of the Constitution (论良性违宪)" (1996) *Legal Studies* (法学研究) 90. Hao dealt with the problem of benign violation of the written PRC Constitutions and held a quite positive view about its necessity and legitimacy, hence the adjective "benign." For skeptical views, see Donald C. Clarke, "China: Creating a Legal System for a Market Economy," Asian Development Bank, 2007, available at scholarship.law.gwu.edu/cgi/viewcontent.cgi?article=2258&context=faculty_publications; Zhiwei Tong, "Benign Unconstitutionality

some extent alleviated by the most recent pilot reforms of China's land administration system starting in early 2015 when the NPCSC gave explicit authorization to suspend the enforcement of the LAL and the UREAL in selected localities under the pilot schemes, without affecting the general validity of such laws. Therefore, in China rural land expropriation is now governed by a mixture of statutes, rules and trial policies. While most existing analyses still concentrate on the formal law, it is time for an update.

3.1 Reform and Its Limitations

3.1.1 The Public Interest Prerequisite

As mentioned, under existing law, China's constitutional public interest clause faces definitional, structural and procedural challenges. Over the last decade, no reform measure was taken to tackle the definitional challenge. For one thing, no statutory specification of the public interest clause has been provided. For example, Liang Huixing's enumerative list of public interest in his draft *Property Law* was not incorporated into the finalized version. While the 2011 RECHSL does offer a list of specific items of public interest for state withdrawal of use-rights over state-owned urban land, it is not applicable to expropriation of rural land. As another example, neither has the Chinese legislature nor the judiciary ever intervened to interpret or review the public interestedness of expropriation decisions.

That said, over the past decade, there have been a series of reform measures targeting both the structural and the procedural challenges, which nevertheless are not without serious limitations. To begin with, while the constitutional clauses (specifically Article 10 (1), (2) and (4) of the existing Constitution) that have been interpreted to make expropriation the only lawful way to convert rural land into urban land are neither dropped nor revised, the connection between expropriation and de-agrarianization, i.e. the de-agrarianization challenge, now starts to be removed, although only partially. As mentioned earlier, pursuant to Articles 43 and 63 of the 2004 LAL and Article 9 of the 2009 UREAL, state expropriation is necessitated when noncollective parties want to use collective rural land for nonagricultural purposes. It is also legally forbidden for rural collectives to transfer use-rights of their land on the

Should not be Supported: Different Opinions from Comrade Hao Tiechuan ("良性违宪不宜肯定" – 对郝铁川同志有关主张的不同看法)" (1996) *Legal Studies* (法学研究) 19.

market. However, in 2003 and 2004, China's central Party and government authorities promised for the first time that rural collectives would be permitted to transfer use-rights of rural construction land on the market.[2] Such a pledge from the central authorities was apparently intended to liberalize the rural construction land market. Yet it is not a blanket liberalization because policy documents since 2008 have clarified that marketization would only apply to for-profit rural construction land.[3] As already explained, out of the five exceptional circumstances where collectives are permitted to use rural land for construction, those for local public utilities and peasant housing are classified as nonprofit while those for TVEs and joint ventures are categorized as for-profit. This means that while rural collectives remain barred from transferring rural construction land used for peasant residences and local public utilities, they are allowed to transfer their construction land used for TVEs and joint ventures on the market without first going through expropriation. As a matter of fact, prior to these policy announcements from the central authorities, as early as in 1999, the MLR authorized a pilot project for liberalizing for-profit rural construction land in Wuhu County of Anhui Province. In the ensuing years, local practices spread across the country, though with considerable variation in the absence of a nationwide policy framework.[4] As such tentative and experimental marketization has

[2] Point 9, Opinions on Improving Work of Agriculture and Countryside (关于做好农业和农村工作的意见), promulgated by CCP Central Committee and State Council on January 16, 2003, available at www.xjxnw.gov.cn/c/2012-09-19/545751.shtml; point 10, Decision on Deepening Reform and Enhancing Land Administration (关于深化改革严格土地管理的决定), promulgated by State Council on October 21, 2004, available at www.mlr.gov.cn/zwgk/flfg/tdglflfg/200601/t20060112_642080.htm. Indeed, local pilot projects have been carried out since the mid-1990s, of which the central authorities only gave formal policy recognition retrospectively. See Samson Yuen, "China's New Rural Land Reform? Assessment and Prospects" (2014) *China Perspectives* 61.

[3] Part 3, point 2, Decision on Major Issues concerning Promoting Rural Reform and Development (关于推进农村改革发展若干重大问题的决定), promulgated by CCP Central Committee on October 12, 2008, available at www.gov.cn/test/2008-10/31/content_1136796.htm; part 3, point 11, Decision on Major Issues concerning Comprehensively Deepening Reform (关于全面深化改革若干重大问题的决定), promulgated by CCP Central Committee on November 15 2013, available at www.gov.cn/jrzg/2013-11/15/content_2528179.htm; Opinions on Comprehensively Deepening Rural Reform and Promoting Modernization of Agricultural Industry (关于全面深化农村改革加快推进农业现代化的若干意见), promulgated by CCP Central Committee on January 19 2014, available at www.gov.cn/jrzg/2014-01/19/content_2570454.htm.

[4] For an analysis, see Samson Yuen, "China's New Rural Land Reform? Assessment and Prospects," 61; Shengping Gao and Shouying Liu, "Marketization of Collective Construction Land: Practical and Legal Challenges (集体建设用地进入市场: 法律与现实困境)" (2007) 3 *Management World* (管理世界) 158.

typically been initiated and driven by local governments,[5] it is not unheard of over the years that rural collectives are sometimes forced by local authorities to transfer their construction land to designated private developers, effectively turning marketization into expropriation in disguise.[6]

It was in 2015 that a national reform scheme got underway when the NPCSC ordered that lawful for-profit rural construction land in existence at the time of the 2015 NPCSC decision would become marketizable in 33 localities across the country.[7] This decision is more than an ex post recognition of what had occurred before. For instance, as touched upon previously, Article 9 of the 2009 UREAL stipulates that collective-owned land within urban planning areas must be expropriated and converted into state-owned urban land before it could be marketized. Hence, a 2008 Party policy specified that for-profit rural construction land could be transferred without expropriation only if it was located outside urban planning areas.[8] Despite the fact that not all local practices had complied with this requirement,[9] the formal legal limitation remained in place. The 2015 NPCSC decision ordained that Article 9 of the 2009 UREAL would stop implementation in the named trial areas within the pilot period, finally clearing the legal obstacle for marketization of for-profit rural construction land regardless of its location. Relatedly, enforcement of Articles 43 and 63 of the 2004 LAL was also halted in these designated localities to make way for the trial marketization of for-profit rural construction land. This can be seen as a response to the problem of

[5] Jiang Wan, "State-led Transfer of Collective Construction Land: From Ideal back to Reality (政府主导下的集体建设用地流转：从理想回归现实)" (2010) 32 *Modern Law Science* (现代法学) 27.

[6] Lijian Guo, "Five Abnormalities in Rural Land Circulation (农村土地流转五大乱象)," *People's Daily*, February 18, 2014, available at www.tuliu.com/read-4418.html; for an ethnographic account of this process, see Julia Chuang, "China's Rural Land Politics: Bureaucratic Absorption and the Muting of Rightful Resistance" (2014) 219 *China Quarterly* 649.

[7] Decision on Authorizing the State Council to Temporarily Adjust Implementation of Relevant Legal Provisions in 33 Piloting Administrative Areas including Daxing District of Beijing (关于授权国务院在北京市大兴区等三十三个试点县(市、区)行政区域暂时调整实施有关法律规定的决定), promulgated by NPCSC on February 27, 2015, available at news.xinhuanet.com/2015–02/27/c_1114461294.htm. Since this decision concerns three areas of reform including rural land expropriation, peasant household residential plot land and rural for-profit construction land, the reform is dubbed in the Chinese media as "reform of three pieces of land" (三块地改革).

[8] Part 3, point 2, CCP Central Committee, Decision on Major Issues concerning Promoting Rural Reform and Development.

[9] See Samson Yuen, "China's New Rural Land Reform? Assessment and Prospects," 61.

benign illegality: if violation of existing law is the inevitable cost of reform that needs to be rolled out prior to formal statutory revision, rather than doing it covertly as was done earlier, it is better to openly acknowledge and legitimatize such apparent illegality. This is exactly what the 2015 NPCSC decision purports to achieve. Its own legal basis was laid down by the *Legislation Law* amended in 2015, stipulating in Article 13 that the NPC and the NPCSC may, according to the demands of reform and development, authorize temporary adjustment or suspension of certain statutory provisions concerning certain matters in the area of administrative management in some localities within a period of time.[10] While such vague terms as "certain statutory provisions," "certain matters" and "administrative management" smack of opening the floodgates of blank-check authorization, it is still a better approach to deal with benign illegality since it is more transparent and formalized than before. This is a new way to address the legality deficit in China's tried and tested experimentation-based reform strategy.[11] In this way, the 2015 NPCSC decision paves the legal ground for a new round of land reform in China. Prescribing that the pilot scheme would end by December 31, 2017, the decision requires the State Council and the MLR to summarize experiences of these trial programs in a timely manner and report to the NPCSC. The goal is that if these trial reforms are proven feasible in practice, relevant statutes will be revised accordingly.

In the larger scheme of things, however, the current pilot reform of liberalizing for-profit rural construction land is no more than a baby step toward the grand promises declared by China's central authority since the early 2000s about establishing a "unified market of urban and rural construction land" and realizing "equality in market opportunity, rights and price" for collective-owned and state-owned construction land.[12] Specifically, it is a far from meaningful solution to the structural challenge facing the constitutional public interest prerequisite because the scope of permitted marketization is severely restrained, covering only collective-owned for-profit construction land that is already used for nonagricultural purposes. For one thing, rural agricultural land and

10 This clause was not present in the original 2000 PRC Legislation Law.

11 For an analysis of China's experimental approach to economic reform, see Sebastian Heilmann, Policy Experimentation in China's Economic Rise (2008) 43 *Studies in Comparative International Development* 1.

12 CCP Central Committee, Decision on Major Issues concerning Promoting Rural Reform and Development; CCP Central Committee, Decision on Major Issues concerning Comprehensively Deepening Reforms.

nonprofit construction land (such as peasant household residential plots) are still excluded from the market. For another, the land targeted by this round of pilot reform was in fact the legacy of China's TVE boom between the 1980s and the mid-1990s when rural collectives were allowed to use their land to set up enterprises. The pilot reform does not license rural collectives to claim new land for TVEs, which can then become transferrable on the market.[13] This means that the size of liberalized for-profit rural construction land is fixed. An official at China's top government-backed think tank revealed that by 2013 stock rural for-profit construction land was 42 million *mu*, which was confirmed by the MLR in 2017.[14] This accounts for just 13.5 percent of rural construction land (310 million *mu*) and 6.36 percent of rural land (660 million *mu*) in China.[15] In this situation, even if the current local pilot reform ultimately goes national, more than 90 percent of rural collective land will remain under stringent use control and expropriation will still be required for its conversion or marketization for most nonagricultural purposes, some of which cannot be easily squared with the constitutional public interest requirement. Hence, the de-agrarianization challenge largely persists and so does the so-called "paradox of expropriation."

Besides opening up limited space for rural land liberalization, which, as explained, hardly addresses the problem of expropriating rural land for nonpublic purposes, there have been reform measures that try to tackle the structural challenge in a more head-on way over the past decade. In 2010, the MLR mandated trial reform in seven cities – Tianjin, Chongqing, Wuhan, Chengdu, Changsha, Shenyang and Foshan – to "narrow down the scope of rural land expropriation" (*suoxiao zhengdi fanwei*). The main objective was to limit the circumstances where the takings power is invoked so as to ensure that it is just used for

[13] Hua Gui, "After Marketization of For-profit Rural Construction Land Will Small Property Houses be Protected (集体经营性建设用地入市 "小产权房"受保护吗)," June 22, 2016, available at sike.news.cn/statics/sike/posts/2016/06/219500696.html.

[14] Explanatory Report on Draft Amendment to Land Administration Law (关于《中华人民共和国土地管理法(修正案）(征求意见稿）的说明), promulgated by MLR on May 23, 2017, available at www.gygov.gov.cn/art/2017/5/23/art_11894_1174759.html.

[15] Xingqing Ye, "Reconstructing Property Rights in For-profit Rural Collective Construction Land (农村集体经营性建设用地的产权重构)," May 27, 2017, available at www.p5w.net/news/xwpl/201505/t20150527_1068050.htm. The author is the head of the Department of Agricultural Studies of the Development Research Center of State Council. See also Guoxiang Li, "Rural Land Property System Expecting Substantial Reform in the Thirteenth Five Year Plan Period（集体产权制度"十三五"迎大改）," September 25, 2015, available at politics.people.com.cn/n/2015/0925/c70731-27631521.html.

truly public interest purposes. The approach taken by these cities was basically twofold: developing a public interest catalogue and replacing expropriation with transfer for purposes outside that catalogue.[16] For example, in Wuhan, a public interest land use list was drawn based on the 2001 *Catalogue of Allocated Land Use*. For purposes outside this list, rural land will be transferred directly from the collectives to private developers without expropriation.[17] In late 2013, the Decision of the Third Plenum of the Eighteenth Party Congress (Third Plenum Decision) reaffirmed that "narrowing down the scope of rural land expropriation" is on the agenda of China's land reform.

As noted in Chapter 2, to create an enumerative list of what counts as public interest was once recommended to cope with the definitional challenge to the constitutional public interest prerequisite. The 2007 *Property Law* did not adopt such a proposal, although a list of this kind did appear in the 2011 RECHSL with regard to urban land withdrawal. While the obvious difficulty in pinning down what public interest entails contributes to the absence of such a catalogue with respect to rural land expropriation, the biggest obstacle lies in the structural challenge: since under the present LAL and UREAL most nonagricultural use of rural land necessitates state expropriation regardless of the particular purposes expropriated land serves in individual cases, no public interest list could constrain the scope of rural land expropriation. What the seven-city trial reform did was therefore, strictly speaking, unlawful, a problem only to be resolved by the 2015 NPCSC decision. Nevertheless, as the extent to which a public interest catalogue can meaningfully narrow down the scope of rural land expropriation is essentially a function of the degree of rural land marketization, namely how much rural land can be transferred for nonagricultural ends without expropriation, and given that the latest reform liberalizes less than 10 percent of rural land in the entire country, it is not surprising that any public interest list, however delicately drafted, will not take us very far in reducing the scope of rural land expropriation and guaranteeing the public interestedness thereof.[18]

[16] Hongling Ye, "The Shock of Reform of Rural Land Expropriation System: Assessing the Reform Prospects of Narrowing Down the Scope of Rural Land Expropriation from Pilot Projects in Seven Cities (征地制度改革冲击波 – 从七城市试点看"缩小征地范围"的改革前景)" (2014) 4 *China Land* (中国土地) 6.

[17] Ibid.

[18] For instance, it has been reported that the latest land reform still faces considerable difficulties in reducing the scope of rural land expropriation. See Changmei Ou, "Three Pilot Projects of Rural Land Reform Start, Narrowing Down Scope of Rural Land

With respect to the procedural challenge to the constitutional public interest precondition, a change took place in 2004 when pre-application notice and consultation were introduced. Prior to 2004, as noted in the preceding chapter, the expropriated were not given the chance to know about the expropriation initiatives before they were approved. Since 2004, the State Council has required that prior to submitting their expropriation application, the initiating governments should inform the expropriatees-to-be of the proposed expropriation and the planned compensation and resettlement arrangements. The procedure thus changed from "two notifications and one registration" to "three notifications and one registration." In the meantime, a pre-application land survey shall also be carried out, the result of which must be verified by the condemnees. In order to make sure that these procedural requirements are followed, it is required that the expropriatees' knowledge about the expropriation application, compensation and resettlement plans, as well as the land survey results, should be recorded in written forms and that such documents should be included in the application materials submitted to provincial or central government for approval. Furthermore, before turning in the application, if requested by the expropriated, the initiating government needs to hold public hearings.[19]

Admittedly, conferring upon the expropriatees the right to know about expropriation initiatives at the pre-application stage is an important progress. But in no way does this mean that the condemnees are given any say in the actual expropriation decision-making. Unfortunately still, in practice, even the meager right to know about expropriation proposals has often been violated without effective remedy. A 2010 survey conducted in 17 provinces across China found that in 29 percent of all the cases farmers were not notified in advance of expropriation.[20] When such procedural illegality occurs, there is no rule providing for any negative consequence with regard to the validity of expropriation decisions. Also, many local governments waste no time in forging documents to cover

Expropriation Faces Difficulties (农村土改三项试点全面启动, 征地范围缩小"存在困难")," July 8, 2015, available at news.163.com/15/0708/11/AU0EIGLR00014AED.html.

19 Point 14, State Council, Decision on Deepening Reform and Enhancing Land Administration.

20 Keliang Zhu and Jeffrey Riedinger, "'Chinese Farmers' Land Rights at the Crossroads – Findings and Implications from a 2010 Nationwide Survey," World Bank, April 18, 2011, available at http://siteresources.worldbank.org/INTIE/Images/475494-1294353056366/ZhuLandRightsPres4.pdf.

up procedural illegality.[21] As to the right to request hearings at the pre-application stage, it was made clear that such hearings are only to deal with objection to the proposed compensation and resettlement arrangements, not the expropriation initiatives.[22] In other words, expropriation decision-making, especially the issue of whether or not public interest is present, remains closed to public participation and contestation.

To summarize, the last decade witnessed limited reform to deal with the definitional, structural and procedural challenges that have tucked away the teeth, as it were, of the constitutional public interest clause in China. In comparison, more substantial progress has been achieved regarding compensation and resettlement. However, as will be shown in the next section, reform on this front is also restrained.

3.1.2 Compensation and Resettlement

Cognizant of the widespread discontent among the expropriated and its destabilizing effect, the central authority in China started to tinker with the compensation regime a decade ago along two lines – one on compensation and the other regarding resettlement.

With respect to compensation, the adjustment is twofold. One is that the State Council stated in a 2004 policy document that if keeping the peasants' original living standards requires more than 30 times the average annual output, local governments shall provide additional compensation with the revenue obtained through post-expropriation land transfers.[23] This is precisely the exception to the 30-times cap provided by the final paragraph of Article 47 in the 2004 LAL. While it might appear that the State Council acted swiftly to take up this statutory exception as the relevant policy document was issued just two months after the LAL was revised in August 2004, it actually took six years for it to bring this exception into effect because the 1998 version of the LAL had already granted that exception (also in Article 47). At any rate, the outcome of such a policy change is that there is no longer a fixed upper

[21] For a recent example, see Chuanjiao Xie, "Land Deal Contested by Villagers is being Investigated," March 25, 2014, available at www.chinadaily.com.cn/china/2014-03/25/content_17378436.htm.

[22] Point 11, Guiding Opinions on Improving Compensation and Resettlement System in Land Expropriation (关于完善征地补偿安置制度的指导意见), promulgated by MLR on November 3, 2004, available at www.mlr.gov.cn/zwgk/flfg/tdglflfg/200506/t20050617_68344.htm.

[23] Point 12, State Council, Decision on Deepening Reform and Enhancing Land Administration.

limit for the amount of expropriation compensation. The other change concerns the calculation of compensation. Since 2005, the statutory formula established by Article 47 of the 2004 LAL based on "average annual output × multiplier" has been replaced by "expropriation uniform annual output standard" (*zhengdi tongyi nianchan zhi biaozhun*) and "comprehensive land section price in expropriation" (*zhengdi qupian zonghe dijia*).[24]

The gist of the new system is "same land with same compensation" (*tongdi tongjia*) as local governments down to the county level classify land within their jurisdiction into different segments at different grades, for which various standards of compensation are formulated and published as local rules of expropriation compensation – the higher the grade, the more the compensation, but for the same grade compensation is the same. Specifically, this has effected the following changes. First, since compensation is no longer determined ad hoc by local governments in individual cases but according to pre-published general rules, it enhances the consistency and transparency of the compensation regime. Second, within the same area, compensation holds constant regardless of future post-expropriation use, intending to make the compensation regime more equitable.[25] Third, the expropriation uniform annual output standard is determined by the dominant farming pattern

[24] There are three follow-up policy documents issued by the MLR to explain in detail the methods of evaluation and calculation for these two new standards. See Guiding Opinions on Improving Compensation and Resettlement System in Land Expropriation (关于完善征地补偿安置制度的指导意见), promulgated by MLR on November 3, 2004, available at www.mlr.gov.cn/zwgk/flfg/tdglflfg/200506/t20050617_68344.htm; Notice on Starting Working on Formulating Expropriation Uniform Annual Output Standard and Comprehensive Land Section Price in Expropriation (关于开展制订征地统一年产值标准和征地区片综合地价工作的通知), promulgated by MLR on, July 23, 2005, available at www.mlr.gov.cn/zwgk/zytz/200508/t20050812_69436.htm; Notice on Effective Publication and Implementation of Expropriation Uniform Annual Output and Comprehensive Land Price in Expropriated Areas (关于切实做好征地统一年产值标准和区片综合地价公布实施工作的通知), promulgated by MLR on June 22, 2008, available at www.pkulaw.cn/fulltext_form.aspx?Gid=219351&Db=chl. For an analysis of these new standards in a Chinese municipality, see Chuanhui Wang, *The Constitutional Protection of Private Property In China: Historical Evolution and Comparative Research* (Cambridge: Cambridge University Press, 2016), pp. 225–27.

[25] Unavoidably there will be borderline cases where the difference in compensation between adjacent pieces of land is difficult to justify. Conversely, there will also emerge a new type of inequity for "different land same price," as land classified in the same area may well have different values. Actual compensation might be lower to some peasants whose land has higher value than others' land located in the same section. For a critique, see Wang, *The Constitutional Protection of Private Property in China*, pp. 227–30.

at a particular location, not the actual use of a land parcel. And the multipliers are no longer determined on a case-by-case basis, but are fixed for different areas. In this way, compared with the traditional statutory standard, the expropriation uniform annual output standard minimizes the possibility that local governments suppress compensation through manipulating the average annual output and/or the multiplier. Fourth, factors other than the annual agricultural output start to be taken into consideration in setting comprehensive land section price in expropriation. In particular, the location of expropriated land, supply and demand in the local land market as well as the level of local economic development and living standards are now factored in. Fifth, when setting uniform compensation standards, local governments can no longer act unilaterally as they used to do, but are obligated to hold public consultations and hearings.[26] Last but not least, as mandated by the State Council, the new standards shall not be lower than the original one, leading to a general rise in expropriation compensation across the country.

Besides adjusting and increasing compensation standards, how compensation is paid and how expropriatees are resettled have also been under reform. Cash payment of compensation and resettlement fees has proven to be inadequate and ineffective in sustaining the expropriatees in the long run.[27] Whilst the low standard is certainly to blame, the fact that compensation and resettlement fees were usually paid as a one-off lump sum is also culpable since it has been documented that land-losing peasants either quickly squander the compensation received or are

[26] Art. 12, Rules on Public Hearings of Land Resources (国土资源听证规定), promulgated by MLR on January 9, 2004, available at www.mlr.gov.cn/pub/mlr/documents/t20040625_83923.htm. No empirical research has been conducted so far to check if local governments do hold public hearings and how meaningful and participatory they are. But a case in Zhengzhou in 2009 shows that holding a public hearing does not necessarily guarantee that peasants are duly consulted. See Qingli Chen, "Public Hearing Held by Zhengzhou Land Bureau after the New Standards Becoming Effective Suspected to be a Mere Formality (郑州国土局被疑走过场,新标准已执行才开听证会)," July 9, 2009, available at news.sohu.com/20090709/n265095742.shtml.

[27] For example, it has been estimated that the compensation could support the peasants for only six or eight years after expropriation. See Xiangzhi Kong and Zhiqiang Wang, "Compensation to Land-losing Peasants in Urbanizing China (我国城镇化进程中失地农民的补偿)" (2004) 5 *Economic Theory and Economic Management* (经济理论与经济管理) 61; Daochi Qiu, Hongmei Yang, Chuanhua Zhang, Wei Yuan and Banghua Li, "Study of Expropriation Compensation Standard: Shapingba District of Chongqing as the Example (征地补偿标准研究 – 以重庆市沙坪坝区为例)" (2005) 30 *Journal of Southwest China Normal University* (西南师范大学学报) 569.

unable to find new employment.[28] In response, since 2004, the Chinese central authority has begun to demand that local governments properly resettle the expropriated to secure their "long-term livelihood" in ways other than merely handing out monetary compensation.[29] In other words, with regard to expropriation compensation and resettlement, the requirement of maintaining the original living standard has been supplemented by the principle of securing a long-term livelihood. Over the years, scores of measures have been implemented to supply the expropriated with continuous social welfare supports such as pensions, unemployment benefits, urban residence permits and so on.[30] Alternatively, government may resettle expropriatees by way of moving them to other locations with government-supplied housing. A third, particularly popular model practiced in many localities over the years is "resettlement through land retention" (*liudi anzhi*), which became recognized and recommended by the central government for the first time in early 2014.[31] Despite variation in local practices, the core idea behind this

[28] Chengang Miu and Zhiliang Huang, "Investigation of the Life and Development of Land-losing Peasants in Pearl Delta Suburbs and Countermeasures (珠三角城郊失地农民生存发展状况调查与对策研究)" (2008) 36 *Journal of Anhui Agricultural Science* (安徽农业科学) 6556.

[29] Point 13, Guiding Opinions on the Work of Providing Occupational Training and Social Security to the Expropriated Peasants (关于做好被征地农民就业培训和社会保障工作的指导意见), promulgated by State Council and Ministry of Labour and Social Security on April 10, 2006, available at www.chrs.gov.cn/page247?article_id=383; point 2, Notice on the Questions relevant to Strengthening Land Control (关于加强土地调控有关问题的通知), promulgated by State Council on August 31, 2006, available at www.gov.cn/zwgk/2006-09/05/content_378186.htm; Notice on the Questions relevant to Guarantee Social Security for Expropriated Peasants (关于切实做好被征地农民社会保障工作有关问题的通知), promulgated by Ministry of Labour and Social Security and MLR on April 28, 2007, available at www.gov.cn/zwgk/2007-05/22/content_621918.htm. It should be noted that this is preceded by extensive local experiments started in the 1990s of replacing one-time payment of compensation with continuous provision of social welfare, including pension and unemployment benefits. See Furong Wang, "Problems and Solutions on Social Security of Land-losing Peasants in China Today (当前我国失地农民社会保障问题与对策)," Master's Thesis, Nanjing Normal University (2012), chapter 3.

[30] The MLR has recommended four measures including providing the peasants with agricultural land to work on, employment or free occupational training, opportunity to share the return of commercial or industrial projects built on the expropriated land and migration. See Guiding Opinions on Improving Compensation and Resettlement System in Land Expropriation (关于完善征地补偿安置制度的指导意见), promulgated by MLR on November 3, 2004, available at www.mlr.gov.cn/zwgk/flfg/tdglflfg/200506/t20050617_68344.htm.

[31] Part 4, point 20, CCP Central Committee, Opinions on Comprehensively Deepening Rural Reform and Promoting Modernization of Agricultural Industry.

model is letting the expropriated retain part (usually 10–15 percent) of the land subject to expropriation, which can then serve as a reliable long-term source of revenue for the expropriatees either as in-kind contributions to future commercial development on the expropriated land or through being rented out directly by the expropriated collectives themselves.[32]

Overall, since the early 2000s, the policy changes toward a more consistent, transparent, equitable, broad-based, generous and sustainable expropriation compensation and resettlement regime have clearly demonstrated the commitment of the Chinese central authority to improving the insufficient and unjust compensation and resettlement system, evidenced more recently by the Third Plenum Decision in 2013 that proclaimed the development of a reasonable, regularized and multi-dimensional mechanism for resettling the expropriated peasants. This is surely progress to be welcomed. Yet, reform in this regard is still critically limited for the following reasons. To begin with, it has rightly been pointed out that the original living standards approach does not take us very far because to duplicate peasants' pre-expropriation income levels will not ensure their economic support once they lose land and become incorporated into the urban economy, with glaring urban-rural income disparity and higher living costs in cities in China.[33] Aware of this problem, the central Party announced in 2012 that expropriation compensation and resettlement should not just maintain but must also improve the original living standards of expropriated peasants.[34] The principle of maintaining original living standards has therefore been turned into the requirement of raising living standards. Yet without any specification, this new mandate is as unclear and immeasurable as the previous approach. To what degree the living standards of the expropriated shall be improved, whether or not it needs be comparable

[32] Jian Tang, Zhengui Li, Qingbin Wang and Boyuan Wang, "Steadily Promoting Resettlement through Land Retention according to Local Conditions: a Survey of 10-odd Provinces" Practices (因地制宜地稳妥推进留地安置 – 基于对10余省份留地安置的调研)" (2014) 28 *China Land Sciences* (中国土地科学) 91.

[33] Valerie Jaffee Washburn, "Regular Takings or Regulatory Takings: Land Expropriation in Rural China" (2011) 20 *Pacific Rim Law & Policy Journal* 108.

[34] Several Opinions on Accelerating Development of Modern Agriculture and Further Invigorating Rural Development (关于加快发展现代农业进一步增强农村发展活力的若干意见), promulgated by CCP Central Committee and State Council on 31 December 2012, available at www.mlr.gov.cn/xwdt/jrxw/201302/t20130201_1180243.htm.

to that of urban residents and how long really is "long term" all remain undefined. Moreover, as the MLR requires that in every two to three years the uniform standards should be revised to reflect changing circumstances,[35] understandably many expropriatees consider compensation unfair when standards published two or even three years ago are applied in their case.[36]

Finally, yet most significantly, although the improved compensation and resettlement system goes beyond the original use criteria and in principle discards the 30-times cap,[37] it still does not explicitly suggest that (at least part of) expropriation surplus will be shared with the expropriated peasants. Admittedly, the State Council did request that local governments offer additional subsidies to condemnees from the revenue generated from post-expropriation land transfers so as to maintain their original living standards, which was in fact urging that some expropriation surplus be allocated to the expropriated. Nevertheless, the central government provided no guidance whatsoever about how much should be distributed. Available evidence suggests that local governments are not so keen to share expropriation surplus by way of providing extra compensatory subsidy. For instance, the only national data published by the Ministry of Finance so far shows that in 2009 only 1.3 percent of the revenue from land use-rights transfer was used to subsidize the expropriated peasants.[38] It was further reported that in 2011 Shaanxi Province used just 0.5 percent of post-expropriation land transfer income to preserve the expropriatees' original living standards.[39]

A breakthrough came in late 2012 when China's central authority for the first time avowed to increase the proportion of condemnees' share of the land value increment caused by expropriation and conversion of

[35] MLR, Notice on Effective Publication and Implementation of Expropriation Uniform Annual Output and Comprehensive Land Price in Expropriated Areas.

[36] This is not to mention the frequent lag of adjustment among local authorities. For instance, it was reported that Jiangsu Province did not adjust its 2004 compensation standards until 2011. See Wang, *The Constitutional Protection of Private Property in China*, p. 227.

[37] There are exceptions where local governments continue to implement the 30-times cap. See ibid., p. 230.

[38] "Basic Situation of National Land Transfer Revenue of Expenditure (全国土地出让基本收支情况)", April 13, 2010, available at www.mof.gov.cn/zhengwuxinxi/caizhengshuju/201004/t20100413_286852.html.

[39] "Shaanxi Made 24.3 billion out of Selling Land and Subsidized 122 million to Expropriated Peasants Last Year (陕西去年卖地收入243亿补助被征地农民1.22亿)," September 27, 2012, available online at gz.house.163.com/12/0927/23/8CEP6DO900873C6D.html.

rural land.[40] A year later, the Third Plenum Decision reconfirmed that a distributional mechanism of the post-expropriation land increased value would be set up to balance the interests of the state, collectives and individuals via *reasonably* increasing individual expropriatees' gain and granting the peasants a *fair* share in the expropriation surplus (emphasis added).[41] Worth noting is that in April 2016 the Ministry of Finance and the MLR jointly issued *Temporary Administration Measures on Collection and Use of Adjustment Fee from Land Increment Value of Rural Collective For-profit Construction Land*, establishing a nationwide framework for the allocation of increment value of the now marketized for-profit rural construction land between collectives and local governments. It is provided that local governments may collect 20–50 percent of the increased land value as adjustment fee (*tiaojie jin*) and another 3–5 percent as deed tax. In other words, 23–55 percent of the income brought about by transferring for-profit rural construction land will be reaped by local states and the remaining 45–77 percent goes to collectives and peasants. However, to date there has been no detailed national standard about reasonable and fair distribution of increment value in rural land expropriation. The vague criteria of original living standards and long-term livelihood are here to stay. And it is still up to local governments to decide if the original living standards of the condemnees are appropriately maintained or improved, whether their long-term livelihood is properly secured and in what proportion the increased land value is shared between the government, future land-users and the expropriated. In contrast, the market value standard tries precisely to move such decisions out of the government's hands. But it has not been adopted so far.

3.1.3 Procedural Rights Concerning Compensation and Resettlement

As mentioned in the previous chapter, it is rather difficult under existing law for the expropriated to challenge compensation and resettlement arrangements fixed by local states. In fact, the locally set compensation and resettlement standards are not open to challenge in court because they are promulgated as local rules regarded as abstract administrative

40 CCP Central Committee and State Council, Several Opinions on Accelerating Development of Modern Agriculture and Further Invigorating Rural Development, part 5, point 2.

41 CCP Central Committee, Decision on Major Issues concerning Promoting Rural Reform and Development, points 11, 22.

acts with general binding force, which are immune to administrative litigation.[42] Nevertheless, during the last decade, there have been two policy adjustments that grant the expropriated more procedural rights concerning expropriation compensation and resettlement arrangements.

First, since 2004, alongside the requirement of pre-application notification of a proposed expropriation project, the initiating governments have been asked by the State Council to consult with the expropriated about proposed compensation and resettlement arrangements before submitting their expropriation applications for approval.[43] As mentioned, since that same year, the local governments have also been required to formulate and promulgate local compensation and resettlement rules. For each individual expropriation initiative, the initiating government should now include in the application package a draft compensation and resettlement plan, indicating the local compensation and resettlement rules to be applied to the expropriation initiative. At this stage, upon the request of potential expropriatees, the initiating government shall hold public hearings to address compensation-related concerns and objections.[44] However, this does not mean that the government-set compensation rules can be challenged. At most the expropriated could disagree with how these rules are applied to their specific cases. Worse still, similar to the right to be notified about the proposed expropriation in advance, the right to be consulted about the proposed compensation and resettlement arrangements at public hearings has frequently been violated in practice. A 2010 survey shows that in 58 percent of the cases surveyed the takees were not consulted on compensation beforehand.[45] According to the MLR, procedural deficiency of this kind does not affect the validity of the compensation decisions.[46] And even when such public hearings are held, the government has no obligation to give any feedback.

Second, as mentioned earlier, once the detailed compensation and resettlement plan is approved by the initiating government, any remaining dispute must first be mediated and adjudicated by the government

42 Jun Fang, "On Ways of Legal Remedies to Disputes of Expropriation Compensation and Resettlement (论征地补偿安置争议的法律救济途径)," in Songnian Ying and Huaide Ma (eds.), *Sources of Modern Administrative Law* (当代行政法的源流) (Beijing: Fazhi Press, 2006).

43 Point 14, State Council, Decision on Deepening Reform and Enhancing Land Administration.

44 Art.19, MLR, Rules on Public Hearings of Land Resources.

45 Zhu and Riedinger, "Chinese Farmers" Land Rights at the Crossroads – Findings and Implications from a 2010 Nationwide Survey".

46 Art.34, MLR, Rules on Public Hearings of Land Resources.

before going to court. The MLR stated in 2006 that in the mediation process both the legality and rationality of compensation and resettlement arrangements could be reviewed.[47] Given that the courts can only review the legality of compensation decisions, which effectively means that they can only review whether or not the local compensation rules are faithfully followed in individual cases, this may seem to be an improvement. But the MLR has made it clear that the rationality review will focus on whether the maintenance of the original living standards and guaranteeing of long-term livelihoods are realized, which, as explicated, is anything but clear and measurable. More importantly, since the mediating authority is the same agency that approves the detailed compensation and resettlement plan in the first place, the impartiality and the effectiveness of the mediation mechanism are highly questionable. Indeed, this was recognized as problematic by the MLR itself, which promised in 2006 that "impartial organizations" would be brought in to evaluate the reasonableness of compensation and resettlement arrangements.[48] More than a decade has now passed, but there is no development in this respect.

In short, despite a series of reform measures rolled out over the last ten years,[49] the expropriation compensation and resettlement regime in China remains far from ideal. Substantively, the ambiguous principles of original living standards and long-term livelihood have not been replaced by the more objective fair market value standards, leaving much discretion for local governments to determine compensation and resettlement as well as distribution of increased land value. Procedurally, the expropriated continue to have little room to participate in making compensation and resettlement arrangements or to challenge such decisions. This is not very different from the lack of breakthrough in the reform related to the constitutional public interest prerequisite described in the last section. Why has the much-anticipated reform stagnated? Why does the existing rural land takings law persist?

[47] Part 2, point 2, Notice on Accelerating the Establishment of the Mediation and Adjudication System for Disputes on Land Expropriation Compensation and Resettlement (关于加快推进征地补偿安置争议协调裁决制度的通知), promulgated by MLR on June 21, 2006, available at www.lawtime.cn/info/zhengdi/zdcqzc/201011083114_3.html.

[48] Ibid.

[49] For an in-depth study of how popular protests through the petitioning system have shaped and influenced the policy changes in this area, see Christopher Heurlin, *Responsive Authoritarianism in China: Land, Protests, and Policy Making* (New York: Cambridge University Press, 2016), chapter 4.

3.2 Land Finance as the Explanation

The foregoing account illustrates the persistently weak constitutional and legal limitations over the state's rural land takings power in China. In the American context, the hurdles government must overcome to wield the takings power are conceptualized as administrative costs of eminent domain, which include, inter alia, the costs to lobby the legislature to grant the power of eminent domain, procedural costs required by the Fifth and Fourteenth Amendments and state laws, costs associated with professional appraisal services, costs to guarantee condemnees' rights such as public hearings on the condemnation's legality and the amount of compensation required, as well as potentially the costs of lengthy law suits challenging the exercise of condemnation.[50] All these costs and burdens render eminent domain in America a very cumbersome and expensive process, from which governments in the United States usually choose to shy away.[51]

In striking contrast, administrative costs of rural land expropriation in China are significantly lower, for reasons discussed previously. This constitutes a prima facie explanation as to the endurance of the current expropriation law. But when one looks closer, it is easy to find that the costs of rural land takings are by no means low in contemporary China since "demoralization costs" and "settlement costs" are extremely high.[52] The former connotes the present and future monetized loss of the uncompensated property losers and their sympathizers as well as other observers disturbed by the thought that they themselves may be subjected to similar treatment. The latter refers to the costs of time, effort and resources to reach compensation settlements adequate to offset demoralization costs. As demonstrated, with expansive practices of expropriation and compensation widely perceived as inadequate and unjust, China's government faces increasing resistance against expropriation and mounting pressure to reform the existing law. Put another way, the costs of preserving the status quo are rising rapidly, and the persistence of the present law cannot be solely or even primarily explained by the low costs involved. For a better explanation, we need to look at the other side of the equation, namely the benefits brought about by rural land expropriation. In brief, it has been immensely beneficial for Chinese local governments in fiscal terms to expropriate. Their reluctance and

50 Thomas Merrill, "The Economics of Public Use" (1986) 72 *Cornell Law Review* 77.
51 Ibid., 80.
52 Frank Michelman, "Property, Utility and Fairness: Comments on the Ethical Foundations of 'Just Compensation' Law" (1967) 80 *Harvard Law Review* 1214.

opposition are now regarded as the most significant barrier that holds off deeper reforms in this area.

As already shown, under China's present land administration system, the government monopolizes the right to convert rural land to urban land through expropriation, a process leading to both augmented land rights and increased economic profitability. But the expropriation surplus did not exist prior to the late 1980s. Back then, China's land system had two key features. First, under a planned economy, land was not treated as a commodity but as production means administered by the state, which allocates (*huabo*) land, free of charge and without term limitation, to government agencies, state-owned enterprises (SOEs), social groups and public–private joint ventures on a need basis.[53] To charge rents or fees for allocated land use-rights was then considered by the central government to "unnecessarily raise the production cost of the enterprises, swell the state budget and incur administrative formalities."[54] Second, sale, lease, mortgage and any other type of transfer of allocated land use rights were strictly prohibited.[55]

Into the opening and reform era, as China embarked on the mission of developing a market economy, the traditional land system became both undesirable and untenable. To start with, since land allocation involved no costs and term limits, users had basically no incentive to economize on land use, giving rise to widespread land waste. Second, the land allocation system aggravated price distortions in the economy and undermined competition. Third, bureaucratic procedures for land allocation were inflexible and could not respond to rapid economic, social and technological change. Consequently, there were considerable imbalances in supply and demand of land, which was further exacerbated by the prohibition of land transaction. Last but not least, in a capital-scare economy, local governments lacked funds to support urban infrastructure-building.[56]

[53] Part 5, Comprehensive Reply on Several Questions concerning the Implementation of the Measures on Land Requisition for State-led Construction (关于执行国家建设征用土地办法中几个问题的综合答复), promulgated by Ministry of Domestic Affairs on April 27, 1954, available at china.findlaw.cn/fagui/p_1/212345.html.

[54] Part 1, Reply on the Issue of Charging Land Use Fee or Rent on Suburban Land used by State-operated Enterprises, State Agencies, Military, Schools and so on (关于对国营企业、机关、部队、学校等占用市郊土地征收土地使用费或租金问题的答复), promulgated by Central Administrative Committee on February 24, 1954, available at www.mlr.gov.cn/xwdt/jrxw/200911/t20091102_126780.htm.

[55] Hin Ling Li, *Urban Land Reform in China* (London: Macmillan Press, 1999), p. 16.

[56] Mark T. Kremzner, "Managing Urban Land in China: The Emerging Legal Framework and its Role in Development" (1998) 7 *Pacific Rim Law & Policy Journal* 611; David E. Dowall, "Establishing Urban Land Markets in the People's Republic of China" (1993) 59 *Journal of the American Planning Association* 182.

Change to the old land system was initially introduced in 1979, when local governments started to charge Sino–foreign joint companies site use fees – a euphemism for land rent that was still regarded as capitalistic and therefore inappropriate for socialist China at the time.[57] In the years that ensued, many cities began to impose land use fees on domestic enterprises. But the real breakthrough came in 1987 when Shenzhen, drawing on Hong Kong's experience in public land lease and motivated primarily by the need to raise capital for infrastructural development, carried out the first competitive public auction of urban land use-rights in order to generate fiscal revenue for local infrastructure development and capital investments.[58] Strictly speaking, this was unlawful because both the 1982 Constitution and the 1986 LAL prohibited land use-rights transaction. It was yet another example of benign illegality. By separating ownership and use-rights over land, it freed up room for the commodification of urban land in China without touching the political fault line of socialist public land ownership. Constitutional and legal recognition ultimately came when the 1988 constitutional amendment and the 1998 revision to the LAL authorized local governments to lease out use-rights of state-owned urban land.[59] The early 1990s witnessed further institutionalization of urban land marketization: in addition to the traditional authority to allocate land use-rights,[60] China's local governments have since been permitted to transfer land use-rights to private parties with charge[61] and mortgage the land to secure loans.[62]

57 Sino-foreign Equity Joint Ventures Law (中外合资经营企业法), art. 5; art. 1, Interim Provisions on Use of Construction Land by Sino-foreign Cooperative Joint Ventures (关于中外合营企业建设用地的暂行规定), promulgated by State Council on July 26, 1980, available at www.chinalawedu.com/falvfagui/fg22016/11561.shtml.

58 For a detailed documentation of the policy experimentation in Shenzhen and its subsequent expansion to other localities, see Xiaofang Shen and Songming Xu, "Shenzhen Special Economic Zone: A Policy Reform Incubator for Urban Land Market Development," in Xiaofang Shen and Xiaolun Sun (eds.), *Untying the Land Knot: Making Equitable, Efficient, and Sustainable Use of Industrial and Commercial Land* (Washington, DC: World Bank, 2012).

59 One sentence was added to Article 10 of the 1982 Constitution, reading, "land use-rights can be transferred according to law." This is another well-known example of the above-mentioned "benign illegality."

60 Interim Measures for the Administration of Allocated Land Use Right, art. 4; 2004 LAL, art. 54; 1994 UREAL, art. 23.

61 1990 *Interim Regulation on the Allocation and Transfer of the Use Right of the State-owned Urban Land* (城镇国有土地使用权出让和转让暂行条例), promulgated by State Council on May 19, 1990, available at www.mlr.gov.cn/zwgk/flfg/tdglflfg/200601/t20060119_72175.htm; 2004 LAL, art. 54. Note that different English translations have been adopted for the Chinese word *churang* such as grant and conveyance.

62 It should be noted that local governments are not permitted to pledge urban land use-rights directly. Yet, since the 1990s they have set up arms-length legal entities, usually

Against this background we can make sense of "land finance," which is widely recognized as the central impetus propelling China's local states to expropriate rural land extensively and to resist relevant reforms.[63] A loosely defined umbrella term, land finance captures at least three ways in which local states in China capitalize on rural land expropriation for financial benefits.

First and foremost, local governments obtain huge amounts of fiscal revenue through land transfer fee (*tudi churang jin*) paid as a lump sum by commercial land-users, to whom use-rights of state-owned urban land are transferred via public competitive tender, auction or listing.[64] Although 30 percent of the revenue is supposed to go to the central government,[65] the lion's share is kept by local governments. As noted earlier, there is a huge gap between expropriation compensation and

under the name of "land reserve center" or "land development center," to pledge the expropriated land to obtain bank loans. For an in-depth examination of this process, see Jianbo Lou and Jinpin Jin, *Legal Institutions of Land Reserve and Primary Land Development* (土地储备及土地一级开发法律制度) (Beijing: Fazhi Press, 2009).

63 Hongmei Liu, Zhibin Zhang and Keqiang Ma, "A Review of the Research on Revenue from Land Finance in China (我国土地财政收入研究综述)" (2008) 1 *Research on Development* (开发研究); Shouying Liu, Xingsan Jiang and Qing Li, *China's Land Policy Reform: Policy Evolution and Local Implementation* (中国土地政策改革– 政策演进与地方实施) (Shanghai: Sanlian Press, 2010); Guangzhong Cao, Fei Yuan and Ran Tao, "Land Finance, Industrial Structure Changes and Rapid Tax Revenue Growth (土地财政、产业结构演变与税收超常规增长)" (2007) 12 *China Industrial Economy* (中国工业经济) *13*; Ju Wang, Chunmei Lv and Shungxing Dai, "Land Finance and Development of Real Estate Sector (土地财政与房地产业发展)" (2008) 10 Local Fiscal Research (地方财政研究) 14; Feizhou Zhou, "Creating Wealth: The Role of Government and Farmers in Land Development and Transfer (生财有道: 土地开发和转让中的政府和农民)" (2007) 1 *Sociological Studies* (社会学研究) 49; Feizhou Zhou, "Land Finance and the Behaviour of Local Government (大兴土木: 土地财政与地方政府行为)" (2010) 3 *Comparative Economic and Social Systems* (经济社会体制比较) 77. For a detailed documentation of how local governments resisted reform of the law on urban land withdrawal, see Heurlin, Responsive Authoritarianism in China, pp. 158–62.

64 Another way to transfer the use-rights over state-owned land is non-public negotiation. In order to guarantee that the state-owned land is transferred at a fair price, from the early 2000s the central authority demanded that all state-owned land transfer for for-profit projects must go through public competitive tender, auction and listing. See art. 4, Rules of Public Tende, Auction and Listing of State-owned Land Use Rights (招标拍卖挂牌出让国有土地使用权规定), promulgated by MLR on April 3, 2002, available at www.mlr.gov.cn/zwgk/flfg/dfflfg/200504/t20050406_636761.htm. See also art. 4, Rules of Public Tender, Auction and Listing of State-owned Construction Land Use Rights (招标拍卖挂牌出让国有建设用地使用权规定), promulgated by MLR on September 21, 2007, available at www.mlr.gov.cn/zwgk/zfgw/zfwj/200712/t20071212_96998.htm.

65 1998 LAL, art. 55; 2004 LAL, art. 55. For more detailed rules on management of land transfer revenue, see Measures of Administration of Receipts and Disbursements of Revenues from State-Owned Land Use-Rights Transfer (国有土地使用权出让收支管

transfer revenue, rendering land transfer immensely lucrative. It was estimated that, on average, land transfer fees comprised almost one-third of budgetary revenues of prefectural level cities in 2010.[66] Some cities were reported to have an even higher proportion (up to 70 percent) of income coming from land transfer fees.[67]

Second, besides generating enormous amounts of land transfer fees, rural land expropriation and subsequent transfer can also boost the local tax base in both the short and the long term. This is especially the case in localities where land price is relatively low and high land transfer fees are not immediately available. But by expropriating and converting rural land for nonagricultural uses, local governments can expect to collect corporate and income taxes paid by real estate companies involved in land development.[68] In some cases, instead of using land for short-term revenue generation, local states intentionally transfer land at very low prices, or even zero fee, in order to attract manufacturing investors in the hope that it will create a steady revenue stream in the future from various kinds of taxes, including value added tax (VAT), business tax, income tax and so forth.[69]

The third type of financial benefit comes from local governments using expropriated land as collateral for bank loans. Article 28 of the 1995 *Budget Law* prohibits local governments from resorting to market borrowing such as bank loans. In practice, however, local authorities all over the country have set up arms-length financing platforms and allocate

理办法), promulgated by Ministry of Finance, MLR and People's Bank of China on December 31, 2006, available at www.mof.gov.cn/zhengwuxinxi/caizhengwengao/caizhengbuwengao2007/caizhengbuwengao20075/200805/t20080519_26378.html. For a historical analysis of the evolving central-local distribution of land transfer revenue, see Qingyong Zhang, "Vertical Fiscal Competition, Price Bargaining and Central-local Distribution of Land Revenue: A Review of Land Revenue in China since the 1980s (纵向财政竞争讨价与中央-地方的土地收入分成 – 对20世纪80年代以来土地收入的考察)" (2008) 4 *Institutional Economics Research* (制度经济学研究) 115.

66 Christine Wong, "Paying for Urbanization: Challenges for China's Municipal Finance in the 21st Century," in J. Linn, R. Bahl and D. Wetzel (eds), *Metropolitan Government Finances in Developing Countries* (Cambridge, MA: Lincoln Institute for Land Policy, 2013), p. 292.

67 It was suggested that in 2010 land transfer revenues accounted for 70 percent of total local revenue for Beijing and 60 percent for Shanghai. See Bin Wu, Shujie Yao and Jian Chen, *China's Development and Harmonization: Towards a Balance with Nature, Society and the International Community* (London: Routledge, 2013), p. 143.

68 Zhou, "Land Finance and the Behaviour of Local Government."

69 Ran Tao, Fubing Su, Mingxing Liu and Guangzhong Cao, "Land Leasing and Local Public Finance in China's Regional Development: Evidence from Prefecture-level Cities" (2010) 47 *Urban Studies* 2224.

use-rights of expropriated land to these platforms, which will then be mortgaged to secure bank loans.[70] It is expected that such loans are going to be paid by future land transfer revenues.[71]

Land finance in the above three senses is now generally considered as the root cause behind stagnant reform of rural land expropriation law. However, one might wonder why Chinese local states have become such revenue seekers. Most existing literature points to the 1994 tax-sharing reform, which significantly altered the central–local relationship in China.[72] This story has been well told, and hence will be sketched out only briefly here.[73]

In the pre-reform era between 1949 and the late 1970s, the Chinese fiscal system was highly centralized, whereby all budgetary decisions were made from the top. With little discretionary fiscal power, subnational governments received operating budgets from the center and spent according to top-down mandates. Local fiscal surpluses had to be handed to and deficits covered by superior governments. Under a stringently planned economy a system of this sort worked just fine. But it became more and more incompatible with China's reform toward market economy from the late 1970s onward. It was well understood, then, that

[70] Yinqi Liu and Tao Sun, *Local Government Financing Platforms in China: A Fortune or Misfortune?* (IMF Working Paper, 2013), available at www.imf.org/external/pubs/ft/wp/2013/wp13243.pdf.

[71] A recently published report surveying 23 provinces across the country demonstrates the astonishing extent to which Chinese local governments have their bank loans backed up by future land transfer revenue (from slightly over 20 percent to more than 66 percent). See Debing Liu, "Ranking of Reliance on Land Finance for 23 Provinces (二十三个省份土地财政依赖度排名)," April 14, 2014, available at finance.sina.com.cn/china/20140414/174318792509.shtml.

[72] Ye'an Zhou, "Theories and Practices of Reform of the Fiscal Expenditure Management at the County Level (县乡级财政支出管理体制改革的理论与对策)" (2000) 5 *Management World* (管理世界) *122*; Deyuan Zhang, "What is the Problem of Land Acquisition (征地问题是什么问题)" (2006) 10 *The World of Survey and Research* (调研世界) *30*; Ying Xie, "Understanding the Land Enclosure Fervor from Fiscal and Land Transfer System (从财政制体制和土地出让制度看圈地热)" (2006) 11 *China Land* (中国土地) 9; Defu Tu and Yunlong Tu, "Analysis of the Land Finance Behaviour of Chinese Local Governments (我国地方政府的土地财政行为分析)" (2007) 1 *Modern Business* (现代商业) 70; Biliang Luo, "Tax-sharing System, Fiscal Pressure and Government's Preferences for Land Finance (分税制、财政压力与政府"土地财政"偏好)" (2010) 10 *Academic Research* (学术研究) 27.

[73] For detailed discussion, see Chunli Shen, Jing Jin and Heng-fu Zou, "Fiscal Decentralization in China: History, Impact, Challenges and Next Steps" (2012) 13 *Annals of Economics and Finance* 4; Joyce Yanyun Man and Yu-Hung Hong (eds.), *China's Local Public Finance in Transition* (Cambridge, MA: Lincoln Institute of Land Policy, 2010), pp. 4–8.

economic revival would be impossible without at least some local initiative and autonomy, which was smothered by the pre-reform fiscal system. Therefore, in the 1980s, a series of fiscal reforms were implemented in order to solve this problem. Despite differences in details, all these reforms aimed at establishing a revenue-sharing system, under which the central and local governments started to "eat in separate kitchens" and the local states were permitted to varied degrees to retain and spend fiscal surpluses created in their jurisdictions. This gave rise to what was famously dubbed "local state corporatism" in China, where local governments were greatly motivated to encourage developmental undertakings and promote economic growth within their administrative region. The TVE boom in the 1980s emerged as a result of local governments acting as critical sponsors to these rural collective enterprises, from which taxes and surcharges were collected.[74]

Despite its success in boosting the Chinese economy, the revenue-sharing system in the 1980s led to a sharp decrease in the central government's share of overall fiscal income. Hoping to mobilize revenue collection at the local level, the central government returned a growing portion of revenue to local governments.[75] By 1993, the central share of total fiscal revenue fell to just 22 percent, compared with 38.4 percent in 1985.[76] It was then warned that an acute decline of central government's extractive capacity would enfeeble its ability to practice macroeconomic control.[77] In response, an overhaul of the fiscal system was launched in 1994, the centerpiece of which was the introduction of the tax-sharing system. Crucially, this system mandates that VAT, the most productive of

[74] Jean C. Oi, "Fiscal Reform and the Economic Foundations of Local State Corporatism in China" (1992) 45 *World Politics* 99; Jean C. Oi, *Rural China Takes Off: Institutional Foundations of Economic Reform* (Berkeley and Los Angeles: University of California Press, 1999). Since the 1980s, rural China has gone through decollectivization, and hence local governments could no longer resort to agricultural sector for fiscal revenue. Meanwhile, because of the political taint still associated with private enterprises and the uncertain political winds from the top towards private entrepreneurs, developing rural collective industries became the most lucrative and least problematic strategy politically for local governments to seek revenue-generating sources.

[75] Other reasons include local governments hiding and retaining the revenue that should have been remitted to the center and granting tax exemptions without proper central authorization. For a more detailed record, see Shaoguang Wang and Angang Hu, *Report of Chinese State Capacity* (中国国家能力报告) (Beijing: Liaoning People's Press, 1993), chapter 3.

[76] Man and Hong, *China's Local Public Finance in Transition*, p. 5.

[77] Shaoguang Wang, "China's 1994 Fiscal Reform: An Initial Assessment" (1997) *Asian Survey* 801.

all existing taxes (to date), shall be shared at the fixed rate of 75 percent going to the central government and 25 percent to local governments. It also established a national tax system that was separated from local tax administration to collect national taxes, especially VAT, in order to avoid poor local tax-collection efforts.[78] These measures successfully recentralized revenues. In just one year, the center's share jumped from 22 percent to about 56 percent, and has remained at around 50 percent since.[79] However, this reform dealt only with income sharing and left out expenditure sharing when subnational governments remain responsible for providing a wide range of public goods and services, including education, health and other social services. The tax-sharing reform therefore created a huge fiscal imbalance between revenue and expenditure for local governments, which on average account for 79 percent of total government expenditure but only 47 percent of total government revenues.[80] It has also left many centrally imposed mandates unfunded.[81] In this situation, it is argued that such a mismatch between revenues and expenditure responsibilities has financially squeezed subnational governments and forced them to seek land-based income and borrowing in order to fund, inter alia, local infrastructural development.[82]

That being said, as much as the 1994 tax-sharing reform is culpable for pushing local governments toward more expropriation, it should be noted that massive rural land takings in China did not begin there. As a matter of fact, prior to this reform, China's local governments had already engaged in pervasive rural land expropriation. Between the late 1980s and early 1990s, local governments across the country fell for what is called "development zone fever" that gave rise to a huge wave of land expropriation and widespread protests of displaced peasants unsatisfied with low compensation.[83] This trend continued well into the late 1990s

78 For more details of these measures, see Christine Wong, "Central-local Relations Revisited: the 1994 Tax Sharing Reform and Public Expenditure Management in China" (2000) 31 *China Perspective* 52.

79 Shen, Jin and Zou, "Fiscal Decentralization in China: History, Impact, Challenges and Next Steps," 12.

80 Man and Hong, *China's Local Public Finance in Transition*, p. 5.

81 Kai-yuen Tsui and Youqiang Wang, "Between Separate Stoves and a Single Menu: Fiscal Decentralization in China" (2004) 177 *China Quarterly* 85.

82 Hongyou Lu, Guangping Yuan and Sixia Chen, "The Root of Land Finance: Competitive or Compelled? (土地财政根源：竞争冲动还是无奈之举)" (2011) 1 *Comparative Economic and Social Systems* (经济社会体制比较) 88.

83 Carolyn Cartier, "'Zone Fever', the Arable Land Debate, and Real Estate Speculation: China's Evolving Land Use Regime and its Geographical Contradictions" (2001) 10 *Journal of Contemporary China* 465; F. Frederic Deng, "Development Zones and Urban

and the early 2000s.[84] The underlying logic of this phenomenon has already been explicated: local governments expropriate rural land to build development zones in order to promote export-oriented industries and attract foreign investment. Oftentimes they do not hesitate to transfer land use-rights to industrial investors at low or even zero prices. Although a loss is incurred on the balance book in the short term, in the long run it enhances local employment, tax revenue and GDP growth. These, as argued by some, are the key indicators for the "political tournaments" local officials in China participate in, a consequence of the current cadre evaluation and promotion system characterized by target-based, top-down control. Local governors are not only required to achieve what is assigned from above, but are also expected to outperform their counterparts in other locales. Local leaders with higher local employment ratios, tax income and GDP growth in their jurisdiction stand a better chance to be assessed more favorably over their peers and thereby promoted by the superior.[85] In this sense, massive expropriation at the local level is not just a consequence of fiscal pressure induced by the 1994 tax-sharing reform. It is also, as many have suggested, an instrument used consciously and actively by local officials to advance their own political careers.[86] The lack of more substantive reform has therefore been blamed on provincial officials' resistance as deeper policy reforms might inhibit their ability to generate tax revenues or to promote economic growth.[87]

More recently, some scholars have dismissed the political tournament thesis. Their fieldwork shows that growth of local fiscal revenue and GDP

Land Reform in China" (2003) 22 *Asian Geographer* 19; Yanzhong Huang and Dali L. Yang, "The Political Dynamics of Regulatory Change: Speculation and Regulation in the Real Estate Sector" (1996) 5 *Journal of Contemporary China* 177.

84 Mingxing Liu, Ran Tao, Fei Yuan and Guangzhong Cao, "Instrumental Land Use Investment-driven Growth in China" (2008) 13 *Journal of the Asia Pacific Economy* 317.

85 Hongbin Li and Li-an Zhou, "Political Turnover and Economic Performance: the Incentive Role of Personnel Control in China" (2005) 89 (9–10) *Journal of Public Economics 1743*; Ye Chen, Hongbin Li and Li-an Zhou, "Relative Performance Evaluation and the Turnover of Provincial Leaders in China" (2005) 88(3) *Economics Letters 421*; Li-an Zhou, "Governing China's Local Officials: An Analysis of Promotion Tournament Model (中国地方官员的晋升锦标赛模式研究)" (2007) 42 *Economic Research Journal* (经济研究) 36; Cao, Yuan and Tao, "Land Finance, Industrial Structure Changes and Rapid Tax Revenue Growth"; Zhen Jiang and Jun Xin, "How Did the Land Finance of Local Governments Come into Existence (地方政府土地财政是如何产生的)" (2011) 1 *Macroeconomics* (宏观经济研究) 20.

86 Wang, *The Constitutional Protection of Private Property in China*, p. 174.

87 Heurlin, *Responsive Authoritarianism in China*, p. 183.

is not formally included in the cadre evaluation index. Hence, they argue that the real impetus behind land finance and expropriation lies in local governments' desire to maximize discretionary fiscal power because land-based revenues are extra-budgetary and can be amassed and spent with lesser top-down control.[88] More empirical work is needed to pinpoint exactly how fiscal shortage, cadre's political competition and an appetite for discretionary fiscal power have influenced Chinese local governments' behavior in land finance. Nevertheless, it is now widely agreed that expropriation-based local financing has led to a whole host of side effects, such as swelling local government debt, high risk of government default in case of a property bubble burst and a lack of sustainable revenue sources to support long-term development.[89] Meanwhile, the received wisdom holds that the huge benefit gained through expropriation, be it economic or political, propels China's local governments to fiercely resist reforms aimed at increasing the administrative costs of expropriation through instituting more robust substantive and procedural constitutional and legal constraints. As already noted, since the early 2000s, there has been much scholarly discussion about and societal demand for deeper reform toward better refined and narrower definition of the public interest, higher and fairer compensation and resettlement standards and more open and participatory expropriation procedures. Yet the lure of land finance seems too hard to offset, even when the political and social costs of rural land takings become ever more pronounced. In the meantime, the central government has also been somewhat tentative and cautious in dishing out reform measures, being acutely aware of the potential risk of local financial crises once the benefits from low-cost expropriation dry up.

[88] Ran Tao, Xi Lu, Fubing Su and Hui Wang, "China's Transition in the Evolving Regional Competition: Reflections on Fiscal Incentives and Development Model (地区竞争格局演变下的中国转轨：财政激励和发展模式反思)" (2009) 7 *Journal of Economic Research* (经济研究) 21; Ran Tao, Fubing Su, Xi Lu and Yuming Zhu, "Does Economic Growth Lead to Promotion: A Logical Challenge against and an Empirical Re-examination at the Provincial Level of the Promotion Tournament Theory (经济增长能够带来晋升吗 – 对晋升锦标竞赛理论的逻辑挑战与省级实证评估)" (2010) 12 *Management World* (管理世界) 13.

[89] Shouying Liu and Xingsan Jiang, "Financial Risks of Land Financing by Local Governments: Case Study of a Developed Area in East China (土地融资与财政和金融风险 – 来自东部一个发达地区的个案)" (2005) 5 *China Land Science* (中国土地科学) 3; Liu, Jiang and Li, *China's Land Policy Reform: Policy Evolution and Local Implementation*, pp. 8–10; Zhou, "Creating Wealth: The Role of Government and Farmers in Land Development and Transfer."

Against this backdrop, there is an increasing realization that to revise rural land expropriation rules alone is far from adequate. Wider and deeper reforms are needed to remove or mitigate land finance, including rebalancing central–local distribution of fiscal powers and expenditure responsibilities, adjusting the cadre evaluation system and authorizing local governments to issue bonds or levy property tax to raise the needed fiscal revenue.[90] As a matter of fact, pilot projects of imposing property tax upon owners of spacious, expensive and multiple homes have been implemented in Shanghai and Chongqing since 2011. But these experimental schemes are obviously limited in scope and are primarily for the sake of curbing runaway housing prices and real estate speculation. More recently, the central government announced that no more pilot programs would be carried out until the promulgation of a national law on property tax.[91] Nevertheless, it is still widely anticipated that once China's local governments become no longer as financially reliant upon rural land expropriation as they have been, further reform of the relevant law will be underway and the constitutional promise of constraining the takings power and protecting land rights will be eventually fulfilled.

To recap, the previous two chapters presented the conventional wisdom about China's rural land expropriation law from descriptive, normative and prescriptive angles. Descriptively, it has been shown that in dealing with essentially the same power of state to acquire private property, while China has a constitutional takings clause no so different from its American counterpart in entrenching a public purpose prerequisite, an obligation to compensate and a due process requirement, its below-constitution takings law and policy in the reform era, especially since the 1990s, have largely failed to honor the constitutional promise (the conceptual and temporal assumptions under the TP). Normatively, it is held that the American law of eminent domain, despite its internal contradictions and controversies, constitutes a more advanced model worthy of imitation, if not replication, to China, particularly in giving

[90] Liu and Jiang, "Financial Risks of Land Financing by Local Governments: Case Study of a Developed Area in East China"; Liu, Jiang and Li, *China's Land Policy Reform: Policy Evolution and Local Implementation*, pp. 266–68; Research Center of China Land Survey and Planning Institute, "Removing Local Over-reliance on Land Finance from an Institutional Perspective (从体制上消除地方过度依赖"土地财政")" (2006) 7 *China Land* (中国土地) 11.

[91] Liyan Qi, "China Not Planning to Expand Pilot Property-Tax Program," March 19, 2014, available at www.wsj.com/articles/china-not-planning-to-expand-pilot-property-tax-program-1395213798. For an introduction to this topic, see Joyce Yanyun Man, "China's Property Tax Reform: Progress and Challenges" (2012) *Land Lines* 15.

teeth to the public interest prerequisite, enhancing due process and adopting fair market value standards for expropriation (the teleological assumption). Prescriptively, it is suggested that the long-awaited reform to bring China's rural land takings law closer to the American model is forestalled by the peculiar problem of land finance and that broader adjustments to alleviate and eradicate land finance are needed before the lackluster reform performance over the last decade can finally pick up (the developmental assumption). As mentioned in Chapter 1, this book challenges such a received position, especially in terms of what I call the Transition Paradigm. This is not to say that the existing analyses and criticisms are erroneous or that further reform is unnecessary. Rather, the argument is that by focusing on how the Chinese law on rural land expropriation measures up to or could move closer to the American ideal, the TP obscures more than it reveals the dynamics of the relevant law, i.e. why and how it has become what it is today. We therefore embark on a journey toward an immanent and sympathetic understanding of the law in its own historical context. And that journey starts with China's original constitutional takings clause in 1954, which serves a perfect test case to call into question some core assumptions of the TP.

4

Original Constitutional Takings Clause

Origin, Meaning and Purpose

Article 13 of the 1954 Constitution reads, "The state may, in the public interest, compulsorily purchase, requisition or nationalize urban and rural land as well as other means of production on the conditions provided by law."[1] In spite of being widely quoted as the first constitutional takings clause of the PRC and regarded as the foundation for the current constitutional takings clause of 1982, this article has never been subject to scholarly scrutiny. This is probably because it ceased to be effective long before the opening and reform period and is thereby relegated as insignificant to the analysis of China's present rural land expropriation law, conceptualized primarily as a post-reform problem. Yet a closer look immediately distinguishes it from its 1982 successor in two important aspects. For a start, while the 1982 clause deals with the power of expropriation (*zhengshou*), the 1954 clause lists three kinds of takings powers – compulsory purchase (*zhenggou*), requisition (*zhengyong*) and nationalization (*shougui guoyou*). Moreover, the original takings clause of 1954 has no explicit requirement to compensate. These two characteristics make China's original constitutional takings clause rather unique not only domestically but also internationally, with no parallel in any other country around the world. Where does China's original constitutional takings clause come from? What does it mean? And what is it for?

Regrettably, these questions have never been raised, let alone addressed. But there is no straightforward answer. Well known is that the 1954 PRC Constitution was drafted mainly out of two reference texts: the 1936 USSR Constitution for its orthodox socialist/communist doctrines and the 1949 Common Programme for its representation of China's indigenous revolutionary experiences. Interestingly, however,

[1] The Chinese reads, "国家为了公共利益的需要，可以依照法律规定的条件，对城乡土地和其他生产资料实行征购、征用或者收归国有."

there is no analogue whatsoever in these two documents for the 1954 takings clause. Articles 5–12 of the 1936 USSR Constitution and Article 3 of the Common Programme deal with property and basic economic relationships under socialism. Yet none even mentions the power of takings. Looking further back, no trace could be found in the 1924 Soviet Constitution either. Is it possible, then, that China's first takings clause is actually made in China? Or is there some source of inspiration other than the socialist big brother? This chapter starts by investigating the origin of the 1954 constitutional takings clause and finds that it was most likely transplanted from Article 23 of the 1949 East German Constitution. The second section uncovers the meaning of the original takings clause by discussing the four critical differences between it and its East German counterpart. The third section reveals that the central purpose of the original takings clause lies in the confirmation of the state takings power, which is normatively underpinned by a socialist principle that equates public interest with state interest and prioritizes public/state interest over private interests. Finally, this chapter concludes with the observation that some of the core features of the original takings clause and the land takings law of the 1950s have largely been preserved to this day. This fact invites us to call the TP into question.

4.1 Origin of Original Constitutional Takings Clause

Since the archival records of 1954 Constitution are yet to be published, we need to use available sources to piece the puzzle together. Constitution-making in 1954's China was a six-step process spanning ten months. The first phase was the writing of an initial draft by a team led by Mao Zedong between December 1953 and February 1954. It was followed by a review and revision procedure by the Politburo and CCP Central Committee members in Beijing from mid-February to March 1954. Then came the deliberation of the adopted draft by the constitutional drafting committee. Subsequently, the draft was sent out to the Chinese People's Political Consultative Conference (CPPCC) and provincial and military leaders for comments from late March, before being approved by the Central Government Committee. The fifth step was publication of the draft in June to solicit comments from the general public for three months. The sixth and final step came in September when the then newly founded and elected National People's Congress passed the Constitution. In the draft constitution submitted to the constitutional drafting committee on March 23, 1954, Article 12 was basically the same as Article 13 in the final version.[2] This means that the original takings clause had been settled by that time. Therefore, in order to figure out where the 1954 takings clause came from, we need to examine all the possible sources of reference available by late March 1954. While it is known that on December 27, 1953, Mao Zedong led a drafting team comprised of his three personal secretaries to Hangzhou with two cases of reference materials;[3] however, it has never been disclosed what exactly were contained and consulted. Yet there is one notable exception coming from Mao himself. In a telegraph cabled from Hangzhou back to Beijing on January 15, 1954, he assigned the following reading list:

> In order to facilitate discussion (of the draft constitution) by the Politburo in mid-February, I would like every Politburo member and Central Committee member now in Beijing to start at once to find time to read each of the following main reference documents:
>
> (1) the 1936 Stalin Constitution and Stalin's report (in a single volume);
>
> (2) the 1918 Russian Soviet Federated Socialist Republic Constitution (read Volume One of the Collected Materials on Constitution and Electoral Law edited by the Government Office);
>
> (3) the Romanian, Polish, German, and Czechoslovakian Constitutions (read the Complied Constitutions of People's Democratic States published by the People's Press. The various national constitutions collected in this volume are similar to each other with only minor variations. The Romanian and Polish Constitutions are selected for being relatively new; German and Czechoslovakian Constitutions are selected for being relatively detailed and having characteristic differences. If you have time, read the other constitutions included);
>
> (4) the 1913 Temple of Heaven Draft Constitution, the 1923 Cao Kun Constitution, the 1946 Chiang Kai-shek Constitution (read Volume Three of the Collected Materials on Constitution and Electoral Law. They represent three models: ministerial system, federalist system, and presidential dictatorship);
>
> (5) the 1946 French Constitution (read Volume Four of the Collected Materials on Constitution and Electoral Law. This represents a comparatively progressive and complete capitalist ministerial system constitution).[4]

[2] Dayuan Han, *1954 Constitution and Constitutionalism in New China* (1954年宪法与新中国宪政) (Beijing: Hunan Renmin Press, 2004), p. 631. It reads, "国家在公共利益需要的时候，可以根据法律所规定的条件，对城乡土地和其他生产资料实行征购、征用或收归国有."

[3] Ibid., p. 70.

[4] Mao Zedong, "Working Plan of Drafting Constitution (宪法起草工作计划)," in *Collected Works of Mao Zedong* (毛泽东文集) (Beijing: Renmin Press, 1993), vol. 6, p. 320.

Additionally, from January 7–March 9, 1954, as recalled by Dong Chengmei, a young graduate from Renmin Law School working under the constitutional drafting committee at the time, the drafting team led by Mao prepared the first 100-article draft and edited a three-volume *Reference Materials on Constitution*. Volume 1 contains the 1918 Soviet Russian Constitution and the 1924 USSR Constitution. Volume 2 includes American, British, German and Swiss constitutions. Volume 3 covers constitutions and constitutional documents enacted by the Qing Dynasty, the Beiyang warlords and the Kuo Min Tang (KMT)/nationalist government. These volumes were published by the General Office of the Central People's Government Committee and distributed to all members of the constitutional drafting committee and relevant working staff.[5] Therefore, we can be fairly certain that these three official compilations – two mentioned by Mao,[6] and one by Dong[7] – had been used as reference materials for constitution drafting by March 1954.

Still, there are three more possible sources of reference. One is the 1940 Mongolian Constitution, which was once referred to by Tian Jiaying, Mao's secretary and one of the three members of the drafting team, when he discussed the constitutional right to freedom of movement.[8] Another is a book edited by the Chinese Society of Political and Legal Studies.[9] It is likely a source of reference for two reasons. On the one hand,

[5] Han, 1954 Constitution and Constitutionalism in New China, pp. 773–74.

[6] Legal Committee of Central People's Government (ed.), *Compiled Constitutions of People's Democratic States* (人民民主国家宪法汇编) (Beijing: Renmin Press, 1953). It includes constitutions of Bulgaria, Czechoslovakia, Korea, Hungary, Democratic Germany, Albania, Poland and Romania. General Office of Central People's Government (ed.), *Collected Materials on the Constitution and Electoral Law* (宪法及选举法资料汇编), (Beijing: General Office of Central People's Government, 1953). Volume 1 includes 1918 and 1924 Constitutions of Soviet Russia. Volume 2 covers Constitutions of Poland, Romania and Democratic Germany. Volume 3 contains Chinese Constitutions or draft Constitutions in 1908, 1911, 1912, 1913, 1914, 1923, 1930, 1931 and 1946. Volume 4 includes constitutions of America, Britain, France, Weimar Germany and Swiss.

[7] General Office of Central People's Government (ed.), *Reference Materials on Constitution* (宪法参考资料) (Beijing: General Office of Central People's Government, 1954). Volume 1 covers 1918 and 1924 Soviet Russian Constitutions. Volume 2 includes constitutions of America, Britain, France, Weimar Germany and Swiss. Volume 3 contains Chinese Constitutions or draft Constitutions in 1908, 1911, 1912, 1913, 1914, 1923, 1930, 1931 and 1946.

[8] Han, 1954 Constitution and Constitutionalism in New China, p. 255.

[9] Chinese Society of Political and Legal Studies (ed.), *Breakdown of Reference Materials of Constitutions* (宪法分解参考资料) (Beijing: Renmin Press, 1954). It includes the constitutions of the Soviet Union, Poland, Czechoslovakia, Bulgaria, Romania, Hungary, Albania, Mongolia, Korea, Vietnam, France and America.

the editor is an organization led by such prominent political figures as Dong Biwu and Qian Duansheng, who themselves participated in drafting the 1954 Constitution. On the other hand, the book was published in July 1954, one month after the draft constitution was made available for consultation, as a reference guide to educate the public and give them the necessary knowledge to make informed comments. A third possible source is the 1931 Constitutional Outline of the Chinese Soviet Republic, which was not included in any of the previously mentioned books but was considered by Mao as the forerunner to the 1954 Constitution.[10]

Admittedly, in no way can we be completely sure that these materials exhaust all sources of influence over the 1954 Constitution. But they are what we presently have based on available materials. As already mentioned, the original takings clause came neither from the Russian Constitutions nor from China's own Common Programme. Excluding the two, our search for a possible source for the original takings clause is thus reduced to a total of 31 written constitutions or constitutional documents, which can be found in Appendix 1.

Out of these 31 texts, two have prescriptions most similar to Article 13 of the 1954 Constitution: Article 18 of the 1931 Provisional Constitution of the Political Tutelage Period of the Republic of China, and Article 23 of 1949 Constitution of the German Democratic Republic.[11] They both use the term "public interest" (*gonggong liyi*) rather than its abbreviated form (*gongyi*) or social interest (*shehui liyi*) or public welfare (*gonggong fuli*). And both include the phrase "in accordance with law."[12] However, for the following three reasons, the odds are that the latter was the source of inspiration to Article 13. First, well known is the fact that, upon establishing the new People's Republic, the CCP announced the complete abolition of the legal *ancien régime* under the nationalist government,[13]

10 Han, 1954 Constitution and Constitutionalism in New China, p. 389. For this reason Mao rejected the notion that the 1954 Constitution was the first Chinese Constitution.

11 The comparison is done according to the translated Chinese version of these foreign constitutional texts.

12 It should be noted that the Chinese version of this phrase is slightly different in these provisions. It was "根据法律" in Article 23 of the 1949 East German Constitution and "依法律" in Article 18 of the 1931 provisional Constitution. In comparison, the 1954 constitutional takings clause uses the phrase "依照法律规定的条件"; its draft version on March 23, 1954, uses the phrase "根据法律所规定的条件." Nevertheless, these renderings essentially share the same meaning, which is not present in the takings clauses found in the remaining 29 constitutional documents.

13 Order on the Abolition of Six Laws System of the Nationalist Party and Establishing the Judicial Principles in the Liberated Areas (关于废除国民党六法全书与确定解放区的

making it highly unlikely that the 1954 Constitution would bring anything back from what was already regarded as a reactionary "falsely-legitimated legal order" (*wei fatong*). Second, two of the initial drafters, Chen Boda and Tian Jiaying, both suggested that the drafting of the 1954 Constitution had extensively drawn on the constitutions of other socialist countries in Eastern Europe.[14] Third, Article 13 of the 1954 Constitution was followed by the stipulation (Article 14), "The state forbids anyone to use private property to the detriment to the public interest."[15] The 1931 Provisional Constitution does not have any similar content. In contrast, Article 23 of the 1949 East German Constitution was followed by a similar provision (Article 24) reading, "Property entails obligations. Its use must not run counter to the public interest."[16]

Does this mean, then, that the true origin of China's original takings clause actually lies in the East German Constitution? According to currently available evidence, the answer is in the positive, albeit with two reservations. First, it may well be the case that the Chinese Constitution-makers came up with an analogous takings clause independently without making recourse to or even having any knowledge of the East German takings clause. On this we may never know, unless any direct evidence is unearthed. But chances are that they did get the inspiration from the East German Constitution because almost none of those who had their fingers on the draft constitution by March 1954 received any legal education.[17] This was why Mao Zedong had to assign a reading list to his comrades in the Central Committee in order to prepare them for constitutional deliberation. This was also why the main initial drafter, Tian Jiaying, was recorded to have prepared himself

司法原则的指示), promulgated by CCP Central Committee on February 28, 1949, available at cpc.people.com.cn/GB/64184/64186/66650/4491574.html.

14 Han, 1954 Constitution and Constitutionalism in New China, p. 225; Bian Dong, Deshan Xin and Zi Zeng (eds.), *Mao Zedong and his Secretary Tian Jiaying* (毛泽东和他的秘书田家英) (Beijing: Zhongyang Wenxian Press, 1996), p. 21. This was also corroborated by Dong Chengmei. See Han, 1954 Constitution and Constitutionalism in New China, p. 774.

15 The Chinese translation reads, "国家禁止任何人利用私有财产破坏公共利益."

16 The Chinese translation reads, "所有权负有一定义务，其使用不得违反公共利益."

17 This includes the three initial drafters, all the Central Party Committee members and the eight-membered constitutional team that had revised the draft Constitution by March 1954. The only exception was Dong Biwu, who went to Japan in 1914 to study law and might have become familiar with the 1889 Japanese Constitution. However, its takings clause (art. 27) is very different from and could not be the source for Article 13 of the 1954 Constitution. Its Chinese translation reads, "日本臣民之所有权不得侵犯. 因公益需要之处分，依法律之规定."

by meticulously studying constitutions of the Eastern European socialist states before plunging into constitutional drafting in December 1953.[18] Therefore, in light of all available evidence, Article 13 was most probably a transplant from the East German Constitution highlighted by Mao in his reading list, not an invention by the Chinese constitutional drafters. However, whilst acknowledging that China's original takings clause took its cue from Article 23 of the 1949 East German Constitution, the former is by no means an exact copy of the latter. Article 13 reads, "The state may, in the public interest, compulsorily purchase, requisition or nationalize urban and rural land as well as other means of production on the conditions provided by law." Article 23 of the 1949 East German Constitution reads, "Restrictions on private property and expropriations may be imposed only for the benefit of the general public and on a legal basis. They shall take place against reasonable compensation unless the law provides otherwise. If the amount of compensation is in dispute, recourse to the ordinary courts shall be open insofar as a law does not provide otherwise."[19] These two constitutional takings clause are different in grammatical structure, objects to be taken, kinds of takings powers and provisions on compensation and dispute resolution. Making sense of these four differences will lead us to the meaning of China's original takings clause.

4.2 Parsing the Original Constitutional Takings Clause

To start with, the tones of the two takings clauses are very different. Article 23 of the 1949 East German Constitution is in the impersonal passive voice, whereas Article 13 of the 1954 PRC constitution is in the active voice. Indeed, on this point Article 13 diverges from most other constitutional takings clauses in the world as it speaks from the standpoint of the state rather than private property. There are two reasons for this: one formal, the other substantive. The latter will be expounded later in this chapter. The formal reason is that Article 13 is located in the first chapter of the 1954 Constitution – i.e. General Principles, which sets out state policies on a variety of issues. In particular, Articles 5 to 15 deal with

[18] Panshi Ding, "A Memory of the Old Contributor to China Youth Tian Jiaying (忆《中国青年》的老作者田家英)," in Bian Dong, Deshan Tan and Zi Zeng (eds.), *Mao Zedong and his Secretary Tian Jiaying* (毛泽东和他的秘书田家英) (Beijing: Zhongyang Wenxian Press, 1996).

[19] English translation of the 1949 East German Constitution is available at cvce.eu/content/publication/1999/1/1/33cc8de2-3cff-4102-b524-c1648172a838/publishable_en.pdf.

the economy, and almost all of them are written from the state's perspective. For example, Articles 5 to 10 provide for four different types of ownership of production means in the PRC and the state's different attitudes and strategies toward each of them. Articles 11 and 12 stipulate that the state protects citizens' ownership of lawful income and means of subsistence and protects in accordance with law their rights of inheritance. Article 13 is the takings clause, and Article 14 prescribes that the state prohibits anyone using private property to the detriment of public interest. Article 15 is about the state's economic planning. Except for Articles 13 and 14, the other articles are more or less the same as their counterparts in the 1936 Soviet Constitution, which are written in the active voice from the viewpoint of the state. Therefore, even though it might have come from a different source, Article 13 adopts a similar sentence pattern so as to be consistent with other articles in the same chapter.

Second, the objects of takings are different in these two clauses. In the East German case, it is private property in the broad sense, including both the means of production and that of subsistence. In contrast, Article 13 concerns only the takings of "urban and rural land and other means of production." This is particularly curious considering that the surrounding Articles 12 and 14 both implicate private property in the general sense.[20] In fact, it had been suggested during the deliberation over the draft constitution that Article 13 should be expanded to cover the takings of private means of subsistence such as privately owned houses as above-ground attachments, edible oil and grain.[21] The reason given at the time was threefold. First, these means of subsistence could also be compulsorily purchased for public interest, for which Article 13 was too narrow to provide a constitutional basis. Second, expanding the takings power in this way would not agitate the public too much because it was still supposed to be "in the public interest" and "in accordance with the conditions set by law." Third, the constitutional takings clauses in other socialist countries did cover private property in the broad sense.[22] However, these considerations were ultimately not accepted, for which no official explanation has been provided. But it is unlikely that they were just overlooked. This is because when asked, in May 1954, why Article 13

[20] Article 12 reads, "The state protects citizen's right of inheritance to private property according to law." Article14 reads, "The state forbids anyone to use private property to the detriment to the public interest."

[21] Han, 1954 Constitution and Constitutionalism in New China, pp. 142, 356.

[22] Ibid., p. 356.

only covers the takings of production means during constitutional deliberation, Tian Jiaying replied that although state-led construction might also require compulsory purchases of privately owned houses, that was not to be provided for directly by the Constitution but by specific statutes (*danxing fa*).[23] The specific statute he alluded to was the 1953 *Measures on Land Requisition for State-led Construction* (1953 MLRSC), which prescribed that for the purpose of state-led construction, houses and other attachments on rural and urban land can be requisitioned by the state alongside the land with compensation.[24] Therefore, it seems to be more of a conscious choice on the part of the constitutional makers not to expand the targets of takings power beyond means of production.

As a matter of fact, it was not until the 2004 amendment to the 1982 Constitution that this extension was finally realized.[25] This means that for half a century, from 1954 to 2004, takings of privately owned houses and other means of subsistence were completely left out of the written constitution and underpinned only by below-constitution statutes. Does this point to some sort of unconstitutionality all the way through? Why is Article 13 limited to the takings of land and other production means? To decode of these puzzles, we now turn to the third difference between the Chinese and East German takings clauses.

Whilst Article 23 of the 1949 East German Constitution deals with the power of expropriation (*enteignungen*, typically translated as *zhengshou* in Chinese), Article 13 includes three kinds of takings powers: compulsory purchase, requisition and nationalization. No official interpretation has ever been given about what exactly these terms stand for; there is hardly any relevant academic discussion, either. Nevertheless, none of those terms were novel at the time of constitution-making around 1954. Out of the three, requisition was most familiar. As noted earlier, the 1953 MLRSC was mentioned once by Tian Jiaying over the course of constitutional deliberation. More crucially, on March 23, 1954, at the first assembly of the Constitutional Drafting Committee, Mao Zedong himself explicitly acknowledged that the 1953 MLRSC was reflected in the 1954 Constitution.[26] In light of this, the odds are that requisition in the

23 Ibid., p. 142.

24 Measures on Land Requisition for State-led Construction (国家建设征用土地办法), arts. 8, 9 and 17. The Chinese text is available www.fxtxls.com/ShowArticle.shtml?ID=200771019184043400.htm.

25 Art. 13. The Chinese reads, "国家为了公共利益的需要，可以依照法律规定对公民的私有财产实行征收或者征用并给予补偿."

26 Han, 1954 Constitution and Constitutionalism in New China, pp. 224–25.

original takings clause came from the 1953 MLRSC, in which requisition means compensatory takings of land (and the houses thereon).[27] It could be exercised for "the construction of national defense projects, factories and mines, railways, transportation, water conservancy projects, municipal works and other economic and cultural initiatives."[28] Requisition in this sense is usually considered as interchangeable with expropriation/ *enteignungen* in the East German Constitution.[29] Its origin could be traced back to a series of rules promulgated in the communist revolutionary border regions during the 1930s.[30] In the early years of the PRC, the power of land requisition was also retained in a number of local and central regulations.[31]

That said, it should be noted that in the early 1950s land requisition took on a couple of slightly different meanings. On the one hand, it was interpreted as the taking of land use-rights rather than ownership.[32] On the other hand, it was defined to require varying levels of compensation according to the class status and living conditions of those

[27] The only exception was that requisition of urban land that belongs to landlords is non-compensatory. Yet if such land was rented out to peasants, the tenant peasants should be compensated for the crops and fixture thereover. See 1953 MLRSC, art. 17. Clearly this was under the influence of the class-based land reform, which will be further discussed very shortly in this section.

[28] 1953 MLRSC, art. 2

[29] It will be shown later on that the two are not completely interchangeable because the scope of Chinese land requisition as prescribed in the 1953 law was much more expansive than expropriation in Germany.

[30] Art. 25, Draft Regulation on Land Rights of Shan'ganning Border Region (陕甘宁边区地权条例草案), promulgated by Shan'ganning Border Region Government in April 1939; art. 13, Land Rights Regulation of Shan'ganning Border Region (陕甘宁边区地权条例), promulgated by Shan'ganning Border Region Government in December 1944; art. 12, Special Regulation on Land Rights of Taiyue Region (太岳区地权单行条例), promulgated by Taiyue Regional Government on April 15, 1945; art. 19, Provisional Land Regulation of Northeastern Region (东北区土地暂行条例), promulgated by Northeastern People's Government on October 17, 1950); art. 14, Regulation on Land Reform in Suburban Areas (城市郊区土地改革条例), promulgated by PRC Government Administrative Council on November 10, 1950.

[31] Provisional Land Regulation of Northeast Region, Provisional Land Regulation of Northeastern Region, art. 19; PRC Government Administrative Council, Regulation on Land Reform in Suburban Areas art. 14.

[32] Reply to Henan People's Government on the Interpretation of Expropriation, Requisition, Compulsory Purchase, Compulsory Rent in Article 10 of the Provisional Measures of Land Use for Urban Construction in Central-South Region (关于城市建设使用土地暂行办法第十条内征收征用征购征租等的解释 – 给河南省人民政府函), promulgated by Central-south Administrative Committee on February 13, 1953.

requisitioned.[33] Landlords with good living conditions were not to be compensated, while middle and poor peasants or those with poor living conditions would be compensated and rich peasants were to be compensated only for the land they themselves toiled on. Such discrimination in compensation based on class status was apparently a consequence of the then-ongoing land reform, which aimed at land redistribution from the landed classes to the landless. Yet these two meanings were soon abandoned. By the end of the land reform movement in 1952, the practice of class-based compensation stopped. The 1953 MLRSC demanded compensation for all those requisitioned regardless of their class identity. Meanwhile, the same legislation resumed the conception of requisition as takings of land ownership. It took another 51 years for the idea of requisition as takings of land use-rights to reappear in the 2004 constitutional amendment.

Compared with requisition, the term "compulsory purchase" is more difficult to pin down and had at least three known meanings by 1954. First is compulsory purchase of grain (*liangshi zhenggou*), a party policy establishing state monopoly over production and circulation of grain. Although the policy was promulgated by the CCP Central Committee just two months before Mao went to Hangzhou with his drafting team,[34] for two reasons it is unlikely that compulsory purchase in the constitutional takings clause bears the same meaning. To begin with, grain was considered at the time to be a kind of means of subsistence rather than means of production.[35] As already shown, the takings clause targeted only the production means. Furthermore, an intentional choice was

33 Measures of Managing Land Use for Railway Construction by Huainan Mines (关于淮南煤矿修铁路所用的土地的处理办法), promulgated by CCP Central Committee on April 6, 1950; art. 2, Provisional Measures of Land Requisition for Road Construction in East-China Region (华东区修建公路征用土地暂行办法), promulgated by East-China Military and Administrative Committee on September 18, 1950; art. 2, Provisional Measures of Land Requisition for Road Construction in Middle-south Region (中南区修建公路征用土地暂行办法), promulgated by Middle-south Military and Administrative Committee on November 29, 1950; art. 3, Instructions of South-west Military and Administrative Committee on Land Use for Public Factories in Land Reform (西南军政委员会关于在土地改革中解决供应工厂用地的指示), promulgated by South-west Military and Administrative Committee on June 27, 1951.

34 Decision on the Planned Purchase and Provision of Grain (关于实行粮食计划收购与计划供应的决议), promulgated by CCP Central Committee on October 16, 1953.

35 Note that in 1950 Mao suggested that grain could be regarded as means of production when it was confiscated from the landlords; otherwise, it is means of subsistence produced by the peasants with the means of production. Mao Zedong, "On Revising the Report of Land Reform (关于修改土地改革问题的报告)," in *Collected Works of Mao Zedong* (毛泽东文集) (Beijing: Renmin Press, 1999), vol. 6, p. 63.

made by the CCP Central Committee that the term "compulsory purchase" would not be employed in the context of grain procurement to avoid reminiscence of what had been done by the Japanese invaders.[36] As a result, "planned purchase" (*jihua shougou*) and "unified purchase" (*tonggou*) were chosen as the official terms.[37] Therefore, compulsory purchase in the sense of takings of grain could not possibly be reintroduced into the 1954 takings clause.

In contrast, the other two meanings of "compulsory purchase" at the time were related to land. In July 1946, the CCP Central Committee issued a policy recommendation to its local branches in the liberated areas about adopting compulsory purchase as the alternative measure to compensationless confiscation (*moshou*) in the land reform campaign.[38] It was suggested that on top of confiscating landlord's land local governments might also choose to compulsorily purchase such land that exceeded a certain set maximum. In reality, however, this proposal was implemented in just a few localities[39] before its abortion in 1947.[40] In the ensuing years, until 1952, compulsory purchase was never again adopted in the land reform campaign. Yet the term "compulsory purchase" was not completely out of circulation, which could be found in a series of central and local rules promulgated in the early 1950s, albeit with a different meaning.[41] According to these documents,

[36] Bo Yibo (ed.), *Review of Several Important Decisions and Events* (若干重大决策与事件的回顾) (Beijing: Zhongyang Dangxiao Press, 1991), vol. 1, p. 266.

[37] Chen Yun, "Implementing Unified Purchase and Sale of Grain (实行粮食统购统销)," in *Selected Works of Chen Yun* (陈云文选) (Beijing: Renmin Press, 1995), vol. 2, p. 217.

[38] Recommendation to the Governments of Liberated Areas for Realizing Land to the Tillers (为实现耕者有其田向各解放区政府的提议), promulgated by CCP Central Committee on July 19, 1946.

[39] Zexue Sun, "On Peacefully Achieving Land-to-the-tiller through Compulsory Purchase with Public Debt by the Communist Party of China (论中共和平实现耕者有其田中的公债征购)" (2010) 11 *Study of the History of Communist Party of China* (中共党史研究) *78*.

[40] Xiaowei Ren, "Experiment and Abandonment of Peaceful Land Reform Policies by the Communist Party of China 1946–1947 (1946–1947年中国共产党对和平土改政策的尝试及其放弃)" (2010) 39 *Journal of Shanxi Normal University* (陕西师范大学学报) *112*.

[41] Art. 6, Measures of Land Reservation for Railway (铁路留用土地办法), promulgated by Central Administrative Committee on June 24, 1950; points 1, 4, Interpretation on the Measures of Land Reservation for Railway (关于铁路留用土地办法的几点解释), promulgated by the Central Administrative Committee on September 16, 1950; art. 2, East-China Military and Administrative Committee, Provisional Measures of Land Requisition for Road Construction in East-China Region; arts. 1 and 3, Provisional Measures of Use of Suburban Land for Urban Construction (关于市政建设适用郊区土地暂行办法), promulgated by Beijing People's Government on October 19, 1950; art. 4, Provisional Measures of Land Use for Urban Construction in Central-south

compulsory purchase of land was not for land reform but for the development of infrastructure and municipal works. Compulsory purchase in this sense then looks very similar to requisition as defined in the 1953 MLRSC. In fact, when Tian Jiaying suggested that compulsory purchase of private houses could be governed by specific statutes rather than the constitution, he seemed to have mistaken "compulsory purchase" for "requisition" because at that time there was no specific statute on the former but one on the latter. However, if these two terms did mean the same, why were they listed separately in the 1954 takings clause?

The real distinction between these two kinds of takings powers does not lie in their purposes but in two other attributes. First is the procedure and the parties involved. Requisition starts with land-using entities (*yongdi danwei*), namely end-users of land for purposes specified in Article 2 of the 1953 MLRSC, applying for approval from central or local government.[42] With the assistance of land-using entities, the approving government should first announce and explain the decision of requisition to those to be affected,[43] before organizing and presiding over negotiations about compensation between the land-using entities and the original owners.[44] Once the amount of compensation is settled, the government might make the payment on behalf of land-using entities.[45] A process of this kind makes requisition center around a two-party relationship between government as the requisitioner and landowners as the requisitionee. Land-using entities are no more than an interested third party in this relationship.

Conversely, compulsory purchase could only be applied when voluntary negotiation between land-using entities and landowners leads to no agreement.[46] Land-using entities should approach and bargain with land owners before petitioning the government for compulsory purchase. This means that compulsory purchase involves a three-party relationship in which voluntary exchange between land-using entities and landowners must be attempted. Only if that fails could the government step in to compulsorily purchase land.

Region (中南区城市建设使用土地暂行办法), promulgated by Central-south Military and Administrative Committee on December 18, 1951.

[42] 1953 MLRSC, art. 4. [43] Ibid., art. 5. [44] Ibid., art. 8. [45] Ibid., art. 14.

[46] Beijing People's Government, Provisional Measures of Use of Suburban Land for Urban Construction, art.3; Central-south Military and Administrative Committee, Provisional Measures of Land Use for Urban Construction in Central-south Region, art. 10.

The second difference between requisition and compulsory purchase is to be found in compensation. For requisition, land-using entities might negotiate with landowners about compensation, but the exact amount is legally set at the total output value of the land during three to five years prior to requisition.[47] On top of that, as a matter of principle, the requisitioning government is required to resettle the peasants according to their living and production conditions. If appropriate resettlement is not available, land requisition should be postponed or relocated.[48] More specifically, if the peasants lose the land they cultivate, the requisitioning government is responsible for providing them with agricultural land on which they can continue to work or helping them to find other jobs in order to prevent unemployment or homelessness. If possible, land-using entities should also recruit the land-losing peasants.[49]

Contrarily, with very limited exceptions,[50] in the early 1950s, compensation in compulsory purchase was either to be negotiated by land-using entities and landowners with reference to local market prices, or to be determined according to standardized land prices set by local governments taking local market price into account. There was no additional requirement that land-losing peasants should receive employment assistance from the government or land-using entities.[51] In fact, provisions of this sort could be traced back to the 1940s when the market price of land was used as the benchmark to calculate compensation for compulsory purchase during the land reform campaign. Back then it was stipulated that land compensation should be agreed upon by local governments,

[47] 1953 MLRSC, art. 8. [48] Ibid., art. 3. [49] Ibid., art. 13.

[50] In a central regulation promulgated in 1950, compensation was explicitly set to be conditional upon the class status of those impacted in areas undergoing land reform. See Central Administrative Committee, Interpretation on the Measures of Land Reservation for Railway, point 1. In three other central and local Regulations, there were no specific compensation standards. See Central Administrative Committee, Measures of Land Reservation for Railway; East-China Military and Administrative Committee, Provisional Measures of Land Requisition for Road Construction in East-China Region; Beijing People's Government, Provisional Measures of Use of Suburban Land for Urban Construction.

[51] Art. 11, Central-south Military and Administrative Committee, Provisional Measures of Land Use for Urban Construction in Central-south Region; point 1, Reply of the Central-south Administrative Committee to Civil Affairs Department of Hunan People's Government on Interpretation of Three Questions in the Provisional Measures of Land Use for Urban Construction in Central-south Region (中南行政委员会关于中南区城市建设使用土地暂行办法中三点异议的解释 – 给湖南省人民政府民政厅函), promulgated by the Central-south Administrative Committee on August 29, 1953.

landlords and peasants' representatives based on its market price, although landlords would be paid only part of the full price.[52]

In this light, compensation for compulsory purchase is distinct from requisition compensation in that the former has more to do with the market price of land while the latter is predicated on the output value of land and the living conditions of those affected. It may be argued that such difference was unknown to the constitutional makers at the time and therefore could not have been intended by the 1954 constitutional takings clause. Otherwise, Tian Jiaying would not have had compulsory purchase and requisition conflated. But their nuanced distinction in terms of compensation was indeed acknowledged by Zhang Youyu, then vice mayor of Beijing and a participant in constitutional drafting.[53] Explaining the draft constitution to the Party cadres from Beijing in June 1954, he made the following observation:

> Compulsory purchase is buying with money, but it is coercive and you cannot refuse to sell. Requisition is substantively different from compulsory purchase. Requisition is the state compulsorily taking the land from its owners. It is not an exchange relationship, but in reality it is similar [to compulsory purchase] because it also requires monetary payment [to landowners]. Yet such payment is called indemnity (*buchang jin*), which is not always the same as the price (*jiage*) of land.[54]

Following Zhang's terminology, while compensation for requisition is considered as "indemnity" for the loss imposed upon landowners, compensation for compulsory purchase shall be called "price" as it clearly bears more resemblance to voluntary market exchange.

Overall, despite the fact that they are both coercive, compulsory purchase is more akin to market transaction than requisition. For

52 Point 5, CCP Central Committee, Measures of Managing Land Use for Railway Construction by Huainan Mines; arts. 6 and 8, Draft Regulation on Compulsory Purchase of Landlords' Land of Shan'ganning Border Region (陕甘宁边区征购地主土地条例草案), promulgated by Shan'ganning Border Region People's Government on December 13. 1946; art. 8, Provisional Regulation on Land Reform in Shandong Province (山东省土地改革暂行条例), promulgated by Shandong People's Government on October 25, 1946.

53 Zhang was then leading the constitutional drafting group in Beijing to provide comments and suggestions on the draft Constitution to the central constitutional drafting committee in June 1954. He had also briefed both central and Beijing Party leaders for many times on the draft, probably because he was one of the few high-level Party cadres who had been legally trained. See Youyu Zhang, *Ten Years in Beijing* (十年京兆) (Beijing: Aolinpike Press 1990), part 4. Zhang was later the leading figure in the making of the 1982 Constitution.

54 Youyu Zhang, *Essays on Constitutionalism* (宪政论丛) (Beijing: Qunzhong Press, 1986), vol. 2, p. 41.

compulsory purchase, voluntary negotiation between land-using entities and landowners is a procedural precondition to nonvoluntary acquisition by government, which is only triggered when no deal is reached. Compensation is negotiated or formulated on the basis of the market price of the land. The government or land-using entities are not required to offer land-losing peasants long-term resettlement assistance such as alternative employment opportunities. In contrast, requisition does not presuppose negotiation and its compensation does not reflect the market price but is calculated according to the output value of the land. Also, the government and land-using entities are required to resettle land-losing peasants with arranged employment.

Similar to compulsory purchase and requisition, nationalization, the third enumerated takings power in the 1954 takings clause, was also practiced prior to the making of the 1954 Constitution. The 1950 *Land Reform Law* enacted to legitimatize and guide the land reform campaign in the early 1950s provided in Article 10 that "any confiscated (*moshou*) or expropriated (*zhengshou*) land and other means of production, unless it is prescribed to be nationalized by this law, shall be taken over (*jieshou*) by peasant associations at the county level." In this light, nationalization is one of the consequences following land confiscation and expropriation during the land reform movement. Articles 2–6 of the same law prescribed that whilst confiscation applied to landlords and expropriation targeted other landed classes, they both were coercive and noncompensatory, meaning that the resultant nationalization is also noncompensatory.

However, non-compensatory nationalization was not only practiced in the land reform campaign. The other incident where the power of nationalization was invoked around the time of the 1954 constitution-making was the campaign of socialist transformation of capitalism. When commenting on the draft constitution between May and June of 1954, Li Weihan, then head of the United Front Work Department of the CCP Central Committee and member of the constitutional drafting committee, pointed out that nationalization could also be applied to private enterprises (and their land) under ripe conditions.[55] He was undoubtedly referring to the then-ongoing movement of socialist transformation of capitalist industry and commerce, to which he and his department were most instrumental.[56] Those familiar with the PRC's

[55] Han, 1954 Constitution and Constitutionalism in New China, p. 142.

[56] The policy document that started the socialist transformation campaign in June 1953 was based on the research done by the United Front Work Department. See Li Weihan,

history would know that during the socialist transformation campaign private enterprises were not outright confiscated but "bought out" (*shumai*) by the state, the main reason being that the rural-based communist party was at the time so inexperienced in running an industrial and commercial urban economy that it felt the need to keep, for an interim period, owners and managers of private businesses intact. Note that the phrase "buying out" was used here. It might therefore be tempting to think that the socialist transformation movement was compensatory – but that cannot be further from the truth. The socialist transformation campaign was not carried out by way of the state paying compensation from its own pocket to the capitalists. In fact, as early as in 1951, Liu Shaoqing rejected purchasing land from capitalists with payment to implement the socialist transformation movement, as he believed that it would create too great a financial burden upon the state.[57] Eventually this movement was executed through what was called "state capitalism," or, more technically, "public–private joint management" (*gongsi heying*), under which private owners were permitted to retain a small portion of the profit generated by the companies they once owned for a set period of time. After that period, previously privately owned businesses would be fully rendered into state ownership, i.e. nationalized.[58] In this sense, nationalization in socialist transformation of capitalism campaign is different from that for land reform only in the fact that it took a bit more time to complete. They were fundamentally the same in terms of being noncompensatory.

On the basis of the foregoing analysis, we can now deal with the two puzzles previously identified regarding the objects of the 1954 takings clause: Why was it confined to means of production? Was the taking of subsistence means between 1954 and 2004 unconstitutional? The reason that Article 13 focused merely on takings of land and other production means is twofold. First, two of the three takings powers entrenched in Article 13 had been exercised for some state-led social movement that aimed to disrupt and transform the ownership structure of production

Memories and Research (回忆与研究) (Beijing: Zhongong Dangshi Press, 1986), vol. 2, pp. 739–43.

57 Liu Shaoqi, "Speech at Chun Ou Zhai (春藕斋讲话)," in Central Archival Research Institute (ed.), *Liu Shaoqi on Economic Development in New China* (刘少奇论新中国经济建设) (Beijing: Zhongyang Wenxian Press, 1993), pp. 211–12.

58 Resolution on the Transformation of Capitalist Industry and Commerce (关于资本主义工商业改造问题的决议), promulgated by CCP Central Committee on February 24, 1956, available at cpc.people.com.cn/GB/64184/64186/66662/4493100.html. The time period was fixed at ten years from 1956.

means in China. Specifically, nationalization was deployed to carry out the land reform campaign and socialist transformation movement; so was compulsory purchase in land reform. In the meantime, while requisition was not used directly to execute these social transformation programs, it had always been used to supply land for state-led construction and development since the 1930s.

This, however, is not to say that it was simply unconstitutional to take means of subsistence. As mentioned, prior to the 1954 Constitution, practices of requisition, compulsory purchase and nationalization had entailed takings of subsistence means, particularly private houses on the taken land. But it seems that to the Chinese constitutional framers in 1954 the taking of means of subsistence was secondary in significance to warrant any explicit mention in the written constitution. The reason for that will be explored more fully later in this section. Suffice it to say here that this should not lead to the conclusion that the state's taking of privately owned subsistence means was unconstitutional until it was overtly mentioned after the 2004 constitutional amendment. This is because Article 13 of the 1954 Constitution did not grant the takings power to the communist party-state, which had already employed such power over the means of production and subsistence before the founding of the PRC. The absence of any mention of the power to take subsistence means in the written constitution is therefore not to be interpreted as denying the constitutionality thereof. Instead, it should stand for tacit acknowledgment and acceptance of what had already been in existence.

The fourth and final distinction between the 1954 takings clause and its counterpart in the 1949 East German Constitution is that the former does not contain the requirement of making compensation or any provision about resolving compensation disputes through courts. This becomes readily understandable from previous discussion in this section. The Chinese original takings clause does not contain a requirement of compensation because it involves a total of three kinds of takings power, only two of which were compensatory (requisition and compulsory purchase). Since the power of nationalization is compensationless, a general requirement of compensation would not be suitable. Meanwhile, settling expropriation disputes in courts had not been embraced by the Chinese communist party-state by that time. Indeed, it would be both unnecessary and unhelpful to involve the judiciary in the process of revolutionary campaigns characterized by massive land takings. Moreover, as the socialist transformation campaign was still underway in 1954, there was no reason for the constitutional framers to import such alien experiences from the East German Constitution.

In summary, the above analysis demonstrates that China's original constitutional takings clause is neither purely homegrown nor completely transplanted. Essentially, it was a hybrid of both foreign and indigenous elements and a fusion between past and future. While inspired by the 1949 East German Constitution, it also grew out of and indeed reflected the native experiences of revolution and development in China over the first half of the last century. Specifically, compulsory purchase originated as an alternative approach to confiscation in the land reform movement in the 1940s before being turned into a measure to secure land for public works in the early 1950s. As compensatory takings of land for public works, requisition was initially practiced in the 1930s and 1940s in the communist revolutionary border regions and was subsequently entrenched in the 1953 MLRSC to provide land for state-led development. Nationalization figured prominently in the land reform campaign until the early 1950s and was subsequently revived for the socialist transformation movement, which was then still in progress. Therefore, as much as being an embodiment of the past, the original takings clause in 1954 also projected into what would come in the future, be it state-led construction or socialist transformation movement.

On March 23, 1954, Chen Boda, personal secretary of Mao Zedong and one of the three original drafters of the 1954 Constitution, delivered an explanatory report on the draft constitution at the first meeting of the constitutional drafting committee. He revealed that the guiding principle for constitution-making at that time was to achieve the following objectives: (1) to reflect the great transformation of social relations from the outset of people's revolution and the founding of the People's Republic; (2) to sum up the main experiences of struggling for and organizing these transformations; (3) to perpetuate the people's revolution; (4) to fully express the fundamental mandate for China to gradually proceed toward socialism and to demonstrate the possible and appropriate way through which the Chinese people strive to realize that goal; and (5) to adopt international practices on constitutional law, especially those of the USSR and other socialist countries while relying also on China's own experiences.[59] From its original meaning revealed by previous analysis,

[59] Han, 1954 Constitution and Constitutionalism in New China, pp. 223–24.

the 1954 takings clause could be said to have achieved all these objectives through weaving together the historical and the future, the local and the international. First and foremost, by containing all three takings powers that were once deployed in the pre-PRC era, the takings clause represents and entrenches China's native revolutionary traditions. Furthermore, through pointing to the then-ongoing campaign of socialist transformation, it expresses the mandate for China to move closer to a more advanced stage of socialism as understood at the time. Last, but by no means least, it draws on the takings clause of the 1949 East German Constitution, thereby imbuing the Chinese Constitution with international constitutional experiences. From this point of view, the original takings clause adopts a multidimensional perspective that is at once both inward and outward, backward and forward looking. It is only against this background that we can explain why Article 13 was confined to takings of production means and especially land without even mentioning takings of subsistence means. To the Chinese constitutional makers in 1954, it was the taking of land and other production means for the land reform campaign and socialist transformation movement that had represented the "great transformation of social relations," the main revolutionary experiences and the future direction of the Chinese people's revolution. Compared with the taking of means of subsistence, it is much more worthy of being expressly highlighted in the written constitution.

As noted at the beginning of this chapter, there was not any comparable provision to the original takings clause in either the 1949 Common Program or the 1936 USSR Constitution, the two main reference texts for the 1954 PRC Constitution. The preceding texts show that all three enumerated takings powers had already been practiced extensively by the Chinese communist party-state prior to the 1954 Constitution. This is in line with the generally held view that the takings power is an inherent attribute of the sovereign state that is antecedent to and regardless of the existence of a written constitution. The mainstream understanding of the Fifth Amendment to the US Constitution is that it does not confer such power upon the government, but is there to place constitutional limitations on such pre-existing sovereign power.[60] Was China's original constitutional takings clause intended for the same purpose? What was its *raison d'etre*?

[60] Philip Nichols, *The Law of Eminent Domain: A Treatise on the Principles which Affect the Taking of Property for the Public Use* (Albany: Matthew Bender & Co., 1917), vol. 1, p. 58.

4.3 Purpose of Original Constitutional Takings Clause

No official interpretation of Article 13 of the 1954 Constitution has ever been published. The best source for clues is a set of constitutional law textbooks and monographs published between 1954 and 1957.[61] These works are authoritative because they were written or edited by influential research institutions or sometimes by government leaders. The reason for stopping at 1957 is because the anti-rightist movement in that year was widely viewed as putting a brake on the implementation of, and indeed any serious attention to, the 1954 Constitution. Therefore, the books published before 1957 are the most reliable basis for an "uncontaminated" reading of the 1954 takings clause.

In all these books, Article 13 was regarded as the exemplification of a three-pronged socialist principle. First, the public interest, sacrosanct and supreme in a socialist society, is always over and above private interests, which must conform to the needs of public interest.[62] Second, public/collective/social interest is permanently consistent with private interest in a socialist society. Indeed, public interest is the fundamental and long-term interest of each and every individual. Without public interest, there is no private or personal interest. Without general development of the society, there will be no increase in the interests of individuals. This is why private interests must always comply with public interest.[63] Third, the PRC is a socialist state under the rule of all people, which represents the common interest of them all. All state policies and measures aim to maintain and create common benefit for the entire population. Therefore, national or state interest is the public/common

[61] A list of these works can be found in Binwen Xing, "Book Collections: Constitutional Studies in Early People's Republic (新中国制宪初期的宪法学)," April 29, 2012, available at xingbinwen.fyfz.cn/b/700546.

[62] Xiu Lin, *On Several Issues of Our Draft Constitution* (谈谈我国宪法的几个问题) (Beijing: Zhongnan Renmin Press, 1954), p. 31; Bangyan Lou, *Basic Knowledge of PRC Constitution* (中华人民共和国宪法基本知识) (Beijing: Xinzhi Press, 1955), p. 94; Da Li (ed.), *Lectures on PRC Constitution* (中华人民共和国宪法讲话) (Beijing: Renmin Press, 1956), pp. 84–85; Chun Gao (ed.), *A Plain Introduction to Constitution* (宪法通俗讲话) (Beijing: Hebei Renmin Press, 1955), p. 31; Defeng Wu (ed.), *Lectures on PRC Constitution* (中华人民共和国宪法讲话) (Beijing: Hubei Renmin Press, 1956), p. 70; State Law Teaching and Research Office of Central Political-Legal Cadres School (ed.), *Teaching Materials on the PRC Constitution* (中华人民共和国宪法讲义) (Beijing: Falv Press, 1957), p. 158; Peihua Liu (ed.), *Outlines of Lectures on the PRC Constitution* (中华人民共和国宪法讲课提纲) (Shenyang: Liaoning Renmin Press, 1957), pp. 80–81.

[63] Gao, A Plain Introduction to Constitution, p. 33; State Law Teaching and Research Office of Central Political-Legal Cadres School, Teaching Materials on the PRC Constitution, p. 158; Liu, Outlines of Lectures on the PRC Constitution, p. 81.

interest of all people, which is also consistent with their individual personal interest. The state guarantees private interests for the sake of public interest.[64] The gist of this socialist principle is that public interest, always represented by the socialist state, is ontologically prior to, axiologically superior than and yet fundamentally consistent with private interests. It can be best illustrated by the following schematic formula: public interest = state interest ≥ private interests.[65]

Under this apparently paradoxical socialist principle, land taking is seen to be necessarily in the public interest for being exercised by the socialist state, which always represents the public interest. Consequently, in a socialist society, land taking for private interests is a logical impossibility. While it may result in the loss of private interests of those whose land is taken away, it is an obligation for the takees as socialist citizens to accept, if not welcome state land takings, not only because their private interests must yield to public interest but also because that is in their own fundamental and long-term private interests.[66]

A story told in a 1955 book is particularly illustrative in this regard. In the early 1950s an entire village in Hebei Province was asked to make way for the construction of a water reservoir by the government. Initially the villagers were reluctant to do so since they did not want to leave their homeland. But they moved eventually and their land was acquired by the state. After being relocated to a new place, the villagers actually found that their situation improved because they were looked after very well by the local government, which built better accommodation for them and provided them with land more fertile than that they used to have. The conclusion derived from this episode was that the personal interest of every individual socialist citizen is intrinsically in complete harmony with public interest guaranteed by the state. Whenever state/public interest requires it, every socialist citizen should comply with such requirements without reservation and will in the end find him/herself better off.[67]

[64] Liu, Outlines of Lectures on the PRC Constitution, p. 80; State Law Teaching and Research Office of Central Political-Legal Cadres School, Teaching Materials on the PRC Constitution, p. 158.

[65] Note that "≥" means "greater than and equal to," which is apparently a paradoxical relationship. For an insightful analysis of the usefulness of paradoxes in Chinese legal and political discourses, see Samuli Seppänen, *Ideological Conflict and the Rule of Law in Contemporary China: Useful Paradoxes* (Cambridge: Cambridge University Press, 2016).

[66] Liu, Outlines of Lectures on the PRC Constitution, p. 80; State Law Teaching and Research Office of Central Political-Legal Cadres School, Teaching Materials on the PRC Constitution, p. 158.

[67] Gao, A Plain Introduction to Constitution, pp. 32–33.

In this light, the aim of China's original constitutional takings clause in 1954 is in no way to limit the state's takings power. While it is neither power-granting, as already demonstrated, it is essentially power-confirming. This is the substantive reason why Article 13 is located in the first chapter among various other macro-level state policies. Compulsory taking is constitutionally and fundamentally conceptualized and affirmed as a state policy toward private ownership of land and other means of production, the normative foundation of which lies in the socialist principle just expounded. In this light we can better understand the commonality shared by all three types of takings powers specified in the 1954 constitutional takings clause: as public interest should be represented exclusively by the state and could not be opposed but only accepted, the takees were not offered any role in the decision-making process, nor could they challenge the takings decisions in any formal, institutionalized way.

4.4 The Transition Paradigm Reconsidered

The Chinese original constitutional takings clause, as just explained, presents a case that cannot be easily fitted into the prevailing TP. Most notably, the conceptual assumption is not applicable to the original takings clause, which has a much broader notion of the takings power. For one thing, it can be used not only for the construction of public works but also for such purposes as land reform and socialist transformation. For another, making compensation is not a general requirement, but applies only to compulsory purchase and requisition. Nationalization in the original takings clause is compensationless. Second, the teleological assumption does not hold in respect of the original takings clause. Far from being power-constraining and aimed at protecting private property against government encroachment, it constitutionally confirmed the expansive takings power already deployed by the Chinese state, which is precisely the opposite to the Fifth Amendment of the US Constitution. It would be a grave mistake to conflate the two or to envision one as the other's future.

Yet, one may argue that none of this detracts from the validity and utility of the TP by pointing out that the current takings clause in the 1982 Constitution departs profoundly from its 1954 predecessor. Whereas the latter might have supplied the semantics and vocabulary for the latter, there is a radical and fundamental rupture between the two. After all, the original takings clause was formulated in the midst of an unfinished revolution that was set to abolish all private land ownership and to establish a planned economy. In sharp contrast, the present constitutional takings clause was adopted, and should therefore be interpreted, against a backdrop wherein China navigates toward a market economy and promises that the state respects and protects human rights.[68] These two clauses should be regarded as holding drastically divergent positions about what the takings power entails and what its purpose is. Hence, as far as existing rural land expropriation law is concerned, the conceptual, temporal, teleological and developmental assumptions under the TP all remain valid and appropriate.

Whether or not the 1982 constitutional takings clause is actually a fundamental break from the 1954 clause will be discussed in much more detail in Chapters 6 and 7. Suffice it to highlight here that it is hard to ignore the imprints left by the original takings clause on the current rural land expropriation law. In terms of the public interest prerequisite, the present takings law inherits at least three crucial features from the original takings clause. First, no clear-cut definition of public interest is proffered. Second, the scope of public interest today seems no less extensive than that in 1954. Third, today those affected by land takings are still largely excluded from the decision-making process and prevented from challenging the decisions of land takings. Furthermore, with regard to compensation, under the original takings clause, the annual output value and living conditions of takees were used as benchmarks, which is preserved by the current LAL.

None of this is to say that the existing expropriation law is simply a repetition of what went before. The enormous changes taking place in China since the 1950s are undisputable. No longer are land reform and socialist transformation objectives for land takings. More crucially, in the current 1982 Constitution, the power to compulsorily take ownership of land is reduced from three to one: only compensatory requisition was left, which, as mentioned in Chapter 1 was renamed as expropriation by the 2004 constitutional amendment. The power of compensationless nationalization is removed from the takings clause and indeed the Constitution. Also gone is the requirement of exhausting voluntary negotiation before involuntary takings. In fact, the idea of taking land for public construction through exchange-like compulsory purchase has been almost completely forgotten. All this results in the collapse of

68 1982 Constitution (as amended in 2004), art. 33.

the internal structure of increasing coerciveness from "compulsory purchase" to "requisition" to "nationalization" in the original takings clause. Consequently, the market price of land, once used to determine compensation for compulsory purchase prior to the early 1950s, is no longer a consideration in calculating expropriation compensation during the post-reform era. It was not until fairly recently that market price began to creep back into the calculation formula of compensation. In this sense, perhaps somewhat surprisingly, the popular reform proposal to adopt fair market value as the compensation standard over the last decade is calling not just for a legal transplant from America, but also a revival of China's own historical practice.

That said, on balance it is not unfair to conclude that the original takings clause in 1954, though long out-of-effect and neglected, has laid down the foundation for China's takings law today. The past six decades witnessed the disappearance of some features of, but no substantial alteration to, the takings law. There is a deep-lying tradition of expansive, nonparticipatory and unchallengeable takings power with compensation and resettlement determined by current use of land and living conditions of those affected, which well predates the reform era and is still alive and kicking today. Such a historical lineage is too important to ignore. In this situation, the temporal assumption under the TP must be transcended and our investigative horizon must be broadened. Specifically, the following question shall be addressed: why have certain pre-reform features of the takings law endured into the reform era when others disappeared along the way? The original constitutional takings clause investigated in this chapter serves the entry point from which we delve into the rich and complex history of rural land takings law in modern China. But before turning to the post-1954 period, it is necessary to go further back and dwell more on what gave shape to the 1954 clause. As shown by this chapter, it deviates from both the conceptual and teleological assumptions of the TP as it involves three distinctive types of takings powers and is normatively legitimatized under a power-confirming socialist principle. Already demonstrated is that this was the result of past revolutionary and developmental experiences of the Chinese communist party-state. Yet given that the party-state is supposed to always exercise takings power in the public interest, which is superior to and fundamentally in harmony with individuals' private interests, why doesn't the original takings clause just say that the state may take land and other means of production? What is the point of having a seemingly restrictive clause not so dissimilar to the counterpart in the 1949 East German Constitution if the aim is to confirm rather than limit the takings power? Why is the original takings clause power-confirming at all? To answer these questions, we now turn to the theoretical foundations of land takings power in modern China.

5

Theoretical Foundations of Land Takings Power

Competing Traditions and Common Legacy

The previous chapter shows that the power of rural land takings had been exercised by the Chinese communist party-state long before the 1954 Constitution, a fait accompli that became constitutionally confirmed by the original takings clause. It went beyond the conventional conception of compensatory land takings for public works to include three distinct types of takings powers – nationalization, requisition and compulsory purchase. As explained, compensationless nationalization was the iconic measure of the CCP in its revolutionary campaigns between the late 1920s and the early 1950s. Later in the 1950s and 1960s, it was envisaged as a way to implement the socialist transformation of capitalist industry and commerce. Compensatory requisition for public works dated from the 1930s in the revolutionary border regions and was retained after 1949, most notably in the 1953 MLRSC. Compulsory purchase was briefly tried out in the late 1940s as an alternative and complementary measure to confiscation during the land reform campaign. After the establishment of the PRC, it morphed into acquisition for public works more akin to market transaction, to which voluntary negotiation between land-using entities and landowners was a procedural precondition. What had given rise to such unique experiences of land takings that eventually shaped the 1954 constitutional takings clause?

This chapter presents and analyzes the theories that had justified and guided the exercising of these takings powers. For the following two reasons, however, the main focus will be on noncompensatory nationalization in the pre-PRC era and compensatory requisition. First, nationalization for socialist transformation of capitalism primarily involved takings of urban land rather than in rural areas because the capitalist industries were then largely located in urban areas. In this sense it lies outside the purview of this book. Second, compulsory purchase for land reform or public works existed very briefly in history. It will be discussed only when relevant.

The remainder of this chapter proceeds in three sections. Section 5.1 deals with the power of nationalization and is divided into two parts. The first part discusses the socialist tradition of land nationalization by way of compensationless confiscation. The second part presents the competing program of land nationalization devised by the nationalist party, especially by its founding father Sun Yat-sen. Section 5.2 discusses the origin and evolution of the theories underpinning the power of compensatory land takings in China. As mentioned, this concept was captured by the term "requisition" in the original takings clause in 1954, which was substituted by "expropriation" according to the 2004 constitutional amendment. Therefore, for the sake of being consistent with the analysis of contemporary Chinese rural land takings law, this chapter adopts the term expropriation, which should be considered to be interchangeable with requisition. The chapter concludes with the observation that, notwithstanding their notable differences, the competing foundational theories of land takings power in modern China were based on similar conceptions of private land ownership and the state–individual relationship, which gave rise to a distinctive Chinese understanding of land takings power very different from the liberal notion prevailing in the West today. This helps us understand why the power-confirming takings clause in the 1954 Constitution took the power-restricting form from its counterpart in the 1949 East German Constitution, which, as noted at the end of previous chapter, does not make much sense at first sight.

5.1 Land Nationalization: A Tale of Two Traditions

5.1.1 Socialist Tradition of Land Nationalization

5.1.1.1 Mandate from Classic Marxism

According to the founding charter of the CCP in 1921, one of the Party's top priorities was to abolish bourgeoisie private property and confiscate all the means of production, including land. This was but one of many proclamations of the Party on its commitment to land nationalization over the course of its revolutionary struggle, the inspiration of which came from classic Marxism.

In the 1848 *Communist Manifesto*, Marx and Engels suggested that the theory of the communists could be summed up in one sentence: abolition of private property. This is rooted in the Marxian interpretation of human history, seen as centering on class struggle between those exploited and oppressed and those exploiting and oppressing. The defining feature of a certain class is its relationship with the means of production, i.e. the instruments and objects of labor such as factories, machines and land. Those who own the means of production and control human labor are thereby the ruling and exploiting class of a society. Those who own no means of production and whose labor power is under control constitute the class ruled and exploited. Axiomatic to this differentiated class structure is struggle rather than cooperation. By definition, revolution is the struggle by exploited classes against exploiting classes and "revolutions are the locomotives of history."[1] Propelled by successive class revolutions, human society progressed from primitive communism, slave society and feudalism to capitalism. Like all previous social systems, the capitalist society is characterized by class antagonism between the bourgeoisie and the proletariat. It will ultimately be replaced by socialism when class exploitation intensifies to such an extent that the working class can no longer sustain itself and the proletarian revolution becomes inevitable. However, different from all its predecessors, under a socialist society, class distinction and oppression will, for the first time in human history, be ended because private property in the means of production will be completely abolished.[2]

More specifically, for the following three reasons, classic Marxism holds that private land ownership is doomed.[3] First, Marx utterly rejected the proposition that private land ownership constitutes a natural right. He took such rights-based justification as no more than a cloak used by the conquerors to disguise the fact of conquest and domination on the one hand, and to legitimatize their possessions "through the instrumentality of Laws imposed by themselves" on the other.[4] Second, Marx remarked, "Landed property is based on the monopoly by certain persons over definite portions of the globe." Such monopoly is economically realized through the rent paid to landed proprietors, who can thereby "pocket a product of social development created without their help."[5]

[1] Karl Marx, "The Class Struggles in France, 1848 to 1850," in *Marx and Engels Collected Works* (Moscow: Progress Publishers, 1969), vol. 1, p. 205.

[2] Karl Marx and Friedrich Engels, "Communist Manifesto," in *Selected Works of Marx and Engels* (Moscow: Progress Publishers, 1969), vol. 1, p. 98.

[3] Karl Marx, "Rent of Land," in *Economic & Philosophic Manuscripts of 1844* (Moscow: Progress Publishers, 1959), available at www.marxists.org/archive/marx/works/1844/manuscripts/rent.htm.

[4] Karl Marx, "The Nationalization of the Land" (1872) 11 *The International Herald*, available at www.marxists.org/archive/marx/works/1872/04/nationalisation-land.htm.

[5] Karl Marx, *Capital* (New York: International Publishers, 1959), vol. 3, p. 442.

Therefore, just as capitalist profit is an extortion of surplus labor value, land rent is also a form of unearned income indicative of exploitation. Meanwhile, as Marx argued, it also constitutes "one of the greatest obstacles to a rational development of agriculture" because "the tenant farmer avoids all improvements . . . for which he cannot expect complete returns during the term of his lease."[6] Third, in line with the Marxist historiography, Engels argued that the abolition of private land ownership is necessitated by the advancement of human society. In primitive societies land was under common ownership, which was turned by agricultural development into a fetter on production and was therefore replaced by more productive private land ownership. Yet, with further development of agriculture in the capitalist society, private property in land in turn becomes a hindrance on production and is bound to be transformed into "a far higher and more developed form" of common ownership.[7] This new form of common land ownership, as imagined by Marx, is land nationalization, a "social necessity" that is inexorable.[8]

In order to realize such a social necessity, the *Communist Manifesto* asks the proletariat to "wrest, by degree, all capital from the bourgeoisie" to accomplish a double mission: (1) to "centralize all instruments of production in the hands of the state" and (2) to "increase the total productive forces as rapidly as possible." Upon the victory of proletariat revolution, according to the *Communist Manifesto*, class distinction will disappear and all production will be in the hands of "a vast association of the whole nation" or "associated individuals."[9]

The logic behind this revolutionary vision and projection is readily understandable. As noted, in Marxian theory a class is fundamentally defined by its relationship with the means of production. Therefore, if the proletariat is to become the ruling class, it must seize production means. To achieve this they need organize themselves into a state and take the means of production into the hands of that state. Once the production means is concentrated in the state, the capitalist mode of production is destroyed and the entire social structure it underpins is transformed. This will not only liberate the productive forces but also sweep away

[6] Ibid.

[7] Frederick Engels, *Anti-Dühring: Herr Eugen Dühring's Revolution in Science* (Moscow: Progress Publishers, 1947), part 1, chapter 13.

[8] Marx, "The Nationalization of the Land."

[9] The difference in formulation is a result of different editions. The former phrase was used in the 1888 English edition edited by Engels while the latter was used in the German editions.

class antagonism, and indeed classes themselves. Over this process, the nature of the state changes profoundly. During the revolution, the state is the organized proletariat as a separate class struggling in a divided class society, famously called by Marx as the "dictatorship of the proletariat."[10] After the revolution, the society will be rid of antagonistic class structure and the state will be turned into "a vast association of the whole nation" or "associated individuals."

Notwithstanding the enormous power and lucidity with which the ultimate objective of land nationalization was pronounced, these highly abstract theoretical sketches of classic Marxism were rather ambiguous on two points. On the one hand, as acknowledged by Marx and by Engels, there is a tension internal to the double mission between the long-term benefits of nationalization to and its short-term damage on the economic productivity of a society. They conceded that in the beginning nationalization would involve "means of despotic inroads" on property rights and the conditions of bourgeois production, which would be economically destructive and untenable. Even though they did insist that this was necessary in the long run to revolutionize the mode of production and unleash greater productive forces,[11] they did not spell out how to solve this supposedly temporary tension in practice. On the other hand, classic Marxism offered no concrete specification about what a nationalized land regime would look like. The founding fathers never adumbrated any specific institutional form of state land ownership that could reflect and accommodate the fundamental transformation of state and society that they had envisaged.

For all their theoretical and practical importance, the above ambiguities were by no means the most urgent issues facing Marxist revolutionaries of the nineteenth century. Rather, of absolute urgency was the question of initiating a revolution. The *Communist Manifesto* suggests that land nationalization is applicable only to the most advanced capitalist countries, where the "forces of production have been developed to the point where enough could be developed for all" and private ownership of production means has already hindered further development. In those societies, abolition of private land ownership becomes "not only possible but absolutely necessary."[12] However, at the time of Marx and

[10] Karl Marx, "Marx to Joseph Weydemeyer in New York," in *Karl Marx and Frederick Engels: Collected Works* (New York: International Publishers, 1982), vol. 38, pp. 401–3.

[11] Marx and Engels, "Communist Manifesto," chapter 2.

[12] Friedrich Engels, "The Principles of Communism," in *Selected Works of Marx and Engels* (Moscow: Progress Publishers, 1969), vol. 1.

Engels, most European countries were predominantly agricultural and landlords owned most of the land. Capitalism was yet to be developed, let alone assume dominance. The natural question, then, is can land nationalization occur in these pre-capitalist societies?

5.1.1.2 Land Nationalization in Pre-capitalist Societies: Engel's Plan

Both founders of classic Marxism believed that small-scale agriculture was destined to be replaced by capitalist production and the peasants be turned into proletariat. Once capitalism dominates the countryside, conditions will become ripe for the proletarian revolution toward land nationalization.[13] Without this being the case in the nineteenth century, however, Marx and Engels did not consider it an objective process that would be automatically set off or should be waited for. The critical issue to them was how the proletariat could initiate a revolution in the countries that were economically backward and populated mainly by the peasant mass.

For Marx and Engels, the key was to establish a proletariat–peasant alliance. Marx argued in the 1870s that "the proletariat must, as the government, take measure whereby the peasant sees his situation immediately improved and which therefore win him over to the revolution."[14] In 1894, Engels made similar remarks when he extended his support to the French socialists' attempt to win over the mass peasantry: "No lasting revolutionary transformation is possible in France against the will of the small peasant."[15] In fact, he suggested that a worker–peasant alliance must be created with urgency, as "the greater the number of peasants whom we can save from being actually hurled down into the proletariat ... the more quickly and easily the social transformation will be accomplished."[16]

However, to win over the peasantry was no easy task. The reason is that the land-owning peasantry was largely conservative, if not reactionary, in being inclined to defend their private ownership of land against not only

[13] Karl Marx, "David Ricardo's Theory of Rent," in *Theories of Surplus-Value* (Moscow: Progress Publisher, 1968), vol. 2; Frederick Engels, "The Peasant Question in France and Germany," in *Selected Works of Marx and Engels* (Moscow: Progress Publishers, 1970), vol. 3.

[14] Karl Marx, "On Bakunin's Statism and Anarchy," cited in Jon Elster, *Making Sense of Marx* (Cambridge: Cambridge University Press, 1985), p. 442.

[15] Engels, "The Peasant Question in France and Germany." [16] Ibid.

capitalist accumulation but also proletarian nationalization.[17] Devising a strategy to revolutionize the conservative peasantry turned out to be central to the revolutionaries of later generations in less developed countries such as Russia and China. But in classic Marxism it was Engels who developed the first and only detailed plan for such a mission in *The Peasant Question in France and Germany*, published in 1894, one year before his death.

To Engels, the socialist revolution depended much on mobilizing the peasantry held back by its deep-rooted sense of private property. Sympathetic to the French socialists' pragmatic consideration to "bring the peasant under their influence," he nevertheless adamantly criticized their attempt to do so by promising to maintain the small-holding peasant ownership. He argued that to the true socialists this was "a promise which we ourselves know we shall not be able to keep." Instead, the socialists should first try to transform small peasants' private enterprise and land ownership into cooperative ones.[18] This ought to be done not by coercion but "by dint of example and the proffer of social assistance," which would make the peasants understand that their property could only be preserved through being converted into "co-operative property operated co-operatively." At the end of the day, however, collectivization is just the intermediate stage toward nationalization of land. During the transitional period, the state may claim formal title over land, with the production activities being carried out collectively by local communities.[19]

For land owned not by peasants but by landlords, however, Engels proposed to confiscate and transfer it to the state without compensation. Yet he did not completely rule out the possibility of compensation by acknowledging that Marx had repeatedly said to him that the socialists "would get off cheapest" if they could buy out the landlords. Engels further argued that whether to pay such compensation in nationalization would depend on "the circumstances under which the socialists obtain power, and particularly upon the attitude adopted by these gentry, the big landowners, themselves."[20]

To summarize, in classic Marxism, especially according to Engels, land nationalization as a socialist ideal should not be compromised by the pragmatic concern to bring the peasants around through pledging to retain their private land ownership. Instead, their private land shall be collectivized voluntarily and gradually, before ultimately being

17 Marx and Engels, "Communist Manifesto."

18 Engels, "The Peasant Question in France and Germany." 19 Ibid. 20 Ibid.

surrendered to the state. Meanwhile, forceful confiscation without compensation should be applied to the landlords, who could also be bought up with compensation when the circumstances permit. All this laid down the general theoretical framework under which land nationalization was to be carried out by the revolutionaries of subsequent generations. As is well known, it was the Russians that made the first avowed attempt.

5.1.1.3 The Russian Way: From Lenin to Stalin

As noted, classic Marxism ordained two tasks for the Russian revolutionaries: to initiate a revolution toward land nationalization in underdeveloped Russia, and to develop rules and institutions of state land ownership. The following texts present the revolutionary program devised by Vladimir Lenin, before introducing the nationalized land regime under Joseph Stalin.

In Lenin's view, land nationalization in Russia would come in two stages. In 1894, commenting on the proposal to confiscate and redistribute land from landlords to peasants, he admitted that it was a progressive bourgeois-democratic demand. The social-democrats (the Russian Marxists at the time) should adopt such a program insofar as it promoted the abolition of private land ownership of the landlords and the elimination of feudalism in Russia. However, Lenin warned that this program was not of a socialist nature for preserving small landed proprietorship, which was to the advantage of capitalism, not socialism. The socialist revolution must transcend that, but only later.[21] This shows that while echoing Engel's insistence on land nationalization, Lenin diverged from him in accepting the need for land redistribution to the peasantry, at least temporarily. More specifically, he conceived that the revolution would start from a land-to-the-tiller bourgeois-democratic phase before progressing to a full-blown socialist stage of land nationalization. In the first phase, the revolution was to be carried out by an alliance of workers, peasants and capitalists to eradicate feudalism and the landlord class through land confiscation and redistribution. In the second stage, the proletariat would unite with the peasants to fight the bourgeois and capitalism. Only at the second stage could private land ownership be eliminated and all land be transferred to the state.[22]

[21] Vladimir Lenin, "What the "Friends of the People" are and How They Fight the Social-Democrats," in *Lenin's Collected Works* (Moscow: Progress Publishers, 1972), vol. 1, pp. 290–91.

[22] Vladimir Lenin, "To the Rural Poor: An Explanation for the Peasants of What the Social-Democrats Want," in *Lenin's Collected Works* (Moscow: Progress Publishers, 1964), vol. 6.

There are three points in Lenin's two-stage theory of land nationalization worthy of further attention. First, the road toward nationalization of land began with confiscation of landlords' land without compensation. Marx's advice to buy out landlords was not heeded. In fact, Lenin explicitly rejected it. He argued that to give landlords compensation constituted "treason to socialism and imposition of a new tax on the laboring and exploited masses."[23] Second, it was out of highly pragmatic concerns that Lenin endorsed temporary redistribution of confiscated land to the peasants. He recognized that "general redistribution" of land had long been a popular request among Russian peasants, who had not yet realized that nationalization of land was truly in their objective interests. In order to mobilize this conservative peasantry, Lenin considered it necessary "to remove any idea that the workers' party wants to impose upon the peasantry any scheme of reforms against their will and independently of any movement among the peasantry." Therefore, the nationalization agenda should not be immediately pronounced, and land redistribution should be adopted first.[24] Third, Lenin insisted on the eventual transition from the first stage to the second. He cautioned that at the first democratic-bourgeoisie stage, "we cannot under any circumstances flatly reject nationalization of the land; but we must specify the particular political conditions without which nationalization might be detrimental to the proletariat and the peasantry."[25] Such political conditions, as envisioned by Lenin, would come about when "the decisive victory of the present revolution brings about the complete sovereignty of the people, i.e., establishes a republic and a fully democratic state system."[26]

Conducive political conditions of this sort were hardy present when Lenin delivered his famous and immensely impactful *April Theses* in 1917. Nonetheless, he claimed in that speech that "the specific feature of the present situation in Russia is that the country is passing from the first stage of the revolution – which . . . placed power in the hands of the bourgeoisie – to its second stage, which must place power in the hands of

[23] The exact words were adopted in "Theses on the Agrarian Question" (Minutes of the Second Congress of the Communist International, 1920), available at www.marxists.org/history/international/comintern/2nd-congress/doc03.htm. The expression was first coined by Lenin in "Preliminary Draft Theses on The Agrarian Question," in *Lenin's Collected Works* (Moscow: Progress Publishers, 1965), vol. 31, pp. 152–164.

[24] Vladimir Lenin, "Revision of the Agrarian Program of the Workers' Party," in *Lenin's Collected Works* (Moscow: Progress Publishers, 1965), vol. 10, pp. 165–95.

[25] Ibid., p. 194. [26] Ibid., pp. 194–95.

the proletariat and the poorest sections of the peasants."[27] The most important reason for Lenin to call for a socialist revolution ahead of schedule, as it were, was his acute awareness of the fact that the popular demand for land reform was not satisfied by the provisional government in power at the time.[28] He saw this as a great opportunity to be seized in order to win over the peasants through satisfying their wants. In this situation, the following land program was pronounced: All landed estates should be confiscated and all land immediately nationalized and disposed of by the local soviets ("council" in Russian) of peasants' deputies. Model farms would be set up on large estates and put under the control of local democratic bodies to engage in collective agricultural production activities.[29]

In promoting land nationalization and collectivized agricultural production, this plan of Lenin's definitely pointed toward socialism characterized by abolition of private property in production means. However, with a decentralized land use system in which the power to arrange agricultural production resided with local peasant soviets, it also placated the Russian peasants' long-held desire to have a greater say in how land was used. That made it precisely more attractive and successful than all alternative proposals advanced by competing forces in winning the hearts and minds of the Russian peasantry. The combination of state ownership, local administration of land use and collective production was subsequently adopted in the Bolshevik Party's *Resolution of on the Agrarian Question*[30] and then in the 1917 *Land Decree*, which demanded in formal legal terms that private land ownership be abolished and all land become part of the national land fund, and with the right to use land accorded to all citizens insofar as that they are able to cultivate it.[31]

Despite the fact that land nationalization was legally mandated, the reality in the immediate aftermath of the Russian revolution was that

27 Vladimir Lenin, "The Tasks of the Proletariat in the Present Revolution," in *Lenin's Collected Works* (Moscow: Progress Publishers, 1964), vol. 24, pp. 19–26.

28 Jules Townshend, *The Politics of Marxism: The Critical Debates* (London: Leicester University Press, 1996), pp. 67–68.

29 Vladimir Lenin, "The Tasks of the Proletariat in the Present Revolution."

30 Vladimir Lenin, "*Resolution on the Agrarian Question (The Seventh (April) All-Russia Conference of the RSDLP(B), 29 April 1917)*," *in Lenin Collected Works* (Moscow: Progress Publishers, 1965), vol. 10.

31 Points 1, 6, and 8 in "The Peasant Mandate on the Land," in *Decree on Land (passed at the Second Congress of Soviets of Workers', Soldiers', and Peasants' Deputies, 8 November 1917)*. The Peasant Mandate on the Land published in August 1917 was incorporated as part of the law.

most confiscated land was neither nationalized nor collectivized, as the socialist project requires, but partitioned among peasants for individual farming.[32] While the ensuing years did witness accelerating collectivization in Soviet Russia, the New Economic Policy between 1921 and 1928 effected a radical U-turn. In particular, the 1922 *Land Code* granted permanent tenure to villages and other rural groups of all land in their possession on the date of the promulgation of the law. No longer privileging any kind of socialist land tenure, it promised equal standing to all existing forms of land tenure, including individual holdings.[33]

On the theoretical level, this could be seen as the Russian response to the abovementioned tension between the socialist revolution's long-term gain and short-term damage to economic productivity. From the early 1920s, the economic conditions of Russia were extremely dire after years of civil war. The Soviet government was forced to rely, at least temporarily, on peasant farming to supply agricultural products vital to the national economy – or, so to speak, to alleviate the short-term damage to the economy caused by revolution. Against this background, for practical reasons, under the New Economic Policy, Russian peasants were allowed more freedom to choose forms of land tenure for themselves.[34] Unsurprisingly, the majority selected independent individual farming.[35] However, as Lenin himself explicitly acknowledged, the New Economic Policy was just a strategic retreat from the socialism that was the long-term goal.[36] When Stalin came to power in 1928, Soviet Russia reverted to collectivization.[37] For what it's worth, although Lenin followed Engels in recommending gradual and peaceful collectivization via persuasion and encouragement,[38] it is widely known that what happened under Stalin was precisely the opposite.[39]

[32] Vladimir P. Timoshenko, "The Agrarian Policies of Russia and the Wars" (1943) 17 *Agricultural History* 205.

[33] Ibid., 206. [34] Ibid.

[35] Stanislaw J. Sawicki, *Soviet Land and Housing Law: A Historical and Comparative Study* (New York: Praeger Publishers, 1977), p. 42.

[36] Vladmir Lenin, "The New Economic Policy and The Tasks Of The Political Education Departments," in *Lenin's Collected Works* (Moscow: Progress Publishers, 1965), vol. 33.

[37] By no means is this to claim that an ideological factor is the only reason for Stalin to initiate large-scale collectivization. Another well-known crucial impetus was that the soviet government was propelled by economic crisis to take more control over agricultural production, especially grain collection through collectivization.

[38] Dorothy Atkinson, *The End of the Russian Land Commune, 1905–1930* (Stanford: Stanford University Press, 1983), p. 214.

[39] On this we only have to refer to Stalin's famous article "Dizziness with Success," in which he acknowledged that the collectivization campaign was oftentimes coercive. J. V. Stalin,

More pertinent here, though, is the institutional form of a nationalized land regime in Soviet Russia. As noted earlier, classic Marxism is unclear on this point. Nor did Lenin live to devise any detailed plan. It was after the collectivization campaign and under Stalin's rule that Soviet Russia's socialist land system finally settled down, the main characteristics of which are as follows.

First and foremost, state ownership of land is both exclusive and absolute. It is exclusive because the state is the sole subject of the right to land ownership. Alienation of land ownership through sale or barter is outright prohibited. State ownership of land is absolute because the state as the owner has unrestricted and indisputable powers over land. Specifically, through organs of the government, the state determines the economic purpose of land, effects its planned distribution and exerts control over its proper use.[40]

Second, land use-right/tenure can be held by nonstate actors but is a right sui generis conferred by the state, in its capacity as the exclusive owner of all land, upon persons natural or juridical to utilize a piece of land. Specifically, land use-rights are allocated/allotted either to the state itself represented through its enterprises and agencies or to nonstate collective organizations and private individuals. Such allotment/allocation of land use-rights is free of charge because land is an asset of the whole people. Land tenure can last for a limited period of time or, more usually, in perpetuity. Moreover, land is functionally divided into six categories: agricultural land, habitation land, industrial land, land covered by woods and forests, land covered by waters and unused land. Any land must be used in accordance with the function designated by the state. Therefore, the right to use land also entails the legal duty to use it according to government-set purposes. For example, a collective farm that has received land for agricultural production cannot deviate from such purposes unless authorized by the competent government authority. This is for the purpose of guaranteeing the implementation of land policies under a socialist planned economy, defined as a system of measures taken by state agencies aiming to achieve the most rational and efficient use of land according to economic planning. Market transaction of land use-rights such as lease is forbidden. Land tenure is

"Dizzy with Success: Concerning Questions of the Collective-Farm Movement," in *Collected Works of J. V. Stalin* (Moscow: Foreign Languages Publishing House, 1955), vol. 12, pp. 197–205.

40 P. S. Romashkin (ed.), *Fundamentals of Soviet Law* (Moscow: Foreign Languages Publishing House, 1962), pp. 290–94.

protected by law. But the normative justification for that is less about respecting land-users' rights than about protecting the social public interests in the orderly utilization of land as an economic resource.[41]

Third, land management is carried out by state administration. The authority to allocate land use-rights for different purposes is shared within the government hierarchy among executive committees of village, city, district and provincial soviets and the national council of ministers. Restriction of land use to designated purposes is enforced through supervision and control by a variety of government agencies.[42]

Fourth, the state can withdraw land use-rights if allocated land is not used within two years of allocation, or used for undesignated ends, or is to be expropriated. Withdrawal of land in the case of expropriation can be initiated by the executive committee of the national council of ministers or provincial/city soviets. Expropriation shall be exercised only when a necessity arises for state or social needs and with the consent of the expropriated. But courts do not have the authority to pass judgment on the legality of withdrawal. Furthermore, while expropriation compensation has to be paid for any cost spent on improvement of land such as crops, seeds, houses and buildings thereon, there should be no compensation for the expropriated land use-right as it is initially assigned to land-users by the state as a gratuitous right free of charge.[43]

In the words of a Soviet Russian jurist, the socialist land system established under Stalin was "an aggregate of rules which regulate the entire system of land relations arising from the nationalization of land and developing with an eye to a fairer and more efficient use of land . . . as the exclusive property of the state, in the interest of socialist and communist construction in the USSR."[44]

Enough has been said about the socialist tradition of land nationalization from classic Marxism to the Russian model. We now demonstrate how such an imported tradition informed the Chinese experiences over the twentieth century.

[41] F. J. M. Feldbrugge, G. P. Van den Berg and William B. Simons (eds.), *Encyclopedia of Soviet Law* (Leiden: Martinus Nijhoff Publishers, 1985), pp. 435–37, 656–58; Romashkin, *Fundamentals of Soviet Law*, pp. 294–301; Sawicki, *Soviet Land and Housing Law: A Historical and Comparative Study*, pp. 55–57.

[42] Feldbrugge, Berg and Simons, *Encyclopedia of Soviet Law*, pp. 435–39.

[43] Ibid., p. 438; William B. Simons (ed.), *The Soviet Codes of Law* (Netherlands: Sijthoff and Noordhoff, 1980), vol. 23, pp, 879–80.

[44] Romashkin, *Fundamentals of Soviet Law*, p. 290.

5.1.1.4 Land Nationalization in Pre-reform China

It is necessary to say at the outset that for most of the last century the CCP broadly followed the socialist tradition of land nationalization (introduced in the last section), until the opening and reform in the late 1970s. This is borne out not only by its policies during the revolutionary years but also by the land system established in the PRC.

In terms of its land policies over the revolutionary period, facing a backward agricultural country, the CCP came to terms with the significance of a worker–peasant alliance and strived to win over the conservative mass peasantry. Particularly, inspired by Lenin's two-stage theory, confiscation and redistribution of land instead of nationalization was chosen as the first step. In his famous 1939 essay, Mao Zedong divides the Chinese revolution into two stages. The initial stage is a bourgeois-democratic revolution, or what he calls the "new democratic revolution," and the second is the proletarian-socialist revolution. The new democratic revolution purports to overthrow the landlord classes through land confiscation and redistribution. But it is not socialist because it achieves no more than clearing the way for capitalist development and thereby preparing the conditions for socialism. According to Mao, accomplishing the bourgeois-democratic revolution and upgrading to the socialist phase was the twofold task facing the CCP in the 1930s.[45]

However, this is not to say that the CCP was simply executing a preordained blueprint to every last detail. Just as the Russian revolutionaries did not strictly follow classic Marxism, the CCP deviated from both classic Marxism and the Russian model, most notably in three cases. Yet, it will be shown that these cases affirm rather than negate the impact of the aforementioned Marxist–Soviet tradition.

The three deviations from the revolutionary script by the CCP are all well known. First, as noted, Engels set land nationalization as a nonnegotiable objective for revolution. Lenin stopped short of distributing land ownership and granted only use-rights to the peasants. In marked contrast, the CCP conferred not just land use-rights but also ownership upon the peasants through land confiscation and redistribution.[46] Second, from 1937 to 1946, the CCP suspended land confiscation and redistribution and turned to the more modest measure of imposed rent reduction.

[45] Mao Zedong, "The Chinese Revolution and the Chinese Communist Party (中国革命和中国共产党)," in *Selected Works of Mao Zedong* (毛泽东选集) (Beijing: Renmin Press, 1991), vol. 2.

[46] 1947 Outline of Land Law, art. 11; 1950 Land Reform Law, art. 10.

Third, while Engels considered it acceptable to buy out the landlords to "get off cheapest," Lenin rejected it as "treason to socialism." But, as mentioned in the preceding chapter, the CCP did, though just for a short while during the land reform campaign, buy off landlords through compulsory purchase. How to make sense of these cases of deviation?

The decision to grant land ownership to the peasants rather than just use-rights was not made until 1931. Although as early as in 1921 the CCP called for confiscation of all production means in the founding Party charter, full-scale land confiscation was not attempted prior to 1927. Before then, the Party's agrarian policies went no further than compulsory reduction of land rent[47] or confiscation of land that exceeded a certain set maximum.[48] Between 1927 and 1931, driven by the KMT to remote mountainous rural areas, the CCP finally came to realize the importance of the mass peasantry as an indispensable revolutionary force in China. As a consequence, the 1928 *Jinggangshan Land Law*, 1929 *Xingguo Land Law* and 1930 *Soviet Land Law* demanded confiscation and redistribution of land use-rights to the toiling peasantry. Yet, they all fell short of ownership redistribution in prescribing that the ownership of confiscated land went to local soviet governments. It was in 1931 that the CCP eventually changed course and opted for privatization of ownership in confiscated land. The reason behind this was twofold. First, it became increasingly clear to the Party that what the peasants wanted was not just use-rights but full ownership of land. To mobilize them to support the disruptive land revolution, it was necessary to put on offer what was actually sought after. Moreover, it turned out that lacking full ownership rights left many peasants feel uncertain about the stability and

[47] Manifesto of the Second Congress of the Chinese Communist Party (中国共产党第二次全国代表大会宣言), promulgated in July 1922, available at cpc.people.com.cn/GB/64162/64168/64554/4428164.html; Draft Charter of the Chinese Communist Party (中国共产党党纲草案), promulgated in July 1923, available at cpc.people.com.cn/BIG5/64162/64168/64555/4428212.html; Statement of the Chinese Communist Party on the Current Situation (中国共产党对于时局之主张), promulgated in November 1924, available at www.marxists.org/chinese/reference-books/ccp-1921-1949/01/064.htm; Resolutions on Peasant Movement (农民运动议决案), promulgated in July 1926, available at www.marxists.org/chinese/reference-books/ccp-1921-1949/02/042.htm.

[48] Plan of the Chinese Communist Party on the Present Practical Problems (中国共产党对于目前实际问题之计划), promulgated in November 1922, available at www.marxists.org/chinese/reference-books/ccp-1921-1949/01/020.htm; Declaration of the Chinese Communist Party and Communist Youth League: To People Now Fighting for National Liberation (中国共产党中国共产主义青年团宣言: 告此次为民族自由奋斗的民众), promulgated in January 1925, available at www.marxists.org/chinese/reference-books/ccp-1921-1949/01/091.htm.

sustainability of their newly acquired land tenure. Crucially, in the spring of 1931 it resulted in widespread reluctance of the peasants in the revolutionary regions to start agricultural work, which lead to a sharp decrease of agricultural output.[49] Against this backdrop, the long-term goal of land ownership nationalization became detrimental to the revolution in the short run. It not only, as just mentioned, dampened the Party's efforts to win around the mass peasantry, but also undermined economic productivity in the revolutionary areas, which was most vital to the Party's survival at the time. Therefore, the CCP conceded that adherence to private land ownership was in the peasants' nature, and during the democratic revolution stage land nationalization would only be a slogan for propaganda, not a policy for implementation. Only until the revolution succeeded on the national level and the entire country was put under a proletariat–peasant dictatorship would nationalization of land ownership be in motion.[50]

In this light, for the CCP the conferral of private land ownership upon the peasantry was by no means a principled decision but a choice of expediency based on the practical need to attract peasant allegiance and mitigate the disturbance of land redistribution on productivity. But it was through Lenin's two-stage theory that this deviation from classic Marxism and the Russian practice became ideologically justified. In fact, up until the mid-1950s, private land ownership by the peasants was officially recognized and constitutionally enshrined. Article 8 of the 1954 Constitution states that the state guarantees the peasant's land ownership according to law. However, it could not be further from the truth to think that the Party intended to have private land ownership by the peasantry perpetuated. As a matter of fact, the CCP never made any promise to such effect. On the contrary, time and again it cautioned against the belief that private land ownership would be preserved in the long run and emphasized emphatically the socialist future in land collectivization and nationalization.[51] In the eyes of Mao, private land

[49] Land Question and Strategy of Anti-rich-peasants (土地问题与反富农策略), promulgated by Central Party Bureau of Soviet Area on February 8, 1931; Mao Zedong, "Opinions on Strengthening the Work of Spring Ploughing (关于加强春耕工作的意见)," in *Works of Mao Zedong* (毛泽东文集) (Beijing: Renmin Press, 1993), vol. 1; Mao Zedong, "Our Economic Policy (我们的经济政策)," in *Selected Works of Mao Zedong* (毛泽东选集) (Beijing: Renmin Press, 1991), vol. 1.

[50] Central Party Bureau of Soviet Area, Land Question and Strategy of Anti-rich-peasants.

[51] Ibid.; Outline of the Land Question (土地问题提纲), promulgated by Committee of the Chairmen of the Provincial County and District Soviet Governments in Jiangxi in March 1931; Biwu Dong, On the Questions of Rural Production and Burden after

ownership was fundamentally a transient product at the new democratic stage of revolution, which ought to be abandoned once the revolution progressed to the next stage. It was only for pragmatic reasons that private land ownership was accepted.

The same logic also applies to the Party's suspension of land confiscation and distribution between 1937 and 1946. This period witnessed the formation of a national united front between the KMT and the CCP to jointly fight the anti-Japanese invasion war. Internal unity of the Chinese nation as a whole became so imperative to sustaining the war effort that the CCP chose to exempt the landed classes from confiscation in order to reduce domestic friction and consolidate as much support as possible.[52]

The third deviation of the CCP from the Marxist–Soviet tradition of land nationalization was that compulsory purchase for landlords was briefly tried out during the land reform campaign between 1946 and 1947. Such "treason to socialism," in Lenin's view, was accepted by the Party not on the grounds that Marx and Engels once commended it. Rather, it was due to practical reasons not so different from the two cases explained above. As touched upon in the preceding chapter, the CCP Central Committee issued a recommendation in July 1946 to advise local Party agencies to buy out the landlord's land above a certain set maximum while leaving the rest intact.[53] This was employed as the alternative measure to full-scale and noncompensatory confiscation. On this, the Party Central Committee clarified that compulsory purchase of landlords was for fending off criticisms against ruthless land confiscation from "democratic personages" (*minzhu renshi*) and "middle forces" (*zhongjian shili*), namely those political players who were caught in the crossfire between the CCP and the KMT at the time.[54] Hence, it is apparent that

the Land Reform (关于土地改革后农村生产与负担问题), August 21, 1947, available at www.xibaipo.gov.cn/system/2012/05/24/006840706.shtml; Instructions on Developing Rural Production after Land Reform (关于土地改革后农村发展生产的指示), promulgated by Jinchaji Party Bureau on May 6, 1948.

52 Telegraph by the CCP Center to the Third National Congress of the KMT (中共中央给中国国民党三中全会电), promulgated on February 10, 1937, available at cpc.people.com.cn/GB/64184/64186/66641/4490185.html; Task of the CCP during the Anti-Japanese Period (中国共产党在抗日时期的任务), promulgated on May 3, 1937, available at www.marxists.org/chinese/maozedong/marxist.org-chinese-mao-19370503.htm.

53 Recommendation to the Governments of Liberated Areas for Realizing Land to the Tillers (为实现耕者有其田向各解放区政府的提议), promulgated by CCP Central Committee on July 19, 1946.

54 Instructions to Zhou Enlai and Dong Biwu on Explaining Our Party's Land Policies to Members of China Democratic League (关于向民盟人士说明我党土地政策给周恩来董必武的指示), promulgated by CCP Central Committee on July 19, 1946.

choosing moderate and compensatory compulsory purchase over radical and noncompensatory confiscation was more about appeasing the potential allies and consolidating political support than about constraining the practice of confiscation and mitigating its harshness. This was manifested again in a letter from the party branch of the Jinjiluyu revolutionary area to the central Party upon receiving the latter's 1946 instruction:

> [compulsory purchase of land] is somewhat not urgently needed for our region because we adopt a more direct and egalitarian approach to solve the land question here. Everyone agrees that redistribution of land is right and an irresistible trend. Confiscation is about redistributing land (which in the peasants' eyes is returning land to them) and is considered legitimate and reasonable by both landlords and peasants. But to stipulate for compulsory purchase poses no harm and will help solve the land question for families of Party cadres and democratic personages.[55]

Clearly, the less harsh measure of compulsory purchase was intended for the landlords who happened to be related to Party members or allies-to-be. This means that to compulsorily purchase landlords' land had nothing to do with respecting their land rights. Quite the contrary – in 1947 the Party stressed emphatically that to regard compulsory purchase for land reform campaign as purely a transactional relationship was a grave mistake. Instead, it should be deemed as complementary to confiscation, which ought to be the main method to implement redistributive land reform. The moderate measure of compulsory purchase was used mainly to better mobilize the peasants, particularly when they felt uncertain about the legitimacy of sweeping confiscation.[56] In this sense, the CCP chose compulsory purchase only as a stopgap to "get off cheapest." When the civil war broke out in early 1947, the CCP dropped compulsory purchase and reverted to confiscation. The rest is history: the land redistribution movement spread across the country and the mass Chinese peasantry were granted not just land use-rights, but full ownership. Privatization instead of nationalization was the *zeitgeist* of this era.

But that did not last very long. From 1952, the CCP started the socialist transformation movement, the core objective of which was to replace

55 Yibo Bo, "Report on Land Reform in Jinjiluyu Region (薄一波关于晋冀鲁豫地区土地改革情况的报告)," in State Archival Administration (ed.), *Selected Files on Land Reform in Revolutionary War Period* (解放战争时期土地改革文件选编) (Beijing: Zhongyang Dangxiao Press, 1981).

56 Notification on Experiences of Trial Projects on Public Land Debt in Various Locales in Central Shan'ganning Border Region (中共中央陕甘宁边区若干地方试办土地公招经验的通报), promulgated on February 8, 1947.

private ownership of the means of production with a completely public one.[57] The second stage of revolution was triggered and the peasants' recently gained private land ownership was doomed. As noted in the preceding chapter, the 1954 Constitution was set to "fully express the fundamental mandate for China to gradually proceed towards socialism." Article 4 stipulates that the state "guarantees gradual abolishment of exploitive system and establishment of a socialist society through socialist industrialization and socialist transformation." How was this agenda reflected in property-related articles in general, and the original takings clause in particular?

To start with, following the Marxist tradition, the 1954 Constitution devised a property regime rooted in a decisive distinction between the ownership of production means and that of the means of subsistence. The *Communist Manifesto* famously suggested that socialism "deprives no man of the power to appropriate the products of society; all that it does is to deprive him of the power to subjugate the labor of others by means of such appropriations." Accordingly, socialism does not call for abolishment of private property in the general sense. Private property in subsistence means, i.e., the resources that are necessary for survival and used for personal consumption, is not to be abandoned under socialism. Hence, Articles 11–12 of the 1954 Constitution stated that citizen's lawful ownership and right to inheritance of the means of subsistence, including wages, savings and housing, should be guaranteed by the state. In fact, in the pre-reform era, citizens' private property in means of subsistence was called "personal property" (*geren caichan*), so as to differentiate from private property (*siyou caichan*) that bears a more negative connotation because socialism does not tolerate private ownership of the means of production, which is considered intrinsically and inescapably exploitive.[58] Four types of ownership of production means were enumerated in Article 5 of the 1954 Constitution. First, state ownership or ownership of all people (*quanmin suoyou*) is ascribed the utmost priority by Article 6, which obligates the state to guarantee preferential treatment toward the development of state-owned economy. The reason is that state ownership of production means represents the socialist nature of

[57] This was called the Party's "general line during the transitional period" (过渡时期总路线), which was first formulated by Mao Zedong in 1952 and formally elevated to be a Party policy in early 1954.

[58] Yong Xia (ed.), *Towards an Era of Rights: the Development of Chinese Civil Rights* (走向权利的时代: 中国公民权利发展研究) (Beijing: Chinese University of Political Science and Law Press, 1999), p. 295.

the country and is the leading force in the national economy as well as the material basis for China to fulfill socialist transformation. There is consequently no temporal or substantial limitation over state ownership of production means as it is going to last in the long run and will always be in line with the public interest. Article 101 of the 1954 Constitution further emphasizes that public property is sacred and nonviolable and that every citizen has an obligation to cherish and protect it. In the meantime, collective ownership by the working mass is regarded as the other form of socialist property, which according to Article 7 is guaranteed by the state and will be used to transform private ownership of production means in individualized farming and handicraft industries. But, compared with state ownership, collective ownership is not as much prioritized as the state is required constitutionally only to encourage, guide and assist the development of collective economy. In contrast to these two socialist property types, according to Articles 8–10, private ownership of means of production by individual laborers (including peasants, handicraftsmen and so on) and capitalists are nonsocialist and therefore ought to be transformed into collective and state ownership eventually. Yet, during the transitional period such private ownership would still be protected by the state according to law. The underlying reason, however, was not that they are intrinsically worthy of state protection. Instead, as explained by a prominent Party leader in 1956, the main purpose was to keep those private owners incentivized enough to continue work over this transition.[59]

It is therefore apt to say that the property regime established by the 1954 Constitution was intrinsically hierarchical and transitional. Private property in the broad sense could not possibly be recognized as a basic constitutional right. While private ownership of means of subsistence is guaranteed in the long run, private ownership of means of production is to be transformed and ultimately eliminated. This explains why in the 1954 Constitution the abovementioned articles setting out the property system are located in the first chapter on macro state policies rather than in the third chapter on citizen's basic rights and obligations.[60] Private property, in its most crucial aspect related to the means of production,

[59] Da Li (ed.), *Lectures on PRC Constitution* (中华人民共和国宪法讲话) (Beijing: Renmin Press, 1956), p. 85.

[60] For alternative explanations, see Chaoying Gan, "A Historical Review of Constitutional Property System in New China (新中国宪法财产制度的历史回顾)" (2010) 4 *China Legal Science* (中国法学) 144.

was conceptualized more as a state policy toward economic resources than as a right enjoyed by individual citizens vis-à-vis the state.

Against this background, we can understand why China's original takings clause is power-confirming. As mentioned earlier, it applies exclusively to land and other production means. More specifically, under the property system just explained, the state's takings power enshrined in Article 13 targets production means, including land, owned by nonstate actors such as the peasants, capitalists and rural collectives. All these ownership types are inferior to state ownership, and private ownership by peasants and capitalists are inferior to public ownership by the state and collectives. In this situation, transferring private land into the hands of the state by definition strengthens state property, which, as demonstrated above, sits at the pinnacle of the property hierarchy for representing both the nature and the future of the country. In taking land from nonstate owners, the state is not only fulfilling its constitutional duty to prioritize the development of state-owned economy over other forms of ownership, it also pushing forward socialist transformation. Moreover, taking rural agricultural land into the hands of the state was also considered to facilitate China's development from a backward agrarian country into an advanced industrial one.[61] As is well known, China underwent state-driven industrialization in the pre-reform era. Thus, the change of hands of land from individual peasants and rural collectives to the state was typically accompanied by a change of industry from agricultural to industrial production, which is precisely what socialist industrialization is about. Last but not least, it was pointed out that the least-favored private property of production means, apart from being restrained temporally in the sense that it would eventually be abolished, should also be subject to substantive limitations over the transitional period in both negative and positive terms. While Article 14 sets the negative limitation that it cannot be used to harm public interest, Article 13 lays down the positive limitation that it must yield to public interest when facing state takings.[62] Overall, development of state property, industrialization of the country and limitation upon private

[61] Peihua Liu (ed.), *Outlines of Lectures on the PRC Constitution* (中华人民共和国宪法讲课提纲) (Beijing: Liaoning Renmin Press, 1957), p. 80; State Law Teaching and Research Office of Central Political-Legal Cadres School (ed.), *Teaching Materials on the PRC Constitution* (中华人民共和国宪法讲义) (Beijing: Falv Press, 1957), p. 158.

[62] Youyu Zhang, *Essays on Constitutionalism* (宪政论丛) (Beijing: Qunzhong Press, 1986), vol. 2, p. 41; Bangyan Lou, *Basic Knowledge of PRC Constitution* (中华人民共和国宪法基本知识) (Beijing: Xinzhi Press, 1955), pp. 93–94.

property were all part of the fundamental mandate of socialist industrialization and transformation and are therefore manifestations of the public interest. Hence, state land takings are supposed to be necessarily in the public interest and the purpose of the original takings clause could be nothing but power-confirming.

That being said, it is well known that the PRC has never gone so far as to nationalize all land. The USSR's experience was not duplicated and the socialist revolutionary project of complete land nationalization did not quite reach the projected end state in China. On the contrary, to this day, collective land ownership stays side by side with state ownership and the possibility of full-scale nationalization is dim, the reason for which will be explored more fully in the next chapter. Suffice it to say here that in terms of its post-revolution land system, China had basically imported the Soviet Russian model. First, considered as a critical economic resource, land was managed exclusively by the state according to economic planning, making land administration an integral part of the state's economic administration. Urban land was allocated by local governments free of charge to state agencies, SOEs, public–private joint ventures and so forth, on a need basis.[63] In rural areas, although the collectives formally owned land after the collectivization movement, in most cases it was actually the state that had the final say on the use and disposal of rural collective land because the collective leaders were usually appointed by and therefore acted as agents of the state. In this situation, urban and rural land effectively became a state-managed resource for the purposes of production or welfare provision to urban and rural residents.[64] Second, under an exclusively state-run land administration system, both urban and rural land markets were closed down and voluntary transactions of land forbidden. Given that land could not change hands freely, if there was an adjustment of the economic plan that necessitated alteration in the

[63] Part 1, Central Administrative Council, Reply on Several Issues of Charging Deed Tax or Rent on Requisition of Privately Owned Land and Use of State-owned Land by State-owned Enterprises, Public-Private Joint Ventures, Private Enterprises and so on (答复关于国营企业、公私合营企业及私营企业等征用私有土地及使用国有土地缴纳契税或租金的几个问题), promulgated by Ministry of Domestic Affairs on March 8, 1954, available at www.110.com/fagui/law_58160.html; part 5, Comprehensive Reply on Several Questions concerning the Implementation of the Measures on Land Requisition for State-led Construction (关于执行国家建设征用土地办法中几个问题的综合答复), promulgated by Ministry of Domestic Affairs on April 27, 1954, available at china.findlaw.cn/fagui/p_1/212345.html.

[64] Xueyang Cheng, "How was the Rural Land Collectivized (农村土地是如何被集体化的)," January 29, 2014, available at www.zgxcfx.com/Article/63660.html.

current use of a piece of urban land, the state would have to withdraw such land first and then re-allocate it.[65] Third, following the USSR model, withdrawal of state-owned land was noncompensatory, though the state shall properly resettle those affected and compensate for any properties on such land.[66] It is worth noting that while the first two features have changed dramatically in the reform era, the noncompensability of urban land withdrawal has persisted and was only changed in recent years, which will be discussed in the next chapter.

To summarize, despite several notable deviations driven by pragmatic considerations in light of local conditions, the Marxist–Soviet tradition of land nationalization in both its revolutionary strategies and the post-revolution land regime was largely adhered to in pre-reform China. Previous discussion shows that the original takings clause in 1954 was shaped by, and in turn epitomized, such a tradition. Worth noting is that the socialist program was only half of the historical experiences of land nationalization in modern China. As is well known, the rival nationalist party also avowed to realize nationalization of land.

5.1.2 Nationalist Tradition of Land Nationalization

At first sight, the nationalist land program devised by Sun Yat-sen might appear quite similar to the communist one since it also claimed to pursue nationalization of land. As will be demonstrated, however, they were different in both philosophy and policy.

Similar to the Marxist position, Sun Yat-sen was dismissive of private land ownership. He considered it an intrinsic injustice because land is a naturally given material that predates and outlasts human beings and should belong to all equally.[67] On a more practical note, convinced by the American political economist Henry George, Sun regarded private

[65] Parts 3–4, Notice on Correcting and Stopping Waste in Land Requisition for State-led Construction (关于纠正与防止国家建设征用土地中浪费现象的通知), promulgated by State Council on January 24, 1956, available at china.findlaw.cn/fagui/p_1/163304.html; art. 21, Revised Draft Regulation on the Work in the Rural People's Communes (农村人民公社工作条例修正草案), promulgated by CCP Central Committee on September 27, 1962, available at www.360doc.com/content/15/0118/10/20762552_441736973.shtml.

[66] Regulation on the Administration of Land Use for Buildings in Villages and Townships (村镇建房用地管理条例), art. 13; 1953 MLRSC, art. 9; 1958 MLRSC, art. 18.

[67] Sun Yat-sen, "Speech to the Chinese Socialist Party in Shanghai (在上海中国社会党的演说)," in *Collected Works of Sun Yat-sen* (孙中山全集) (Beijing: Zhonghua Book Company, 1982), vol. 2, p. 514.

land ownership as undesirable and counterproductive.[68] According to George, there are three productive sources in a society: land, labor and capital. Their products are, respectively, rent, wage and interest, the sum of which constitutes the total output of a society. In this situation, at any given level of productivity, rent is inversely related to wage and interest. Land monopoly and speculation based on private ownership of land will therefore drive up rent and squeeze wage for labor and interest for capital investment.[69] Accordingly, Sun suggested that private land ownership was an impediment to China's industrialization as it diverted capital investment from productive industries to unproductive land speculation.[70] Furthermore, reflecting on his tour of Europe and America in the early 1900s, Sun identified private land ownership as the root cause of endemic inequality and poverty in the West.[71] His favored solution was nationalization of land, which in his view would facilitate industrialization and prevent its attendant misery in China.

But Sun's specific measures to nationalize land were very different from the CCP's. Most notably, he resolutely rejected compensationless confiscation, even though he admitted it to be a strategy of "thorough revolution."[72] This was due to the following three reasons. First, Sun saw confiscation as a sure way to generate great resistance from the landowners, which he believed would devastate the fledgling revolution.[73] Second, Sun thought that China was not ready for land confiscation and nationalization. He remarked that even Russia had to adopt the New Economic Policy to give room for private land ownership because it was too undeveloped economically. Since China was no more developed than

[68] The impact of Henry George on Sun's land program has been well documented and analyzed. See Richard W Lindholm and Sein Lin, *Henry George and Sun Yat-sen: Application and Evolution of their Land Use Doctrine* (Cambridge, MA: Lincoln Institute, 1977); Sein Lin, "Sun Yat-sen and Henry George: The Essential Role of Land Policy in Their Doctrines" (1974) 33 *The American Journal of Economics and Sociology* 201.

[69] Henry George, *Progress and Poverty* (Garden City: Doubleday, Page, & Co, 1912), book 3, chapter 2.

[70] Sun Yat-sen, "Speech at the Welcoming Event of the Press in Guangzhou (在广州报届欢迎会的演说)," in *Collected Works of Sun Yat-sen* (孙中山全集) (Beijing: Zhonghua Book Company, 1982), vol. 2.

[71] Sun Yat-sen, "Speech at the Anniversary Celebration Ceremony of the Ming Paper in Tokyo (在东京明报创刊周年庆祝大会的演说)," in *Collected Works of Sun Yat-sen* (孙中山全集) (Beijing: Zhonghua Book Company, 1982), vol. 1, p. 327.

[72] Sun Yat-sen, "Speech at the Graduation Ceremony of the First Peasant Movement Institute in Guangdong (在广东农民运动讲席所第一届毕业典礼的演说)," in *Collected Works of Sun Yat-sen* (孙中山全集) (Beijing: Zhonghua Book Company, 1986), vol. 10, p. 556.

[73] Ibid., pp. 557–58.

Russia, it should do the same too.[74] Third, on a deeper level, Sun had a different interpretation of human history from Marxism. He rejected the notion that class revolution is the locomotive of history, but held that "the primary force of human evolution is cooperation, not struggle":[75] "The reason for social progress lies in the harmony of the majority of economic interests in a society, not in their conflict";[76] "Class war is by no means the reason for social evolution but a disease that appears in the process of social evolution." "Marx was less a "physiologist" than a "pathologist" of human society."[77] On these grounds, Sun preferred a "slow and peaceful" way to achieve land nationalization. Though he did acknowledge the need for the nationalist party to ally with the mass Chinese peasantry, he held that the interests of landed proprietors should also be attended to and a win-win settlement be strived for.[78]

The win-win settlement for Sun Yat-sen and his nationalist party was three-pronged. The core element was the introduction of a single land tax, initially conceived by Henry George, who famously claimed that:

> Let the individuals who now hold it still retain, if they want to, possession of what they are pleased to call their land. Let them continue to call it their land. Let them buy and sell, and bequeath and devise it. We may safely leave them the shell, if we take the kernel. It is not necessary to confiscate land; it is only necessary to confiscate rent . . . in this way the State may become the universal landlord without calling herself so, and without assuming a single new function.[79]

Following George, Sun proposed imposing land value tax to reduce land monopoly and enhance efficiency in land use.[80] Most critical is the determination of land value as the tax base. Diverging from George, Sun made his original contribution in suggesting that the owners themselves should report to the state such base land value. Naturally this poses a risk of under-reporting, a problem Sun was well aware of. His second

[74] Sun Yat-sen, "First Lecture on the Principle of People's Livelihood under Three Principles of the People (三民主义民生主义第一讲)," in *Collected Works of Sun Yat-sen* (孙中山全集) (Beijing: Zhonghua Book Company, 1986), vol. 9, pp. 391–92.

[75] Sun Yat-sen, *The International Development of China* (New York: Putnam's Sons, 1922).

[76] Sun Yat-sen, "First Lecture on the Principle of People's Livelihood under Three Principles of the People."

[77] Ibid.

[78] Sun Yat-sen, "Speech at the Graduation Ceremony of the First Peasant Movement Institute in Guangdong," pp. 555–58.

[79] George, *Progress and Poverty*, book 8, chapter 2.

[80] Sun Yat-sen, "Speech at the Anniversary Celebration Ceremony of the Ming Paper in Tokyo"; Sun Yat-sen, "Speech to the Chinese Socialist Party in Shanghai." The difference between Sun and George was that Sun did not propose abolition of other types of taxation.

proposal was that the state retains the power to compulsorily purchase (*shoumai*) private land at the reported base value whenever necessary in the future.[81] In Sun's opinion, this would make private landowners report a fair base value: there will be no over-reporting because the reported value is the benchmark for land value tax, and there will be no under-reporting because the reported value will be the price for potential compulsory purchase by the state.

The second measure for land nationalization proposed by Sun was to let the state appropriate all increment of land value,[82] the justification for which was twofold. First, he argued that the rise in land value should not be attributed to its private owners but to external factors such as urban development brought by successful revolution. Therefore, it is unjust for individual owners to harvest all the windfall profits. Second, Sun believed that nationalizing increased land value would purvey the nascent revolutionary government with the much-needed financial resources to cover the costs of public administration and services.[83] The way in which such nationalization of land increment value is going to happen, according to Sun, is that land sale should become a state prerogative and the private land market be prohibited, making state compulsory purchase the only way for landowners to alienate their land at the original reported price. This will ensure that all value increment falls into the public coffer and prevent private landowners from obtaining any unearned benefits.[84]

The third element in the nationalist program of land nationalization is the state's taking of private land. In contrast to the socialist tradition, as mentioned, compulsory purchase, rather than confiscation, was the preferred approach. A further difference is that in Sun Yat-sen's view "not all land should fall into state ownership and it is adequate if the state just owns what it needs."[85] Three scenarios under which the state needs to

[81] Sun Yat-sen, "Speech at the Farware Party with the Nanjing United League Members (在南京同盟会会员饯别会的演说)," in *Collected Works of Sun Yat-sen* (孙中山全集) (Beijing: Zhonghua Book Company, 1982), vol. 2, p. 321.

[82] Sun Yat-sen, "Speech to the Chinese Socialist Party in Shanghai," p. 522.

[83] Sun Yat-sen, "Second Lecture on the Principle of People's Livelihood under Three Principles of the People (三民主义民生主义第二讲)," in *Collected Works of Sun Yat-sen* (孙中山全集) (Beijing: Zhonghua Book Company, 1986), vol. 9, p. 390.

[84] Sun Yat-sen, "The Means of Introducing Local Self-Government (地方自治开始实行法)," in Yan Huang (ed.), *Selected Works of Sun Yat-sen* (孙文选集) (Guangzhou: Guangdong Renmin Press, 2006), vol. 2.

[85] Sun Yat-sen, "Speech to Parliamentarian and Journalists at Xingyuan in Guangzhou (在广州行辕对议员记者的演说)," in *Collected Works of Sun Yat-sen* (孙中山全集) (Beijing: Zhonghua Book Company, 1982), vol. 2.

compulsorily purchase land were suggested by Sun. First is the construction of public works, such as roads and markets, which will be discussed in more detail in the next section.[86] Second is economic development at a general level. Sun envisaged that "in the future, the public authority will definitely need land for local development" and "inevitably provincial capital will be expanded and land be taken for such development."[87] To facilitate such large-scale government-led economic development, he put forth a concrete policy proposal based on the separation between de jure and de facto nationalization. Sun remarked that to build an oriental New York out of Shanghai, the government might not be able to afford to purchase upfront all the land needed. But it could first make the declaration in law to nationalize an entire area without paying any compensation or actually acquiring physical possession. After such de jure nationalization, original landowners in that area lose the right of alienation (i.e. to sell the land), but they can continue using the land until the de facto nationalization – that is, when the state compulsorily purchases their land with compensation and transfer of physical possession. As the initial de jure nationalization effectively freezes the private land market and land value of an area, the state can start with compulsorily purchasing the first allotment of land at the original land price and developing the area. As a result, land value in this area rises and the local government's financial capacity is enhanced. It could then move to the second phase of de facto nationalization by gradually purchasing the rest of the land in that area with enhanced fiscal capability, yet still at the original price frozen under the de jure nationalization.[88] In this way, Sun envisaged that the state would ultimately afford all the land needed for economic development. The third scenario under which the state may find compulsory purchase of land necessary is when it needs stop land speculation and monopoly. Discussing developing the Chinese border regions of Mongolia and Xinjiang, Sun wrote that the state should buy up the land in those regions and divide it into farmsteads, which could then be offered to landless peasants for cultivation. The aim was to "prevent

[86] Sun Yat-sen, "Speech at the Welcoming Event of the Press in Guangzhou," p. 355.

[87] Sun Yat-sen, "Speech to Parliamentarian and Journalists at Xingyuan in Guangzhou," p. 370.

[88] Sun Yat-sen, *The International Development of China*, pp. 34–35. In the same book, he offered a similar analysis in respect of railway construction in Guangdong: "If all the future city sites and mining lands could be taken up by the Government before railway construction is started, the profit would be enormous. Thus no matter how large a sum is invested in railway construction, the payment of its interest and principal will be assured."

the speculators from creating the dog-in-the-manger system that is to the detriment of the public."[89]

In conclusion, diverging from the socialist tradition, Sun Yat-sen came up with his own unique program of land nationalization. As explained, his objective is not to overturn the entire system of private landed property through confiscation, redistribution and public land ownership. Rather, it is to alleviate the negative consequences of private land ownership through a mixture of less radical measures such as land value tax, state appropriation of land value increment and potential compulsory purchase. In his final years, Sun Yat-sen came to realize the crucial importance of winning over the mass peasantry and thus called for "land to the tiller,"[90] a move that made his land policy somewhat closer to that of the communists. But it is mistaken to think that his land program became indistinguishable.[91] As a matter of fact, the banner "land-to-the-tiller" meant very different things to the CCP and to Sun and his nationalist party. Throughout the years when the KMT held power in the mainland, it never went beyond alleviating the burden of tenant peasants through compulsory reduction of land rent to full-scale land confiscation and redistribution.[92] After all, as Sun pointed out, the nationalist party did not want to topple the pre-existing land ownership structure, but only demanded reallocation of land rent and increased land value. This is, in Sun's own words, also communism, though he advocated for "communization of the future" as opposed to "communization of the present" by the communists.[93] Widely known, however, is

89 Ibid., p. 24.

90 Sun Yat-sen, "Speech at the Graduation Ceremony of the First Peasant Movement Institute in Guangdong," p. 555.

91 The KMT and the CCP established the first united revolutionary front in 1924. But when asked if the nationalist party was implementing Russian policies, Sun claimed that what he appreciated about Soviet Russia was merely the organizational aspect of the revolutionary party, not the substantive revolutionary "ism" it upheld. See Yongying Xu, "Meeting Mr. Sun Yat-sen (见孙中山先生记)," in *Materials on Modern History* (近代史资料) (Beijing: Zhongguo Shehui Kexu Press, 1988), vol. 68, pp. 183–84.

92 Sun Yat-sen, "Third Lecture on the Principle of People's Livelihood under Three Principles of the People (三民主义民生主义第三讲)," in *Collected Works of Sun Yat-sen* (孙中山全集) (Beijing: Zhonghua Book Company, 1986), vol. 9; Sun Yat-sen, "Speech at the Graduation Ceremony of the First Peasant Movement Institute in Guangdong," p. 558. It is worth mentioning that the KMT did promise to provide those landless tenant peasants with state-owned land for cultivation. However, this was not implemented before the KMT was defeated in the mainland and driven to Taiwan.

93 Sun Yat-sen, "Second Lecture on the Principle of People's Livelihood under Three Principles of the People."

that the nationalist nationalization program had long been criticized as half-hearted and reactionary by the CCP. Nevertheless, these two traditions of land nationalization share a fundamental commonality, which will be discussed in the end of this chapter. Before that, we now turn to the power of compensatory land takings.

5.2 Land Expropriation: From Classical Liberalism to Socialized Property

As noted in the preceding chapter, the power of compensatory land expropriation for public works in the 1954 constitutional takings clause (the exact term used was "requisition") originated from relevant legislation in the CCP revolutionary border areas in the 1930s. In particular, the *Land Regulation of Shan'ganning Border Region* and the *Draft Regulation on Land Rights of Shan'ganning Border Region*, both passed in April 1939, were the first legal documents enacted by the communist government that provided for land expropriation. Despite the different terms deployed,[94] they both stipulated that the government might take private land with compensation for road, military facilities, public buildings, municipal works and other undertakings in the public interest. Interestingly, since these regulations were passed under the Anti-Japanese United Front when the communist party recognized the KMT government in Nanjing as the sole legitimate national government of China, they explicitly stated that they were made in accordance with the basic principles of the land law promulgated by the Nanjing government,[95] which was the 1930 *Land Law of the Republic of China*. Therefore, to understand the land expropriation law in the communist revolutionary areas, perhaps somewhat surprisingly, we must first make sense of the basic principles of land law in general and land expropriation law in particular under the nationalist regime, the origin and evolution of which are discussed in the following texts.

[94] Expropriation (征收) was used in the Land Regulation of Shan'ganning Border Region (arts. 18–19), while requisition (征用) was used in the Draft Regulation on Land Rights of Shan'ganning Border Region (art. 25). The reason behind this was unclear. But these terms had the same meaning.

[95] Art. 1, Draft Regulation on Land Rights of Shan'ganning Border Region (陕甘宁边区地权条例草案), promulgated by Shan'ganning Border Region Government in April 1939; art.1, Land Regulation of Shan'ganning Border Region (陕甘宁边区土地条例), promulgated by Shan'ganning Border Region Government on April 4, 1939.

5.2.1 Classical Liberal Origin of Land Expropriation Law

It was during the late nineteenth century that the legal concept of land expropriation was imported to China. In an officially commissioned 1888 Chinese translation of the 1804 French Civil Code, Article 545 stated that no one should be compelled to transfer his property to others unless such transfers greatly benefit the public and the owner is fairly reimbursed (*buhuan*) for the value of the property. Far from an accurate rendering,[96] this was nevertheless the first discussion of compensatory land taking as a legal concept in China.[97] However, at that time no specific Chinese term was used to refer to the action of takings. Nearly two decades later, in 1907, through translating the 1900 Japanese Land Acquisition Act (*tochi shuyo ho*) into Chinese, the word acquisition (*shouyong*) was chosen,[98] which was further formalized into the first Chinese legal term for compensatory land takings by the *Land Acquisition Law* enacted by the Beiyang government in 1915.

Following the suit of the 1900 Japanese Land Acquisition Act, for the first time in modern Chinese history, the 1915 *Land Acquisition Law* systematically covered the purpose, procedure, compensation and dispute resolution of land acquisition.[99] It was stipulated that with the approval of the president of the Republic of China and for the purpose

[96] Article 545 in French reads, "Nul ne peut être contraint de céder sa propriété, si ce n'est pour cause d'utilité publique, et moyennant une juste et préalable indemnité." The typical English translation is "No one can be compelled to give up his property, except for the public good, and for a just and previous indemnity." See *The Code Napoleon, or, The French Civil Code* (London: Thomas Davison, 1824), p. 150. But it should be noted that "préalable" is better translated not as "previous" but as "prior" because the article means that indemnity must be paid before expropriation takes place, which was completely missed in the Chinese translation.

[97] Anatole Billequin, *French Statutes of Codification* (法国律例) (School of Combined Learning, 1880), part 3, art. 545, cited in Ruiqing Wang, "The Evolution of the Idea of Land Expropriation in Modern China from the Perspective of Academic Research (学术史视野下近代中国土地征收思想的演进)" (2011) 4 *Journal of South China Agricultural University* (华南农业大学学报) 108. The Qing government tasked the famous School of Combined Learning (京师同文馆) to translate a set of French statutes including the criminal law, civil law, civil procedural law, etc. Code Civil was translated as "minlv," now called "minfa." For a comparison between this earliest translation and later versions, see Guilian Li, "Three Versions of Chinese Translations of the French Civil Code (《法国民法典》的三个中文译本)" (1993) 1 *Journal of Comparative Law* (比较法研究) 86.

[98] *New Translated Collection of Japanese Statutes* (新译日本法规大全) (Shanghai: China Commercial Press, 2008), vol. 6, pp. 86–109.

[99] The Chinese text of this law can be found in *The New Compilation of Laws and Regulation of the Republic of China* (最新编订民国法令大全) (Shanghai: China Commercial Press, 1924), pp. 516–18.

of public interest, the central government and subprovincial governments might compulsorily acquire land (Articles 1 and 25). It copied Article 1 of the 1900 Japanese Land Acquisition Act to include a list of public interest items such as national defense, infrastructure development, educational and charitable enterprises and government buildings (Article 2). Standard of compensation was set to be the market price of land and the fixtures and crops thereon (Article 7). The exact amount of compensation, however, could be negotiated, in the case of acquisition by the national government, between the initiating central governmental department and the local land acquisition appraisal committee comprising representatives of local officials and gentry (Articles 17 and 21), or between the local government and landowners if the acquisition is initiated at the local level (Article 18). Once compensation is settled, the acquirer may request land conveyance within a prescribed period, during which it must also make full payment of compensation to the acquiree (Article 32). Failing to do so without good cause will void the settled agreement of acquisition and entitle the landowners to seek indemnity for any loss incurred (Article 33). If any dispute arises, landowners may choose to pursue administrative petition to the government or file suit in court (Articles 19–20, Article 36). Pending judgment, the acquirer can request urgent conveyance of land when required by the public interest, but the agreed compensation must be paid if demanded by the acquiree (Article 35).

In imposing these substantive and procedural limitations over land takings, the 1915 *Land Acquisition Law* was an embodiment of the classical liberal conception of private property. But for two reasons that was less a homegrown tradition than a result of foreign influence. First, as already noted, the legal concept of compensatory land takings was initially imported into China by way of translating the 1804 French Civil Code, the takings clause of which found its origin in the 1789 Declaration of the Rights of Man.[100] As is well known, these two documents are both canonical texts of classical liberalism. Meanwhile, also already mentioned is that China's own first statutory expression of compensatory land takings in 1915 was a transplant of the 1900 Japanese law. As a matter of fact, the latter was a legal transplant too. The 1889 Meiji constitution of

[100] Lynn Hunt (ed.), *The French Revolution and Human Rights: A Brief Documentary History* (Boston and New York: Bedford/St. Martin's, 1996), p. 79. Article 17 reads, "Property being an inviolable and sacred right, no one may be deprived of it except when public necessity, certified by law, obviously requires it, and on the condition of a just compensation in advance."

Japan prescribes in Article 27 that "The right of property of every Japanese subject shall remain inviolate. Measures necessary to be taken for the public benefit shall be provided for by law." This was an imperfect replica of Article 9 of the 1850 Imperial Constitution of Prussia, which reads, "Property is inviolable. It shall only be taken or interfered with considerations of public weal, and then only in a manner to be prescribed by law, and in return for a compensation to be previously determined."[101] Apparently, the requirement of compensation for property takings was left out by the 1889 Meiji constitution, which was widely perceived as problematic at the time. But before long this problem was addressed, as the 1900 Land Acquisition Act was brought in line with the German model in ordering compensation for land takings (Article 48).[102] As a result of transplanting the Japanese law that was itself a transplant from nineteenth-century German law, the earliest legal expression of compensatory land takings in modern Chinese history found its root in the European classical liberal tradition, a brief discussion of which is warranted here.

Compensatory land takings had existed in Europe since antiquity and had long been taken for granted.[103] Yet, sophisticated theoretical discussion of related issues only emerged in the early seventeenth century, pioneered by none other than the famed Dutch jurist Hugo Grotius. Not only did he coin the term *dominium eminens*, which later became "eminent domain" in English;[104] more importantly, he was the first to formulate a principled justification for compulsory takings by the state based on a theory of the origin of private property. His reasoning can be summarized as follows. Under what Grotius called the "primitive state," people had only use-rights to what was bequeathed by God as the common possession of all men.[105] To the extent that using often

101 Wilhelm Röhl (ed.), *History of Law in Japan Since 1868* (Leiden: Brill, 2005), pp. 207–8.

102 Yixiong Jiang, "On the Compensation System of Public Use Expropriation in Japanese Law (日本法上公用征收补偿制度之探讨)" (1998) 13 *National Chung Chen University Law Journal* (中正大学法学集刊) 9.

103 Susan Reynolds, *Before Eminent Domain: Toward a History of Expropriation of Land for the Common Good* (Chapel Hill: University of North Carolina Press, 2010), p. 85.

104 It should be noted, though, that according to Grotius the term had a much broader connotation to stand for the sovereign's general right over its subjects and their property, including the right of taxation. Ibid., p. 95.

105 Hugo Grotius, *On the Law of War and Peace* (A. C. Campbell tr., New York: M. W. Walter Dunne, 1901), book 1, chapter 1, section 10. It is a common theme in natural law theories that the world exists for the preservation of mankind, which can be traced back to Thomas Aquinas. See Stephen Buckle, *Natural Law and the Theory of Property: Grotius to Hume* (Oxford: Clarendon Press, 1993), pp. 12–13.

amounted to using up, the original use-rights did mean that the initial user could effectively exclude others.[106] But this was not private ownership in the sense of exclusive property, which according to Grotius came into existence only when human beings left the idyllic primitive state characterized by abundance of material goods. Facing increasing conflicts over access to limited resources, people gradually found it necessary to recognize previous private possession of the common inheritance as private property, the objective of which was to secure stable and peaceful enjoyment of resources for all. This eventually gave rise to the positive legal recognition of private ownership.[107] Over this process, people surrendered their natural rights to use resources to the society in exchange for a more organized and thus more reliable property regime. As part of this social contract, individuals are obliged to obey society, which has "a higher right over the property of the citizens than the citizens themselves." To Grotius, who lived in an age of absolutism, it was the sovereign state that should naturally represent the entire society and thereby have the higher right over private properties than their owners. That is the power of compulsory acquisition.[108]

The above justification, however, entails important limitations upon the takings power. Grotius wrote that the sovereign state had the right to dispose of its subjects' property "on all occasions, where the public good is concerned." But it must repair the owners' losses at the public expense.[109] This is because public good is the sole reason for people to enter into organized society and the property regime in the first place. Therefore, it must be the case that "the original framers of society intended that private interests should give way" to the public good. When that happens, Grotius argued that compensation ought to be paid to the sufferers who had contributed their due proportion to the public good.[110]

As it turned out, Grotius paved the way for European theorists of subsequent generations. Some public purpose was since considered a prerequiste to government takings of private property, though it was

106 Buckle, *Natural Law and the Theory of Property*, pp. 13–14.

107 Grotius, *On the Law of War and Peace*, book 2, chapter 2, section 2.

108 Hugo Grotius, *The Introduction to Dutch Jurisprudence* (Charles Herbert tr., London: John Van Voorst, 1845), pp. 72–74.

109 Grotius, *On the Law of War and Peace*, book 3, chapter 20, section 7. A similar statement can also be found in book 2, chapter 14, section 7, "it [eminent domain] must be for some public advantage, and then the subject ought to receive, if possible, a just satisfaction for the loss he suffers, out of the common stock."

110 Ibid.

captured by different theorists with different terms. For instance, while Grotius used "public good," it was "public safety" for Swiss philosopher Emer de Vattel, "public use" for French jurist Jean Domat, "public necessity" for German jurist Samuel Pufendorf[111] and "public utility" for Dutch theorist Cornelius van Bynkershoek.[112] Across the Atlantic, in 1690 the English philosopher John Locke emphatically argued that the government can legitimately exercise authority delegated by the people, including the power to take one's property, only to serve the "public good."[113] That being said, it has been suggested that none of these terms were defined precisely and might have meant very different things.[114] Similarly, while the need to compensate for takings of private property was generally agreed upon, opinions diverged on the underlying rationale, which can be divided into two most representative camps of thought. On the one hand, Pufendorf argued that "natural equity" requires no one to bear a greater burden than others to the public good and that whatever exceeds his just share must be refunded.[115] On the other hand, Montesquieu suggested that, as a matter of principle, individuals should not sacrifice private property to serve public interest because the latter consists in everyone having his property. If takings must take place, the individual shall be regarded "as the whole community" and be indemnified because "the public is in this respect like an individual who treats with an individual."[116]

Despite their obvious differences, these early modern European thinkers were united in classical liberalism in the following three senses. First, they were primarily concerned with the protection of individuals' private property, which to them was the reason people entered into civil society

[111] William D. McNulty, "Eminent Domain in Continental Europe" (1912) 21 *Yale Law Journal* 560.

[112] Michael Taggart, "Expropriation, Public Purpose and the Constitution," in Christopher Forsyth and Ivan Hare (eds.), *The Golden Metwand and the Crooked Cord: Essays in Honour of Sir William Wade QC* (Oxford: Oxford University Press, 1998), p. 95.

[113] John Locke, *Second Treatise of Government* (Indianapolis and Cambridge: Hackett Publishing Company, 1980), p. 8.

[114] William B. Stoebuck, "A General Theory of Eminent Domain" (1972) 47 *Washington Law Review* 586.

[115] Samuel Pufendorf, *De Jure Naturae et Gentium* (trans. Charles Henry Oldfather and William Abbott Oldfather; London: H. Milford, 1934), cited in Stoebuck, "A General Theory of Eminent Domain," 584. See also Pufendorf, *De Officio Hominis et Civis* (Oxford: Oxford University Press, 1927), title 2, chapter 15, section 4, cited in McNulty, "Eminent Domain in Continental Europe," 560.

[116] Montesquieu, *The Spirit of Laws* (Thomas Nugent tr., London: George Bell and Sons, 1912), book 26, chapter 15.

and thereby constitutes the *raison d'être* for legitimate government and law. Second, they shared a conception of property that was both individualistic and absolute. The individualistic conception of property was manifested by Montesquieu when he advised that individual property owners should be treated on a par with the entire community because public interest is no more than the sum of private interests and the collective whole has no conceptual priority over the individual. The same point was made more bluntly by William Blackstone, who suggested that in eminent domain "the public is considered as an individual, treating with an individual for an exchange."[117] Besides, private property was considered as absolute, though not in the extreme sense that it could never be outweighed in any circumstance. Rather, it is absolute for having no positive obligation imposed upon it as a priori. The freedom from external, especially state, interference is the presumed default position, requiring any form of intervention to be justified. Last but not least, as a result of the previous two points, land taking by the state was regarded as an exceptional occurrence under stringent restrictions of one kind or another. For instance, Bynkershoek insisted that public utility is the sole ground for property takings without exception.[118] Grotius argued that the state was never relieved of the burden of compensation and must fulfill such obligation whenever possible.[119]

Such a classical liberal tradition of private property and government power of takings lasted in Europe until the eighteenth and nineteenth centuries, which was embodied in texts no less influential than the 1789 Declaration of Rights of Man,[120] the 1804 French Civil Code[121] and the 1850 Prussian constitution.[122] As noted earlier, both the ideas and the

[117] William Blackstone, *Commentaries on the Laws of England in Four Books* (Philadelphia: J.B. Lippincott Co., 1893), vol. 1, book 1, chapter 1.

[118] Cornelius van Bynkershoek, *Questions of Public Law* (Tenney Frank tr., London: Clarendon, 1930), book 2, chapter 15. He suggested that expropriation to gratify the pleasure of the public or for the adornment of public places was illegitimate even with compensation.

[119] Grotius, *On the Law of War and Peace*, book 3, chapter 20, section 7.

[120] Apart from Article 17 (the expropriation clause cited above), Article 2 reads, "The aim of every political association is the preservation of the natural and imprescriptible rights of man. These rights are liberty, property, security, and resistance to oppression."

[121] The above-cited Article 545 was the takings clause. Article 544 reads, "Property is the right to use and control things in the most absolute manner provided this use and control are not prohibited by the law."

[122] In addition to Article 9 of the takings clause, Article 42 reads, "The right of free disposal of the landed property is subject to no other restrictions than those of the general legislation."

legal rules of compensatory land expropriation in early-twentieth-century China were in one way or another influenced by these documents, exemplified most vividly by the 1915 *Land Acquisition Law* analyzed above. However, it was not long before the classical liberal tradition turned out to be a pill too difficult to swallow for the nationalist government, and it was consequently replaced by a different theory of private property and takings power.

5.2.2 Evolution to the Theory of Socialized Property

Recall that under the nationalist program of land nationalization conceived by Sun Yat-sen the state may compulsorily purchase land at the original reported price for such ends as building public works, facilitating and funding local economic development and stopping land monopoly and speculation. As promised in the manifesto of the KMT's first national congress in 1924, this nationalist land program would be legalized through a series of statutes, including one under the name *Land Expropriation Law*.[123] It was not until 1928, when the military campaign of the KMT's Northern Expedition ended and the demand on private land for local infrastructure building began to rise, that the nationalist government felt prompted to promulgate its own land takings law.[124] The draft legislation was prepared by the state legal bureau and was modeled on the 1915 *Land Acquisition Law* passed by the Beiyang government with the same title. However, when submitted to the KMT party center for approval, the draft was significantly revised and the 1915 model was abandoned by the finalized legislation enacted in July 1928.[125] Most notably, the title was changed from *Land Acquisition Law* to *Land Expropriation Law*, with the term "acquisition" (*shouyong*) replaced by "expropriation" (*zhengshou*) in order to be in line with the aforementioned 1924 KMT manifesto.[126] As technical as it seemed at the time, this

[123] Milton J.T. Shieh, *The Kuomintang: Selected Historical Documents, 1894–1969* (New York: St. John's University Press, 1970), p. 84.

[124] Yiguang Tu, *Comparative Study of Land Expropriation* (土地征收之比较研究) (Taipei: Chengwen Press, 1981), p. 98.

[125] The Chinese text of the 1928 Land Expropriation Law is available at wk.baidu.com.cn /view/ee25b8fb910ef12d2af9e7a8?pu=.

[126] There was a published suggestion to this effect made by one member of the KMT's central political committee on the draft law in 1928, which was obviously taken on board in the end. See Jiqing Zhu, "Opinions on the Land Acquisition Law of the Central Political Committee Member Zhu Jiqing (对土地收用法之意见)" (1928) 6 *Bank Weekly* (银行周报) 52.

terminological adjustment chose expropriation to be the Chinese term for compensatory takings of land ownership, which has nowadays become the established practice across the Taiwan Strait. In addition, there were four differences between the 1915 *Land Acquisition Law* and the 1928 *Land Expropriation Law* that are illustrative of a fundamental shift in the prevailing theory of property in early twentieth-century China.

As a starter, emulating the 1915 *Land Acquisition Law*, the draft version of the 1920 expropriation law prescribed that only the president of the state could approve land expropriation. This, however, was thought to be impractical by the nationalist party center given the rapidly increased demand of land expropriation for development across the country. Therefore, Article 8 of the finalized statute authorized both the Ministry of Domestic Affairs and provincial governments to sanction land expropriation. Second, in terms of the purposes of land expropriation, besides the variety of public interest items already enumerated in the 1915 law, one more was added to the 1928 statute, i.e. expropriation could be used to achieve land redistribution for the sake of developing agriculture and improving peasants' livelihood (Article 1). Relevant legislative records revealed that such an expansion in the legitimate scope of land expropriation was intended to render the 1928 expropriation law compliant with the nationalist party's land nationalization program, which, as noted earlier, conceived that the state could compulsorily purchase land not only for public works and local economic development, but also for preventing land speculation and monopoly.[127] As a consequence, redistribution of land from the haves to the have-nots was transformed from a party policy to a legal mandate. In the meantime, the peculiar element of state compulsory purchase in the KMT's nationalization agenda was incorporated into its expropriation law of 1928. Third, in the 1928 statute, the standard of expropriation compensation was changed from market value of land as prescribed in the 1915 law to original reported land price as required by the nationalist land program (Article 30). Moreover, it was prescribed that expropriation compensation should typically be paid in cash, but if expropriation was for land redistribution or urban and rural redevelopment, maximally one-third of compensation can be paid in government bonds (Article 37). Apparently, these changes in both the standard and the payment of compensation were purported to enhance the affordability of land expropriation to the government, a major

[127] Ibid.

concern for Sun Yat-sen when he devised the plan of expropriation for large-scale economic development based on the division between de jure and de facto nationalization. Last but not least, the procedural rights of the expropriated to seek remedy against expropriation by filing administrative petition and court litigation in the 1915 *Land Acquisition Law* were kept in the 1928 legislation. But they were significantly limited in two ways. It was prescribed that administrative petition and court litigation should be mutually exclusive (Articles 44–45). It was also stipulated that implementation of expropriation decisions would not be suspended by any ongoing dispute resolution process (Article 46).

Taken as a whole, these changes in China's land expropriation law from 1915 to 1928 had considerably loosened up both the substantive and procedural restraints over the state power of expropriation. While the influence from the nationalist land program was definitely a contributing factor, this tendency should not be seen simply as an example of party politics overriding legal principles. In fact, the need to legalize the KMT's land program characterized by more extensive and less constrained expropriation power coincided with, and to a large extent was made possible by, a general change in the prevailing theory of private property at that time. That was the introduction of the theory of private property as social function into China since the late 1910s, which took place somewhat independently from the land politics of the KMT. As will be shown in this section and Section 5.3, this theory had a significant impact not only on the land expropriation law enacted by the nationalist government, but also on the original constitutional takings clause in the 1954 PRC Constitution. A brief discussion of this theory is now in order.

In his 1912 lecture series titled *General Transformations of Private Law Since the Code Napoléon*, the French jurist Léon Duguit famously wrote that "property is not a right; it is a social function," signaling a profound change in the way private property was conceptualized in the European–American world.[128] This change is best illustrated when contrasted with the classical liberal theory of private property, against which Duguit launched his critique.

As already explained, the classical liberal theory of private property, enshrined by such formative texts of Western law as the 1789 Declaration of the Rights of Man of and the 1804 French Civil Code, considers private

[128] Léon Duguit, *Les Transformations Générales du Droit Privé depuis le Code Napoléon* (Paris: F. Alcan, 1920), cited in M.C. Mirow, "The Social-Obligation Norm of Property: Duguit, Hayem, and Others" (2010) 22 *Florida Journal of International Law* 191.

property as the individual's natural rights and sees the raison d'être of government and law as protecting private property from illegitimate external interference. In Duguit's view, however, this theory is metaphysical and individualistic in an undesirable way.[129] It is metaphysical because private property as a natural right cannot be rendered knowable through observation of the world. It exists merely as a normative criterion without any empirical basis.[130] A disciple of the empiricist Auguste Comte, Duguit argued that such a notion contradicts the truly scientific method of positivism (or, in his term, *realisme*) and should be discredited totally in modern societies that have moved from the metaphysical stage to positive stage.[131] Furthermore, the classical liberal take on property is undesirably individualistic because it presumes that individuals exist in isolation.[132] To Duguit, this is far from an accurate description of the social reality: human beings are never isolated from one another. Instead, they are intrinsically social beings that can only live and have always lived in societies.[133] The key feature of social reality is therefore human interdependence rather than independence.[134] In this respect, Duguit was greatly influenced by his colleague and friend, the sociologist Émile Durkheim, who is known for arguing that central to all human societies is social solidarity.[135] In Duguit's words, social solidarity or human interdependence is the "objective law" (*droit objectif*) or "rule of law" (*la règle de droit*) of society. Being descriptive and normative at the same time, such a law should direct and control all members of a society, including the state.[136]

[129] Note that Duguit clarified that his focus was on capitalist property (*propriété capitaliste*) rather than consumption goods (*objets de consummation*). He did not think that the ownership of consumption goods was "evolving in the socialist direction." See Duguit, *Les Transformations Générales du Droit Privé Depuis le Code Napoléon*, pp. 149–50. This is perfectly in line with our focus upon the takings of production means.

[130] Sheila Foster and Daniel Bonilla, "The Social Function of Property: A Comparative Law Perspective" (2011) 80 *Fordham Law Review* 105. Original text can be found at Duguit, *Les Transformations Générales du Droit Privé Depuis le Code Napoléon*, p. 17.

[131] Duguit, *Les Transformations Générales du Droit Privé Depuis le Code Napoléon*, pp. 17–18. See also Martin Loughlin, *Public Law and Political Thought* (Oxford: Oxford University Press, 1992), pp. 107–11, cited in Mirow, "The Social-Obligation Norm of Property: Duguit, Hayem, and Others," 201.

[132] Duguit, *Les Transformations Générales du Droit Privé Depuis le Code Napoléon*, p. 16.

[133] Ibid., p. 18. [134] Foster and Bonilla, "The Social Function of Property," 105.

[135] Émile Durkheim, *De la division du travail social* (Paris: F. Alcan, 1922), cited in Julius Stone, *Human Law and Human Justice* (Stanford: Stanford University Press, 1965), p. 161.

[136] Stone, *Human Law and Human Justice*, pp. 162–63.

Apparently, the nature and purpose of the individual, state and private property conceived by Léon Duguit in the early twentieth century were fundamentally different from classical liberalism. According to Duguit, bound by the objective law of social solidarity, individuals are by no means independent holders of natural rights. They are not the ends but the means of society. Each individual has his or her reason for existence by virtue of the social work he or she does as "a cog of the vast machine which is the social body."[137] Individual human beings' needs are legitimate only insofar as being consistent with the need of the community and any private property can only be utilized to that extent as well.[138] It is in this sense that Duguit remarked that "property is no longer the subjective right of the owner; it is the social function of the possessor of wealth."[139]

Correspondingly, the *raison d'être* of government and law lies not in the protection of individuals' natural rights, as is suggested by classical liberal theorists. Rather, the principal responsibility of political and legal authorities is to further social solidarity.[140] Private property is guaranteed only when it fulfills its social function, thereby enhancing social solidarity. When the opposite happens, private property is to be limited or even prohibited by the state,[141] and private owners can legitimately be forced to make sure that their property satisfies the needs of the community, be it a nation or a collective.[142]

It is certainly debatable whether Duguit's formulation of what constitutes the objective law is in itself metaphysical.[143] And it is quite difficult to see how social solidarity as a social fact can generate normative obligations for both the state and individuals.[144] The more relevant point here, however, is what exactly the social function of private property entails. Apart from suggesting that property owners can be

137 Duguit, *Les Transformations Générales du Droit Privé Depuis le Code Napoléon*, p. 157.
138 Ibid., p. 166. 139 Ibid., p. 158.
140 Léon Duguit, *Law in the Modern State* (trans. Frida Laski and Harold Laski, New York: Howard Fertig, 1970), cited in J. W. F. Allison, *A Continental Distinction in the Common Law: A Historical and Comparative Perspective on English Public Law* (Oxford: Oxford University Press, 2000), p. 62.
141 Duguit, *Les Transformations Générales du Droit Privé Depuis le Code Napoléon*, p. 151.
142 Ibid, pp. 165–66.
143 Hans Kelson suggested that the French doctrine of *solidarité sociale* is merely a typical variant of the natural-law doctrine. See Hans Kelson, *General Theory of Law and State* (trans. Anders Wedberg, New Jersey: The Lawbook Exchange, Ltd., 2009), p. 127. For relevant discussion, see Stone, *Human Law and Human Justice*, chapter 5.
144 Stone, *Human Law and Human Justice*, pp. 162–65.

compelled to put their private property into production instead of wasting or hoarding it, Duguit provided no further details.[145] Nevertheless, it seems that his theory of socialized property did provide the intellectual justification for the KMT to relax those restrictive rules in the 1915 *Land Acquisition Law* underpinned by classical liberal values.

To be clear, Duguit's 1912 lectures were translated into Chinese only in 1935, eight years after the 1928 *Land Expropriation Law*. However, between the late 1910s and mid-1920s, his work on the theory of property as social function was already known to and cited by many Chinese jurists.[146] Among them was Wang Shijie, who obtained his PhD in law from the University of Paris in 1920. He wrote in 1923 that a revolutionary idea of private property had been put forward by Western legal giants such as Duguit, and that countries such as France, America and Germany had all embraced this new trend of socialized property in their laws.[147] Four years later, Dr. Wang was appointed the head of the KMT government's state legal bureau that, as mentioned, was in charge of drafting the 1928 *Land Expropriation Law*. Absent any direct archival evidence, it is hard to pinpoint precisely what kind of impact Wang personally had on the draft and to what extent the theory of socialized property was consciously assimilated into the 1928 statute. What is certain, however, is the deep-level compatibility between this theory and the nationalist land nationalization program the 1928 expropriation law set to legalize. Unlike Marxism, both did not go so far as to demand complete nationalization through confiscation of land. As noted, Sun Yat-sen believed that the driving force of history is cooperation

145 Duguit stated that the consequences of absolute private property included "lands being left without cultivation, city lots without construction, vacant and unmaintained houses, and unproductive capital goods." He also suggested that legal intervention is legitimate to stop property hoarding. Duguit, *Les Transformations Générales du Droit Privé Depuis le Code Napoléon*, pp. 153, 163.

146 Jiahe Zhang, "The Changing Ideas of Ownership (所有权思想之变迁)" (1918) *Taipingyang Journal* (太平洋杂志) 15; Zaorong Xu, "The Materialization of Private Rights (私权之物质化)" (1921) *Journal of Association of Legal Studies* (法学会杂志) 66; Shijie Wang, "New Idea of the Nature of Property Rights (财产权性质之新义)" (1923) *Social Science Quarterly* (社会科学集刊) 1; Tingrui Chen, "New Theory of Liberty, Contract and Property Rights (自由权、契约全、财产权新论)" (1923) *Legal Quarterly* (法学集刊) 465; Zhirang Zhang, "The Evolution from Old to New Legal Principles of the World in the 19th Century (十九世纪中世界法律上新旧两大主义之嬗替)" (1924) *Legal Weekly* (法律周刊) 5; Zhirang Zhang, "Legal Philosophy of the French Scholar Duguit (法儒杜基之法律哲学)" (1924) *Legal Weekly* (法律周刊) 3; Shutang Yan, "Changing Ideas of Property (财产观念之变迁)" (1925) *Social Science Quarterly* (社会科学集刊) 217.

147 Wang, "New Idea of the Nature of Property Rights."

rather than conflict, a point that would be well shared by an adherent to Durkheim's social solidarism such as Duguit. Moreover, seen by many Chinese jurists as the new trend dominating Western legal thinking, the theory of private property as social function provided a timely justification for the KMT government to expropriate land for extensive purposes such as government-led economic development and land redistribution, which go far beyond what is acceptable under classical liberalism.

This last point could be no better demonstrated than by Hu Hanmin's opening speech at the Legislative Yuan of the Republic of China as its first president in December 1928, just a few months after the enactment of the *Land Expropriation Law*. Then president of the national legislature, Hu remarked that according to Sun Yat-sen, human beings are not independent and their rights are not natural. Instead, they must live in societies, from which their rights are derived. Therefore, the public interest of the society, nation and state as enshrined in Sun's *Three Principles of the People* should be the highest guiding principle for any legislation adopted by the nationalist government. Individual rights are recognized and protected only to the extent that they express public interest and can be compelled by law to serve the public interest.[148] In this light, it was no accident that the theory of socialized property replaced classical liberalism to become the normative foundation to the KMT's *Land Expropriation Law* in 1928.

Such a shift was further cemented in the 1930 *Land Law* promulgated by the nationalist government since most expropriation-related clauses in the 1930 law were copied from the 1928 *Land Expropriation Law*. As mentioned earlier, the legal provisions on land expropriation in the communist revolutionary areas in 1939 were claimed to be made in pursuance to the basic principles of the 1930 *Land Law*. Does this then mean that the CCP had by that time also embraced the theory of socialized private property as the normative basis for its own expropriation law? In view of the preceding discussion, the answer should be in the negative. After all, this theory stops at calling for an overall abolition of private ownership of production means and is therefore a mere bourgeoisie agenda, according to the socialist tradition. The reason that the CCP claimed to follow the 1930 *Land Law* of the KMT government more likely rested with the united front between the two parties than with

[148] Hanmin Hu, *Opening Remarks at the National Government's Legislative Yuan* (国民政府立法院开会词), in Secretariat of Legislative Yuan (ed.), *Journal of Legislative Yuan* (立法院专刊) (Shanghai: Minzhi Publisher, 1929), vol. 1, pp. 1–12.

a genuine commitment on the part of the communist party to the theory of private property as social function.

5.3 Common Legacy of Competing Theories

A broad range of theories on land takings power have been presented and examined in this chapter, which run the ideological gamut from the radical left to the progressive center-left to the conservative right. On the far right end, the 1915 *Land Acquisition Law*, the first ever statute on compensatory land expropriation in modern Chinese history, was grounded in classical liberalism, the core concern of which was to protect individuals' private property rights through instituting both substantive and procedural limitations over the power of compensatory expropriation. On the far left end, under the socialist tradition of land nationalization, compensationless land confiscation was utilized as a revolutionary strategy to struggle against the landlord class and disrupt the pre-existing ownership structure. Moving to the center-left, drawing on Henry George and Léon Duguit, Sun Yat-sen and his nationalist party tried to alleviate the evils of private land ownership through more modest measures such as land value tax, nationalization of land increment value and expropriation without thoroughly upsetting the existing property regime.

The difference between these theories cannot be overstated. As noted, in the late 1930s the CCP claimed to abide by the basic principles of the nationalist government's land law, which had then already evolved into the theory of private property as social function. But this is by no means to discount the obvious divergence between the Marxist–Soviet socialist tradition followed by the CCP and the theory of private property as social function developed by Léon Duguit and adopted by the KMT. While the former aims to abolish private ownership of all production means through class struggle and state ownership, the theory of socialized property has nothing to do with all of this.[149] It is more about putting private property at the service of the community than putting it into the hands of the state.

That being said, the palatability of the socialized property theory to the CCP can be attributed to, besides the political necessity to cooperate with the KMT under the national united front, a deep-lying commonality

[149] Foster and Bonilla, "The Social Function of Property: A Comparative Law Perspective," 105.

between the socialist tradition of land nationalization and the theory of property as social function. To begin with, both the socialist tradition and the theory of socialized property reject the notion that private property is an absolute natural right of individuals, the protection of which is the ultimate goal of the state. Quite the contrary – private property, especially that of land, is regarded by both as something to be cautioned against and curtailed, to say the least. Moreover, in the name of some expansively defined notion of public interest, be it societal evolution toward communism or economic development or curbing land monopoly, the state can compel private landed property into sync with the grand scheme of things, to the extent of its extinction. In both these traditions, to borrow Isaiah Berlin's terminology, it is not negative but positive liberty that constitutes the telos of private property in land.[150] After all, as mentioned, Sun Yat-sen once suggested that his land program was also communist. Duguit too called his theory "socialist."[151]

In this situation, the state's taking of private land is not seen as an action to be taken diffusely and occasionally for specific technical purposes such as construction of public works, as is conceived under classical liberalism. It is conceptualized and indeed deployed as an instrument used systematically and frequently in order to achieve such preconceived programs of the state as realizing public land ownership and facilitating economic development. Land taking is therefore not to be framed as an extraordinary event to be strictly limited, but an ordinary occurrence to be encouraged and guaranteed. In short, it is the first rather than the last resort. In the meantime, from the perspective of landowners, since they are socialist citizens (under the Marxist–Soviet socialist tradition) or obligated to discharge their social function (according to the theory of socialized property), dispossession by the state is neither a sacrifice nor a transaction, but an honorable duty that manifests and reaffirms the precedence of the public interest over individual interests.

As demonstrated in the preceding section, since the 1920s, these new "socialist" ideas started to dominate the thinking on both compensationless land nationalization and compensatory land expropriation in China. Arguably, this was another testament to the famous proposition that modern Chinese history oscillated between "national salvation" (*jiuwang*) and "enlightenment" (*qimeng*), but the latter consistently lost

[150] Isaiah Berlin, "Two Concepts of Liberty," in *Four Essays on Liberty* (Oxford: Oxford University Press, 1969).

[151] Foster and Bonilla, "The Social Function of Property: A Comparative Law Perspective," 103.

out to the urgency of the former.[152] In a time of war and crises, the two dominant political forces in China were united in prioritizing national development over individual property. Despite the differences in their specific strategies, both party-states aimed to bring about systemic and profound changes to the most critical element in an agrarian society such as China – the ownership of land, for which land taking served an important tool. I call this the tradition of land takings for state-led social transformation. This is the common legacy bequeathed by the competing foundational theories of land takings power in early twentieth-century China.

Against this background, we can now comprehend why the constitutional takings clause in 1954 is power-confirming but takes a seemingly restrictive form. As explained, it was most probably a transplant from the 1949 East German Constitution, which is suggested to have contained a number of provisions that would not look out of place in a bourgeois constitution so as to be palatable to the West for potential unification of the divided country.[153] As noted, its Article 23 includes the takings clause and Article 24 deals with the obligation of property and prohibition of misusing private property to the detriment of public good. Both these clauses actually found their origin in Article 153 of the 1919 Weimar Constitution of Germany, which was undoubtedly of a capitalist nature.[154] Yet, by expressly entrenching the social obligation of private property, Article 153 of the Weimar Constitution symbolizes a transition from classical liberal conception of property to the theory of private property as social function.

This socialist theory embodied in the capitalist Weimar Constitution was perfectly fit for purpose for the East German constitutional makers in

152 Zehou Li, "Dual Variation of Enlightenment and Nationalism (启蒙与救亡的双重变奏)," in *Essays on Modern Chinese Intellectual History* (中国现代思想史论) (Beijing: Dongfang Publisher, 1987).

153 Inga Markovits, "Constitution Making After National Catastrophes: Germany in 1949 and 1990" (2009) 49 *William and Mary Law Review* 1317.

154 Ibid. Article 153 reads, "Property is guaranteed by the Constitution. Laws determine its content and limitation. Expropriation may only be decreed based on valid laws and for the purpose of public welfare. It has to be executed with appropriate compensation, unless specified otherwise by Reich law. Regarding the amount of the compensation, the course of law at general courts has to be kept open in case of a controversy, unless Reich laws specify otherwise. Expropriations by the Reich at the expense of the states, communities or charitable organizations may only be executed if accompanied by appropriate compensation. Property obliges. Its use shall simultaneously be service for the common best." The English translation of Weimar Constitution is available at www.zum.de/psm/weimar/weimar_vve.php.

1949 who intended to write a constitution that could stride both worlds. While the 1949 East German Constitution stipulates in Article 22 that private property is constitutionally guaranteed, such constitutional protection of private property is immediately followed, and indeed qualified by Article 23 and Article 24, which establish both positive and negative limitations upon private property. On the positive side, according to Article 23, constitutionally guaranteed private property can be expropriated for public benefit, with appropriate compensation and according to law. On the negative side, in pursuance to Article 24, constitutionally protected private property is prohibited from harming the public good. As it turned out, these positive and negative provisos qualifying private property were assimilated into Articles 13–14 of the 1954 PRC Constitution.[155] It was unclear whether or not the Chinese constitutional makers at the time realized the aforementioned critical difference between the Marxist–Soviet tradition and the theory of socialized property. But given the deep-level congeniality between the two, the takings clause in Article 23 of the 1949 East German Constitution, in spite of its restricting form, is still perfectly appropriate for the socialist constitution of China. Its ostensibly restrictive public interest prerequisite and requirement of legality[156] are kept in the 1954 constitutional takings clause not to straightjacket the takings power of the state, but to highlight and reinforce the idea that the government and the law of a socialist country represent the public interest and therefore should take precedence over private property of individuals. As a matter of fact, when Chinese commentators in the 1950s suggested that the original constitutional takings clause had profoundly upset the absolute sacrosanctity of private property in the capitalist societies[157] and that in a socialist society private property was not only a right but also generated duties and obligations to the owner,[158] they could not be closer to Duguit.

It might be argued that, interesting as it may be in historical terms, what has been unearthed by the previous two chapters is basically a story of a bygone era. Indeed, as the conventional wisdom in the field of Chinese law goes, the existing Chinese Constitution of 1982 constitutes

155 The explicit expression "property entails obligation" was left out, which is probably because that notion was felt to be too esoteric.

156 As mentioned, the compensation requirement was omitted given that the power of nationalization listed out in the 1954 Constitutional takings clause is non-compensatory.

157 Liu, *Outlines of Lectures on the PRC Constitution*, p. 80.

158 Zhang, *Essays on Constitutionalism*, p. 41.

a drastic departure from its 1954 predecessor, with the former being a "reform constitution" and the latter a "revolution constitution."[159] Still, it is difficult to disagree that the social, economic and political backgrounds of these two constitutional takings clauses are a world away from each other. Whereas the 1954 takings clause was made under a planned economy by a party-state that stressed class struggle and aspired to abolish private ownership of production means, the 1982 provision came into being when the party-state decided to shift its focus from class struggle to economic development, to which private property of production means is presumably of crucial importance. Therefore, the *prima facie* case is that the constitutional basis of land takings power in China has been fundamentally renovated in the reform era and has become equivalent to the Fifth Amendment of the American Constitution, concerned primarily with restraining the takings power and protecting landed property. But if that is true, how can it be reconciled with the fact that the salient characteristics of the land takings law in the 1950s have been preserved until today when the expropriation power remains expansive, nonparticipatory and unchallengeable, and the expropriation compensation standard is still affected by current land use and living conditions of the expropriatees? It may be suggested that the new promise made by the 1982 constitutional takings clause is not duly delivered due to the deficiencies in the existing rural land expropriation law exposed in Chapters 2 and 3. In other words, nonimplementation of the Constitution or the unconstitutionality of the present rural land expropriation law is to be blamed. Yet the next chapter will demonstrate that this narrative of unconstitutionality is historically unfounded, as the 1982 constitutional takings clause was intended to be a continuation of the historical legacy illustrated above.

159 Yong Xia, "Basic Theoretical Issues in China's Constitutional Reform: From 'A Reform Constitution' to a 'Constitutionalist Constitution' (中国宪法改革的几个基本理论问题: 从改革宪法到宪政宪法)" (2003) 2 *China Social Science* (中国社会科学) 48.

6

The 1982 Constitutional Takings Clause Re-examined

New Wine in an Old Bottle

This chapter examines the takings clause in the existing Constitution of 1982, which has been the focus of academic attention for years. In the conventional understanding, the third paragraph of Article 10 is the presently effective constitutional takings clause. The original 1982 version of Article 10 had the following five paragraphs:

> Urban land is owned by the state.
>
> Rural and suburban land is owned by collectives except for those portions that belong to the state in accordance with law.
>
> The state may in the public interest expropriate land in accordance with law.
>
> No organization or individual may appropriate, buy, sell, lease, or unlawfully transfer land in other ways.
>
> All organizations and individuals who use land must make rational use of it.[1]

Apparently, Article 10 deals with issues beyond land takings, including the ownership, alienation and use of land. In fact, it is the only, and the most comprehensive, clause on land-related matters in the entire constitution. Hence, it is generally regarded as the constitutional land clause. But for reasons that will be elaborated in this chapter, Article 10 should instead be seen as the constitutional takings clause *sensu lato* and its third paragraph the constitutional takings clause *sensu stricto*. A deeper understanding of the present constitutional basis for rural land takings in China requires a sound grasp of both of these senses and their interrelationship.

The best way to analyze the existing constitutional takings clause is to juxtapose it with the original takings clause of 1954 explored in Chapter 4. Starting with the 1982 takings clause *sensu stricto*, i.e. the

[1] The Chinese version reads, "城市的土地属于国家所有. 农村和城市郊区的土地，除由法律规定属于国家所有的以外，属于集体所有. 国家为了公共利益的需要，可以依照法律规定对土地实行征用. 任何组织或者个人不得侵占、买卖、出租或者以其他形式非法转让土地. 一切使用土地的组织和个人必须合理地利用土地."

third paragraph of Article 10, one finds that nationalization and compulsory purchase were no longer in place, leaving expropriation the only type of takings power expressly enumerated in the written constitution.[2] Scant attention has been paid to this adjustment in the existing literature, and no explanation has ever been offered. Why were the powers of nationalization and compulsory purchase removed from the constitutional takings clause? Extending our analysis to the takings clause *sensu lato*, namely Article 10 in its entirety, we find three new additions. To begin with, it was declared that urban land belongs to the state while rural and suburban land belongs to the collectives. Furthermore, sale, lease and other ways of land transfer were prohibited. Last but not least, rationality was announced as the guiding principle for land use. None of this was present in the 1954, 1975 and 1978 Constitutions, or indeed in any Chinese constitutional documents since the early 1900s. That makes the 1982 clause unprecedented in the modern Chinese constitutional history. It is also unparalleled globally because there has never been any similar constitutional stipulation concerning land matters around the world. Where does it come from? What does it mean? And what is it for?

This chapter addresses these puzzles in four sections. The first three sections analyze the abovementioned three additional parts in Article 10 of the 1982 Constitution, i.e. the rural-land ownership structure, the ban on land transactions and the rational use principle. On that basis, the fourth section exposes the nature and purpose of the 1982 constitutional takings clause as well as the reason why nationalization and compulsory purchase were removed.

6.1 "Urban Land Is Owned by the State": A Reinterpretation

6.1.1 Land Ownership Clause or Nationalization Clause?

From the perspective of the Marxist–Soviet tradition of land nationalization surveyed in Chapter 4, the land ownership structure specified in the first two paragraphs of Article 10 is somewhat puzzling. The existing literature has discussed these provisions rather extensively,[3] but the

[2] These two types of takings power were kept in the 1975 and 1978 Constitutions.

[3] Junfeng Yang, "The Origin and Evolution of State Ownership of Urban Land in China (我国城市土地国有制的演进与由来)" (2011) 1 *Journal of Gansu Academy of Administration* (甘肃行政学院学报) 100; Qiren Zhou, "The Puzzle of Nationalization of Urban Land ("城市土地国有化"之谜)," *The Economic Observer* (经济观察报), October 15, 2012; Qiren Zhou, "Nationalization of Urban Land is the First Step in Nationalization of All Land (城市土地国有是全盘土地国有第一步)," *The Economic*

following questions have hardly been addressed. For one thing, as state ownership of land is a time-honored orthodox socialist mandate, why did it take more than three decades for the PRC to constitutionalize it? What was so special about 1982? This is all the more curious given that it was not the two highly ideological PRC Constitutions passed during the Cultural Revolution that established state ownership of land. For another, in relation to nationalization, neither classical Marxist theory nor Soviet Russian practice distinguished between urban and rural land. Why does Article 10 provide for state land ownership only in the urban area, but not the rural area?

Before we move on to decode these puzzles, a few words are needed to explain the pre-1982 urban land ownership regime in the PRC. When the triumphant CCP took over the cities in 1949, it was estimated that 20 percent of the urban land was owned by foreign capitalists and bureaucratic bourgeoisie and 10 percent by national bourgeoisie. The remaining 70 percent was held by individual owners.[4] Between 1949 and 1966, three different policies were adopted based on the class status of the landowner and the land use.[5]

Overall, private landowners were categorized into three categories: foreign capitalists and bureaucratic bourgeoisie (*guanliao ziben jia*); national bourgeoisie (*minzu ziben jia*); and noncapitalist individual owners. First, confiscation and nationalization were applied to urban land owned by foreign capitalists and bureaucratic bourgeoisie, seen as reactionary enemies of the people and the state.[6] Second, a more moderate

Observer (经济观察报), October 25, 2012; Xueyang Cheng, "The Origin of Nationalization of Urban Land (城市土地国有规定的由来)" (2013) 6 *Yanhuang Chunqiu* (炎黄春秋) 35. For an earlier discussion, see Liang Fan, "On the Procedural Problem after "Urban Land Belongs to the State" (谈城市的土地属于国家所有后的程序问题)," May 22, 2001, available at www.china-week.com/info/00612.htm.

4 Yuan Li (ed.), *China's Land Resources* (中国土地资源) (Beijing: Zhongguo Dadi Press, 2000), p. 339.

5 A similar approach was taken in the suburban context. See Regulation on Land Reform in Suburban Areas (城市郊区土地改革条例), promulgated by Central Administrative Committee on November 10, 1950, available at www.ce.cn/xwzx/gnsz/szyw/200705/25/t20070525_11491301.shtml. For the sake of brevity, only the urban land policies will be analyzed here.

6 Instructions on Confiscating the Property of War Criminals, Traitors, Bureaucratic Bourgeoisie and Counter-revolutionaries (关于没收战犯、汉奸、官僚资本家及反革命分子财产的指示), promulgated by Central Administrative Committee on February 4, 1951, available at www.110.com/fagui/law_220.html; Provisions on Confiscating the Property of Counter-revolutionary Criminals (关于没收反革命罪犯财产的规定), promulgated by Central Administrative Committee on June 22, 1951, available at bianke.cnki.net/web/article/G118_1/SDZB195106033.html.

approach was taken with regard to land owned by the national bourgeoisie. It was not immediately confiscated but went through the socialist transformation movement in two ways dependent upon land use.[7] With respect to their land used for industrial purposes and large-scale leasing business, the so-called public–private joint management (*gongsi heying*) was adopted where private property of land and business thereon were taken over by the government though the original owners were allowed to retain part of the profit generated. As already demonstrated in Chapter 4, it was in effect nationalization without compensation. And the profit sharing stopped at the outbreak of the Cultural Revolution. Alternatively, concerning their land used for small-scale leasing business above a certain government-set threshold,[8] the socialist transformation movement was carried out through what was called "state trusteeship" (*guojia jingzu*), which was virtually the same as public–private joint management because the state would first manage and rent out the property on behalf of the original owner and then distribute 20 percent to 40 percent of the rent back to the owner for a limited period of time.[9] Similar to the imposed public–private joint management schemes, the original private owners were not allowed to withdraw from state trusteeship and were ultimately deprived of their ownership. Third, land owned by national bourgeoisie used for leasing business of a scale below the government-set threshold and the land owned by noncapitalist individual owners used for their own residential uses were left intact and private ownership of such land was permitted to stay.

Yet, before long this three-pronged policy was swept away by the Cultural Revolution. In 1967, several central ministries jointly announced that all urban land, regardless of owner or use, should be indiscriminately nationalized.[10] In reality, the private land and houses of

[7] Opinions on the Current Situation of Urban Private-owned Buildings and their Socialist Transformation (关于目前城市私有房产基本情况及进行社会主义改造的意见), promulgated by CCP Central Committee on January 18, 1956), available at znzg.xynu.edu.cn/a/2017/07/21484.html; Report on the Socialist Transformation of Leased Private-owned Real Estate (关于私有出租房屋社会主义改造问题的报告), promulgated by State Real Estate Administration Bureau on January 13, 1964, available at www.law110.com/law/lishi/28016.htm.

[8] Different thresholds were stipulated in different cities. Overall, it was set at 50 ㎡ for small cities and towns, 100 ㎡ for middle-sized cities and 150 ㎡ for big cities. See Zhou, "The Puzzle of Nationalization of Urban Land."

[9] In practice, the payment of rent to the original owners stopped in 1967. Ibid.

[10] Record of the Reply from State Real Estate Administration Bureau, National Taxation Bureau of the Ministry of Finance on the Nationalization of the Land in Cities and Towns (国家房管局、财政部税务总局答复关于城镇土地国有化请示提纲的记录),

millions of urban residents across the country were confiscated, oftentimes in spontaneous and unauthorized raids by the Red Guards. For instance, it was reported that in Beijing alone about 50,000 privately owned or rented houses of 7,650,000 ㎡ were taken from their original owners during the Cultural Revolution, amounting to more than one-third of all the houses in that city.[11]

That being said, at the time the constitution was passed in December 1982, private ownership of urban land remained in existence in China. In other words, not all private urban land had been nationalized over the course of the Cultural Revolution. This was confirmed by the 1978 Constitution, passed two years after the Cultural Revolution, which provides in Article 6 that the state may nationalize urban land. If all urban land were already nationalized by then, there would have been no point in making such a prescription. In addition, a more direct and explicit confirmation could be found in a central ministerial order issued in March 1982, in which the State Bureau of Urban Development urged carrying out examination and verification of land ownership in the urban area, including private land ownership of individual citizens.[12] In this situation, why was it announced just months later that all urban land is owned by the state?

The answer can be found in the legislative process of the 1982 Constitution that began in September 1980, marked by the formation of the Constitutional Amending Committee (CAC) that was put in charge of constitutional drafting.[13] In the two constitutional drafts prepared before March 1981, there was no prescription on land ownership. In March 1981, the secretariat under the CAC proposed for the first time that a clause on land ownership by all people and land ownership by the

promulgated on November 4, 1967, available at www.pkulaw.cn/fulltext_form.aspx?Gid=357&Db=chl.

11 Provisions on Implementing the Policies on Private Houses Taken Over during the Cultural Revolution (落实"文革"中接管的私房政策的若干规定), promulgated by Beijing Municipality People's Government on March 11, 1983, available at www.chinalawedu.com/falvfagui/fg22598/160435.shtml.

12 Provisional Rules on Administration of Property Rights and Registry of Houses and Land in Cities and Towns (关于城市（镇）房地产产权、产籍管理暂行规定), promulgated by State Bureau of Urban Development on March 27, 1982, available at china.findlaw.cn/fagui/p_1/211778.html.

13 The official term used for 1982 constitutional making was "comprehensive revision" (全面修改); hence, the name constitutional amendment committee. But it is widely agreed that this revision was so comprehensive that the 1982 Constitution was effectively a constitution remade. Therefore, the concepts of constitutional making and constitutional makers in 1982 will be used in this chapter.

collectives should be inserted in chapter 1 of the constitution on general principles. It was suggested then that since land is a kind of production means and a natural resource of immense importance, its ownership should be prescribed in the written constitution, a matter left unspecified in all previous PRC Constitutions.[14] By the end of 1981, the land ownership clause as we know it today had been written into the draft constitution. In December that year, vice chairman of the CAC Peng Zhen remarked that although the land ownership system in China had not been provided for in the constitutions and laws in the past, urban land had always been treated as owned by the state and rural land as owned by the collectives, which became overtly confirmed and entrenched by the 1982 Constitution this time.[15] Similarly, according to the explanatory note on the draft constitution published by the CAC secretariat in February 1982, the land ownership clause was "a reflection of the actual conditions" in China.[16] In light of this, it seems that the ownership clause is no more than the constitutional acknowledgment and entrenchment of a fait accompli.

But that is difficult to square with what has been demonstrated above: private ownership of urban land was countenanced in the PRC between 1949 and 1966 and still existed even after the Cultural Revolution, at the time of the 1982 constitutional drafting. Were the constitutional makers ignorant of this fact? The legislative records between February and April of 1982 show that they were not. Quite the opposite – they were fully aware that there was still privately owned urban land but nevertheless made a conscious decision after deliberation to declare that all urban land belongs to the state.[17] Why?

There were two competing viewpoints among the Chinese constitutional makers of 1982 on the draft land ownership clause that established state ownership of urban land and collective ownership of rural land. One view criticized it as inadequate for leaving rural land in the hands of collectives. It was advised that all land should be state owned while the peasant collectives retain just use-rights over rural land.[18] The central concern for the proponents in this camp was that collective ownership of rural land would constitute a serious obstacle to state-led nonagricultural

[14] Cheng, "The Origin of Nationalization of Urban Land," 38. [15] Ibid.

[16] Chongde Xu, *The Constitutional History of the PRC* (中华人民共和国宪法史) (Fuzhou: Fujian Renmin Press, 2003), p. 619.

[17] The detailed records can be found in Xu, *The Constitutional History of the PRC*, chapter 18.

[18] Ibid., pp. 645, 680.

construction and development. For instance, the then vice chairman of the CPPCC Rong Yiren warned that collective ownership of rural land would make it very difficult for the state to develop new mines, build army horse-breeding farms, extract oil and so on. Geng Biao, Minister of National Defense, remarked that since all military airports of the air force and the navy were built in suburban and rural areas, the constitution should not set up a land ownership regime that hinders future construction of these airports.[19] Similar concerns were voiced by others, namely that collective ownership of rural land would spawn disputes when the state needs to acquire rural land to build satellite cities, exploit natural resources, construct new ports, etc.[20] In this regard, the most illustrative comment was made by Fang Yi, then chairman of the State Scientific and Technological Commission:

> The contradiction between these two kinds of ownership is increasingly intensified and severe. The state enterprises and undertakings need to be developed, which requires land. But land is limited. Collective ownership of suburban and rural land becomes a way for [the rural collectives] to rip off the state and make a windfall. For one mu of land, ten thousand yuan was demanded. By selling the land the production teams [of the rural collectives] can secure their members a good life for this generation and the next two, who don't ever have to work anymore. Although the draft constitution prescribes that no organization or individual can sell the land, [rural collectives] can still do so in disguised forms by setting conditions [for them to accept state land takings] such as establishing factories that will recruit their peasant members to become workers and provide for them for life ... the national fiscal expenditure becomes a bottomless pit ... if this continues, it will enrich the peasants at the expense of the entire population, making the contradiction even more intense.[21]

It should be noted at this point that Geng Biao's concern was neither novel nor totally unfounded. At the two NPC sessions in 1980 and 1981 that preceded the one at which the 1982 Constitution was passed, multiple motions were tabled that a piece of legislation on land expropriation should be promulgated with urgency to deal with widespread holdouts by rural collectives against state land expropriation by demanding unreasonable compensation from SOEs, coal mines and the army.[22] In fact, as early as in 1956, Mao Zedong made the following comments:

[19] Ibid., p. 637. [20] Ibid., p. 680. [21] Ibid., pp. 644–45.

[22] Secretariat of the Third Session of the Fifth PRC National People's Congress (ed.), *Motions and the Review Comments of the Third Session of the Fifth PRC National People's Congress* (中华人民共和国第五届全国人民代表大会第三次会议提案及审查

> A few years back, there was an airport to be built in a locality of Henan province. No resettlement arrangement was provided to the peasants. The local government neither negotiated with nor explained clearly to the people [about the imminent land taking] but attempted to evict them forcefully. According to the peasants of that village, if you use a stick to strike down a bird nest to the ground, the birds will voice out their protest ... The people in that locality set up three defense lines ... Those sent there to survey the land was forced away. The peasants won the battle. Later on, the government explained to the peasants clearly and made resettlement arrangements for them. They moved their homes and the airport was built finally. There are many incidents like this ... people oppose them [the cadres] by throwing stones to them and beating them with hoes. The cadres deserve it. I welcome it ... the communist party should learn its lesson.[23]

Ironically, but perhaps unsurprisingly, this shows that the socialist principle that underpins the constitutional takings clause had not always been accepted or complied with in socialist China. The win-win result of state land-taking portrayed in the 1955 book noted in Chapter 4 turned out to be the exception that proves the rule. In practice, it was more often the case that the peasants did not regard being expropriated by the state as a glorious duty to embrace but, rather, an unwanted burden to reject, sometimes with violence, especially when there was no satisfactory compensation and resettlement arrangement. This is what Geng Biao meant by the contradiction between state land ownership and collective land ownership, and why he was so worried about it. Since the late 1970s, such contradiction became much more intense as the CCP decided to change its priority from class struggle to economic development and the pace of state-led nonagricultural development picked up dramatically. This was thrown into sharp relief by the official explanatory note of a new *Regulation on Land Requisition for State-led Construction* promulgated in May 1982 (1982 RLRSC), just months prior to the enactment of the 1982 Constitution:

> The 1958 Measures on Land Requisition for State-led Construction was once having positive effect upon supplying land for state-led construction.

意见) (Oakton: Center for Chinese Research Materials, 1989), pp. 408, 469; Secretariat of the Fourth Session of the Fifth PRC National People's Congress (ed.), *Motions and the Review Comments of the Fourth Session of the Fifth PRC National People's Congress* (中华人民共和国第五届全国人民代表大会第四次会议提案及审查意见) (Beijing: Renmin Press, 1983), p. 1838.

23 Mao Zedong, *Selected Works of Mao Zedong* (毛泽东选集) (Beijing: Renmin Press, 1977), vol. 5, p. 325.

> However, in the last twenty-odd years, with the economic and population growth in our country, there have emerged some new circumstances in respect to land requisition for state-led construction. The Measures on Land Requisition for State-led Construction promulgated in 1958 has long become unable to adapt to the changed circumstances, resulting in a "lawless" situation in the operations of land requisition for state-led construction over recent years ... due to the lawlessness, administration of land expropriation has been very chaotic. During recent years, compensation for land expropriation has hiked in some localities and there are some cadres making too much concession to the demands of peasants and making increasing land expropriation compensation as a way to get the peasants rich ... governments in some localities used the occasion of land requisition for state-led construction to get petty advantages at the expense of the state ... some lawbreakers committed corruption, bribery and extortion to subvert socialism. Many construction units have postponed the due dates for construction time and again because they could not satisfy the demands for land expropriation raised by rural collectives, hindering state-led construction ... various local governments and state departments have strongly urged that a new Regulation and in recent couple of years motions in this respect have been put forward at sessions of the national people's congress and people's political consultative conference ... in 1977 the State Council entrusted the State Construction Commission to draft a new Regulation on the basis of the 1958 Measures on Land Requisition for State-led Construction, which after rounds of research and survey and solicitation of opinions from provincial governments and state departments finished the draft Regulation on Land Requisition for State-led Construction.[24]

In this light, the reason that a new expropriation law was found necessary from the late 1970s and was eventually promulgated in 1982 is twofold. For a start, the 1958 MLRSC, the supposedly governing law in this area, was not adaptive to changed circumstances. This is likely a euphemism for the fact that although the 1958 MLRSC was never formally repealed, its implementation had stopped, or at least been severely disrupted, during the tumultuous Cultural Revolution. Consequently, this lawless situation caused havoc for smooth state land expropriation at the time, especially through rural collectives and collusive local governments gaining petty advantages at the expense of the state. Against this background, the need to reduce impediments to land expropriation and accelerate state-led development was felt more acutely than ever before, which occasioned the call by some constitutional

[24] Kebai Lv, "Explanatory Report on the Draft Regulation on Land Requisition for State-led Construction (关于《国家建设征用土地条例(草案)》的说明)," April 28, 1982, available at bianke.cnki.net/web/article/G116_2/GWYB198210001.html.

makers for complete state ownership of land to be written into the incoming Constitution. This is why even though land nationalization is a long-standing socialist mandate, only in 1982 was it constitutionally enshrined for the first time in the PRC.

Alternatively, the other camp of opinion among the Chinese constitutional makers in 1982 accepted the draft land ownership clause, arguing that rural land had better stay in the hands of rural collectives. This is obviously contrary to the Marxist–Soviet tradition of indiscriminate land nationalization. But three very practical considerations were voiced in support. First, it was suggested that nationalization of rural land would not alleviate, let alone resolve, the holdout problem because taking state-owned land requires compensation too. For instance, Yang Shangkun, deputy chairman of the Central Military Commission, noted that even if all land becomes state owned, disputes over land takings would not go away. He gave the example that whilst urban land was already owned by the state, there were still households holding out in Tianjin and Beijing.[25] Second, the concern was expressed by Yang Xiufeng, vice chairman of the Legal Affairs Commission of the NPC, that nationalization of rural land should not be carried out unless the following questions are thought through: How will the state-owned rural land be administered? Who will administer it? And who may use it?[26] He was apparently unconvinced that these matters had received adequate deliberation by that time. Last, yet most importantly, some of the participants in constitutional deliberation, including the two leaders of the CAC secretariat Hu Qiaomu and Peng Zhen, were of the view that to nationalize rural land that had been owned by peasant collectives would cause unwanted shock and disruption to the rural population, who had rallied around the CCP because of land redistribution and fought very hard for land rights for a long time.[27] Yang Shangkun remarked that to prescribe that only urban land belongs to the state in the constitution was an interim step to minimize possible disturbance and state ownership of urban land; plus, the new regulation on land requisition would be adequate to deal with the problem of holdouts against state-led construction.[28]

Despite their differences with regard to nationalization of rural land, the above two camps were united in constitutionalizing state ownership of urban land. In fact, throughout the entire deliberation process of the

[25] Xu, *The Constitutional History of the PRC*, p. 681. Hu Qiaomu and Peng Zhen shared this view. See ibid., pp. 666, 681.
[26] Ibid., p. 681. [27] Ibid., pp. 666, 681–82. [28] Ibid., pp. 681–82.

1982 Constitution, no opposition was ever raised against this initiative. As hinted, this was not because the constitutional makers believed that all urban land had already fallen into the state's hands. Quite the opposite – Jiang Hua, then head of the SPC, unequivocally pointed out in April 1982 that the urban real estate holdings that had gone through socialist transformation were very different from those that had not: the former had become state owned, but the latter remained in private ownership. Such a critical distinction would vanish if all urban land were pronounced to be state owned.[29] Although Jiang's concern was never echoed by any other participants in constitutional deliberation, we can still confidently conclude that the constitutional provision that urban land is owned by the state was not a result of the constitutional makers' misperception of the status quo at the time, but was intended as a partial nationalization when there was still privately owned urban land in China. It was one step back from full-scale nationalization due to the highly pragmatic reasons just explained, and was framed by Peng Zhen as merely an interim and transitional (*guodu*) situation.[30] It is in this sense that I consider the first paragraph of Article 10 to be as much a nationalization clause and thereby part of the constitutional takings clause *sensu lato* as it is about the land ownership system.

6.1.2 *Land Ownership Clause or Nationalization Clause?*

The legitimacy of the 1982 nationalization clause has been subject to heated debate in recent years, on which there are two conflicting views. The mainstream position is that it has dubious legitimacy. First, as already mentioned, overall nationalization of urban land was pronounced during the Cultural Revolution, which had already been dismissed as a national disaster by the CCP itself in 1981. Hence, it was noted that the 1982 Constitution should not have constitutionalized the legacy of the Cultural Revolution by stipulating that urban land belongs to the state.[31] Second, without paying any compensation to or even consulting those affected, and in the absence of any statutory basis, the state had no right to simply declare away the private property on urban land.[32] A third argument is that private urban land used for residential purposes should be categorized as subsistence means, not means of

[29] Ibid., p. 681. [30] Ibid., p. 681.

[31] Cheng, "The Origin of Nationalization of Urban Land," 41.

[32] Yang, "The Origin and Evolution of State Ownership of Urban Land in China," 105; Qiren Zhou, "Property Rights on Rural Land and the Land Acquisition System: A Critical

production. As noted in the previous chapter, according to classical Marxism, socialism is tolerant of private ownership of subsistence means, which will not be nationalized.[33] The competing minority view is that it is legitimate because it was an exercise of the constitutional amending power. As long as it is done in pursuance of lawful procedures, which was the case in 1982, it can abolish private ownership of urban land.[34]

I am in favor of the minority view, but for a different reason. Of course, it was by amending the previous constitution that the 1982 Constitution nationalized all urban land that was still in private ownership. But to say that merely scratches the surface of the issue and has at most verified only the formal legality, not the substantive legitimacy of the nationalization clause. On a more fundamental level, I argue, it was an exercise of the long-held power of the party-state, i.e. nationalization to achieve social transformation. It is therefore essentially the same as the land reform movement and the socialist transformation movement that came before it. To be sure, this is not to say that it was simply a repetition of history. First, the specific goal in 1982 was no longer systematic restructuring of the ownership system, as in the previous two cases of nationalization. Supplying land as much as possible for state-led economic development was the objective this time around. Second, unlike the two revolutionary movements, nationalization in 1982 did not involve any extensive nationwide campaign and was virtually nationalization through declaration. Third, different from the socialist transformation movement which was explicitly mandated in the 1954 Constitution (Article 4), nationalization in 1982 was not expressly ordained in the constitutional text, as the power of compensationless nationalization was removed from the constitutional takings clause and the clause on state ownership of urban land only provides for nationalization in 1982 in a rather veiled fashion. Fourth, there was no law or regulation promulgated to authorize or regulate nationalization of urban land in 1982, which differed from the land reform movement that had been statutorily underpinned by both the 1947 *Outline Land Law* and the 1950 *Land Reform Law*. Fifth, and

Choice for China's Urbanization (农地产权与征地制度 – 中国城市化面临的重大选择)" (2004) 4 *China Economic Quarterly* (经济学季刊) 197.

33 Zhou, "The Puzzle of Nationalization of Urban Land."

34 Rui Zhang, "The Basis of the Legitimacy of the Land Ownership Clause of the 1982 PRC Constitution: Analysis based on Theories of Social Justice and Market Economy (八二宪法中土地所有权条款的正当性基础 – 基于社会正义与市场经济理论的分析)" (2013) 19 *Rule of Law and Social Development* (法制社会发展) 91.

finally, the 1982 nationalization covered all urban land, including that used for individual citizens' residences. It therefore went further than the socialist transformation movement of the 1950s, which, as mentioned, covered only urban land used for commercial leasing business while leaving private household residences intact.

Nevertheless, for the following reasons, none of the above five differences makes nationalization by declaration in 1982 any less legitimate than those preceding land-based nationalization through campaign. First and foremost, the 1982 nationalization is no different in nature from its predecessors. The change in the content of the party-state's social transformation project from class revolution to economic development did not affect the fact that the power of nationalization had been used ever since the land reform campaign as a means to accomplish such macro transformative projects. Second, though absent a nationwide campaign, in 1982 private ownership of urban land was not simply declared away in a stealthy manner, as suggested by some commentators.[35] On the contrary, the draft Constitution containing the nationalization clause was actually published for nationwide public consultation from late April to August of that year. It was recorded that within two months of its publication, 1538 letters of comments and suggestions were sent to the CAC secretariat, some of which were about the land ownership/nationalization clause.[36] Third, while the 1982 nationalization seemed to lack either constitutional or statutory basis, it is nothing new. Well known is that the land reform movement was not constitutionally mandated and the socialist transformation movement was carried out by party orders instead of statutes. Anyone familiar with the CCP's history understands that initiating hugely impactful programs without constitutional or statutory basis has been a long-established practice of the Party. Fourth, it cannot be stressed enough that the 1982 nationalization clause was anything but the legacy of the Cultural Revolution. For one thing, it was evidently not intended to be a revival of the Cultural Revolution politics because during the deliberation the framers of the 1982 Constitution never even mentioned the Cultural Revolution. For another, as noted in the preceding chapter, nationalization of land has been a socialist decree ever since classical Marxism. The call for land nationalization over the course of the Cultural Revolution does not render it a product thereof.

[35] Weiluo Wang, "A Stealth Land Revolution in 1982: How Private Land in China became Nationalized? (1982 年的一场无声无息的土地"革命" – 中国的私有土地是如何国有化的)" (2007) 10 *Land Resources* (国土资源) 64.

[36] Xu, The Constitutional History of the *PRC*, p. 719.

Last but not least, in the Marxist tradition land is always regarded as the quintessential production means. The *Communist Manifesto* made no distinction between land as a means of production and land as a means of subsistence, but insisted on abolishing private landed property generally. In China, the 1954 Constitution (Article 13), 1975 Constitution (Article 6) and 1978 Constitution (Article 6) all classified land as a production means. Admittedly, land can be and has been used for nonproductive ends such as household residence, which is undoubtedly a kind of subsistence means in Marxian terms. But that confirms rather than repudiates the notion that land is essentially a subject of human labor, namely a kind of means of production, on which human labor creates such means of subsistence as individual household residence. This point had long been recognized in China. In 1979, the central authority openly acknowledged that residential houses of rural collective members are means of subsistence and should be owned by them. Yet it was not suggested that land used for such houses should therefore be owned by the collective members.[37] Such a distinction and indeed separation between private residence and the land beneath applies equally to urban land and actually persists in today's Chinese real estate law, as urban residents legally own the property they live in without owning the land thereunder, to which they have just use-rights. At a fundamental level, this artificial if not arbitrary division is instituted to strike a balance between the need to accommodate millions of households and the necessity to keep the socialist public ownership of land as a production means in place. Land used for private residence has therefore always been framed as a means of production, not a subsistence means in the People's Republic. The argument that the socialist transformation movement in the 1950s did not nationalize urban land used for household residence because such land was seen as a means of subsistence is historically unsound. In August 1949, on the dawn of the military success of the CCP, *People's Daily*, the prominent party mouthpiece, published an article to explain to the public the People's Liberation Army's announcement earlier in that year that "urban

[37] Report on the National Conference on the Work of Rural Housing Construction (全国农村房屋建设工作会议的报告), promulgated by State Construction Committee, State Agriculture Committee, Ministry of Agriculture, Ministry of Construction Materials and Industry and State Bureau of Construction Industry on March 14, 1980, available at www.law110.com/law/jianshe/2354.htm.

housing and land should not be treated in the same way as the rural land problem":[38]

> In terms of private urban housing, the reason that it should not be treated like rural land is because ... rural land is a product of nature, which human beings can only exploit but not create. Therefore landlords occupy land and use it to exert extremely cruel exploitation over the peasantry and such land ownership is feudalistic ... and must be abolished ... it is a basic task of new democratic revolution. But the urban housing problem is different. Houses are not products of nature but products of labor. In a society of commercial production, houses are a kind of commodity that requires certain investment and frequent refurbishment and renovation ... that is why the ownership of urban housing by private owners is generally not feudalistic but of a capitalistic nature. In new democratic revolution, such capitalistic housing ownership should be protected ... as to land ownership associated with urban housing, because urban land needs leveling and involves some investment and after several rounds of transactions urban land becomes a inseparable part of the housing property, which is different from rural land.[39]

To what extent urban housing ownership is really capitalistic as opposed to feudalistic and why urban land ownership is inseparable from urban housing ownership are admittedly debatable. The justification provided above seems rather crude and unconvincing. But one thing was made crystal clear here: urban land, even if owned and utilized by private citizens for residential purposes, was not conceptualized by the CCP as a means of subsistence, otherwise the ownership of it could not have been labeled as being capitalistic given that the Marxian analysis of different modes of production focuses solely on production means. Hence, urban land used for household residence was left untouched during the socialist transformation campaign not because it was seen to be a subsistence means. The real reason was hinted in the same *People's Daily* piece:

> Only by doing so [recognizing and protecting private ownership of urban housing] can we ensure that there is enough housing for urban residents. If we adopt the opposite strategy, as some cities once mistakenly confiscated urban houses during the land reform movement ... there will be

38 The announcement appeared in the Notice of the Chinese People's Liberation Army (中国人民解放军布告), promulgated on April 25, 1949, available at www.marxists.org/chinese/maozedong/marxist.org-chinese-mao-19490425.htm.

39 "On the Nature and Policy of Urban Real Estate and Lease (关于城市房产、房租的性质和政策)," *People's Daily*, August 11, 1949, available at www.360doc.com/content/10/1228/22/3063062_82158769.shtml.

> no one willing to pay for new houses and the stock houses will be left unattended, unrenovated and even squandered at will. The result is that the people do not have adequate housing for residence, which in turn harms the people.[40]

In this light, it was for this pragmatic consideration that the CCP decided to exclude private urban housing land from the socialist transformation movement and nationalization, which was obviously an option of expediency not intended to last in the long run. Indeed, as was made clear by the *People's Daily* article, all urban housing properties ought to be deemed as property of the entire society, over which the state should provide proper stewardship so as to ensure that the stock of urban housing increased and no one faced difficulty in finding a place to live. This would then prepare favorable conditions for eventually realizing socialist public ownership of urban housing and the land below in the future.[41]

To summarize, the above discussion demonstrates that nationalization in 1982 should be regarded at least as legitimate as the land reform and socialist transformation movements that had once featured heavily in the communist party-state's struggle to trigger social transformation. If one is to challenge the legitimacy of the former, it is logical to also challenge the legitimacy of the latter. In theory this is certainly possible. Yet, thus far, none of those who have questioned the legitimacy of the 1982 nationalization clause have done so. Nor are they likely to if asked. That is because their real concern is less about what kind of normative judgment should be passed on the 1982 nationalization clause as a historical event than about what shall be done to the structural challenge that clause seems to pose to the constitutional public interest prerequisite today. As noted in Chapter 2, the constitutional prescription that "urban land is owned by the state" effectively makes it impossible to guarantee the public interestedness of rural land expropriation decisions because expropriation is understood to be necessitated whenever rural land is converted into urban land. In order to revolve this urbanization challenge, many scholars have proposed either abolishing or radically reinterpreting the 1982 nationalization clause by questioning or even denying its legitimacy.[42]

40 Ibid. 41 Ibid.

42 Xueyang Cheng, "Chinese System of State Ownership of Land from a Public Law Perspective (公法视角下的中国国有土地制度)" (2011) 25 *China Land Science* (中国土地科学) 20; Zhenyuan Zheng, "Urban Land should not only be Owned by the State (城市土地应不仅属国家所有)," October 15, 2012, available at finance.jrj.com.cn/opinion/

While echoing such a concern, I disagree with the suggested solution. My argument is that the urbanization challenge can be tackled without going so far as to reject the legitimacy of the 1982 nationalization clause. Section 6.1.3 will show that the 1982 nationalization clause does not necessitate state expropriation when rural land is converted into urban land. The widely perceived urbanization challenge is more apparent than real, and it is a myth derived from misreading the 1982 nationalization clause and misunderstanding its true legacy.

6.1.3 Legacy of the 1982 Nationalization Clause

6.1.3.1 Defining Urban Land

In early 1982, when the draft constitution was out for public consultation, a party cadre from Hunan cautioned that "urban land belongs to the state" was "not easy to explain clearly and difficult to enforce." His reason is that, first, the boundaries of existing urban areas are constantly changing due to urban expansion. Second, it is sometimes very difficult to have a clear-cut demarcation between urban and suburban areas, the latter of which according to the draft constitution belong to rural collectives. Third, he envisioned that in the future more and more counties and towns designated as rural areas would be upgraded and recognized as cities. Would their land then be nationalized as a result?[43] Essentially, two questions are raised here. How is "urban land" defined and demarcated? And what practical implications does the 1982 nationalization clause have for urban land? These questions are apparently of enormous magnitude in terms of both constitutional interpretation and constitutional implementation. Yet presently available constitutional legislative records offer no answer to any of them. This section attempts alternative ways to shed light on these questions.

First of all, what is urban land? The only authoritative definition available so far is to be found in the official interpretation of the 1998 LAL published by the Committee of Legal Work under the NPCSC. In China both the NPC and the NPCSC have the legislative power to enact statutes. The NPCSC legislates outside the NPC session, which happens once

2012/10/15185714515992.shtml; Jiming Cai, "The Top-level and Systematic Design of China's Land System Reform (我国土地制度改革的顶层和系统设计)" (2013) 7 *Economic Review* (经济纵横) *18*; Xueyang Cheng, "On the Constitutional Interpretation of "Urban Land Belongs to the State" (论"城市土地属于国家所有"的宪法解释)" (2014) 1 *Rule of Law and Social Development* (法制与社会发展) 169.

[43] Xu, *The Constitutional History of the PRC*, p. 721.

every year. The agency that is in charge of law drafting under the NPCSC is its Legal Work Committee. The 1986 LAL and its subsequent amendments were all drafted by the NPCSC Legal Work Committee and passed by the NPCSC. In this situation, it is fair to say that the NPCSC Legal Work Committee has the most intimate and authoritative understanding of the provision on urban land ownership in the LAL. In its official interpretation of the 1998 LAL, it suggests that the provision on urban land in Article 6 of the 1986 LAL is in line with the 1982 nationalization clause and that, notwithstanding minor adjustments, Article 8 of the 1998 LAL is essentially the same as Article 6 of the 1986 LAL.[44] Therefore, we may take the NPCSC Legal Work Committee's interpretation of Article 8 in the 1998 LAL as the most reliable proxy at hand for an authoritative definition of urban land in the 1982 nationalization clause.

Specifically, it is suggested that following Article 6 in the 1986 LAL, Article 8 of the 1998 LAL prescribes that land in the "urban districts of cities" (*chengshi shiqu*) is owned by the state. Urban land is explicated as land in the urban districts of the cities here. What, then, is land in the urban districts of the cities? First of all, as to the definition of city, the NPCSC Legal Work Committee suggests that according to paragraph one of Article 3 of the 1989 *Urban Planning Law*, the legal term "city" stands for a municipality directly under the central government (*zhixia shi*), a prefecture (*shi*) or a town (*zhen*), all of which are established by the state according to administrative division.[45] Moreover, concerning what constitutes an urban district, the NPCSC Legal Work Committee admits that the present law offers no precise definition. But it clarifies that in practice it is typically understood to be the "built-up areas" (*jiancheng qu*) of cities.[46]

Three points are worth considering with regard to these definitions. To start with, the establishment of a city in China is a government decision. While the national government, i.e. the State Council, has the authority to grant a particular locality the legal status of municipality directly under the central government or that of prefecture, provincial governments may do so with regard to a town.[47] Against this backdrop,

[44] Yaowu Bian (ed.), *Explanation of the PRC Land Administration Law* (中华人民共和国土地管理法释义) (Beijing: Falv Press, 1998), p. 59.

[45] The Chinese text reads, "本法所称城市，是指国家按行政建制设立的直辖市、市、镇."

[46] Bian, *Explanation of the PRC Land Administration Law*, p. 59.

[47] Arts. 4–5, Rules on Administration of Administrative Division (关于行政区划管理的规定), promulgated by State Council on January 15, 1985, available at www.gov.cn/test/2009-03/30/content_1272329.htm.

"city" in the 1982 nationalization clause is not about the socioeconomic characteristics of a particular locale but its administrative classification or legal status. Second, an administratively designated city in China usually contains within its boundary not only a smaller and urbanized city proper but also a larger suburban and rural part in socioeconomic terms. The term "urban land," therefore could have two meanings. On the one hand, the broad sense covers all the land inside the administrative boundaries of those municipalities directly under the central government, prefectures and towns. On the other hand, the narrow sense of urban land covers only the land within the urbanized city proper of such cities. Which meaning is adopted by the 1982 nationalization clause? Third, the 1986 and 1998 LAL specifies, as expounded by the NPCSC Legal Work Committee, that the phrase "urban land" in the 1982 Constitution stands for land in the urban districts of cities. The NPCSC Legal Work Committee further acknowledges that urban district conventionally means the built-up area of a city. According to the Chinese national standard of planning terminology, a built-up area refers to the area within a city's boundaries that is actually developed and covered with urban public service facilities and infrastructures.[48] It is usually considered as the truly urbanized area inside a city that avoids the distortion of administrative classification.[49] In this light, "urban land" in the 1982 constitutional nationalization clause means the narrow sense of the phrase, namely the land in the urbanized parts of the municipalities directly under central government, prefectures and towns in China.

Without doubt, urban land as defined in the above sense is constantly changing in scope as urbanized areas grow when existing cities expand and new cities are established, a process typically known as urbanization. In China, ever since the early 1950s, urban planning is supposed to precede and guide the actual development of infrastructure in the cities.[50] Specifically, according to Article 29 of the 1984 *Urban Planning Regulation*, before a certain area is developed and turned into an urban built-up area, it should first be earmarked in the city's urban planning scheme as an "area under planning control" (*guihua kongzhi qu*). Simply

[48] Point 3.0.6, Standard for Basic Terminology of Urban Planning (城市规划基本术语标准), promulgated by Ministry of Construction on August 13, 1998.

[49] George C.S. Lin, *Developing China: Land, Politics and Social Conditions* (London: Routledge, 2009), p. 15.

[50] For a historical survey of the urban planning practice in the pre-reform era in China, see Fulong Wu, *Planning for Growth: Urban and Regional Planning in China* (London: Routledge, 2015), chapter 2.

put, today's built-up area is yesterday's area under planning control, and the area under planning control today will become a built-up area tomorrow. Therefore, from a dynamic point of view, urban land can take two forms: while the built-up area is the actual urban district, the area under planning control is the potential urban district. Combined, these are called the "planned urban areas" (*chengshi guihua qu*) of a city.[51] From this perspective, urban land in the 1982 nationalization clause refers to land in the planned urban areas of cities, including both those already urbanized parts and those expected to be developed under urban planning schemes. The next question is: what impact does the 1982 constitutional nationalization clause have on such land? Given that urban land is expanding in scope, we start by looking at its impact on urban land existing at the time that the 1982 Constitution came into effect (December 4, 1982), before examining urban land coming into being afterwards.

6.1.3.2 Impact on Urban Land in Existence by the 1982 Constitution

Under the definition just given, urban land existing by the enactment of the 1982 Constitution could be in two forms. Broadly speaking, it included the land both in areas already built up and in areas earmarked for future development in the cities at the time. Narrowly speaking, it included only the built-up areas by then. For two reasons, the narrow definition should prevail here. For one thing, urban planning stopped during the Cultural Revolution.[52] It was only in 1980 that the CCP Central Committee and State Council urged all cities to compile their own urban master plan by 1982.[53] Yet, by 1986, most cities had not finished making.[54] That means that by the time the constitution was passed in December 1982, most Chinese cities were yet to have their urban master plans. For example, Beijing had its urban master plan only in July 1983. Shanghai had its plan approved even later in 1986. This means that in those cities without an urban master plan, there was no

[51] 1984 Urban Planning Regulation, art. 29; 1989 Urban Planning Law, art. 3; 2007 URPL, art. 2.

[52] Zongbo Tan, *Introduction to Urban Planning and Design* (城市规划) (Beijing: Tsinghua University Press, 2005), p. 412.

[53] Minutes of the National Conference on the Work of Urban Planning (全国城市规划工作会议纪要), promulgated by State Council on December 9, 1980, available at www .chinabaike.com/law/zy/xz/gwy/1332020.html.

[54] Tan, *Introduction to Urban Planning and Design*, p. 413.

area under planning control at all. In this situation, it is fair to say that urban land existing by the 1982 Constitution refers to the land in those already developed areas in the cities.

What was the effect of the 1982 nationalization clause on such land, especially the land that was still owned privately at the time? Evidently it did not deprive the original owners of their possession or use-rights as there was neither revocation of old private land title certificates nor physical transfer of the land, which is understandable because, as mentioned, the 1982 nationalization of urban land was intended to be an expedient measure falling short of overall nationalization to minimize disturbance. This also explains why there was hardly any fuss or objection to this round of nationalization. As a matter of fact, there was no legal or policy documents promulgated to spell out the exact effect of the nationalization clause for many years. It was only in 1989 that the State Bureau of Land Administration announced that those who had been lawfully using state-owned urban land through either inheriting such land or accepting as gifts the buildings thereon should be considered to have lawful use-rights over state-owned urban land.[55] One year later, the same agency gave a more direct answer regarding what kind of rights the original owner still had to the land they once had since the 1982 nationalization. In an internal reply to the SPC, the State Bureau of Land Administration stated, "After the 1982 Constitution prescribes that urban land belongs to the state, citizens should naturally enjoy use-rights over the urban land they originally owned."[56] Eventually, in 1995, the formal legal confirmation came with the *Provisions on Determining Land Ownership and Use-rights*: "Those who had used private land through buying houses or land or renting land before state ownership of urban land was implemented and has continued to use such land afterwards till the present day should be regarded to have the use-rights over the now state-owned land."[57] In view of this, nationalization in 1982 was

55 Art. 15, Opinions on the Issue of Determining Land Rights (关于确定土地权属问题的若干意见), promulgated by State Bureau of Land Administration on July 15, 1989, available at www.pkulaw.cn/fulltext_form.aspx/pay/fulltext_form.aspx?Db=chl&Gid=240645.

56 Reply on the Ownership and Use-rights of Urban Household Residential Plots (关于城市宅基地所有权使用权等问题的复函), promulgate by State Bureau of Land Administration on April 23, 1990, available at www.law-lib.com/law/law_view.asp?from=androidqq&id=51720.

57 Art. 28, Provisions on Determining Land Ownership and Use-rights (确定土地所有权和使用权的若干规定), promulgated by State Bureau of Land Administration on March 11, 1995, available at www.mlr.gov.cn/zwgk/flfg/tdglflfg/200411/t20041125_39415.htm.

considerably less intrusive upon private property compared with the land reform campaign and the socialist transformation movement that came before, which were characterized by immediate or shortly postponed dispossession.

Nevertheless, this is by no means to say that the impact of the 1982 nationalization clause was merely nominal. As mentioned, wholesale land nationalization was proposed during constitutional deliberation in 1982 for the sake of better facilitating state-led construction and development. In the end, the less disruptive option of partial nationalization targeting only urban land was adopted. One particular argument against nationalization of rural land raised at the time was that it would not make much of a difference since takings of state-owned land also required compensation and there remained the possibility of holdouts. If the partial nationalization in 1982 had only a nominal effect on urban land, it seems that there was little sense in introducing it into the written constitution. What, then, is the substantive impact of the 1982 nationalization clause on urban land in existence at the time?

The legacy can be best understood with reference to the distinction between de jure and de facto nationalization first conceptualized by Sun Yat-sen. As explained in the preceding chapter, de jure nationalization means that the state acquires the legal title of land from its original owners without paying compensation or taking physical possession. As far as the use of land is concerned, it is business as usual. But once they have lost the title, original owners can no longer sell the land. Up to this point, nationalization in 1982 is basically the same as Sun's plan. The two diverge when it comes to de facto nationalization, i.e. the state's taking actual possession of the land. While Sun Yat-sen suggested that the state should pay for de facto nationalization at the original reported land price with revenues generated through reaping increased land value, the PRC does not pay for the land at all. This is because, after nationalization, taking the nationalized land from its original owners is no longer expropriation of land ownership but withdrawal of use-rights over urban state-owned land. As noted in the preceding chapter, following the Soviet model, withdrawal of state-owned land has been noncompensatory in the PRC since the 1950s and the original owners are compensated only for their private property on the land, such as houses. No official justification has ever been proffered for such a policy. Yet, an illuminating parallel can be drawn from the Soviet law, which denied compensation for state-owned land withdrawal for the reason that land use-rights were conceptualized in law as a gratuity assigned free of charge by the state.

In a similar vein, it can be argued that the original owners' continuous possession and use of their land after the 1982 nationalization have not been seen as a residual extension of their previous ownership but a gratuitous benefit bestowed by the state without charge. Therefore, no compensation is to be paid when the state merely takes back what it ought to have possessed in the first place. Since the late 1980s, use-rights of state-owned land became marketized and private land-users could pay the government with land transfer fees to purchase such rights for a specified period of time. In this situation, the 1994 UREAL (Article 19) and the 2007 *Property Law* (Article 148) prescribe that if the state withdraws transferred use-rights before the lease term expires, it should compensate for the remaining term and refund part of the transfer fee to the land-users. However, apparently the owners of private urban land prior to 1982 did not obtain their use-rights over subsequently nationalized land from paid transfer. Consequently, they are not to be compensated for such use-rights. In this situation, by reducing the costs of urban land withdrawal, the 1982 nationalization clause does achieve its intended purpose, which is to facilitate state-led construction and development.

More recently, the noncompensability of urban land withdrawal was somewhat changed by the 2011 RECHSL, which prescribes in Article 19 that compensation for expropriating houses above state-owned land shall not be lower than the market price of comparable real property at the date when the expropriation decision is announced. As the price of real property consists of both land price and the price of aboveground structures, and the fact that these two are basically inseparable, in predicating compensation for expropriating houses above state-owned urban land on the price of comparable real property, the 2011 RECHSL manages to bring land price back into the equation and thereby renders land use-rights compensable. Nonetheless, the compensability of urban land use-rights in state withdrawal yet remains to be explicitly provided for in the 2011 RECHSL. The shadow of nationalization in 1982 lives on.

6.1.3.3 Impact on Urban Land Coming into Existence after the 1982 Constitution

Precisely what effect the 1982 constitutional clause proclaiming that urban land is owned by the state has had upon urban land coming into existence after it was enacted has been a much disputed issue, and one on which there are three contending views. One view is that land in the planned urban areas is automatically nationalized.[58] The second view, which is currently the more prevalent position in the literature, holds that such land will not be automatically nationalized, but that the state is obligated to expropriate it eventually. Hence, there is the urbanization challenge to the constitutional public interest prerequisite.[59] Still others suggest that such land will not be nationalized automatically, nor is the state obligated to expropriate it, and that the 1982 nationalization clause only covers urban land in existence at the time.[60] I argue that the last is the correct interpretation, and the so-called urbanization challenge is actually nonexistent. To put it differently, there is no tension or contradiction between the first and third paragraphs of Article 10 in the 1982 Constitution.

First off, the proposition that automatic nationalization applies to land within planned urban areas is untenable primarily because it does not fit the reality. Since the 1982 Constitution, in the vast majority of cases, the fact that an area is marked as a planned urban area per se has led to neither de jure nor de facto nationalization of the land thereof. Admittedly, there seems to be one exception, wherein the City of Jiyuan in Henan Province pronounced in 1992 that all collective-owned land within its planned urban area would be nationalized from the last day of that year. Furthermore, it was stipulated that if not used for state-led construction, the nationalized land would continue to be used by its original owners.[61] One is quick to note the resemblance of this local rule to the 1982 nationalization clause. In fact, the legal basis cited for this Jiyuan rule was none other than the 1982 constitutional clause stating that urban land belongs to the state.[62] But I argue that this is based on

58 Wang, "A Stealth Land Revolution in 1982: How Private Land in China became Nationalized," 99.

59 Zhou, "Property Rights on Rural Land and the Land Acquisition System: A Critical Choice for China's Urbanization," 193.

60 Yang, "The Origin and Evolution of State Ownership of Urban Land in China," 105; Chen Chen, "Apply Correctly the Prescription "Urban Land Belongs to the State" (正确运用"城市的土地属于国家所有")" (2012) 3 *Land and Resources* (资源导刊) 40; Zhen Yuan, " "Study on the Scope of Collective Land Ownership (论集体土地所有权客体范围的确定)" (2012) 11 *Hebei Legal Science* (河北法学) 43; Liantai Liu, "The Constitutional Space for Reforming the System of Collective Land Expropriation (集体土地征收制度变革的宪法空间)" (2014) 3 *Studies in Law and Business* (法商研究) 10.

61 Notice on Issues concerning Nationalization of Collective Land within the Planned Urban Areas (关于城市规划区内集体土地国有化有关问题的通知), promulgated by Jiyuan People's Government on December 8, 1992.

62 Ibid.

a misreading of the constitution and is therefore, strictly speaking, unconstitutional. As touched upon in Section 6.1.2, while the constitutional takings clauses in the 1954, 1975 and 1978 Constitutions all provided for the state's power of nationalization, such a provision was removed from the 1982 constitutional takings clause. The underlying reason for this will be discussed in Section 6.4. Suffice it to say here that this should be seen as a constitutional change of momentous significance because the constitutional power of nationalization has since been formally revoked and the Chinese state can no longer practice noncompensatory nationalization based on the constitution. It is therefore unconstitutional for local governments such as that of Jiyuan to simply nationalize land in the planned urban area while claiming that it is legitimatized by the 1982 nationalization clause.

There is, however, one possible counterexample in this regard. Article 2 (5) of the 1998 LALIR states that when all members of a rural collective are converted into urban residents, the land originally owned by the rural collective belongs to the state. Under the Chinese household registration (*hukou*) system, the change of one's status from rural residents to urban residents is basically a government decision. Over the years, citing the just-mentioned prescription as the legal basis, a number of local governments in China have nationalized rural land by reclassifying the original peasant owners as urban residents.[63] The two most notable cases are Guangzhou in 2002 and Shenzhen in 2004.[64] Local practices of this kind seem to attest to the fact that through converting the peasant landowners into urban residents, local governments may still lawfully nationalize rural land even after the 1982 Constitution.

This, however, turns out to be an unlawful practice based on an incorrect understanding of the law rejected by China's central authorities. In 2005, less than a year after Shenzhen nationalized a large area within its jurisdiction, a clarification was issued jointly by the State Council Office of Legislative Affairs and the MLR on the meaning

[63] Su Chen, "Generalized Nationalization of Collective Land in Urbanization (城市化过程中集体土地的概括国有化)" (2000) 3 *Legal Studies* (法学研究) *108*.

[64] Point 2 (1), Several Opinions on Reform of Villages within Cities (关于"城中村"改制工作的若干意见), promulgated by General Office of Guangzhou CCP Committee and General Office of Guangzhou People's Government on May 24, 2002, available at www.flzx.com/fagui/difang/201301/18663.html; art. 2, Administration Measures on Urbanized Land in Bao'an and Longgang Districts of Shenzhen Municipality (深圳市宝安龙岗两区城市化土地管理办法), promulgated by Shenzhen Municipal Government on June 26, 2004, available at www.gsfzb.gov.cn/FLFG/ShowArticle.asp?ArticleID=597.

of the aforementioned Article 2 (5) of the 1998 LALIR. It suggests that instead of allowing local governments to nationalize rural collective land via reclassifying rural land owners as urban residents, that particular provision means that when a rural collective has undergone land expropriation and all of its members have consequently been converted into urban residents, any land in small quantity left in the hands of the collective may then be expropriated by the state.[65] It is crystal clear that rural land cannot be nationalized as a result of *hukou* reclassification. Besides, during the last decade, the Chinese central authority repeatedly and expressly stressed that rural land nationalization via altering the *hukou* classification of its original peasant owners is strictly forbidden.[66] The Shenzhen incident reportedly received central approval ex post facto only on the condition that it would never happen again.[67] If one still wonders why the 1998 LALIR has included such a misleading provision in the first place, chances are that it originates from Article 14 of the 1995 *Provisions on Determining Land Ownership and Use-rights*, which states, "If a rural collective is disbanded or all of its members are converted into nonagricultural population because of land requisition for state-led construction, its remaining land that is yet to be expropriated belongs to the state." While this certainly demonstrates that conversion of *hukou* classification does not authorize local governments to nationalize rural land, it was not made clear in what way the remaining collective-owned land could become state-owned. Hence, the 1998 provision gives a false impression that it will be automatically nationalized. However, as the 2005 clarification points out, the remaining collective-owned land can only be expropriated.

This brings us to the second view on the impact of the 1982 nationalization clause on the urban land that came into being after the 1982

[65] Interpretation Opinions on Article 2 (5) of the Implementation Regulation of the PRC Land Administration Law (关于对《中华人民共和国土地管理法实施条例》第二条第(五)项的解释意见), promulgated by State Council Office of Legislative Affairs and MLR on March 4, 2005, available at china.findlaw.cn/fagui/p_1/204288.html.

[66] Point 10, Decision on Deepening Reform and Enhancing Land Administration (关于深化改革严格土地管理的决定), promulgated by State Council on October 21, 2004, available at www.mlr.gov.cn/zwgk/flfg/tdglflfg/200601/t20060112_642080.htm; point 3 (8), Notice on Actively and Reliably Promoting Reform of Household Registration System (关于积极稳妥推进户籍管理制度改革的通知), promulgated by General Office of State Council on February 26, 2011, available at www.gov.cn/zwgk/2012-02/23/content_2075082.htm.

[67] Yanzheng Lu, "The Exceptional Case of Nationalization of Agricultural Land in Shenzhen (深圳农地国有化特例)," November 3, 2006, available at finance.people.com.cn/GB/70392/4996685.html.

Constitution, which maintains that such land will not be automatically nationalized, but the state is obligated to expropriate it. It has long been the mainstream position that gives rise to the widely accepted urbanization challenge thesis. After all, paragraph one of Article 10 states rather plainly and bluntly that urban land belongs to the state. When a collective-owned land parcel is earmarked under the urban planning scheme to be within the planned urban area, it becomes urban land and should therefore be owned by the state. As the previous analysis shows, the state cannot simply nationalize (de jure or de facto) such land anymore after the 1982 Constitution. Nor can the state purchase land as land transaction is banned by the constitution. So, the only way for the state to comply with the first paragraph of Article 10 is to exercise expropriation. If not, there is a prima facie case for constitutional violation. Yet, as noted in Chapter 2, if the state does expropriate all the land located in the planned urban area, as required by the first paragraph, although that will not necessarily break the public interest prerequisite for land expropriation prescribed in the third paragraph of the same article, it does render any check on the public interestedness of expropriation structurally meaningless.

To tackle this urbanization challenge, two kinds of proposals have been advanced in the existing literature. One is to abandon the public interest requisite, which is not generally accepted. The other is to decouple expropriation from urbanization, which can be realized in two different ways. As noted in Chapter 2, many commentators have suggested that the first paragraph should be removed, which I consider unnecessary if the goal is to decouple expropriation from urbanization as a result of planning decisions. Alternatively, over more recent years, it has been argued that paragraph one need not be abolished, but reinterpreted in a way that relieves the state of the obligation to expropriate land classified as urban due to planning decisions. This is the third view on the effect the 1982 nationalization clause has upon the post-1982 urban land: it does not lead to automatic nationalization, nor does it demand eventual expropriation by the state. As touched upon above, this understanding is correct.

So far, there are three points of view in support of this interpretation. First, it has been argued that paragraph one should not be interpreted as requiring the state to expropriate all urban land because the necessary connection between expropriation and planning-induced urbanization was not the original intent of the constitutional makers in 1982 and has resulted in widespread and serious violations of the peasants' land rights.[68] Second, it is suggested that the phrase "urban land *is* owned by the state" should be interpreted as "urban land *can* be owned by the state" rather than "urban land *shall* be owned by the state."[69] The reason provided is that the latter interpretation produces undesirable consequences such as state monopoly of rural–urban land conversion through expropriation and all the attendant problems and crises. Still others have submitted that paragraph one has had no real impact on urban land that has come into being after the 1982 Constitution. Although it did nationalize urban land in existence by constitutional enactment on December 4, 1982, it places no duty on the state to ensure that the land subsequently marked as urban according to planning decisions is ultimately owned by itself.[70] In other words, the 1982 nationalization clause applies only to the urban land in history. Yet, there is no specific reason offered as to why this should be the correct reading.

Sympathetic to their objective, I find that the first two propositions bring very little to the table in terms of argument. The consequentialist argument is largely question-begging because although highlighting the undesirable consequences of the link between expropriation and planning-induced urbanization establishes *why* it is necessary to reinterpret the 1982 nationalization clause in a way that differs from the conventional wisdom, that does not clarify *how* it should be reinterpreted. Furthermore, it is definitely right to point out that based on the available historical materials surveyed earlier in this chapter, it is more likely that the constitution-makers in 1982 did not intend the urbanization challenge and were not even aware of any possible tension between the first and third paragraphs in the same constitutional article. They never discussed in detail what urban land means and how it should differentiated from rural and suburban land. Nor did they seem to be particularly concerned about the constantly changing and sometimes fuzzy boundaries of urban areas. Peng Zhen actually advised that the distinction between urban and nonurban land should be left ambiguous given that

[68] Qianfan Zhang, "Urbanization does not Necessitate Land Expropriation: Clearing the Misunderstanding of the Constitutional Dual Structure of Urban and Rural Land (城市化需要征地: 清除城乡土地二元结构的宪法误区)" (2012) 6 *Legal Science* (法学) 19.

[69] Cheng, "On the Constitutional Interpretation of 'Urban Land Belongs to the State'."

[70] Yang, "The Origin and Evolution of State Ownership of Urban Land in China," 105; Chen, "Apply Correctly the Prescription 'Urban Land Belongs to the State'" 41; Zhen Yuan, "Study on the Scope of Collective Land Ownership," 43; Liantai Liu, "The Constitutional Space for Reforming the System of Collective Land Expropriation," 10.

such a distinction was only an interim measure.[71] Hence, it is reasonable to infer that the nationalization clause was conceived only to cover what was already in the urban areas at the time of constitutional making, but not to be applicable to the ever-growing urban areas that would come in the future.

That being said, the original intent of the constitutional makers in 1982 has never been used as the ground to validate the existence of the urbanization challenge. One may well argue that even if it was not in the original design, the urbanization challenge still looks perfectly tenable simply because it is what the first paragraph of Article 10 says literally. It is then very tenuous to maintain that it suggests urban land *can* be owned by the state, not least because that clearly deviates from the plain text meaning. More crucially, such an interpretation also contradicts the fact that the 1982 nationalization clause did mean that urban land existing by the time of constitutional enactment *should* be owned by the state. A reinterpretation of this kind effectively creates an unnecessary rupture within the same clause: on the one hand, it means that urban land in existence by the 1982 Constitution *should* be and indeed did come to be owned by the state; on the other hand, it means that urban land coming into being after the 1982 Constitution *can* be but *not should* be owned by the state. In this situation, the better understanding of the 1982 nationalization clause is that it is applicable just to urban land existing by 1982 and not to urban land coming into existence afterwards, which the state is not obligated to expropriate or nationalize. The reason, however, is not that this will remove the urbanization challenge. Instead, it is that such a challenge is a myth that is more apparent than real in the first place.

6.1.3.4 Demystifying Urbanization Challenge

As early as January 1984, just one year after the 1982 Constitution came into force, the first-of-its-kind statute on urban planning in the PRC – the *Regulation on Urban Planning* – was promulgated and contained the following provisions. Article 31 reads, "any organization and individual that engages in various kinds of development (*gexiang jianshe*) within the planned urban areas, if needing to use state-owned land or to expropriate collective-owned land, shall apply to the government department in charge of urban planning for approval of use of construction land."

[71] Xu, The *Constitutional History of the PRC*, p. 681. For the thesis of deliberate institutional ambiguity in China's land system, see Peter Ho, "Who Owns China's Land? Policies, Property Rights and Deliberate Institutional Ambiguity" (2001) 166 *The China Quarterly* 387–414.

Article 33 states, "Within the planned urban areas, if there is a need to expropriate collective-owned land for development, the city people's government shall follow the national regulation on land requisition for development and requisition such land from the rural collectives." Article 35 stipulates, "If those rural collectives that locate within planned urban areas are to build or expand their residential settlements, enterprises and public facilities, they shall report to and seek approval from the government department in charge of urban planning about the location and scope of such proposed land use."

Two obvious conclusions follow from these provisions. First, following the 1982 Constitution, land within the planned urban areas is not automatically nationalized. Collective-owned land still exists inside these areas. Otherwise, Articles 31 and 33 would not have prescribed that for the sake of "various kinds of development" collective-owned land within the planned urban areas could be expropriated by the state.[72] Furthermore, according to Article 35, rural collectives could still use their land within the planned urban areas for their own construction of residence, enterprises and facilities, if approved by the planning authority. Yet it is not obvious when there is a need to expropriate collective-owned land within the planned urban areas. Article 31 provides that such needs arise when collective-owned land is demanded for "various kinds of development." What does that mean? Does it exhaust all possible scenarios under which the state expropriates collective land in the planned urban areas? When can the rural collectives carry out development on their own without having to go through state expropriation? These questions can only be answered in the light of China's land administration system back at the time.

Prior to the 1986 LAL, China's rural land administration system was set out in the 1982 *Regulation on the Administration of Land Use for Building Construction in Villages and Townships* (Rural Construction Regulation). On the one hand, it prescribes that rural collectives may, upon government review and approval, use their own land to build the following: (1) member peasants' household residences, (2) public utilities such as open courtyards, roads, green space and (3) collective enterprises (*shedui qiye*). On the other hand, no noncollective entities, including government department, enterprise, public institution or individual

[72] This point is reconfirmed by Article 8 of the 1994 UREAL and Article 9 of the 2009 UREAL, both of which prescribe that collective-owned land within the planned urban areas must first be expropriated and converted into state-owned land before its use-rights can be transferred with compensation.

citizen is allowed to use rural land for construction without permission. If they want to use such land, they have to do so according to the national 1982 RLRSC.[73] Based on these provisions, the 1982 *Rural Construction Regulation* effectively means that the rural collectives can use their own land only for those nonagricultural purposes enumerated in law. All other nonagricultural uses of rural land must first undergo state expropriation.

It is impossible to neglect the striking similarity between the present Chinese land administration system and that in the early 1980s. As explained in Chapter 2, rural land in China is now placed under a stringent use control regime characterized by what I call the presumption of state expropriation in nonagricultural use of rural collective land, which poses the de-agrarianization challenge to the constitutional public interest prerequisite. Specifically, the 2004 LAL stipulates that apart from being used for building peasant household residential plots, local public utilities as well as the TVEs (in the form of joint ventures or as a result of bankruptcy or merger of such enterprises), rural collective land cannot be utilized for other nonagricultural purposes unless being expropriated by the state and turned into state-owned land. In view of the previous discussion, it was precisely the same situation back in the early 1980s when rural collectives were prohibited from putting their land to nonagricultural purposes other than those legally specified. The overwhelming majority of nonagricultural development could only take place over state-owned land. This is what is meant by "various kinds of development" in Article 31 of the 1984 *Regulation on Urban Planning*.

The upshot of all this is that according to the 1984 *Regulation on Urban Planning*, expropriation of collective-owned land is required not by virtue of the fact that such land falls within the planned urban areas and is therefore designated as urban land. As already shown, ownership of such land may still be lawfully left with the rural collectives. Yet, when and only when such rural collective land is to be used for nonagricultural development that cannot be carried out by the collectives themselves, state expropriation is necessitated. There is sufficient ground to consider the 1984 *Regulation on Urban Planning* in line with the 1982 Constitution because the former was promulgated shortly after the latter and there was no reason that only one year later the Chinese central authorities passed a law that invalidates the constitutional provision on state ownership of

[73] Regulation on the Administration of Land Use for Buildings in Villages and Townships (村镇建房用地管理条例), arts. 5, 7, 9–11, 16.

urban land. In this situation, the sensible conclusion is that the 1982 nationalization clause does not obligate the state to expropriate collective land within the planned urban areas unless it is needed for nonagricultural development that cannot be conducted by the rural collectives. In this sense, the urbanization challenge never really exists. The false perception that it exists is derived from the reality that land in the urban built-up areas is usually owned by the state, as was acknowledged by the aforementioned NPCSC Legal Work Committee's interpretation of the 1998 LAL. The foregoing analysis has now made it clear that this is not because the state has a legal duty to expropriate the collective-owned land in the urban built-up areas. Rather, it is because the state has to expropriate such land first so that it can be used for constructing urban infrastructures and facilities, including commercial developments, which cannot be done by rural collectives. That will turn a particular area into an urban built-up area, the land in which is already state-owned by that time. Therefore, what really exists is the de-agrarianization challenge to the public interest prerequisite for expropriation, not the urbanization challenge.

To summarize, based on the above analysis, the first paragraph of Article 10 of the 1982 Constitution bears three layers of connotation. First and foremost, it was an exercise of the power of nationalization, which was not so different from the land reform movement and socialist transformation campaign prior to the 1950s. Although it was de jure nationalization without immediate conveyance of physical possession from the original owners, it did have a tangible substantive impact as urban land title exchange became out of the question and, more importantly, withdrawal of the use-rights over the now nationalized urban land turned noncompensable. Second, as shown by the legislative record, the nationalization of urban land in 1982 was more of an interim compromise than a final and stable solution. If not for the pragmatic consideration to avoid too much disruption, the constitutional makers might well have decided to nationalize all land in China. At the end of the day, comprehensive nationalization is a classic socialist mandate. Some commentators do predict that the PRC will one day fulfill this imperative and nationalize all land.[74] Nonetheless, given that the 1982 nationalization itself was motivated primarily by pragmatic instead of ideological concerns, it is very unlikely that full-scale nationalization will be adopted

[74] Zhong Huang, "Urbanization and the Ownership of "Urbanized" Collectively-Owned Land (城市化与"入城"集体土地的归属)" (2014) 4 *Legal Studies* (法学研究) 57.

unless certain concrete circumstances dictate so. More importantly, since compensationless nationalization as a kind of land takings power has been removed from the written constitutional text, it can no longer be invoked as a constitutional power. There is presently only one type of constitutional land takings power left and that is expropriation. Transfer of collective land to the state in any other manner is therefore unconstitutional. Third, the 1982 nationalization clause applies only to land in the urban built-up areas existing by the time the 1982 Constitution was enacted. It neither leads to automatic nationalization of nor demands the state to eventually expropriate the land incorporated into urban planned areas under planning decisions after the 1982 Constitution came into effect. The broadly acknowledged urbanization challenge is actually a myth that should now be put to rest.

Before we move on, attention should be directed to four points of objection raised in the existing literature against seeing the 1982 nationalization clause as affecting only the urban land in existence prior to 1982.[75] First, it is argued that if seen as applicable only to urban land in history, the first paragraph is reduced to a mere descriptive provision, not a prescriptive one that regulates behavior in the future. This falls foul of the supposedly normative nature of the written constitution. Second, if it indeed meant to nationalize all urban land in existence by the enactment of the constitution in 1982, it violated the principle of *lex prospicit non respicit* for targeting urban land that used to be privately owned before the 1982 Constitution. Third, such an interpretation tells us nothing about what to do with post-1982 urban land. Fourth, since it is impossible for people today to accurately delineate the boundaries of urban land by 1982, it is infeasible to work out what exactly had been nationalized back then.

None of these arguments holds up. First, the 1982 nationalization clause seen as applicable just to urban land in history is by no means purely descriptive. Precisely the opposite; it is prescriptive in the sense that it did have actual legal effects upon such land and does requires recognition and acceptance of that fact from the society. If any dispute arises over the ownership of a piece of land in one city, the issue whether or not it was within the cities at the time when the 1982 Constitution was passed must be dealt with. Besides, even if we concede that it is descriptive instead of prescriptive, there is nothing intrinsically wrong with

[75] Cheng, "On the Constitutional Interpretation of 'Urban Land Belongs to the State'," 173.

a constitutional article being so. Instead, it is simply mistaken to think that the 1982 Constitution contains only prescriptive provisions. An easy counterexample is its Article 136, which reads, "the national flag of the PRC is the red flag with five stars." It is the same with Article 137, which states that the national emblem of the PRC is Tiananmen in the center illuminated by five stars and encircled by ears of grain and a cogwheel; and with Article 138,which suggests that the capital of the PRC is Beijing. Apparently, these provisions are no more prescriptive than the 1982 nationalization clause, but no one will deny their status as proper constitutional clauses. Second, in nationalizing all urban land in existence by 1982, the nationalization clause is in no way an ex post facto law. This is because it took effect precisely from the day when the 1982 Constitution came into effect, not any time before. Third, the 1982 nationalization clause alone does admittedly tell us little about what to do with post-1982 urban land. But that is what we need to figure out by analyzing other parts of the Constitution and relevant laws and regulations. There is nothing problematic about one constitutional clause not telling us about everything. Fourth and finally, it is actually possible nowadays to work out the exact scope of nationalization in 1982 if we successfully identify all the urban built-up areas existing at the time. Even if that is a difficult task to achieve, it is far from a fatal flaw.

6.2 Forbidding Voluntary Land Transaction

The fourth paragraph of Article 10 of the 1982 Constitution stipulates, "No organization or individual may appropriate, buy, sell, lease, or unlawfully transfer land in other ways." As shown in Chapter 5, prohibition of voluntary land transaction is part of the Marxist–Soviet tradition of land nationalization, which featured prominently in the post-revolution land administration system of the USSR. Demonstrated earlier in this chapter is that since the 1960s, transaction of both rural and urban land was banned in the PRC. Against this background, the just-cited provision seems to be no more than a constitutional confirmation of the long-held socialist tradition as well as the status quo by that time. But why did such confirmation not appear earlier, in the 1975 or 1978 Constitution? And why did the change happen in 1982?

Signs of this constitutional change in late 1982 can be seen in a series of central policies and laws promulgated between 1981 and 1982. In April 1981, the State Council issued a sternly worded rescript to make the following statement:

> It must be reconfirmed that land of the rural people's commune and production teams is owned by the collectives. The member peasants have only use-rights over land allocated to them as household residential plots, land (hills) allotted to them for private use and cultivated land contracted out to them, which is prohibited to be leased, sold or transferred without permission.[76]

In January 1982, the State Council reconfirmed that land allocated to peasants as their household residential plots is owned by the rural collective and cannot be unlawfully sold, leased or transferred.[77] The *Rural Construction Regulation* enacted in February 1982 stated in Article 4 that "sale, lease and unlawful transfer of land for buildings are strictly proscribed." The 1982 RLRSC prescribed in Article 2 that "it is forbidden that any entity buys or rents land directly or in disguised forms from rural collectives." In fact, this was the first time since the 1960s that the Chinese central authority openly reaffirmed its long-held commitment to prohibiting voluntary land transaction. What prompted such reprioritization?

The clue is to be found in the aforementioned legislative explanation on the 1982 RLRSC. As noted in Section 6.1.1, in revealing the motivation and consideration behind promulgating a new law on land expropriation, it highlighted the legal vacuum caused by the lack of enforcement of the 1958 MLRSC, which heightened the contradiction between state ownership and collective ownership of land and became all the more acute at the beginning of the reform era when the scale and pace of state-led construction increased. In the meantime, the legislative explanation further warned that as a consequence of such a legal vacuum, "free price bargaining" (*ziyou yijia*) – sales and leases of rural land in disguised forms – had taken place, which had left the principle embedded in the 1978 Constitution that the state may expropriate land according to law unimplemented in practice on the one hand and exacerbated the waste of cultivated land on the other. It was against this backdrop that the 1982 RLRSC was drafted and enacted to prohibit land-using entities from buying or leasing land from the rural collectives.[78] In this light, the Chinese central authority's re-emphasis on closing down the rural land

76 Point 3, Urgent Notice on Stopping Appropriation of Cultivated Land for Rural Housing Construction (关于制止农村建房侵占耕地的紧急通知), promulgated by State Council on April 17, 1981, available at www.law-lib.com/law/law_view.asp?id=44537.

77 Minutes of the Second National Conference on the Work of Rural Housing Construction (第二次全国农村房屋建设工作会议纪要), promulgated by State Council on December 29, 1981, available at www.gov.cn/zhengce/content/2016-10/18/content_5121011.htm.

78 Kebai Lv, "Explanatory Report on the Draft Regulation on Land Requisition for State-led Construction."

market in the early 1980s was motivated primarily by two concerns. First, due to the ineffective enforcement of the statute on state land expropriation, voluntary rural land transaction emerged and proliferated, resulting in the nonimplementation of the constitutional principle of state expropriation according to law. Second, free transaction of rural land had also aggravated the waste of cultivated land. In this situation, a new legislation on land expropriation was desperately needed to re-instate the ban on the rural land market.

To contemporary readers, these two concerns are far from self-explanatory. For one thing, why was rural land transaction incompatible with the constitutional principle of state expropriating rural land according to law? Are they not supposed to be mutually independent and exclusive – i.e., where voluntary transaction stops, state expropriation steps in? For another, why was rural land transaction considered to have worsened the problem of cultivated land waste? Isn't voluntary transaction supposed to be efficiency-boosting instead of waste-generating? To make sense of these puzzles, it is necessary to look at the Chinese law on land expropriation and administration all the way back to the 1950s.

The 1982 RLRSC is the third statute on land expropriation in the PRC, preceded by the 1953 and the 1958 MLRSCs. Judging from their titles, a commonality shared by these three pieces of legislation is that "state-led construction" is set as the purpose for land expropriation. In Chinese the term is *guojia jianshe*, which literally translates as "state/national construction." Why is a different term, "state-led construction," adopted here as the English translation? What does the Chinese term actually mean? More detail can be found in Article 2 of these three statutes. In 1953, it was prescribed that land can be expropriated when needed for building national defense facilities, factories, mines, railways, public transportation, water conservancy and irrigation projects and municipal works, as well as development of other economic and cultural initiatives. In 1958, it was stipulated that the state could expropriate land to build factories, mines, public transportation, water conservancy and irrigation projects and national defense facilities, as well as to carry out cultural, educational, public health, municipal works and other undertakings. In 1982, it was provided that land could be expropriated for the state to execute economic, cultural and national defense construction and to develop public welfare projects. None of these provisions tell us much about the exact meaning of *guojia jianshe* except that it may take a variety of forms. What, then, is the common denominator for all these various initiatives and undertakings? As noted in Chapter 4, the power of expropriation is typically understood to be interchangeable with the German concept *Enteignungen*. Both are believed to entail some sort of public construction projects that are usually and to a large extent justifiably undertaken by the state itself. After all, the Chinese term "state construction" has at least two literal connotations. One is construction *by* the state, represented through its affiliated entities such as government agencies and SOEs. The other is construction *for* the state that is supposed to represent the public interest. In listing particular items such as national defense facilities, railways, public transportation, municipal works and public welfare undertakings that fit these two criteria very nicely, the above provisions in the Chinese statutes on land expropriation between the 1950s and early 1980s have reinforced the belief that land expropriation in China served construction projects conducted by the state for the public interest.

However, such conventional wisdom is far from the truth as land expropriations under these laws were intended for purposes well beyond what is commonly understood as construction projects by the state for the public interest. As a matter of fact, ever since the 1950s, state expropriation has become the only channel via which rural land could be provided for all kinds of construction and development projects that rural collectives are not permitted to engage in. A word of explanation is now in order.

To begin with, notwithstanding its presence in all the statutory titles, construction by the state for the public interest was not the sole end for land expropriation. According to Article 19 of the 1953 MLRSC, private enterprises in need of land for their own use shall file applications to governments above the provincial/prefectural level. Once their application is approved, the local government within whose jurisdiction the sought-after land is located should expropriate such land on behalf of the applying private enterprise. In 1954, clarifying how to implement the 1953 MLRSC, the Ministry of Domestic Affairs noted that state agencies, SOEs, public–private joint ventures and *private enterprises* might all request land expropriation.[79] This clearly shows that land expropriation

[79] Point 1, Reply on Several Issues of Charging Deed Tax or Rent on Expropriation of Privately Owned Land and Use of State-owned Land by State-owned Enterprises, Public-Private Joint Ventures, Private Enterprises and so on (答复关于国营企业、公私合营企业及私营企业等征用私有土地及使用国有土地交纳契税或租金的几个问题), promulgated by Ministry of Domestic Affairs on March 8, 1954, available at www.110.com/fagui/law_58160.html; point 5, Comprehensive Reply on Several Questions concerning

could be exercised to provide land not only for entities affiliated with the state, but also for private enterprises upon their initiation and with government authorization. Interestingly, the 1958 MLRSC did not have any provision similar to Article 19 of its 1953 predecessor. The reason, however, was not that the state could no longer expropriate land for private enterprises, but that by that time the socialist transformation campaign was accomplished and all private enterprises were considered eliminated and prohibited in the PRC.[80] It was only in 1987 that the legitimacy of private enterprises became officially recognized by the party-state again.[81] Hence, the 1982 RLRSC did not have any prescription on expropriation for private enterprises, either.

But that does not mean that land expropriation was not deployed for private purposes following the end of the socialist transformation campaign in the mid-1950s. Quite the contrary – the 1983 *Measures on Administration of Building Residence for Individuals in Prefectures and Towns* prescribes that when residents of cities and towns need land to build residences they ought not to use such land without government permission. Instead, they must apply for state expropriation according to the relevant national stipulation,[82] which certainly refers to the 1982 RLRSC. Three conclusions follow from this 1983 provision. First, it confirms the proposition established above that the 1982 nationalization clause neither automatically nationalizes urban land nor obligates the state to expropriate it. This is because two different terms are used in the 1982 RLRSC to connote state land takings. According to its Articles 2 and 31, collective-owned land is "expropriated" and state-owned land is "withdrawn." The fact that the 1983 provision stipulates that residents in prefectures and towns should apply for state expropriation rather than withdrawal demonstrates that collective-owned land still existed within

the Implementation of the Measures on Land Requisition for State-led Construction (关于执行国家建设征用土地办法中几个问题的综合答复), promulgated by Ministry of Domestic Affairs on 27 April 1954, available at china.findlaw.cn/fagui/p_1/212345.html.

80 The final success of the socialist transformation of capitalist industry and commerce movement was pronounced at the Eighth CCP National Congress in 1956.

81 Further Deepening the Rural Reform (把农村改革引向深入), promulgated by Politburo of CCP Central Committee on January 22, 1987, available at www.51wf.com/print-law?id=1164257.

82 Art. 4, Measures on Administration of Building Residence for Individuals in Prefectures and Towns (城镇个人建造住宅管理办法), promulgated by Ministry of Construction on June 4, 1983, cited in Lewei Cai, "From Fiction to Nullity: the Evolution of Public Interest in Land Expropriation (从拟制走向虚无: 土地征收中"公共利益"的演变)" (2012) 6 *Tribune of Political Science and Law* (政法论坛) 51.

prefectures and towns at the time and was not automatically nationalized by the 1982 constitutional nationalization clause. Second, the 1983 provision also shows that collective-owned land in prefectures and towns shall be expropriated when needed for private residences for individual citizens. The state is therefore obligated to expropriate the collective-owned land within prefectures and towns not by virtue of its location, but because it is demanded for nonagricultural construction and development, such as building residences for individual urban dwellers. Third, of more relevance here is that, as clearly attested by the 1983 provision, state land expropriation could be deployed to serve purposes other than construction by state agencies for the public interest.

That said, one might argue that land expropriation for private enterprises and individuals only existed for a very short period of time in the 1950s and the 1980s. It was therefore a mere exception, whereas the rule was that state expropriation was practiced primarily to support public construction. However, that cannot be further from the truth. Attention should be directed to a 1959 central party announcement, which specified that land used for highways, railways, factories, mines and other kinds of basic construction (*jiben jianshe*) should all be expropriated according to the national stipulation on land expropriation, unless such construction projects are carried out by the rural collectives, which should then supply land for themselves.[83] Worth noting here is that this party document substituted "basic construction" for "state construction" as the purpose of land expropriation. Was that an expansion or a contraction of scope? The answer is the former. The 1952 *Interim Measures of the Work on Basic Construction*, the first-of-its-kind legislation concerning this matter in the PRC, defines "basic construction" as the "expanded reproduction of fixed assets" in a diverse array of areas including manufacturing, mining, transportation, agriculture, finance, trade, culture, education, public health, etc.[84] Derived from Marxist economic theory, the phrase "expanded reproduction" originally stands for the way in which the accumulation of capital occurs.[85] Yet in the Chinese context, according to the just-cited 1952 law, expanded reproduction of fixed assets simply

83 Point 5 (2), Eighteen Issues concerning the People's Communes (关于人民公社的十八个问题), promulgated by Politburo of CCP Central Committee on April 20, 1959, cited in Cai, "From Fiction to Nullity: the Evolution of Public Interest in Land Expropriation."

84 Art. 1, Interim Measures of the Work on Basic Construction (基本建设工作暂行办法), promulgated by State Council Committee of Finance and Economic Affairs on January 9, 1952, available at www.pkulaw.cn/fulltext_form.aspx?Gid=159996.

85 Karl Marx, *Capital* (New York: International Publishers, 1959), vol. 2, chapter 21.

means *all sorts of* construction works. Hence, the more common and indeed more accurate rendering of the term is "capital construction." Apparently capital construction is much broader in scope than state construction in the conventional understanding.

According to the aforementioned 1959 provision, rural collectives could use their own land to engage in basic construction. Yet no national or local policy or law was ever promulgated to spell out the exact type of basic construction that could be undertaken by the rural collectives. A textbook on finance and accounting of the people's communes published in 1960 suggested that they could carry out basic construction in both productive and nonproductive areas.[86] Productive construction stands for agricultural, industrial and transportation construction; nonproductive construction means the construction of public welfare facilities within the rural collectives including member peasants' household residences, hospitals, schools, nursing homes, kindergartens, canteens and so forth. While this list might appear fairly extensive and it seems that rural collectives could also undertake industrial construction, the fact is that in the pre-reform era the basic construction that rural collectives could conduct by themselves on their own land generally fell into two categories: agricultural production and public facilities. This was no accident. It is, rather, an inevitable result of the well-known fact that under the pre-reform political economy characterized by a rigid rural/urban division, rural collectives in China were assigned only a limited role that focused almost exclusively on agricultural production and welfare provision for their member peasants, while industrialization was more or less the sole responsibility of the state. To be sure, this is not to say that rural industrialization did not take place at all prior to the opening and reform policy. The notable exception was of course the Great Leap Forward Movement of 1958, when rural collectives were asked to engage in industrial production, especially steel-making, on their own land.[87] As is well known, however, this radical campaign was soon proven to be economically disastrous and in response the central policies started to demand contraction of rural industrialization from the late 1950s and early 1960s. For example, it was prescribed in the 1959

86 Teaching and Research Group on Finance and Accounting of the Department of Economics at Xiamen University (ed.), *Finance and Accounting of People's Communes* (人民公社财务会计) (Beijing: Nongye Press, 1960), p. 336.

87 Resolution on Several Issues concerning People's Communes (关于人民公社若干问题的决议), promulgated by the CCP Central Committee on December 10, 1958, available at cpc.people.com.cn/GB/64184/64186/66665/4493211.html.

provision cited above that no less than 80 percent of the labor force of the people's communes should be committed to agricultural production and no more than 20 percent to industry.[88] In 1962, it was further requested that rural collectives should stop setting up new enterprises and that remaining collective enterprises ought to be of direct service to agricultural production and peasants' livelihood, carrying out basic construction projects related to irrigation, afforestation as well as soil conservation and improvement.[89] Before long, the central authorities made it crystal clear that in rural areas initiatives of ancillary production (*fuye*), i.e. nonagricultural production, should in principle be for the sake of better serving agricultural production. Otherwise it should at least not interfere with agricultural production or compete with SOEs for raw materials.[90] In this situation, it is fair to say that during the pre-reform era, non-agricultural production was in the monopolistic hands of the state. Except for minimal extent industrial development and public goods provision for the member peasants, such as residential plots, roads and other public facilities, rural collectives could not use their land for non-agricultural construction unless first expropriated by the state.[91] Put differently, even though there was no formal policy or law explicitly imposing stringent use control upon rural land, the presumption of state expropriation in nonagricultural use of rural collective land was already in place from the 1950s, only to be provided for in legislation during the 1980s. This means that the de-agrarianization challenge to the constitutional public interest prerequisite was already extant in the pre-reform period.

The implications of this finding will be explored more fully in the next chapter. The issue of more immediate relevance here is how did the state decide to expropriate rural collective land? It is notable that by following

[88] Politburo of CCP Central Committee, Eighteen Issues concerning the People's Communes, point 12.

[89] Points 11, 13, 19, Revised Draft Regulation on the Work in the Rural People's Communes (农村人民公社工作条例修正草案), promulgated by CCP Central Committee on September 27, 1962, available at www.tdzyw.com/2013/1204/33698.html.

[90] Decision on Developing Ancillary Production in Rural Areas (关于发展农村副业生产的决定), promulgated by CCP Central Committee and State Council on November 22, 1962, available at www.china.com.cn/guoqing/2012-09/12/content_26747227.htm. Similar requirements were repeated in 1965. Article 5, Instruction on Greatly Developing Ancillary Production in Rural Areas (关于大力发展农村副业生产的指示), promulgated by CCP Central Committee and State Council on September 5, 1965, available at guoqing.china.com.cn/2012-09/06/content_26448136.htm.

[91] As shown in the previous section, this was formally legalized through the 1982 Rural Construction Regulation and the 1982 RLRSC.

the Soviet model, since the early 1950s China had instituted a comprehensive planning system of capital construction.[92] Put briefly, that system required capital construction projects of various scales to be planned and authorized in advance by the competent central or local planning authorities and governments.[93] Correspondingly, the 1953 and 1958 MLRSC both provided in Article 4 that land expropriation should first be reviewed by the planning authority responsible for approving the related capital construction projects and then sanctioned by the competent central or local government. In other words, expropriation decisions were concomitant with the decisions to launch capital construction projects that were made according to state economic planning. Expropriation decisions were therefore part of the economic planning system and served as an instrument to implement state economic plans. Put differently, they were essentially the spatial manifestation of state economic plans. Worth noting is that the state economic planning system did not formally cover the capital construction projects conducted by rural collectives. Nevertheless, rural collectives were also required to make plans for their own capital construction and obtain government authorization for such plans and capital construction projects.[94] Overall, under a system of this kind, the state exercised full control over the use and conversion of rural land for both agricultural and nonagricultural ends. With regard to the latter, as noted, from the 1950s onwards, state land expropriation had been deployed for all kinds of capital construction projects, including those for the private interests of enterprises and individual citizens. It was by no means always undertaken by state agencies or intended for the common good. In this scenario, the Chinese

[92] For a brief historical account of the economic planning system in China in the pre-reform years, see Yingyi Qian, "The Process of China's Market Transition (1978-1998): The Evolutionary, Historical, and Comparative Perspectives" (2000) 156 (1) *Journal of Institutional and Theoretical Economics* 164.

[93] For details of this system, see State Council Committee of Finance and Economic Affairs, Interim Measures of the Work on Basic Construction, chapter 3; Several Rules on Strenghthening the Planning Administration of Basic Construction (关于加强基本建设计划管理的几项规定), promulgated by State Council in May 1962; Several Rules on Improving the Planning Administration of Basic Construction (关于改进基本建设计划管理的几项规定), promulgated by State Planning Commission, State Construction Commission and Ministry of Finance on November 15, 1965.

[94] Point I (1) 4, Illustration on Making the 1960 Measures on Planning Administration of Basic Construction (1960年基本建设计划管理办法的编制说明), promulgated by Bureau of Basic Construction of State Planning Commission in July 1959; Point 11, Revised Draft Regulation on the Work in the Rural People's Communes; arts. 5, 16, Regulation on the Administration of Land Use for Buildings in Villages and Townships.

term *guojia jianshe* present in the titles of China's expropriation laws enacted in the 1953, 1958 and 1982 is translated as "state-led construction" instead of "state construction." In essence, it means that all nonagricultural capital construction was under state management from plan to practice, and land expropriation was but a means for the state to determine when and where rural land should be used for such purposes.[95]

In light of the preceding discussion, we are now in a position to decode the two puzzles mentioned earlier – the incompatibility between the constitutional principle of state expropriation of land according to law and voluntary rural land transaction, and the causal relationship between rural land transaction and waste of cultivated land. Given that in most cases rural land could not be used for nonagricultural purposes unless expropriated by the state according to economic plans, voluntary transaction of rural land ("free price bargaining") undoubtedly bypassed this restriction and the state was prevented from expropriating such land. More importantly, rural land transaction severely disrupted the economic planning system that was supposed to determine the location and timing of capital construction and thereby undermined the state's comprehensive control over the utilization of rural land. The end result was endemic unsupervised and unauthorized conversion of rural land, especially cultivated land into construction land, which was a waste of cultivated land in the eyes of the party-state.

Admittedly, all these problems of cultivated land waste and unauthorized conversion of rural land appeared when the Cultural Revolution stopped the implementation of the 1958 MLRSC and a legal vacuum ensued in this field. But it was only in the late 1970s and early 1980s that the Chinese central authority was prompted to put in place a new law on state land expropriation containing an express ban on rural land transactions. Why? The reason lies in the fact that after the opening and reform policy, rural China took off and there was a rapidly increasing demand for nonagricultural capital construction in the countryside, especially for peasants' residences.[96] Within just a few years, a huge

95 "State-authorized construction" is another possible candidate. However, it is less appropriate than "state-led construction" because it implies a rather neutral or even passive role of the state, which is historically inaccurate in the Chinese context.

96 State Council, Minutes of the Second National Conference on the Work of Rural Housing Construction. Two factors were identified for this boom in rural housing construction. First, after the agricultural reform, the peasants became more financially capable of affording building residences. Second, the Party changed its policy in 1979 to encourage

amount of cultivated land was converted into construction land, alerting the Chinese central authority that it might pose long-term and irreversible risks to a still predominantly agricultural country with a huge population but little arable land. Hence, in 1981 the State Council issued a notice highlighting the pressing need to curb this trend.[97] And in 1982 it became a formal legal requirement that rural collectives must seek approval from the governments at the county level or higher whenever they converted their land to construction land.[98] Meanwhile, besides peasant residences, widespread unauthorized purchases and leases of cultivated land by government agencies and SOEs from rural collectives also exacerbated the problem.[99] Although it was conceded that these state-affiliated entities did so out of real demands for building office blocks, manufacturing sites or employee accommodation, they were criticized for pursuing self-interest at the expense of national interest, and the rural collectives that sold or rent out cultivated land were condemned for trying to gain windfall profits by treating land as a commodity.[100]

Against such a background, as noted earlier, between 1981 and 1982, a series of policy documents and statutes were promulgated, for the first time after the 1960s, to reaffirm and re-emphasize the principle of state expropriation according to law and the prohibition on voluntary land transaction, both of which eventually received constitutional entrenchment in 1982. The preceding analysis reveals that as much as being a Marxist–Soviet tradition, the constitutional ban on the land market was also a pragmatic policy response to the rapid loss of rural agricultural land to construction land from the late 1970s. It was intended to enable the state to regain control over the use and conversion of rural land by

construction of peasant residences, which was previously discouraged and suppressed for being nonproductive. See State Construction Committee, State Agriculture Committee, Ministry of Agriculture, Ministry of Construction Materials and Industry and State Bureau of Construction Industry, Report on the National Conference on the Work of Rural Housing Construction.

97 State Council, Urgent Notice on Stopping Appropriation of Cultivated Land for Rural Housing Construction.

98 Regulation on the Administration of Land Use for Buildings in Villages and Townships, arts. 5, 16.

99 For example, the Beijing municipal government found out in 1983 that this was pandemic in that city. See Notice on Working Harder in Dealing with the Problem of Leases and Sales of Collective Land (关于抓紧处理租赁买卖社队土地问题的通知), promulgated by Beijing Municipality People's Government on November 9, 1983, available at www.110.com/fagui/law_67663.html.

100 Ibid.

ensuring that expropriation remained the only means for nonagricultural use of rural land in most scenarios. It is for this reason that the constitutional clause inhibiting voluntary transaction of land should also be seen as part of the constitutional takings clause *sensu lato*.

6.3 Rational Use of Land

The third change in Article 10 of the 1982 Constitution as compared to Article 13 of the 1954 Constitution is the constitutional requirement that all land-using organizations and individuals ought to do so rationally. At first sight, this clause seems to bear exclusively on the principle of rationality according to which land should be used. The term is *heli* in Chinese, literally meaning reasonably, efficiently or wisely. In fact, however, it was closely related to land takings right from the beginning.

In January 1956, the State Council issued the *Notice on Rectifying and Preventing Waste in Land Requisition for State-led Construction.*[101] It was warned that within just two years of the 1953 MLRSC being enacted, there had emerged a serious problem of massive waste of expropriated land across the country. For example, 40 percent of the land expropriated in Wuhan, Beijing, Hangzhou, Chengdu and Hebei was wasted. This percentage shot up even higher in Changsha, standing at 80 percent. Two causes were identified for such waste in land expropriation.[102] First, the State Council were critical that many land-using entities made unwise capital construction plans and blindly asked the state to expropriate more land than was actually needed or before it was actually needed. Second, the government agencies responsible for reviewing and approving expropriation applications had also been very slack in their jobs, allowing too much concession to the land-using entities. Most crucially, they had failed to regularly check whether and how expropriated land was used in reality by those entities. As a response, the State Council ordered four measures.[103] First, governments at all levels were required to practice thrift in approving land expropriation and ensure that the quantity and location of the land requested to be expropriated fit the general local economic plan. Second, all land-using entities should economize on land use and prepare detailed plans before applying for expropriation.

[101] Notice on Correcting and Stopping Waste in Land Requisition for State-led Construction (关于纠正与防止国家建设征用土地中浪费现象的通知), promulgated by State Council on January 24, 1956, available at china.findlaw.cn/fagui/p_1/163304.html.
[102] Ibid. [103] Ibid.

Applications should be filed only for the amount of land actually needed and only at the time when it is actually needed. Third, governments at all levels had to regularly check whether and how expropriated land is used and rectify any waste. Any land no longer needed by the land-using entities due to change of capital construction plans should be withdrawn without compensation and then re-allocated to other land-using entities or returned to the peasants. Fourth, all land-using entities should give any expropriated land that is no longer used back to the local government. Apparently, these four measures aimed to guarantee rationality in expropriation application, approval and post-expropriation land use. In fact, all of them were already stipulated by Articles 3 and 4 of the 1953 MLRSC, which established the principle of "economizing on land use" (*jieyue yongdi*) in land expropriation. But this was largely to no avail. Why?

There are mainly two reasons. First and foremost, under a centralized planned economy land-using entities did not have to bear any cost incurred in land expropriation and subsequent usage. Although both the 1953 and the 1958 MLRSC did mention that land-using entities should be responsible for paying compensation to the expropriated,[104] given the fact that they were in one way or another affiliated with the state and supported by government funding,[105] the real costs of land expropriation compensation were eventually covered by the public purse.[106] In the meantime, land-using entities did not have to pay for their use of expropriated land because such land was allocated to them free of charge and without term limits. In this situation, to borrow a term from economics, there was a prime example of free riding on the part of the land-using entities, which had no incentive and indeed no opportunity to increase the efficiency of land use as they were neither allowed to marketize the land nor permitted to change land use to more profitable ends.[107]

The second reason for endemic waste in land expropriation is the lack of effective supervision. As noted earlier, expropriation decisions at the time were essentially a spatial manifestation of state economic planning

104 1953 MLRSC, art. 14; 1958 MLRSC, art. 8.

105 Private enterprises were abolished after the mid-1950s. Individual urban residents were supported by their units that are either government agencies or SOEs in building residence and therefore did not have to bear the expropriation cost personally.

106 Jingdong Zhang, "China's Urban Land is not Used for Free: on the Fundamental Cause to Low Efficiency in Land Use (中国城市土地并非无偿使用 – 兼论土地利用效率低的根本原因)" (1992) 5 *Urban Issues* (城市问题) 14.

107 Ibid.

as they were first approved by the planning authorities responsible for approving the capital construction projects for which the expropriated land was supposed to be used. In the pre-reform era, such planning authorities came from the same vertical functional system of government as the expropriation-applying land-using units, known as the *tiaotiao* in Chinese as opposed to the *kuaikuai* that is the horizontal and territorial system of government.[108] In this situation, for example, expropriation applications for irrigation projects would be approved by local departments and the national ministry in charge of agricultural production and water energy. In contrast, expropriation applications for steel factories or coalmines would go to those agencies designated with the task of administering affairs of steel production and coalmine operation. It was observed that out of turf protectionism these planning authorities were very reluctant to impose much constraint upon the land-using entities.[109] Hence, they were chastised by the State Council for being "very slack in their job." Besides, top-down control from superior governments over land expropriation was also less than effective. While the 1953 and 1958 MLRSC both granted governments down to the county level the power to sanction land expropriation depending on the size of the projects, the State Council decided in 1962 to scale such power back up to the provincial level in order to strengthen top-down control over land expropriation.[110] Just two years later, in 1964, however, this approving power was devolved again down to the county level governments for capital construction projects below a certain size threshold. This was because the State Council realized that centralizing the approving authority to the provincial level and above was too administratively cumbersome, which had hindered timely review of an increasing number of expropriation applications and caused undue delay in supplying land to construction and development.[111] In the meantime, acutely aware of the

108 Qian, "The Process of China's Market Transition (1978-1998)," 164.

109 Yuchuan Zou (ed.), *Land Administration in Contemporary China* (当代中国土地管理) (Beijing: Dangdai Zhongguo Press, 1998), vol. 1, p. 91.

110 Comments of the Ministry of Domestic Affairs on the Report on the Use of the Land Expropriated for State-led Construction in Beijing and Tianjin (内务部关于北京、天津两市国家建设征用土地使用情况的报告的批语), promulgated by State Council on April 10, 1962, available at www.china.com.cn/law/flfg/txt/2006-08/08/content_7057984.htm.

111 Notice on Modest Decentralization of the Examining and Approving Power concerning Land Requisition for State-led Construction (关于国家建设征用土地审批权限适当下放的通知), promulgated by State Council on July 20, 1964, available at china.findlaw.cn/fagui/p_1/163002.html.

risk of excessive expropriation, the State Council emphasized in the same decree that after the devolution of the approving power those responsible governments should continue to practice thrift in authorizing land expropriation and that top-down supervision in this area should never be relaxed.[112]

That again turned out to be unsuccessful in reining in wasteful expropriation. In fact, the intractability of this problem was manifested time and again in the subsequent decades. In 1962, 1964, 1970, 1973 and 1979, the above-cited requirements in the 1956 State Council Notice were repeatedly reissued and re-emphasized by the central authority, attempting to crack down on excessive rural land expropriation.[113] That fact itself demonstrates that orders from the top were far from adequate in stopping wasteful expropriation, which was once again thrown into stark relief in the early 1980s when conversion of rural cultivated land into construction land picked up in pace. In this scenario, at a national conference on rural housing construction in December 1981, the Chinese central authority pronounced for the first time that "every inch of land must be cherished and used rationally" should be a basic national policy (*jiben guoce*).[114] A few months later, this was written into Article 3 of the *Rural Construction Regulation* enacted in February 1982 and Article 3 of the 1982 RLRSC promulgated in May 1982. Eventually, in December of the same year the principle of rational use of land became constitutionally enshrined. In view of the historical background just presented, the

[112] Ibid.

[113] State Council, Comments of the Ministry of Domestic Affairs on the Report on the Use of the Land Expropriated for State-led Construction in Beijing and Tianjin; Comprehensive Report of the Ministry of Domestic Affairs on the Inquiries done by Local Governments and Departments on the Use of the Land Expropriated (内务部关于个地方各部门检查征用土地使用情况的综合报告), promulgated by State Council on October 30, 1962, available at www.china.com.cn/law/flfg/txt/2006-08/08/content_7059102.htm; Notice on Issues concerning Land Expropriation by the Military (关于部队征用土地问题的通知), promulgated by General Political Department of the People's Liberation Army on April 20, 1970; Notice on Implementing the State Council's Instruction on Practicing Thrift in Using Land for Basic Construction (关于贯彻执行国务院有关在基本建设中节约用地的指示的通知), promulgated by State Planning Revolutionary Committee and State Basic Construction Revolutionary Committee on June 18, 1973, available at china.findlaw.cn/fagui/p_1/212352.html; Point 11, Decisions on Several Issues concerning Accelerating Agricultural Development (关于加快农业发展若干问题的决定), promulgated by CCP Central Committee on September 28, 1979, available at www.china.com.cn/chinese/zhuanti/jd/493900.htm.

[114] State Council, Minutes of the Second National Conference on the Work of Rural Housing Construction.

constitutional principle of rational use of land applies equally to the land-using entities that apply for state land expropriation and the government authorities with the power to review and approve such applications. Both the applicant for and the approver of expropriation are required to be rational so as to prevent waste of land, especially the much-cherished cultivated land. Therefore, the constitutional entrenchment of rationality as the principle for land use was historically primarily motivated by worry about irrational expropriation. As much as being about land use in the general sense, it also constitutes a component of the 1982 constitutional takings clause *sensu lato*.

6.4 Parsing the 1982 Takings Clause: Nature and Purpose

This chapter began with a distinction between two senses of China's 1982 constitutional takings clause. With the first two paragraphs on public land ownership by state and collective, the fourth paragraph on prohibition of voluntary land transaction and the final paragraph on rational use of land, Article 10 in the 1982 Constitution is typically considered to have much broader connotations than its third paragraph, which is usually regarded as the existing constitutional takings clause. However, as demonstrated by the foregoing analysis, in ways that have been largely overlooked so far, all of these provisions are in one way or another closely related to the state power of land takings. To start with, the first two paragraphs were historically the result of a pragmatic decision made by and indeed a compromise struck among the constitutional framers, falling just one step short of full-scale land nationalization. More importantly, as already demonstrated, the first paragraph stating that urban land is owned by the state was itself an exercise of the power to nationalize the urban land existing at the time of constitutional enactment in 1982, though it neither automatically nationalizes nor obligates the state to expropriate the urban land that has come into existence afterwards. The next paragraph on collective ownership of rural and suburban land defines the subject of state expropriation. Second, via prohibiting land transaction, the fourth paragraph was intended to ensure that state expropriation remains the only way in which rural land could be used for most nonagricultural construction and development projects. It therefore demarcates the scope of state expropriation. Third, the final paragraph spells out the basic principle that should be followed by both the initiators and the decision-makers of land expropriation. For sure, this is not to say that these provisions are exclusively about land takings.

For instance, the rationality principle also applies to post-taking utilization of land. However, the foregoing analysis does show that although usually not regarded to be so, all provisions in Article 10 are indeed related to the state power of land takings. The third paragraph shall be seen as the constitutional takings clause in the narrow sense, which must be comprehended in the light of Article 10 as the constitutional takings clause in the broad sense.

How exactly do these five paragraphs fit together? They are united on two points, from which the nature and purpose of the 1982 constitutional takings clause *sensu lato* can be derived. Above all, all of them are normatively based on the socialist principle discussed previously. The provisions in Article 10 on land expropriation and the ban on voluntary land transaction have constitutionally endorsed the fact that from the 1950s to the 1980s in China expropriation was (or, at least, was supposed to be) the predominant way to supply land to all sorts of nonagricultural construction projects, including those by and for private enterprises and individual citizens. This was normatively legitimized not because these entities and individuals were somehow regarded as representing the state or the public interest. Rather, it was because these construction projects and expropriation initiatives were authorized by the state. Under the socialist principle, the state is the embodiment of public interest, which is superior to and at the same time in harmony with private interests. Land expropriation is necessarily in the public interest for being undertaken by the state to enhance public property, to facilitate industrialization of the country or to limit the least-favored and most suspicious private property. Therefore, so long as a decision of land expropriation is sanctioned by the state, no matter who the applicants are or what ends the expropriated land is subsequently put to, it is considered to be in line with the public interest. Moreover, a similar argument can be made about the 1982 nationalization clause, which was legitimized under the same principle too. From the perspective of private landowners of urban land in 1982, according to the socialist principle, being dispossessed by the state should not be conceptualized as a loss or sacrifice of their property rights in land. Instead, it was an honorable duty for them as socialist citizens to accept nationalization. This point was well articulated by the deputy minister of the State Construction Commission when he delivered the official explanatory note of the draft RLRSC in 1982 and explained how expropriatees should respond to expropriation: "when receiving reasonable compensation and resettlement according to relevant rules, rural collectives and peasants have the obligation to actively support state-led construction."[115] This was confirmed in Article 4 of the finalized 1982 RLRSC: "If a decision of land expropriation complies with the prescriptions contained in this law, members of the expropriated collectives ought to obey the demands of the state and shall not cause any hindrance or obstruction."

In the meantime, all provisions of Article 10 serve the same function of facilitating state-led construction and development. For example, the previous analysis has shown that the clause on state ownership of urban land was originally intended to partially alleviate the difficulty with which the state could acquire land. The no-land transaction clause was put in place to reaffirm the state's exclusive control over conversion of rural land to nonagricultural uses by way of land expropriation. The rational land use clause attempted to put a brake on wasteful expropriation so as to help the course of state-led construction and development. Even the ostensibly restrictive requirement of "in accordance with law" in the takings clause *sensu stricto* was instituted largely to stress that the governing law on rural land expropriation must be obeyed to prevent the legal vacuum in the aftermath of the 1958 MLRSC from reappearing.

In summary, the unprecedented and unparalleled constitutional takings clause of China emerged when the CCP abandoned class struggle and started to commit itself to growing the economy at the dawn of the opening and reform era. It is fundamentally shaped by this historic turn, yet it is not that different from its 1954 predecessor, normatively and teleologically. On the one hand, it is still based on the socialist principle that sees the state as the unquestionable and unchallengeable representative of the public interest. On the other hand, although the specific agenda the state land takings power is supposed to serve is changed from class struggle to economic development, the power-confirming function stays the same. In this sense, the 1982 constitutional takings clause is new wine in an old bottle. It has remained an integral part of the modern Chinese tradition of land takings for state-led social transformation ever since the early twentieth century. It is a world away from the Fifth Amendment to the American Constitution.

In this light, we can now make sense of the change made by the 1982 constitutional takings clause *sensu stricto* to its 1954 counterpart, which is the removal of nationalization and compulsory purchase from the enumerated list of takings power. The reason that the power of nationalization

[115] Kebai Lv, "Explanatory Report on the Draft Regulation on Land Requisition for State-led Construction."

was removed is twofold. First, the socialist transformation of industry and commerce had long been completed back in the 1960s. At the time of constitutional drafting in 1982, there was no longer any ongoing or anticipated revolutionary project that requires compensationless nationalization. But this cannot explain why the power of nationalization was still provided for in the 1975 and 1978 constitutional takings clauses, which brings us to the second reason. At the dawn of the reform era, after decades of seclusion, China urgently needed foreign investment to kick-start its economic turnaround. In order to alleviate the bad taste in the mouths of international investors who had been damaged by sweeping compensationless nationalization, most notably when the CCP took power in 1949, a pledge was consciously and explicitly made in one of the first few statutes enacted in the reform era: the 1979 *Law of Sino-foreign Equity Joint Ventures* stipulates in Article 2 that the state will never nationalize Sino–foreign joint ventures under any circumstances. Against this background, it is reasonable to conclude that erasing nationalization from the 1982 takings clause was also driven by the desire to regain the confidence of overseas investors.

The reason for the disappearance of compulsory purchase is that it is, as mentioned in Chapter 4, procedurally preconditioned on the voluntary negotiation between land-using entities and landowners, which distinguishes it from expropriation. As noted, voluntary transaction of rural land became banned after collectivization in the early 1960s. This made it no longer possible or necessary to differentiate compulsory purchase from expropriation or to treat it as a separate and distinctive takings power. Hence, it was removed from the 1975 and 1978 Constitutions. In the deliberation process of the 1982 Constitution it was advised that since purchase and sale of land is prohibited, compulsory purchase by the state was no longer appropriate.[116] In addition to these practical motivating factors, a more deep-seated conceptual reason is that under the socialist principle dispossession by the state is not conceptualized as a transaction.

Yet, one may argue that what has been revealed in this chapter is no more than a historical reading of the 1982 constitutional takings clause. It is unsurprising that, to a large extent, it still carried the historical legacy from the pre-reform years when the opening and reform policy was just about to unfold. Over the past three decades, however, China has undergone enormous and comprehensive changes, which should have already

[116] Xu, *The Constitutional History of the PRC*, p. 666.

renovated the constitutional basis of rural land expropriation. A good case in point is that the 2004 constitutional amendment openly proclaims that the state guarantees and respects human rights. Another example is the general perception today that it should not be a duty for citizens to actively accept state expropriation and that the decision to expropriate is not always in the public interest. Nevertheless, as will be pointed out in the next chapter, the Chinese law on rural land expropriation in the reform era is not a betrayal but a faithful reflection of the 1982 constitutional takings clause. This is because, to a significant extent, the constitutional basis of rural land expropriation in China today is still what it was more than half a century ago.

7

Rural Land Expropriation Law in the Reform Era

A Story of Continuity

The preceding three chapters have demonstrated that for the best part of the twentieth century, the power of land takings had been conceptualized and exercised as an instrument for the communist party-state to achieve its social transformation program in China, be it proletarian revolution or economic development. This was not only manifested by the relevant laws and policies promulgated by the communist government, but also enshrined in China's constitutional takings clauses in 1954 and 1982. As shown in the previous chapter, whereas the widely discussed urbanization challenge turns out to be an ungrounded myth, the de-agrarianization challenge is real and was in existence from the 1950s. Although the 1954 constitutional takings clause requires expropriation to be in the public interest, the reality was that in most cases rural land could be used for nonagricultural purposes only after state expropriation, regardless of how and by whom it would be used subsequently. Under this presumption of expropriation in nonagricultural use of rural land, it was inevitable that the power of expropriation was permitted in law to be exercised for private individuals or firms, none of which could be easily squared with the public interest in the conventional understanding. Until the early 1980s, that presumption was never formally expressed in a policy or legal document. Instead, it was more of a natural consequence of the Chinese political–economic system in the pre-reform era when the function of the rural collectives was by and large limited to agricultural production and public provision to their member peasants, while nonagricultural construction and development fell within the sole jurisdiction of the state. At the beginning of the reform era, the state's monopoly of nonagricultural development of rural land continued and became overtly expressed for the first time in the 1982 *Rural Construction Regulation* and the 1982 RLRSC, as explained in the previous chapter. Worth noting is that both these statutes were enacted just months prior to and stayed effective after the 1982 Constitution. As demonstrated in Chapter 6, the 1982 constitutional takings clause in the broad sense has actually confirmed and entrenched the presumption of expropriation in nonagricultural use of rural land, which is drastically different from the American Fifth Amendment.

Since then, China has witnessed two legal regimes of land administration and expropriation, from the 1986 LAL to the 1998 LAL, with intermittent amendments in 1988 and 2004. It is undeniable that over this period enormous changes and transformations in economical, social and legal terms have occurred in the People's Republic. One seems to have every reason to believe that the historical theories and practices of rural land takings law examined in the preceding three chapters have largely lost contemporary relevance. This chapter argues precisely the opposite: the Chinese law of rural land expropriation in the reform era shows an amazing level of continuity of its pre-reform roots. The first section exposes the structural continuity of the law by highlighting the lasting presence of various legal provisions from the early 1980s until this day, which demonstrates that rural land expropriation in China persists to be expansive, unchallengeable, poorly compensated and undemocratically determined. The second section discusses the functional continuity of China's rural land expropriation law, which continues to serve the dual purpose, as it did in the pre-reform years, of preserving cultivated land and promoting economic development. The third section focuses on the law's normative continuity in the sense that the socialist principle remains the standard of legitimation behind rural land expropriation. The penultimate section of this chapter turns to the law's foundational continuity by exploring the existing mechanism of expropriation decision-making. It reveals that expropriation decisions are not freestanding ad hoc decisions, but rather the extension of top-down state planning, as was the case in the pre-reform period. Finally, this chapter explains the persistent nonjusticiability of expropriation decisions, especially how it is based on a mistaken reading of the law and why the potential of judicializing the constitutional public interest prerequisite is still limited even if the law is interpreted correctly.

Before delving into the details, it is crucial to clarify at the outset that changes do happen in this area of law, many of which are significant and impactful. This chapter denies none of that and gives them due attention. The argument is that instead of examining these changes, a much more accurate and coherent story can be told through recording, analyzing and explaining a set of enduring characteristics of the law in question. This is because China's rural land expropriation law is deeply rooted in its historical lineage, which this chapter attempts to reconstruct.

7.1 Structural Continuity

7.1.1 1986 LAL and 1988 Revision

In 1986, China promulgated its first comprehensive land legislation, followed by a more detailed implementation rule in 1991. Both kept the presumption of expropriation in nonagricultural use of rural land, albeit in a somewhat inexplicit manner. Pursuant to Articles 36 and 38–41 of the 1986 LAL and Articles 27–29 of the 1991 LALIR, there were a total of six types of nonagricultural use of rural land that could be carried by rural collectives upon government approval without state expropriation. They were: (1) residence construction for collective member peasants, (2) public utilities and welfare initiatives for collectives, (3) TVEs, (4) joint ventures between rural collectives and noncollective entities, (5) residence construction for urban residents without rural *hukou*, and (6) small privately run nonagricultural businesses of peasant households known as "private entrepreneurs" (*getihu*).[1] It was not expressly stated that these six scenarios exhausted all legally permissible nonagricultural purposes for which rural collectives might utilize their land without undergoing state expropriation. However, in light of the structure of both legal documents, that was the case. Specifically, the 1986 LAL contained seven chapters, two of which were about nonagricultural use of land. The fourth chapter covered nonagricultural land use for state-led development and the fifth chapter was about the same for rural collectives. In the fourth chapter, provisions besides Article 36 spelled out the two ways in which land could be secured for state-led development, i.e. state expropriation of rural land from the collectives and withdrawal of state-owned land from private users. Article 36 prescribed that any rural land to be used for joint ventures between collective and noncollective entities should typically be expropriated and converted into state-owned land first. But, if approved by the government at the county level or above, such land might also be used by rural collectives as in-kind contributions to the joint ventures without expropriation and conversion. The fifth chapter of the 1986 LAL included a total of six provisions from Article 37 to Article 42. Articles 37 and 42 specified how nonagricultural use of rural land should be regulated through government

[1] As shown in Chapter 6, the first three categories were already present in the 1982 Rural Construction Regulation, which means that three more were added here. Chapter 2 showed that in total five categories of this kind are specified by the 1998 LAL. The reason for such expansion and contraction in the permitted categories for nonagricultural use of rural land without state expropriation in the reform era will be discussed shortly in this chapter.

planning. Articles 38–41 listed the aforementioned scenarios for nonagricultural use of rural land without expropriation. Similarly, the 1991 LALIR also contained two chapters on nonagricultural land use in a structure similar to their counterparts in the 1986 LAL. The only difference was that one additional scenario for nonagricultural use of rural land free of expropriation was provided for in the 1991 LALIR (Article 29). According to these provisions under the first land law regime, nonagricultural land use could be either for state-led development or for rural collectives. The former is done through expropriation and withdrawal, the end result of which is that state-led development takes place over state-owned land. There are no enumerated specific purposes for which such development may happen. What is stated is just that the state may use land for economic, cultural, national defense and social public undertakings.[2] In stark contrast, the 1986 LAL and the 1991 LALIR included a list of specific purposes for nonagricultural land use by rural collectives. Although it is not overtly suggested that these ends are exhaustive, when compared with the open-ended and expansive prescription on state-led development, it cannot be clearer that nonagricultural use of land for rural collectives is the exception that can happen only for a limited number of specified objectives. For most nonagricultural uses, state expropriation is required.

Relatedly, on concrete issues concerning expropriation, the 1986 LAL also largely continued previous trends. To start with, with respect to expropriation decision-making, the 1986 LAL maintained the mechanism of top-down hierarchical review and approval according to economic planning, though with two changes. Whilst it still delegated the expropriation-approving authority down to the county-level government, a practice that was first started in 1964, as mentioned in the previous chapter, and was adopted by the 1982 RLRSC, the 1986 LAL scaled part of that power up to the provincial level.[3] Furthermore, for the first time in PRC history, the 1986 LAL instituted departments specialized in land administration from the ministerial to the county level, which were called land administration bureaus and were tasked to manage land affairs on behalf of the corresponding governments, including reviewing expropriation applications before submitting them for final government

[2] 1986 LAL, art. 21; 1991 LALIR, art. 17.

[3] 1982 RLRSC, art. 8; 1986 LAL, art. 25. In the 1982 RLRSC, the county governments can authorize expropriation of cultivated land less than 3 *mu* and other kinds of land below 20 *mu*. The 1986 LAL prescribes that the county governments may sanction expropriation of cultivated land below 3 *mu* and other kinds of land below 10 *mu*.

approval.[4] That being said, according to Article 23 of the 1986 LAL, to secure the final government approval, applicants of expropriation must first obtain permission for the capital construction projects the expropriated land would be used for, dependent on conformity with state economic plans. Therefore, expropriation decisions remained the spatial expression of state economic plans.

Second, expropriation compensation standards in these two statutes were identical: the compensation fee for cultivated land was set at 3–6 times the average annual output of agricultural products over the three years before expropriation. The resettlement fee per person was stipulated to be 2–3 times the average annual output, and the maximum resettlement fee per hectare to be 10 times such value. If the land compensation and resettlement fees combined were inadequate to maintain the peasants' original living standards, the provincial government could decide to increase the resettlement fee. However, the sum of the increased resettlement fee and the land compensation fee should not exceed 20 times the average annual output.[5] Last but not least, Article 23 of the 1986 LAL copied Article 4 of the 1982 RLRSC in prescribing that those expropriated should obey the demands of the state and should not cause any hindrance or obstruction. There was no way to challenge the expropriation decisions.

Overall, despite some adjustments, the aforementioned prescription on the scope, decision-making mechanisms, compensation standards and objectionability of land expropriation in the early 1980s was by and large inherited by the 1986 LAL. Without doubt, proximity in time is a contributing factor here. In fact, the central authority had already decided to promulgate a comprehensive land law in 1979,[6] and a draft LAL was prepared in 1981.[7] Thus, unsurprisingly, the finalized version of the LAL was left with an unmistakable imprint of what came just a few years before. Apart from that, a deeper cause for such continuity lies in

4 1986 LAL, art. 5; point 4, Notice on Tightening Up Land Administration and Stopping Unauthorized Occupation of Cultivated Land (关于加强土地管理制止乱占耕地的通知), promulgated by CCP Central Committee and State Council on March 21, 1986, available at www.law-lib.com/law/law_view.asp?id=47245.

5 1982 RLRSC, arts. 9–10; 1986 LAL, arts. 27–29.

6 Decisions on Several Issues concerning Accelerating Agricultural Development (关于加快农业发展若干问题的决定), promulgated by CCP Central Committee on September 28, 1979, available at www.china.com.cn/chinese/zhuanti/jd/493900.htm.

7 Zhongyang Xiang, "Explanatory Report on the Draft PRC Land Law (关于《中华人民共和国土地法(草案)》的说明)," March 15, 1986, available at www.npc.gov.cn/wxzl/gongbao/2000-12/26/content_5001797.htm.

the fact that the 1986 LAL was driven by exactly the same concerns as its precursors from the early years of the opening and reform period. It was demonstrated in the previous chapter that a series of policies and statutes were passed in the early 1980s to reaffirm and re-emphasize the presumption of expropriation in nonagricultural use of rural land and the prohibition on voluntary land transaction, both of which eventually received constitutional entrenchment in 1982. This was done largely in response to the rapid loss of rural agricultural land to nonagricultural development at the time. Four years later, this problem was far from solved, as evidenced by the fact that in March 1986 China's central authority again urged tightening up the control over unauthorized and excessive rural land expropriation and rural land transaction, which were seen to perpetuate the problem of agricultural land loss and waste.[8] The measure adopted this time was a new comprehensive land law,[9] which was intended as an upgrade solution to the same old problem. This explains not only the 1986 LAL's overall similarity to its precursors from the early 1980s, but also the differences. The partial recentralization of expropriation-approving power and the establishment of land administration bureaus in 1986 both reflected a conscious effort to strengthen top-down control over rural land expropriation.

None of the above was changed by the 1988 revision to the LAL or the 1988 constitutional amendment, which nevertheless brought a development of far-reaching impact. The blanket ban on voluntary land transaction was lifted. Recall that the original text of the fourth paragraph of Article 10 in the 1982 Constitution reads, "No organization or individual may appropriate, buy, sell, lease, or unlawfully transfer land in other ways." The 1988 constitutional amendment removed "lease" and added one sentence. The revised clause now reads, "No organization or individual may appropriate, buy, sell or unlawfully transfer land in other ways. Land use-rights can be transferred according to provisions of the law." In the meantime, the term "lease" was also taken out from the second paragraph of Article 2 in the 1986 LAL. In addition, two paragraphs were

[8] Notice on Tightening Up Land Administration and Stopping Unauthorized Occupation of Cultivated Land (关于加强土地管理制止乱占耕地的通知), promulgated by CCP Central Committee and State Council on March 21, 1986, available at www.law-lib.com/law/law_view.asp?id=47245.

[9] Law Commission of the National People's Congress, "Report on the Deliberation Result of the Draft PRC Land Law (对《中华人民共和国土地法(草案)》审议结果的报告)," June 16, 1986, available at www.npc.gov.cn/wxzl/gongbao/2000-12/26/content_5001798.htm.

inserted into that article. The new paragraph four reads, "Use-rights of state-owned land and collective-owned land can be transferred in accordance with law. The concrete measures on transfer of land use-rights will be promulgated by the State Council." Paragraph five states, "The state enforces a system for the use of state-owned land by payment of consideration. The concrete measures on the use of state-owned land by payment of consideration will be promulgated by the State Council." The rest is indeed history: by separating use-rights from ownership, without abandoning the hallmark of socialism that is public land ownership, China has since established a huge and dynamic market for state-owned land. The last 30 years have consequently witnessed a booming real estate industry, enormously improved urban infrastructure and, of course, land finance as explained in Chapter 3. Yet none of this has affected the state monopoly of rural–urban land conversion through expropriation, the nonchallengeability of expropriation decisions, the compensation standard based on multiplied agricultural output or the top-down expropriation decision-making mechanism.

7.1.2 The 1998 LAL and the 2004 Revision

The next, and most recent, comprehensive revision of the LAL took place in 1998, which effectively established the current land law system in China since the more recent 2004 amendment to the 1998 LAL contained just a terminological adjustment from "requisition" to "expropriation" with no substantive alteration. The conventional wisdom is that as the first land law promulgated after China formally committed itself to a socialist market economy in the early 1990s, the 1998 LAL marked a sharp departure from its predecessor to reflect this momentous sociopolitical change. However, while it did include some significant changes, it is a myth to think that it amounted to a radical rupture with the past.

First, as already noted in Chapter 2, the existing LAL prescribes in Articles 43, 60 and 63 that the rural collectives can only use their land, upon government permission, for nonagricultural purposes under five enumerated situations. All other nonagricultural development must take place on state-owned land and therefore involves rural–urban land conversion through expropriation. This is indeed the first time that the presumption of expropriation in nonagricultural use of rural land becomes explicitly and unequivocally stipulated in law. As mentioned earlier, from the 1950s to the early 1980s, this presumption was not mandated in any policy or legal document, but existed primarily as a consequence of China's pre-reform system based on a huge rural–urban divide, under which rural collectives carried out agricultural production to serve industrialization that was the sole responsibility of state government. In that situation, the presumption of expropriation in nonagricultural use of rural land was but a de facto reflection of the state's monopoly of nonagricultural development. After the opening and reform policy, this presumption became formally legalized in the 1982 RLRSC, the 1982 *Rural Construction Regulation* and the 1986 LAL, though in a rather implicit manner. None of these legislations stated that the enumerated circumstances for nonagricultural use of rural land by collectives were all-inclusive and exhaustive, which, as demonstrated in the preceding chapter, was nevertheless the case judging from the structure of all these laws.

It should be noted that even though relevant laws from the 1980s preserved the presumption of state expropriation in nonagricultural use of rural land, nonagricultural use of rural land without expropriation took off in the reform era for the following reasons. To start with, as noted in the preceding chapter, peasant residential construction underwent a huge boom. This was further exacerbated by the aforementioned legal change where the 1986 LAL began allowing citizens with nonagricultural *hukou* to use rural land for housing purposes. In this situation, the size of rural land used for residence construction increased dramatically. It was reported by the *People's Daily* that between 1978 and 1991 eight billion square meters of rural housing were built, two times more than the total amount of rural housing constructed in the previous 30 years.[10] In the meantime, unlike the pre-reform era, rural industrialization was no longer suppressed but encouraged. In 1984, the central authorities announced a new official term for those enterprises run by rural collectives – TVE – and demanded local party and state agencies to treat TVEs with equal support as SOEs.[11]

[10] Xuexiao Wang, "A Historical Leap: Our Country has Strode Three Big Step in Fourteen Years since Opening and Reform (历史性的跨越 – 改革开放十四年我国上了三个大台阶)", *People's Daily*, October 14, 1992.

[11] Notice on Circulating the Report on Opening a New Page for Rural Collective Enterprises by Ministry of Agriculture, Husbandry and Fishing and its Party Branch (转发农牧渔业部和部党组《关于开创社队企业新局面的报告》的通知), promulgated by CCP Central Committee and State Council on March 1, 1984, available at www.china.com.cn/guoqing/2012-09/12/content_26747631.htm. There is a vast amount of literature on the TVE phenomenon in China, yet this is not the place for any extensive discussion. For a bibliography of relevant scholarship, see Hong-yi Chen, "Township and Village Enterprises," February 25, 2016, available at www.oxfordbibliographies.com/view/document/obo-9780199920082/obo-9780199920082-0128.xml.

A more specific change in favor of TVE development regarding land use was made by the 1986 LAL. Different from the 1982 *Rural Construction Regulation* that prohibited rural land to be used, without state expropriation, for joint ventures between rural collectives and noncollective entities or for private peasant entrepreneurs, the 1986 LAL opened up new space for such initiatives. Against such a background, the 1980s witnessed an unprecedented expansion of rural industrialization, which in turn resulted in a great spike in the volume of rural land used for industrial ends without state expropriation. By 1985, the size of rural industrial land was 2.6 times of that in 1978.[12]

Such rapid increase of rural construction land for residential and industrial ends without state expropriation during the 1980s and 1990s should not be seen as a breakaway from the presumption of expropriation in nonagricultural use of rural land. Quite the contrary – it ultimately became the motivating factor behind the explicit legalization of that presumption in the 1998 LAL. Since both residential and industrial uses of rural land had been provided for by the 1982 *Rural Construction Regulation* and the 1986 LAL with the latter being more relaxed in containing more types of permitted nonagricultural uses of rural land, the huge hike in the actual volume of rural land put to such uses was nothing other than the statutorily enumerated exceptions being utilized in practice. Admittedly, as just demonstrated, the amount of rural construction land claimed without expropriation was enormous, and the pressure that put on agricultural land preservation was undeniable. Yet that was not because the said presumption was abandoned and thereby as a principle rural collectives were licensed to use their land for nonagricultural purposes without expropriation. Rather, it was because the approval mechanism supposed to put a check upon permissible nonagricultural uses of rural land without expropriation was largely ineffective at the time. Even though the 1982 *Rural Construction Regulation* (Articles 14, 16 and 18) and the 1986 LAL (Articles 38–41) included provisions requiring permission from local governments to be secured in these circumstances, it was recorded that peasants could easily claim rural land for residential or industrial ends as long as the rural collectives acquiesced.[13]

[12] Yuchuan Zou (ed.), *Land Administration in Contemporary China* (当代中国土地管理) (Beijing: Dangdai Zhongguo Press, 1998), p. 142. The editor was the deputy minister of China's Ministry of Construction.

[13] Division for Agricultural Economics Research under Development Research Center of State Council, *Property Rights Restructuring under Collective Ownership* (集体所有制下的产权重构) (Beijing: Zhongguo Fazhan Press, 2015), p. 114.

It was against this backdrop that the 1998 LAL further tightened up state control over rural construction land. First, it trimmed down the legally permitted exceptions for nonagricultural use of rural land without expropriation, abolishing residential land for people with nonagricultural *hukou* and industrial land for private peasant entrepreneurs that were once present in the 1986 LAL and its 1991 implementation rule. Moreover, it instituted a quota system to impose much more stringent control over rural construction land than before. Although TVEs and joint ventures between rural collectives and noncollective entities are still kept in law as permissible exceptions, in practice it became virtually impossible for rural collectives to be allocated construction land quota from local governments to set up new TVEs or joint ventures.[14] Last, yet most importantly, the 1998 LAL entrenched formally and overtly, for the first time in modern Chinese legal history, the presumption of state expropriation in nonagricultural use of rural land, confirming and highlighting that the state monopoly of rural–urban land conversion through expropriation is now guaranteed by a national law. In consideration of the meaning of the 1982 constitutional takings clause as exposed in the previous chapter, on this front, the 1998 LAL, alongside its predecessors in the 1980s, remains more of a faithful application than a breach of the constitutional mandate.

Second, as to how expropriation decisions are made, the 1998 LAL sets up a so-called "land use regulatory system" (*tudi yongtu guanzhi zhidu*) to replace the previous "system of graded examination and approval according to specified limits" (*fenji xian'e shenpi zhidu*) under the 1986 LAL. But these two systems are in essence the same because in both rural land expropriation decisions were made through a process of top-down review and approval inside the government hierarchy. What was different in 1998, though, is twofold. On the one hand, the 1998 LAL recentralized the expropriation-approving authority back to the provincial level and above. Since then, the subprovincial governments no longer have such power, which is now exclusively within the competence of the State Council and provincial governments. History repeats itself here – as shown in the previous chapter, in 1962 the State Council once scaled such power back up to the provincial level. The second and indeed more significant adjustment in 1998 was that the basis on which governments authorize expropriation initiatives changed. It was noted earlier that

[14] Ibid, pp. 119–20. More detailed analysis of the quota system will be available in Section 7.4.

from the 1950s to the 1986 LAL, compliance with state economic plans was the criterion for approving expropriation applications. In the 1998 LAL, however, with the end of a comprehensive centralized command-and-control state economic planning system in China, the grounds for expropriation decision-making have changed to be an equally comprehensive system of land use planning – hence the name "land use regulatory system." More discussion about this will appear in Section 7.4. Suffice it to note here that the top-down and exclusionary nature of expropriation decision-making has been well preserved under the new system set up by the 1998 LAL. As a matter of fact, as will be shown more clearly in the next part of this chapter, this land use regulatory system was established precisely for the sake of strengthening top-down state control over the conversion of rural land to nonagricultural ends through expropriation. That also explains the recentralization of the expropriation-approving power to the provincial level and above.

Third, with regard to expropriation compensation, there was a noticeable increase in the 1998 LAL compared with the 1986 LAL. For instance, the land compensation fee of cultivated land was increased from 3–6 times to 6–10 times the average annual output of the expropriated land over three years prior to expropriation. The resettlement fee per person was increased from 2–3 times to 4–6 times the average annual output, and the maximum resettlement fee per hectare was raised from 10 to 15 times. It is further stipulated that if the sum of the land compensation fee and resettlement fee is insufficient to maintain the peasants' original living standards, the provincial governments may decide to raise the resettlement fee. The upper limit of the sum was increased from 20 to 30 times the average annual output. Moreover, the 1998 LAL specifies that considering the level of social and economic development and under special circumstances, the State Council may further raise compensation to maintain the original living standard of the expropriated. Of equal if not more importance, alongside the increase of compensation fees, the 1998 LAL triggered a change in the form of resettlement for expropriation. While the 1986 LAL require that the expropriating governments should help the expropriated peasants find new jobs by asking the TVEs or the land-using entities to recruit them,[15] such a provision was removed from the 1998 LAL. That turned out to have an impactful change, which will be explored more fully in the next chapter. At any rate, despite the increase in the quantity of expropriation compensation, the substance of it remains the

[15] 1986 LAL, art. 33; 1988 LAL, art. 31.

same in the 1998 LAL as the principle of maintaining peasants' original living standards was kept in place as the guiding criterion to determine compensation. In fact, the increase of compensation fees could be seen as making up for the abolishment of the legal duty for the expropriating government to resettle the expropriated with post-expropriation re-employment opportunities.

Last, but by no means least, as to the challengeability of expropriation decisions, the 1998 LAL itself does not include any specific prescription. But that was precisely a continuation of the tradition of nonchallengeable expropriation decisions. For sure, as demonstrated in Chapter 2, for all the difficulties, nowadays compensation and resettlement arrangements have been open to judicial review. This was a change brought about by the 1989 ALL. Nonetheless, it will be shown in Section 7.5 that expropriation decisions per se, particularly their public interestedness, are still out of the purview of judicial scrutiny to this day.

Based on the previous discussion, in spite of various changes here and there, it is undeniable that there is a structural continuity from the 1986 LAL to the 1998 LAL where rural land expropriation has persisted to be expansive, unchallengeable, poorly compensated and undemocratically determined. Given that the 1986 LAL carried on the legacy of the relevant law in the early 1980s, it is therefore fair to conclude that over the past four decades China's rural land expropriation law evolved without radical rupture ever since the onset of the reform era and right up to the present day. On a deeper level, however, the continuity in China's rural land expropriation law goes beyond similarly structured statutory provisions across time, as just explained. The texts that follow highlight the endurance of the historical legacy in both the functional, normative and foundational senses. Functional continuity means that the core objectives for the rural land expropriation law have stayed constant to a considerable degree. Normative continuity means that the socialist principle, as explicated earlier, is still the normative foundation to the law in this area. Foundational continuity means that the substantive grounds on which expropriation decisions are made have remained to be top-down state planning schemes.

7.2 Functional Continuity

7.2.1 Farmland Preservation and Food Security

As demonstrated, the 1986 LAL was originally intended as an upgrade solution to the same old problem of cultivated land waste due to excessive and unauthorized land expropriation, which had previously motivated the promulgation of relevant statutes in the early 1980s, when the 1982 RLRSC and the 1982 *Rural Construction Regulation* were enacted to fill the legal vacuum in this area left by the Cultural Revolution to ensure orderly and rational rural land expropriation and use. The 1998 LAL was again intended to achieve precisely the same goal, a point openly acknowledged in its legislative explanation:

> With the deepening of the reform and the changed circumstances, many provisions in the present LAL [the 1986 LAL] are now obviously unfit for the purposes of strengthening land administration and preserving cultivated land effectively. Problems such as unlawful approval of land use, unauthorized occupation of cultivated land and waste of land have occurred from time to time in some localities, resulting in sharp decrease of cultivated land and loss of landed asset . . . attaching great importance to such crucial matters of land administration and preservation of cultivated land that concern not only the present situation of the country but also the future generations of the Chinese nation, the Central Party and State Council issued the Notice on Further Strengthening Land Administration and Effectively Preserving Cultivated Land on April 15, 1997 . . . accordingly, the National Land Administration Bureau prepared the craft Land Administration Law and submitted it to the State Council for approval on August 18, 1997.[16]

One year later, the final version of the 1998 LAL was passed by the NPCSC, which retained and actually enhanced by way of an explicit mention the presumption of state expropriation in nonagricultural use of rural land and set up a more stringent land use regulatory system with recentralized expropriation-approving authority. All of this was supposed to offer an improved and more effective solution than the 1986 LAL to strengthen top-down state control over rural land use and conversion and to rein in cultivated land waste, matters regarded as critical to both the present and future of the country.

It is worth noting that this no waste of arable land imperative has a long history in the PRC, as can be attested by the aforementioned central authority's repeated crackdown on excessive expropriation since the 1950s, which culminated in the entrenchment of rational use of land as a basic state policy and constitutional principle in the early 1980s. Yet what was new in the build-up to the 1998 LAL was an increasing concern for

[16] Yongkang Zhou, "Explanatory Report of the Draft Amended PRC Land Administration Law (关于《中华人民共和国土地管理法》修订草案的说明)," April 26, 1998, available at www.npc.gov.cn/wxzl/gongbao/2000-12/17/content_5003977.htm.

food security in a hugely populous country with relatively meager resources. There is of course a cultural background to this, evidenced by the famous Chinese saying "food is heaven to the people" and the age-old greeting "have you eaten today." Yet, of more contemporary relevance is the fact that China feeds 20 percent of the world's population with only 7 percent of the world's farmland and has a per capita cultivated land standing at only 40 percent of the world average, 12.5 percent the USA, and 40 percent of that in India.[17] It is well known that appalling economic mismanagement and political rigidity in the pre-reform years caused serious a food crisis that exacted a heavy toll of millions of lives.[18] After the opening and reform policy, spectacular economic growth in China has made famine and starvation a distant memory. But the policy agenda about feeding the country actually gained unprecedented momentum in the 1990s. In 1995, the American environmental analyst Lester Brown published *Who Will Feed China*, predicting that by 2030 China's grain production would decline by at least one-fifth due to, among other things, rapid conversion of arable land for urbanization and industrialization.[19] Despite much controversy surrounding its methodology and pessimistic vision,[20] Brown's book became highly influential among the top Chinese policy-makers, probably due to the indelible painful impression the disastrous famine during the pre-reform period had made on the national psyche. In 1996, the State Council published a white paper on food security in China and declared a target of a 95 percent food supply self-sufficiency ratio.[21] In 1997, the CCP Central Committee and the State Council jointly issued the *Notice on Further Strengthening Land Administration and Cultivated Land Protection*, stressing that to protect cultivated land is to protect our "life line" as unauthorized occupation and conversion of cultivated land not only severely hamper grain production and agricultural development, but also harm the health of the national economy and social

17 Ajmal Qureshi, "Food Security in China," *Harvard International Review*, September 15, 2008, available at http://hir.harvard.edu/article/?a=1750.

18 Frank Dikötter, *Mao's Great Famine: The History of China's Most Devastating Catastrophe, 1958–1962* (London: Bloomsbury Paperbacks, 2011).

19 Lester Brown, *Who Will Feed China: Wake-up Call for a Small Planet* (New York: W. W. Norton & Company, Inc., 1995), p. 95.

20 For a more optimistic prediction about China's ability to feed itself, see Jikun Huang, Scott Rozelle and Mark Rosegrant, "China's Food Economy to the Twenty-first Century: Supply, Demand, and Trade" (1999) 47(4) *Economic Development and Cultural Change* 737.

21 State Council Press Conference, "China's Food Problem (中国的粮食问题)," October 1996, available at www.scio.gov.cn/zfbps/ndhf/1996/Document/307978/307978.htm.

stability.[22] To further this mandate, the 1997 revision to the PRC Criminal Code criminalized unauthorized conversion and transaction of cultivated land, which according to the NPC was intended to provide special protection of cultivated land and to guarantee national food security.[23] All of this had laid down the foundation for the 1998 LAL, the core aim of which, as suggested by the aforementioned official legislative explanation, was to enhance top-down control over conversion and use of rural land so that cultivated land can be better preserved. Admittedly, to this day, whether food self-sufficiency is absolutely sine qua non for food security and whether China really needs be self-sufficient in food supply remain debatable – and debated – questions.[24] But there has been no sign of this self-sufficiency policy abating, at least on the level of official discourse.[25] In 2003, at the Third Plenum of the Sixteenth Party Congress, President Hu Jintao declared that the land use regulatory system instituted under the 1998 LAL would be the strictest system of cultivated land preservation in the world to ensure national food security for China.[26] As a result, since the turn of this century, this system has not been reversed but consolidated and refined, the details of which will be discussed in Section 7.4. It suffices to note here that sitting at the center of this system, rural land expropriation remains the only channel for rural–urban land conversion and serves as a tool for the state to maintain tight control over rural land for the sake of arable land conservation and food self-sufficiency.

[22] Notice on Further Strengthening Land Administration and Cultivated Land Protection (进一步加强土地管理切实保护耕地的通知), promulgated by CCP Central Committee and State Council on April 15, 1997, available at www.law-lib.com/law/law_view.asp?id=64630.

[23] The official NPC explanation of the 1997 amendment of the criminal code is available at www.npc.gov.cn/npc/flsyywd/xingfa/2004-10/20/content_337788.htm.

[24] For the general theoretical debate on this issue, see Jennifer Clapp, "Food Self-sufficiency: Making Sense of it, and When it Makes Sense" (2017) 66 *Food Policy* 88; for a critique of China's pursuit of food self-sufficiency, see Yushi Mao, Nong Zhao, Xiaojing Yang, *Food Security and Farm Land Protection in China* (Singapore: World Scientific, 2013).

[25] Qian Wang, "China to Maintain Self-sufficiency in Food Production," April 21, 2014, available at www.chinadaily.com.cn/china/2014-04/21/content_17450136.htm. For recent adjustments concerning this policy, see Hongzhou Zhang, "Feeding the Chinese: Wither the Self-Sufficiency Policy?," *IPP Review*, May 18, 2016, available at ippreview.com/index.php/Home/Blog/single/id/143.html.

[26] The expression that China has the strictest land law system first appeared in 1998 when Geping Qu, then chairman of the Environmental and Resources Protection Committee of the NPC, commented on the draft revision of the LAL. See also Carolyn Cartier, "'Zone Fever', the Arable Land Debate, and Real Estate Speculation: China's Evolving Land Use Regime and Its Geographical Contradictions" (2011) 10 (28) *Journal of Contemporary China* 447.

7.2.2 Economic Growth and Macroeconomic Management

The other key objective for China's rural land expropriation law during the reform period is the pursuit of economic growth, which has been the paramount agenda for the communist party-state in contemporary China. But again, there is a pre-reform legacy to this. As noted, from the 1950s onwards, rural land expropriation decisions were made in accordance with state plans for capital construction and were therefore essentially the spatial manifestation of economic planning. In this situation, rural land expropriation effectively served as the tool with which the state secured land for its planned nonagricultural development. However, right from the outset state expropriation faced peasants' resistance, which in spite of Mao's praise did cause hindrance to the smooth implementation of state economic plans. This problem was further aggravated by the nonenforcement of the 1958 MLRSC during the Cultural Revolution. In response, the 1982 RLRSC was enacted and the (partial) nationalization clause in the 1982 Constitution was designed, both with the intention to facilitate state-led nonagricultural development. Article 23 of the 1986 LAL was particularly illustrative here, with its dual requirement on how rural land expropriation should proceed. Its first half stressed that land-using entities must submit documents of approval for the relevant capital construction projects when applying for expropriation so that rural land expropriation would only happen for construction projects already included in the state economic plans. The second half of Article 23 stipulated that in rural land expropriation the expropriatees should obey the demands of the state and not cause any obstruction. In this light, up to this point, China's rural land takings law functioned to ensure orderly and efficient conversion of rural land, which could then be supplied for state-led industrialization in a planned and nonliberalized economy.

Since then, such practice of expropriation for growth has been largely maintained. In fact, with the marketization of urban land in the late 1980s, it has become all the more intensified and has reached an unprecedented level. As discussed in Chapter 3, over the past three decades, post-expropriation transfer and pledge of urban land use-rights have been the single most significant source of funding and financing benefits to the Chinese local governments, a phenomenon widely known as land finance. With these land-generated resources, local governments across the country have attracted capital investment, stimulated industrialization, boosted urban employment and, most importantly, generated growth – a process depicted by some commentators as China's land-centered development.[27] As early as the beginning of 1990s, the National Bureau of Statistics estimated that for every RMB yuan invested in real estate development China's GDP would increase by 1.34 yuan.[28]

However, the flip side of developing the economy through expropriating and converting more and more rural land into tradable and thereby profitable urban land is that it can be, and indeed has been, overdone. The early years following the commodification of urban land witnessed a "real estate craze" (*fangdichan re*) and a "development zone fever" (*kaifaqu re*) across the country, which were tropes to describe the exponential increase of real estate activities and government-set development zones.[29] It is quite ironic that just a while back it was still a hotly debated issue among many Chinese whether or not leasing land out to foreign investors was repeating the history of humiliation, as when China was forced to carve out concession areas to Western powers.[30] But when Deng Xiaoping's Southern Tour in early 1992 confirmed China's commitment to continuing its journey toward a market economy, and when the CCP Central Committee and State Council declared in June that year to prioritize the development of the real estate sector which "requires comparatively less investment, gets profitable instantly, yields good returns and expands employment capacity,"[31] 1992 became the "year of the real estate industry" (*fangdichan nian*).[32] Compared with

[27] George C.S. Lin, *Developing China: Land, Politics and Social Conditions (Routledge Contemporary China Series)* (London: Routledge, 2009), part 2.

[28] Meg E. Rithmire, "Land Institutions and Chinese Political Economy: Institutional Complementarities and Macroeconomic Management" (2017) 45 (1) *Politics & Society* 134.

[29] For an account of this episode, see Meg E. Rithmire, *Land Bargains and Chinese Capitalism: The Politics of Property Rights under Reform* (New York: Cambridge University Press, 2015), pp. 44–50.

[30] For example, Shanghai municipal government had to explain to the public in a party newspaper that government land lease to overseas investors was fundamentally different from old concession areas and would not lead to exterritorial jurisdiction. See MLR, *Thirty Years of Reform and Development of Land Administration* (国土资源事业改革发展三十年) (Beijing: Dizhi Press, 2008), p. 220. In November of 1989, the State Bureau of Land Administration drafted a reply on behalf of the State Council to opposition raised by some members of the NPCSC and the CPPCC against the "treason-like" decision to lease land to foreign companies. See MLR, *Thirty Years of Reform and Development of Land Administration*, p. 21.

[31] Decision on Further Promoting the Tertiary Industry (关于加快发展第三产业的决定), promulgated by CCP Central Committee and State Council on June 16, 1992, available at www.law-lib.com/law/law_view.asp?id=16055.

[32] Zongrong Feng and Guangzhong You, *Hot Economic Issues and Major Events in Modern Chinese History* (中国近现代经济热点及重大事件) (Beijing: Zhongguo Jingji Press, 1995), p. 531.

just one year previously, on average the volume of capital investment in real estate grew 117 percent and the quantity and size of land parcels transferred increased by 2 and 10 times respectively. Hainan saw a 216 percent upsurge in real estate investment, and 211 percent for Guangdong. Many other provinces also experienced near or more than 100 percent growth, including Inner Mongolia, Liaoning, Jilin, Heilongjiang, Fujian, Henan and Guangxi.[33] The number of real estate films also quadrupled from 3,700 in 1992 to 12,400 in 1993 and 24,372 in 1994. And housing prices underwent a 51 percent spike.[34] In 1992, 22,000 hectares of land were leased, which was three times the area leased in 1991 and eleven times that leased in 1990.[35] During this process, the lucrativeness of land transfer and development attracted a wide variety of participants, including market players such as international investors and those typically nonmarket players such as SOEs, government departments, universities, hospitals and so on.[36]

In the meantime, local governments across the country fell prey to the development zone fever. The idea of carving out large tracts of land for concentrated industrialization with favorable policy conditions was first tested in coastal regions with central government approval in the late 1970s.[37] It gradually became the symbol and model for government-driven economic growth over the 1980s. Yet it was in the early 1990s that the frenzy of setting up development zones spread throughout the country. One estimate put the number of development zones in the country at 117 at the end of 1991, which increased to 1993 by the end of 1992.[38] It was reported that in the second half of 1993 there were 8,700 development zones occupying more land area than the total actual built-up area of five hundred cities.[39] Most of these newborn development zones were established by subprovincial-level governments, including counties and towns, in their great scramble for capital investment. A 1993 report recorded 389 development zones established at the township and village levels in Fujian, a figure 3.5 times higher than the count for 1992.[40] In Hainan, there were 24 centrally and provincially sanctioned

[33] Zangchun Gan (ed.), *Land Macroeconomic Management: Innovative Theory and Praxis* (土地宏观调控创新理论与实践) (Beijing: Zhongguo Caizheng Jingji Press, 2009), p. 17.

[34] Zonghua Bao, *Real Estate: Pioneering Industry and Bubble Economy* (房地产: 先导产业与泡沫经济) (Beijing: Zhongguo Caizheng Jingji Press, 1993), p. 32.

[35] Rithmire, *Land Bargains and Chinese Capitalism*, p. 48. [36] Ibid., p. 46.

[37] Cartier, "'Zone Fever', the Arable Land Debate, and Real Estate Speculation," 454–456.

[38] Rithmire, *Land Bargains and Chinese Capitalism*, p. 44. [39] Ibid., pp. 44–45.

[40] Cartier, "'Zone Fever', the Arable Land Debate, and Real Estate Speculation," 457.

development zones by the end of 1993, which was merely one-fourth the number of development zones created by city and county governments.[41]

An emblematic case of this wave of land development that swept China in the early 1990s can be found in the city of Beihai in Guangxi province. An official recollected that back then the entire city joined the land development bandwagon, hoping to "make fortunes from land, grow the market through land, attract business with land and develop the city based on land."[42] Between early 1992 and June of 1993, the number of real estate companies in Beihai swelled from 6 to 1,056. The total capital investment by these real estate firms amounted to 1.2 billion RMB, equal to the total amount over the previous eight years.[43] From 1992 to 1995, 85 square kilometers were leased, but the actual built-up area of the city was only 17 square kilometers.[44] In 1992 alone, Beihai opened up 17 new development zones, and by September of 1993 two more were added.[45] Nevertheless, it was reported that in Beihai less than one-fifth of all the land leased out for real estate construction and development zones at the time was actually utilized for the designated purposes and that most investors were only eyeing a quick buck through speculatively hoarding and reselling land.[46] More alarmingly, much of the capital poured into land development in Beihai came from bank loans with very high interest rates, typically between 18 and 25 percent.[47]

Before long, it was clear to everyone that there was a huge property bubble and severe economic overheating. According to the statistics published by the central authority, inflation accelerated rapidly from October of 1992, on an average monthly ratio of 10 percent. Between 1992 and 1993, the consumer price index (CPI) went up 12 percent and the producer price index (PPI) increased 43 percent. Net money supply

[41] Luping Xia, *To Choose the Road of Green Development: Retrospect and Reflection on Twenty Years' Development of Hainan* (选择绿色发展之路:海南发展20年的回顾与反思) (Haikou: Nanhai Press, 2004), p. 14.

[42] Committee of Culture, History and Learning of Chinese People's Political Consultative Committee (ed.), *Records of Opening Up of 14 Coastal Cities: Beihai* (十四个沿海城市开放纪实: 北海卷) (Beijing: Zhongguo Wenshi Press, 2015), pp. 153, 156.

[43] Jianming Zhou and Hongjian Ding (eds.), *Theory and Practice of Urban Land Use in China* (中国城市土地利用的理论与实践) (Beijing: Zhongguo Jianzhu Gongye Press, 2009), p. 189.

[44] Rithmire, *Land Bargains and Chinese Capitalism*, p. 45.

[45] Zhou and Ding, *Theory and Practice of Urban Land Use in China, pp. 189–190.*

[46] Ibid., p. 190.

[47] Ibid. The land development fever was also partially driven by the decentralized structure of the financial sector in China back then when local banks enjoyed high degree of independence in lending practices. See Rithmire, *Land Bargains and Chinese Capitalism*, p. 47.

in the first half of 1993 was 58 billion RMB, whereas that figure in the same period of 1992 was only 5.3 billion.[48] In Beihai, the volume of newly developed housing could accommodate more than two million residents, but it had just 500,000 residents at the time.[49] The vacant housing floor area was 1.07 million square meters.[50] Many iconic development projects became "unfinished buildings" (*lanwei lou*), which were left abandoned well into the next century.[51]

At the center of this land development fever was uncontrolled urban land use-rights conversion and transfer. The 1986 LAL,[52] the 1989 *Notice on Competence to Approve Transfers of State-owned Land Use-rights*[53] and the 1990 *Interim Regulation on the Allocation and Transfer of the Use Right of the State-owned Urban Land*[54] required that rural land expropriation and urban land transfer should be approved by governments at the county level and above: expropriating and transferring more than 1,000 *mu* of cultivated land or 2,000 *mu* of other kinds of land ought to be reviewed and sanctioned by the State Council; expropriating and transferring less than 3 *mu* of cultivated land or 10 *mu* of other kinds of land could be authorized by county governments; anything in between should be approved by provincial governments. The same hierarchical approval requirement also applied to the collectives' allocating rural land for the TVEs.[55] In the meantime, it was specifically stressed that initiatives of urban land transfer or rural land expropriation should not avoid scrutiny from superior governments by "breaking up the whole into parts" (*huazheng weiling*). Expropriating rural land without any actual capital investment project in place was also prohibited to prevent land hoarding.[56] These provisions, however, were far from effective in reality. First, entities such as SOEs, government departments, universities and hospitals, which You-tien Hsing called "socialist land masters," started to

[48] Opinions on Current Economic Situation and Strengthening Macroeconomic Management (关于当前经济情况和加强宏观调控的意见), promulgated by CCP Central Party and State Council on June 24, 1993, available at www.chinalawedu.com/falvfagui/fg22016/11287.shtml.

[49] Qi Zhang (ed.), *Urban Economics* (城市经济学) (Beijing: Jingji Ribao Press, 2007), p. 187.

[50] Ming Fan, *Purchase and Sale of Real Property and Real Estate Policies* (房地产买卖行为与房地产政策) (Beijing: Shehui Kexue Wenxian Press, 2012), p. 186.

[51] Ibid. [52] Arts. 23, 25.

[53] Point 1, Notice on Competence to Approve Transfers of State-owned Land Use-rights (出让国有土地使用权批准权限的通知), promulgated by State Council on July 22, 1989, available at laws.66law.cn/law-41736.aspx.

[54] Art. 9. [55] 1986 LAL, art. 39.

[56] 1986 LAL, art. 26; Interim Regulation on the Allocation and Transfer of the Use Right of the State-owned Urban Land, art. 1.

establish land-development companies to rent and transfer land under their control to commercial developers.[57] They obtained land through free-of-charge administrative allocation in the pre-reform era. By putting such land into the real estate market and bypassing government approval they could easily make a profit for themselves. Second, in a race to the bottom to attract capital investment, local governments set up development zones or expropriated and transferred land without going through proper authorization procedures. The then director of the State Bureau of Land Administration conceded in July 1992 that unauthorized and unlawful land transfer and expropriation were pervasive across the country. Some local governments transferred 20 or 30 square kilometers without even informing the State Council, which according to law should have permitted such transfer beforehand. This was done through breaking up one lump-sum transfer into smaller sized transfers. Some local governments illegally delegated the power to sanction land expropriation and transfer to offices of urban land reform or even local government-set real estate development companies.[58] For instance, the former mayor of Beihai recalled rather proudly, "Why could Beihai unleash so much dynamism? That is because we turned one government into ten by delegating the power of approving investment projects to ten development zones, which held investment promotion meetings everywhere and were far more effective than us the prefectural government."[59] Still, there were some local governments that "were too eager to get results in terms of implementing the opening and reform policy and would take whatever offers made by foreign investors," many of which were simply planning to stockpile large amount of land for future speculation.[60] Third, it has been suggested that more than half of the development zones were initiated by local governments at the subcounty levels for their TVEs,[61] with the legally stipulated review and approval procedures sidelined.

In this situation, the State Bureau of Land Administration issued the *Urgent Notice on Reviewing and Approving Land Use Strictly According to*

[57] You-tien Hsing, *The Great Urban Transformation: Politics of Land and Property in China* (New York: Oxford University Press, 2010), pp. 35–38.

[58] Xianjin Wang (ed.), *Land Administration and Reform* (中国土地管理与改革) (Beijing: Dangdai Zhongguo Press, 1994), pp. 241–42.

[59] Haibo Jiang, "Siqi Liang and Xin Zhang, Former Mayor Liguo Shuai Opening up on Beihai after Thirteen Years" Silence (沉默十三年老市长帅立国开口话北海)," December 8, 2008, *China Business News* (中国经营报), available at www.thuedp.com/html/news/media/718.html.

[60] Wang, *Land Administration and Reform*, p. 243.

[61] Hsing, *The Great Urban Transformation*, p. 98.

Law on July 31, 1992, stressing that legal provisions concerning land use approval must be obeyed and that transfer of land use-rights must be "highly monopolized" (*gaodu longduan*) and "approved with only one pen" (*yizhi bi shenpi*).[62] In November of that year, the State Council promulgated the *Notice on Several Issues concerning the Development of Real Estate Industry*[63] and *Urgent Notice on Strictly Forbidding Unauthorized Occupation and Use of Cultivated Land*,[64] urging the enforcement of "five uniforms" (*wuge tongyi*) in land administration: uniform planning, uniform expropriation, uniform development, uniform management and uniform transfer solely by governments at the county level and above.

This policy of five uniforms originated from the city of Zhuhai, one of the first of four Special Economic Zones in China. As recollected by its former mayor, who presided over this then-innovative practice, it was adopted primarily to rein in unscrupulous nonagricultural use of land and to ensure that the prefectural government could recover the costs of infrastructure development, both of which had previously proved to be difficult when land expropriation, development and transfer were conducted dispersedly and disorderly by all kinds of land-using entities.[65] The fact that this local experiment was taken on board by the State Council shows that the core lesson drawn by China's central authority facing the real estate bubble and economic overheating in the early 1990s was that the primary land market should be completely monopolized by the state, represented by local governments down to the county level.[66] In the words of the Minister of Construction at the time, "From now on, the Chinese government will have a monopoly over the land supply to strengthen economic and land planning. When urban land is transferred, the government will control the macro supply of land."[67] In order to

[62] The Chinese text is available at www.chinalawedu.com/falvfagui/fg22016/11780.shtml.

[63] The Chinese text is available at www.gov.cn/xxgk/pub/govpublic/mrlm/201012/t20101219_63321.html.

[64] The Chinese text is available at www.chinalawedu.com/falvfagui/fg22016/11780.shtml.

[65] Kewei Ma (ed.), *China Reform Records 1978–1991: Land System Reform* (中国改革全书(1978–1991): 土地制度改革卷) (Dalian: Dalian Press, 1992), pp. 455–57.

[66] A much-debated issue in the early 1990s was who should represent the state as the owner of urban land. See Institute of Finance, Trade and Economics Research at Chinese Academy of Social Sciences, *Urban Land Use and Administration in China* (中国城市土地使用与管理) (Beijing: Jingji Kexue Press, 1992), pp. 22–24; Institute of Agricultural Economics Research at Chinese Academy of Agricultural Science, *Agricultural Economics and Scientific Development Research* (农业经济与科技发展研究) (Beijing: Nongye Press, 1993), p. 231.

[67] Rithmire, *Land Bargains and Chinese Capitalism*, p. 53.

achieve a soft landing for the economy, alongside tightening up central control over local banks to end easy credit,[68] a plethora of land-related measures were adopted, including centralizing the power to set up development zones for the provincial and central governments, prohibiting unlawful delegation of land use approval authority, requiring land development projects to be backed up by actual capital investment and re-emphasizing state expropriation as the prerequisite for land transfer.[69]

This turned out to be just the first episode where the control of land was adopted as a measure of macroeconomic management (*hongguan tiaokong*). It has been summarized that there are at least four ways land control has served as a policy instrument for macroeconomic management, including expanding construction land supply both nationally or regionally to prompt nationwide or regionally focused growth and using land supply as a form of financial and industrial policy to adjust resources allocation among localities and sectors.[70] The basic idea behind this is that where there is more land to be expropriated and transferred there is a greater economic boost and vice versa. Specifically, this is done via a top-down land use planning and quota system, which determines the pace, volume and location of rural land expropriation and conversion. More discussion on this will come in Section 7.4. Suffice it to say for the moment that since the late 1990s, China has experienced two more notable rounds of macroeconomic management through land control. After the 1997 Asian financial crisis, China faced considerable pressure from the economic downturn, compounded by its then-ongoing systematic overhaul of SOEs that was going to have millions laid off. Zhu Rongji, the newly appointed Premier, announced at a press conference in March of 1998 that housing construction would become a new source

[68] Opinions on Current Economic Situation and Strengthening Macroeconomic Management (关于当前经济情况和加强宏观调控的意见), promulgated by CCP Central Committee and State Council on June 24, 1993, available at www.chinalawedu.com/falvfagui/fg22016/11287.shtml.

[69] Notice on Strictly Approving and Seriously Rectifying Various Kinds of Development Zones (关于严格审批和认真清理各类开发区的通知), promulgated by State Council on April 28, 1993, available at www.law-lib.com/law/law_view.asp?id=56098. See also Notice on Several Issues concerning the Development of Real Estate Industry (关于发展房地产业若干问题的通知), promulgated by State Council on November 4, 1992, available at www.gov.cn/xxgk/pub/govpublic/mrlm/201012/t20101219_63321.html.

[70] Rithmire, "Land Institutions and Chinese Political Economy: Institutional Complementarities and Macroeconomic Management," 134–36. See also Chunhua Wang, *Study on Optimal Allocation of Land Resources and Construction of Conservation-minded Society* (土地资源优化配置与构建节约型社会研究) (Beijing: Huanjing Kexue Press, 2006), pp. 164–71.

of economic growth for China.[71] Before then, urban housing in China was provided by work units as a form of in-kind welfare. In July of the same year, a housing reform (*fanggai*) was initiated to privatize housing by giving the original owners of public housing a right to buy the title of the house. As a result, the use-rights of a vast amount of urban land were reassigned from government organizations and SOEs to new private owners or developers.[72] This was carried out with the aim of removing the heavy burdens of housing maintenance from ailing SOEs, to provide subsidized housing for many soon to be laid-off workers and, most importantly, to help channel individual consumption to the real estate market so that domestic demand could be stimulated in sectors such as construction, home furnishings, home appliances and so on.[73] Similarly, in the wake of the 2007 and 2008 global financial crisis, the General Office of State Council issued *Opinions on Promoting Healthy Development of Real Estate Market*,[74] spelling out a series of government measures to expand social housing construction and encourage private consumption of real property, both of which were to back up or supplant the four trillion RMB stimulus package and were based on more urban construction land supply. As shown in Figure 1.1, there was a noticeable increase in the amount of rural land expropriation in the immediate aftermath of the global financial crisis.

It is not difficult to see that the twin objectives of the law on rural land expropriation in the reform era just discussed are not always mutually compatible. While protection of agricultural land for food security is more of a long-term and stable goal that requires order and restraint in

[71] Yonglie Ye, "The End of Welfare Housing Premier Zhu declared the commodification of housing (福利分房终结者朱总理宣布住房商品化)," January 7, 2003, available at finance.qq.com/a/20081208/002811.htm.

[72] Notice on Further Deepening Urban Housing System Reform and Accelerating Housing Construction (关于进一步深化城镇住房制度改革加快住房建设的通知), promulgated by State Council on July 3, 1998, available at www.china.findlaw.cn/fagui/p_1/352846.html. This explains the sudden increase in urban land supply shown in Figure 7.1. But apparently there was a time lag between stimulus policies and actual economic turnaround, which explains the slow recovery of GDP growth after 1998. For a fuller account of China's housing reform since the late 1990s, see Joyce Yanyun Man (ed.), *China's Housing Reform and Outcomes* (Cambridge, MA: Lincoln Institution of Land Policy, 2011).

[73] Rithmire, "Land Institutions and Chinese Political Economy: Institutional Complementarities and Macroeconomic Management," 136–37; James Lee and Ya-peng Zhu, "Urban Governance, Neoliberalism and Housing Reform in China" (2006) 19 (1) *The Pacific Review* 43.

[74] The Chinese text is available at www.gov.cn/zwgk/2008-12/21/content_1184227.htm.

rural land expropriation, land-centered macroeconomic development and management is comparatively more cyclical and short-term, and demands more expropriation to boost the economy when necessary. In this situation, to promote urban construction and economic growth while simultaneously preserving cultivated land becomes one of the core tensions internal to China's rural land expropriation law, which will be discussed at greater length in the next chapter. Yet again, this is not completely novel as it also has a pre-reform presage when the pendulum swing between devolution and recentralization of the power to approve expropriation as early as in the 1960s testified to the central authority's long-held ambivalence toward rural land expropriation. On the one hand, devolution led to more efficient expropriation and conversion of rural land for state-led nonagricultural development, but at the same time resulted in excessive, unauthorized and wasteful expropriation and agricultural land loss. On the other hand, recentralization tightened up superior control yet gave rise to administrative rigidity and inefficiency. In this scenario, as shown in the previous chapter, rational use of land was elevated to a constitutional principle in 1982 first and foremost to ask for a balanced approach to rural land expropriation.

7.3 Normative Continuity

In addition to strong path dependence in terms of its four structural characteristics and dual functions, China's rural land expropriation bears testimony to the endurance of the past with respect to its normative basis, too. On this front one should not be fooled by the fact that the sternly worded provision that the expropriated shall obey the demands of the state and shall not cause any hindrance or obstruction present in the 1982 RLRSC and the 1986 LAL was removed from the 1998 LAL. As already argued, that provision can be seen as the illustration of the socialist principle that had underpinned the Chinese expropriation law between the 1950s and the 1980s. Does its disappearance from the 1998 LAL imply a critical change in the normative basis of China's takings law? The conventional wisdom among Chinese legal scholars has been that the normative foundation of existing Chinese law on rural land expropriation is the theory of social obligation of private property.[75] The reason provided lies in the widely known fact that the Chinese legal system is

[75] To my knowledge the earliest academic work advancing this view is a 1994 article. See Quansheng Chen, "On the Compensation for Land Requisition (论土地征用之补偿)" (1994) 5 *Legal Science* (法律科学) 56.

generally modeled on its German counterpart,[76] in which the theory of private property as social function plays the crucial role in both justifying and limiting the state takings power.[77] The mainstream position in the existing Chinese literature holds that in expropriation the expropriatees have made a "special sacrifice" (*tebie xisheng*) for the public interest that must be compensated for.[78]

That view, however, is untenable as it is unfounded to assume that the Chinese and German expropriation laws share the same normative foundation simply because of the close relationship between the two countries' legal systems in general. Whereas the theory of social obligation of private property as practiced in German law conceptualizes going through expropriation as a "special/unusual sacrifice" (*sonderopfer*),[79] that is not the case in China – at least, not according to the official narrative that was demonstrated by the aforementioned legislative explanation of the draft LAL in 1998. It was made clear then that land expropriation is a kind of state action and also a duty the peasants should fulfill vis-à-vis the state. It should not be regarded as the peasants selling their land to the state. When the expropriated land is transferred, the difference between expropriation compensation and transfer price is the result of state investment and therefore should in principle be obtained by the state.[80]

[76] The transplantation of German law started from the late Qing period and continued into the Republican Era. In the first three decades of the PRC, this practice was abandoned for being considered bourgeoisie and reactionary. Since the opening and reform era, it was resumed as China's legal system, especially its private law branch, develops rapidly through imitating many aspects of the German legal system. For a historical account, see Jianfu Chen, *Chinese Law: Context and Transformation* (Leiden: Martinus Nijhoff Publishers, 2008), chapter 1.

[77] Rebecca Lubens, "The Social Obligation of Property Ownership: A Comparison of German and US Law" (2007) 24 *Arizona Journal of International & Comparative Law* 389.

[78] Maohui Qu and Hong Zhang, "On Several Issues concerning Expropriation Law (论征收法律制度的几个问题)" (2003) 2 *Law Review* (法学评论) 50; Xiaojun Chen, "Jurisprudential Reflection and Institutional Restructuring on Rural Collective Land Expropriation (农村集体土地征收的法理反思与制度重构)" (2012) 1 *China Legal Science* (中国法学) 34.

[79] For a brief discussion of the *sonderopfer* principle and expropriation in German constitutional law, see Markus Perkams, "The Concept of Indirect Expropriation in Comparative Public Law – Searching for Light in the Dark," in Stephan W. Schill (ed.), *International Investment Law and Comparative Public Law* (Oxford: Oxford University Press, 2010), pp. 130–37. Note that in German law not all expropriation or Regulation of private property is seen to involve special sacrifice on the part of the individual owners. It may well be considered as part of the social obligation of private property and thereby non-compensable. But when it does cause special sacrifice, the state must compensate.

[80] Yongkang Zhou, "Explanatory Report of the Draft Amended PRC Land Administration Law."

Two important conclusions follow from this revealed legislative intent behind China's existing land law. First, the socialist principle has remained the legitimating ground for the current rural land takings law because undergoing expropriation is not conceptualized as a sacrifice borne by the expropriatees but an obligation owed to the state. That is a world apart from the German theory of socialized property, which, as mentioned, conceptualizes expropriation as imposing excessive sacrifice over private property rights. Between sacrifice and obligation there lies a nuanced yet fundamental distinction. Expropriation as an obligation is based on the premise that there is a prima facie case for expropriation unless invalidated and there is a moral and legal duty on the part of the peasants to accept, if not welcome, expropriation by the state, which is deemed as the natural representative of public interest. In contrast, expropriation as sacrifice is predicated on the presumption that there is a prima facie case *against* expropriation unless justified. The moral and legal duty is now on the state, no longer regarded as the necessary embodiment of public interest, to legitimize its own expropriation decisions. Put another way, the logical starting points of these two theories are very different: while the German theory of socialized private property requires by default justification of expropriation as a kind of inference with or invasion into private property, the Chinese socialist principle demands by default compliance with expropriation decisions. A particularly illustrative example on this point is that Article 46 in the 1928 *Land Expropriation Law* passed under the nationalist government reappears more than half a century later in the presently effective 1998 LALIR (Article 25), stipulating that any ongoing dispute resolution process does not suspend the execution of expropriation decisions. Hence, it cannot be clearer that the existing Chinese law on rural land expropriation continues to be based on the socialist principle that confirms and facilitates, instead of constrains, the state takings power.

Secondly, the legislative explanation of the 1998 LAL also explains why maintenance of the peasants' original living standards has been kept as the guiding principle to determine expropriation compensation. Since expropriation should not be regarded as some sort of quasi-transaction between the expropriatees and the state, compensation for expropriation is not going to be the land price that could have been realized under a simulated market condition as if it were a voluntary exchange, as required by the fair market value standard in the USA explained in Chapter 2. Consequently, property in rural land serves not as a return-maximizing investment or commodity, but a source of welfare and social security to the peasants. In this situation, what the state is obligated to do is to ensure continuous welfare and social security provision to the expropriated peasants, just as how the villagers in Hebei were treated in the 1950s, as presented in Chapter 4. In essence, the criterion of multiplied agricultural output is to simulate the situation as if the expropriated peasants had not been subject to expropriation and would have continued agricultural production, i.e. the life they used to live, on the same land for the next 20 or 30 years. Hence, it was made clear that the increased land value in rural–urban land conversion was not to be part of the equation, the reason being that it is not needed to keep the expropriated where they were before expropriation and is seen as a fruit purely from state investment that should be garnered by the state alone.

7.4 Foundational Continuity

As was demonstrated in the second chapter, under the present law the entire decision-making process of rural land expropriation in China takes place inside the government hierarchy under a review and approval mechanism, where the initiating prefectural or county government submit applications of expropriation initiatives to provincial or national government for authorization. As noted, land is legally categorized into three types dependent on usage: agricultural land, construction land and unused land. In theory, therefore, state expropriation of collective land can trigger in total nine kinds of land use conversion, four of which are more typical in practice. Table 7.1 illustrates these four types and the respective competence of central and local governments in approving them.[81]

The above has to date been the focus of the existing literature as far as the decision-making on rural land expropriation is concerned. This is apparently of crucial importance. But the existing literature barely goes beyond the formal distribution of authority inside the government. What is missing in the discussion is the following issue: on what substantive grounds do Chinese central and provincial governments decide to expropriate a piece of collectively owned rural land? To answer this question, one needs to look at China's peculiar land use regulatory system, as it has been called since the 1998 LAL.

According to Articles 20 and 23 of the 2011 LALIR, there are two ways in which expropriation applications can be submitted by prefectural/county government to be reviewed by central/provincial government: one is submission and review in clusters (*fen pici*), which I call "batched

[81] 1998 and 2004 LAL, arts. 21, 44, 45.

Table 7.1 *Competence to sanction rural land expropriation of central and provincial governments*

Effect of Expropriation	State Council	Provincial Governments
Collective agricultural land to state-owned agricultural land	(1) Expropriating prime agricultural land regardless of the amount[82] (2) Expropriating over 35 hectares of cultivated land other than the PAL	Other circumstances
Collective agricultural land to state-owned construction land	(1) Expropriating the PAL regardless of the amount (2) Expropriating over 35 hectares of cultivated land other than the PAL (3) Expropriation for construction projects authorized by the State Council (4) Expropriation for the construction of road, pipeline and large-scale infrastructure projects authorized by central ministries and departments[83] (5) Expropriation for the construction of road, pipeline and large-scale infrastructure projects authorized by provincial governments (6) Expropriation to implement Land Use Master Plans in municipalities directly under central government, provincial capital cities and cities with a population over half a million[84]	Other circumstances

82 According to Article 34 of the 1998 and 2004 LAL, "prime agricultural land" (PAL) is a special kind of cultivated land with particular characteristics earmarked for special preservation by the provincial governments, which is supposed to take up 80 percent of all the cultivated land in a particular province.

83 This is provided for not in the LAL, but in article 1, Measures on Examination of the Application of Construction Land Use for Approval by the State Council (报国务院批准的建设用地审查办法), promulgated by MLR on August 30, 1999, available at www.mlr.gov.cn/zwgk/flfg/tdglflfg/200504/t20050412_66930.htm.

84 Ibid.

Table 7.1 (*cont.*)

Effect of Expropriation	State Council	Provincial Governments
Collective construction land to state-owned agricultural land	Expropriating over 70 hectares	Other circumstances
Collective construction land to state-owned construction land	Expropriating over 70 hectares	Other circumstances

expropriation"; the other is submission and review for individual construction projects (*dandu xuanzhi*), which I call "individual expropriation."[85] The former covers those applications made in order to implement the Land Use Master Plans (*tudi liyong zongti guihua*, LUMPs) and Urban and Rural Plans (*chengxiang guihua*, URPs). The latter refers to those applications made in order to provide land for such centrally or provincially approved individual construction projects as energy, transportation, irrigation, mines and military facilities that need to occupy land other than those designated as construction land in the LUMPs. Apparently, filing and approval of these two kinds of expropriation applications are intimately related to these plans, which are the most crucial elements of China's land use regulatory system. Both plans are formulated nationally and locally to specify, within the planned time frame, the spatial outlook at different localities in China. To understand how the two types of expropriation decisions are made, we shall first make sense of these two kinds of spatial plans.

7.4.1 *Land Use Master Plans*

Starting from 1986, the LUMPs have been formulated to set long-term (usually 10–15 years) land use plans at the national, provincial, prefectural, county and township levels.[86] As a planning instrument, the LUMPs

[85] See also 2004 LAL, art. 44.

[86] The legal basis has been set out in chapter 3 of the LAL since 1986. So far, there have been three rounds of land use planning in China. The first national LUMP covered the time span from 1986 to 2000, the second one from 1997 to 2010 and the present one from 2006 to 2020. The reason for the overlap in time coverage is because the need was felt to make

Table 7.2 *Quota control under land use master plans*

Agricultural land	Quota 1: amount of preserved cultivated land (*gengdi baoyou liang*)
	Quota 2: amount of preserved PAL (*jiben nongtian baohu mianji*)
Construction land	Quota 3: amount of rural and urban construction land (*chengxiang jianshe yongdi guimo*)
	Quota 4: amount of urban industrial and mine land per capita (*renjun chengzhen gongkuang yongdi guimo*)
Land conversion	Quota 5: amount of cultivated land converted to construction land (*xinzeng jianshe yongdi zhanyong gengdi guimo*)
	Quota 6: amount of post-conversion cultivated land supplement (*zhengli fuken kaifa buchang gengdi liang*)

put in place a mechanism that I call "one designation and three controls" – i.e. land-use designation, quota/numeric control, timing control and spatial control. To wit, every land parcel has an officially designated usage under the LUMPs that falls into a tripartite category: agricultural, construction and unused. The scale, timing and location of rural land expropriation and conversion are all effectively determined by the LUMPs. This is done first and foremost through the six binding numeric quotas (*yueshuxing zhibiao*) included in the present national LUMP that covers the period from 2006 to 2020, which are as shown in Table 7.2.[87]

The basic function of these quotas is to set the upper or lower numeric limits for certain kinds of land use during the planning period. The most significant ones appear under the first category, mandating the minimum amount of cultivated land in general and the PAL in particular that ought to be conserved until 2020. Specifically, the minimum amount of cultivated land to be preserved nationwide has been set at 1.8 billion *mu* or 120 million

new plans prior to the expiry of the old plans. Without further specification, the following discussion focuses on the present plan.

87 In the present national LUMP (2006–2020), besides these six binding quotas, there are another nine "anticipatory quotas" (预期性指标) on matters such as the minimum amount of preserved forestland, orchards and grassland as well as the maximum amount of construction land for urban industrial and mining purposes. The difference between the two is that anticipatory quotas have only a guiding effect upon local governments, which are expected to achieve such quotas as much as possible, but not to follow them strictly. See section 2, Outline of National Land Use Master Plan 2006–2020 (全国土地利用总体规划纲要2006–2020), promulgated by State Council on October 23, 2008, available at www.mlr.gov.cn/xwdt/jrxw/200810/t20081024_111040.htm.

hectares, famously known as the "redline" of cultivated land.[88] This figure came about based on the MLR calculating how much arable land ought to be preserved to guarantee food security for China, which came up with an estimate of between 1.7 billion to 1.8 billion *mu*.[89] Eventually the upper limit was chosen, though not without criticism for its accuracy and indeed necessity.[90] Yet ever since it was formalized as a national target, it has become the bedrock to China's land use regulatory system and the center of gravity around which land policies revolve. The minister of land once called it a "sacred mission" to protect the redline.[91]

Understandably, the biggest threat to this target is the inevitable conversion of agricultural land for nonagricultural development during China's still ongoing process of urbanization and industrialization. In fact, the backdrop against which this redline target was initially put in place was the rapid agricultural land shrinkage since the 1990s.[92] To limit the increase of construction land is therefore the other side of the same coin to preserving arable land. Hence, quota 3 sets the maximum amount of rural and urban construction land by the end of the planning period so that not too much agricultural land is converted for construction. As the maximum ratio of urban construction land to actual urban population, quota 4 serves a similar purpose through limiting the speed of construction-land expansion to ensure that it does not outpace urban population growth. The national LUMP actually demands a two-meter-square reduction in 2020 compared with 2010, which means that the increase of the urban population shall be faster than that of urban land.[93]

Quotas in the third category set the maximal amount of cultivated land allowed to be converted to construction land and the minimal amount of

[88] The PAL target is set at 1.56 billion *mu*.

[89] Yuan Xiao, "Making Land Fly: The Institutionalization of China's Land Quota Markets and Its Implications for Urbanization, Property Rights, and Intergovernmental Negotiation," PhD Thesis, MIT (2014), p. 46. Specifically, the redline is what is considered necessary to realize 95 percent self-sufficiency in food supply. See Dong Xiao, "Why is the redline set at 18 mu (红线为何设在18亿亩)," March 12, 2013, available at http://sannong.cntv.cn/20130312/101663.shtml.

[90] A famous critique can be found in Mao, Zhao and Yang, *Food Security and Farmland Protection in China*.

[91] "Minister of Land Resources Xu Shaoshi: Hold Fast to the Redline Target of 1.8 Billion Mu of Cultivated Land (国土资源部长徐绍史: 坚守18亿亩耕地红线目标)," October 10, 2008, available at news.163.com/08/1010/10/4NSUQ1660001124J.html.

[92] Decision on Deepening Reform and Enhancing Land Administration (关于深化改革严格土地管理的决定), promulgated by State Council on October 21, 2004, available at www.mlr.gov.cn/zwgk/flfg/tdglflfg/200601/t20060112_642080.htm.

[93] If complied with, this quota can also enhance land use efficiency. The reason is that the lower the land/population ratio, the more intensive urban land is used.

cultivated land required to be reclaimed in order to supplement the loss of cultivated land as a result of conversion. This is to impose restrictions on the scale of cultivated construction land conversion and to require local governments to reclaim at least the same amount of cultivated land as is converted into construction land. The latter is called the policy of "dynamic balance" (*dongtai pingheng*) or "balance between occupation and reclamation" (*zhanbu pingheng*): since converting cultivated land for nonagricultural development is inevitable and necessary for economic growth, the least that can be done is to ensure that there is no net loss of cultivated land to avoid falling below the set target.

The mechanism of quota control has three crucial features. First, all the above quotas are allocated in a top-down manner and reflected in each and every level of subnational LUMPs. To use quota 1 as an example, the national sum of 1.8 billion *mu* of cultivated land is first divided up and allocated to the thirty-plus provincial governments, which then further distribute their share of the quota to the prefectural governments in their respective jurisdiction. This runs through to the most grassroots township level.[94] Such top-down allocation of land use quotas is carried out through the process of drafting, review and approval of local LUMPs. According to the 2004 LAL, subnational LUMPs are drafted by local governments before being reviewed and approved by superior governments. The LUMPs of provinces, provincial capitals and cities with more than one million population are subject to approval by the State Council. Other local LUMPs are typically reviewed and approved by provincial governments.[95] The most critical condition for lower-level LUMPs to be approved is their compliance with the higher-level LUMPs,[96] which entails, in more concrete terms, that the amount of preserved cultivated land in any local LUMP shall be no less than what is determined by that one level up.[97] It is in this way that the aggregate land use quotas are decomposed and allotted from the national to the township level and that land use under subordinate administration falls within the four corners delineated by superior governments.

94 The breakdown of quotas 1 and 2 to the provincial level can be found in Appendix 2.

95 2004 LAL, art. 21; 2011 LALIR, art. 8.

96 Art. 26, Measures of Formulating and Reviewing Land Use Master Plans (土地利用总体规划编制审查办法), promulgated by MLR on February 4, 2009, available at www.mlr.gov.cn/zwgk/flfg/tdglflfg/200902/t20090211_114416.htm. Note that this is now repealed by the Administration Measures of Land Use Master Plans (土地利用总体规划管理办法), promulgated by MLR on May 8, 2017, but this particular requirement is not changed.

97 2004 LAL, art. 18.

Second, as already mentioned, the six numeric quotas are binding. The implication is that subnational governments are expected and responsible to abide by them, especially the first two quotas as assigned political tasks of cultivated land preservation. While the 1998 LAL requires that provincial governments shall insure no deduction in the total amount of cultivated land within their administrative jurisdiction over the planning term,[98] since 2004 the State Council has made it clear that every level of local government is responsible for keeping the amount of cultivated land and PAL within their jurisdiction as prescribed in their LUMPs and that local government leaders are the "principal subjects of accountability" (*diyi zeren ren*) in this regard.[99] The enforcement of these binding quotas requires not only that provincial governments report their compliance performance to the people's congresses at the same level every year;[100] more importantly, it subjects all local governments to annual reviews and performance evaluations.[101] Noncompliance with the LUMPs, especially violation of the binding quotas, leads to disciplinary action against both the responsible government and individual officials. For example, exceeding the quota in one year will result in quota deduction the next year.[102] And the most seriously offending officials will face criminal punishment of a maximum of seven years' imprisonment.[103]

Third, three of the six binding quotas are not just for the longer-run planning period but are also broken down on a year-to-year basis in the form of Annual Land Use Plans (*tuli liyong niandu jihua*, ALUPs), which include the amount of preserved cultivated land, the amount of cultivated land converted to construction land and the amount of post-conversion cultivated land supplement.[104] Similar to the LUMPs, the ALUPs are also prepared locally but are required to contain the quotas allocated from

[98] 1998 LAL, arts. 18, 21.

[99] State Council, Decision on Deepening Reform and Enhancing Land Administration, point 21.

[100] 2004 LAL, art. 25.

[101] Measures on Reviewing and Evaluating Enforcement of Annual Land Use Plans (土地利用年度计划执行情况考核办法), promulgated by MLR on March 13, 2008. The full text of this document is not published, but a comprehensive summary can be found at www.china.com.cn/policy/txt/2008-04/10/content_14743681.htm.

[102] State Council, Outline of National Land Use Master Plan (2006–2020), chapter 7, section 2.

[103] PRC Criminal Code, art. 410.

[104] Art. 4, Administration Measures of Land Use Annual Plans (土地利用年度计划管理办法), promulgated by MLR on December 19, 2006, available at www.mlr.gov.cn/zwgk/flfg/gtzybl/200612/t20061227_648781.htm. A newer version of this administration measure was issued by MLR on May 12, 2016, available at www.mlr.gov.cn/zwgk/zytz/201605/t20160520_1406065.htm.

above. They imbue the quota control system with a temporal dimension by specifying the limits of land use in a particular year.[105]

On top of the numeric and timing control focusing on the quantitative and temporal aspect of land use, the present national LUMP also contains a layer of spatial control that determines the spatial distribution of designated land use. In other words, while the quota control deals with the question of "how much" and timing control with the matter of "when," the spatial control concerns the issue of "where." It operates through "three boundaries and four zones" (*san jie si qu*):[106]

Table 7.3 *Three boundaries and four zones*

Three Boundaries	Boundary of areas for urban-rural construction land (*chengxiang jianshe yongdi guimo bianjie*)/Boundary allowing construction (BAC): the outer limits of areas allowed for construction land according to the quotas set in the LUMPs
	Boundary of expanded areas for urban-rural construction land (*chengxiang jianshe yongdi kuozhan bianjie*)/Boundary allowing construction conditionally (BACC): the outer limits of areas outside the BAC allowed for construction land conditionally to accommodate further urban development
	Boundary of areas prohibiting construction land (*jinzhi jianshe yongdi bianjie*, BPC): the outer limits of areas where construction is prohibited for the purpose of ecological, environmental and cultural-historical conservation

105 Note that the ALUPs are not just yearly installments of the corresponding LUMPs as annual quotas are not allocated evenly and statically to control and adjust the pace of non-agricultural development.

106 Point 3, Notices on Strictly Implementing and Managing Land Use Master Plans (关于严格土地利用总体规划实施管理的通知), promulgated by MLR on February 22, 2012, available at www.mlr.gov.cn/zwgk/zytz/201202/t20120228_1068266.htm; art. 22, Administration Measures of Land Use Master Plans, promulgated by MLR on May 8, 2017; Guideline for Municipal General Land Use Planning (市(地)级土地利用总体规划编制规程), promulgated by the MLR on June 27, 2010, available at www.mlr.gov.cn/zwgk/zytz/201006/t20100630_153290.htm; Guideline for the County-level General Land Use Planning (县级土地利用总体规划编制规程), promulgated by the MLR on June 27, 2010, available at www.360doc.com/content/16/0601/15/33897771_564206325.shtml; Guideline for the Town-level General Land Use Planning (乡(镇)土地利用总体规划编制规程), promulgated by the MLR on June 27, 2010, available at www.soujianzhu.cn/norm/csgh129.htm.

Table 7.3 (*cont.*)

Four Zones	Zones allowing construction (*yunxu jianshe qu*, ZAC): zones for construction land as prescribed by the LUMPs Zones allowing construction conditionally (*xianzhi jianshe qu*, ZACC): zones outside the BAC but inside the BACC Zones limiting construction (*guanzhi jianshe qu*, ZLC): zones outside the BAC, BACC and ZPC Zones prohibiting construction (*jinzhi jianshe qu*, ZPC): zones where construction is prohibited to protect important natural, ecological and cultural-historical resources

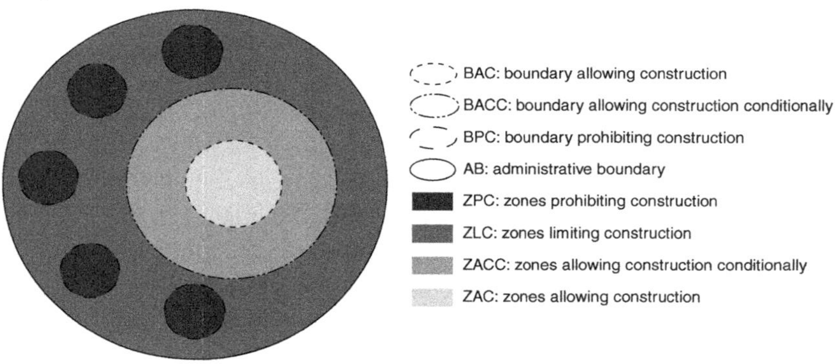

Figure 7.1 Visualization of three boundaries and four zones

These boundaries and zones are visualized in Figure 7.1.[107]

Through conjoining land use designation and quota control with numerical, temporal and spatial dimensions, the LUMPs and the ALUPs effectively dictate permitted land use and especially conversion from agricultural land to construction land across the country both annually and for the entire planning period. However, as noted earlier, this is but one of the two most crucial elements in China's land use regulatory system. The other is the URPs, which is related to but distinctive from the LUMPs.

[107] Taiyang Zhong, "Success or Failure: Evaluating the Implementation of China's National Land Use Plans in Past Twenty Years," Presentation at the University of Waterloo on November 11, 2013, p. 44. The document is on file with the author. There are slight changes in the translation of some Chinese terms.

7.4.2 *Urban and Rural Plans*

The URPs spell out the urban development strategy at the national, provincial, prefectural, county, township and village levels.[108] Subnational URPs are drafted locally and then submitted to the government one level above for review and approval.[109] National and provincial URPs are of a macro nature, setting out urban development layout for the whole country or a particular province. Prefectural, county, township and village URPs hammer out the details.[110] In particular, the URPs at prefectural and county levels establish the spatial arrangement for a locality, including its functional zones, layout of different land uses, areas used for infrastructure and public service facilities, the PAL, historical and cultural heritage and so forth. The township and village URPs specify the layout of residence, roads, water supply and drainage, power supply, garbage collection, livestock and poultry farms and so on.

Typically formulated for a 20-year period,[111] the URPs are broken down into Short-term Construction Plans (*jinqi jianshe guihua*, SCPs) that usually cover five years.[112] With an increasing degree of specificity, subprovincial URPs are categorized into master plans (*zongti guihua*), regulatory plans (*kongzhi xing xiangxi guihua*) and site plans (*xiujian xing xiangxi guihua*). These plans further lay down the nitty-gritty of the functional spatial arrangements of a locality. For example, under the current urban and rural planning system in China, construction land can be used for a total of 43 purposes, including residences, government buildings, shops, restaurants, theaters, factories, roads, parks, plazas and so forth.[113] On the planning map, each and every piece of land is earmarked for a particular use over the planning period. At a general level,

[108] 2007 URPL, arts. 13–18.

[109] 2007 URPL, arts.12–15. The exception is that provincial capital's URP will be approved by the State Council.

[110] 2007 URPL, arts. 17–18. [111] 2007 URPL, art. 17.

[112] 2007 URPL, art. 34; art. 6, Interim Working Measures on Short-term Construction Planning (近期建设规划工作暂行办法), promulgated by Ministry of Construction on August 29, 2002, available at www.360doc.com/content/12/0203/07/7293128_183794880.shtml.

[113] Code for Classification of Urban Land Use and Planning Standards of Development Land (城市用地分类与规划建设用地标准), promulgated on January 1, 2012; Explanation of the Code for Classification of Urban Land Use and Planning Standards of Development Land (城市用地分类与规划建设用地标准条文说明), promulgated on January 1, 2012.

Table 7.4 *Urban rural planning areas*

Built-up areas (*jiancheng qu*)	Areas already developed and covered by basic infrastructure and public service facilities
Areas suitable for construction (*shiyi jianshe qu*)	Areas designated in the URPs to accommodate urban development projects
Areas restricting construction (*xianzhi jianshe qu*)	Areas designated in the URPs as unsuitable for urban development projects; if such development is necessary, the projects shall be in line with the overall development and their nature, scale and intensity must be strictly controlled
Areas prohibiting construction (*jinzhi jianshe qu*)	Areas designated in the URPs that should not accommodate urban development projects for preservation of ecological, natural and cultural-historical environment as well as meeting the needs of infrastructural facilities and public security, etc.

however, the URPs divide a locality into four areas not so dissimilar from the four zones established in the LUMPs (see Table 7.4).[114]

Whether and to what extent the legally required consistency between the URPs and LUMPs[115] is realized in practice is an empirical question that cannot be pursued here.[116] Suffice it to conclude that the current and prospective use of a land parcel, be it state-owned or collectively owned, during the planning period are actually determined by the LUMPs and URPs. Moreover, the ALUPs and SCPs dictate at what time each year and where within a locality conversion of rural agricultural land is going to happen. This is the substantive ground on which rural land expropriation decisions are made in China.

114 Letters on Opinion Solicitation concerning Partial Amendment to the National Standard Urban Planning Basic Terms Standard (关于征求国家标准《城市规划基本术语》局部修订征求意见稿意见的函), promulgated by Ministry of Housing and Urban-Rural Development on July 27, 2005, available at www.csres.com/info/16492.html.

115 2004 LAL, art. 22; 2007 URPL, art. 5.

116 Xiangdong Yin and Yunjing Pan, "Spatial Regulatory Zoning: The Basic Spatial Platform for Planning Coordination (空间管制分区: 规划协调的基础空间平台)," in *Planning Innovation: Collected Papers of 2010 Annual Conference on Urban Planning in China* (规划创新: 2010 中国城市规划年会论文集) (Chongqing: Chongqing Press, 2010).

7.4.3 How Rural Land Expropriation Decisions Are Made

As mentioned, expropriation applications can be filed and reviewed either in batches or individually. Since there may well be multiple expropriation initiatives in a locality at different times over the period of one year, in order to make the whole process more efficient, individual applications are submitted to and reviewed by the approving government in batches. A batched expropriation application package normally consists of "one form and three programs" (*yi shu san fang'an*) (see Table 7.5).[117]

Upon receiving these materials, the central or provincial government will review the batched application and make decisions according to the following criteria. First, the agricultural land conversion program and cultivated land supplementation program must demonstrate that the

Table 7.5 *One form and three programs*

One Form[118]	Application form of construction land projects (*jianshe yongdi xiangmu chengbao shuoming shu*): demonstrates that the proposed expropriation initiative is in line with the relevant LUMPs and URPs
Three Programs[119]	Agricultural land conversion program (*nongdi zhuanyong fang'an*): specifies the type, location, amount and quality of the agricultural land to be expropriated and converted Cultivated land supplementation program (*buchang gengdi fang'an*): specifies the location, amount, quality and time frame of the supplement to the cultivated land and the PAL that are to be expropriated Land expropriation program (*zhengyong tudi fang'an*): specifies the scope, type, amount and rights over the land to be expropriated as well as the compensation and resettlement arrangements

[117] 1998 LALIR, art.20; article 7, Administration Measures on Examination and Application of Construction Land Use (建设用地审查报批管理办法), promulgated by MLR on March 2, 1999, available at www.mlr.gov.cn/zwgk/flfg/gtzybl/200504/t20050426_637326.htm.

[118] MLR, Administration Measures on Examination and Application of Construction Land Use, art. 9.

[119] Ibid., art. 10. If no collective agricultural land is expropriated, there is no need to prepare and submit the agricultural land conversion program and cultivated land supplementation program.

proposed expropriation is in conformity with the LUMPs, especially the quotas set in the ALUPs.[120] Second, the land expropriation program must meet the following three conditions: (1) there is a clear and uncontested demarcation of the location, scope and allocation of rights of the land to be expropriated; (2) the compensation standards are in line with relevant laws and regulations and (3) the resettlement arrangements of those expropriated are feasible.[121] In light of this, so as to be approved by the provincial and central authorities, in addition to making lawful and proper compensation and resettlement arrangements, the most crucial requirement the prefectural or county governments' batched expropriation applications must satisfy is to comply with the aforementioned spatial plans.

As already noted, alongside batched expropriation, prefectural and county governments in China may also submit expropriation applications for centrally or provincially approved construction projects that will take up land other than that which is designated as construction land in the LUMPs. In other words, these individual expropriation decisions lie outside the purview of the LUMPs. That being said, it is mistaken to think that these individual expropriations can contravene the LUMPs. As a matter of fact, applications of individual expropriation require the same materials as the batched expropriation except for one additional document called "land provision program" (*gongdi fang'an*), which specifies the particular construction projects the expropriated land will be used for.[122] This means that an application package of individual expropriation comprises of one form and four programs.[123] When reviewing these materials, the central and provincial governments must also make sure that individual expropriations are in line with the LUMPs.[124] How is this possible? The answer is that the LUMPs will be revised to accommodate these construction projects that are originally not covered in the plans.[125] In this way, whereas batched expropriation follows the spatial plans, especially the LUMPs, *statically*, individual expropriation does so

120 Art. 13, ibid. 121 Art. 14, ibid. 122 Art. 15, ibid.

123 2011 LALIR, arts. 23; Guidelines concerning Approval of Land Use for Individual Construction Projects (单独选址建设项目用地审查办事指南), promulgated by MLR on October 18, 2007, available at www.mlr.gov.cn/bsfw/bszn/td/200710/t20071018_658828.htm.

124 Point 5, Notice on Improving the Work of Examination and Approval of Land Use by the State Council for Individual Construction Projects (关于改进报国务院批准单独选址建设项目用地审查报批工作的通知), promulgated by MLR on January 24, 2009, available at www.mlr.gov.cn/xwdt/zytz/200903/t20090319_116624.htm.

125 MLR, Notices on Strictly Implementing and Managing Land Plans.

in a *dynamic* manner. Notwithstanding this difference, both are supposed to reflect and implement the spatial plans. When and where a piece of rural land is going to be expropriated and converted is already determined when these spatial plans are formulated. To put it differently, rural land expropriation decisions in China are not freestanding decisions made on an ad hoc basis. They are the extension of predetermined spatial planning decisions.

7.4.4 From One Plan to Another

As pointed out in the previous chapter, since the 1950s decisions to expropriate rural collective land in China followed from the decisions to undertake capital construction projects, and therefore constituted part of the economic planning system. Expropriation decisions back then were effectively the spatial expression of state economic plans. In the post-reform era, as China gradually moves toward a market economy, microeconomic planning and management on price, material, output and consumption are no longer practiced. But that by no means signifies a complete retreat of state planning and control. In the area of rural land expropriation, for example, spatial planning has replaced economic planning to become the determining factor as to when, where and how much rural land expropriation takes place. From the old economic planning system to the new spatial planning system, there are at least three points of continuity. To begin with, both operate through some sort of quotas that are allocated and enforced in a top-down fashion. Second, in both, the government planning agency plays a crucial role. The current spatial planning system is far from being monopolized by the land administration agencies. In fact, when formulating the LUMPs and the URPs as well as their annual versions, departments in charge of development and reform (*fazhan yu gaige weiyuanhui*), the successors of pre-reform economic planning commissions, are also significant participants.[126] This actually carries on the tradition of the original land use planning system established in 1987 when the construction land use plan was the product of both the land administration department and the planning commission.[127] Last but not least, the guiding

[126] MLR, Administration Measures of Land Use Master Plans, arts. 26, 34;

[127] Art. 5, Interim Administration Measures of Construction Land Use Plan (建设用地计划管理暂行办法), promulgated by State Bureau of Land Administration and National Commission of Development and Planning on October 15, 1987, available at www.shanxilr.gov.cn/Article/ShowArticle.asp?ArticleID=35.

principle of the spatial planning system today is none other than rational use of land,[128] which still stands as an effective constitutional mandate. In light of this, with its foundation rooted in the top-down planning schemes, rural land expropriation decisions remain the instrument to express and enforce the preconceived program of the party-state.

The preceding analysis of the foundational continuity of China's rural land expropriation law sets the scene for us to make better sense of the aforementioned nonchallengeability or nonjusticiability of expropriation decisions, to which we now turn.

7.5 Persistent Non-justiciability of Expropriation Decisions

It was mentioned in Chapter 2 that the existing literature holds that decisions to expropriate rural land are nonjusticiable primarily for two reasons: they are regarded either as administrative decisions with finality or as abstract administrative acts, both of which are immune to administrative litigation. The following texts first demonstrate that while it does contain a grain of truth, such conventional wisdom overall represents an erroneous understanding of the law on the part of the Chinese judiciary. However, even if the law gets properly interpreted and the courts do start to review provincial expropriation decisions, given the aforementioned foundational continuity, there is still very little room to judicialize the constitutional public interest prerequisite.

Before proceeding, it should be clarified that the nonjusticiability of expropriation decisions themselves does not mean that expropriation is completely closed for judicial review. Quite the contrary – commentators have observed that there has been a tremendous increase in the number of expropriation-related administrative lawsuits in China since the early 2000s.[129] While they did not break down the specific disputes in these expropriation-based administrative cases, the same authors did acknowledge that "people will not oppose the government's right to expropriate land in the abstract ... instead, disputes are usually about compensation."[130] In other words, whereas expropriation compensation

128 2004 LAL, arts. 1, 3; 2007 URPL, art. 4.

129 John Wagner Givens and Andrew W. MacDonald, "Squeezing the Same Old Stone: Suing the Rural Chinese State and the Shift from Tax Reform to Land Seizures," American Political Science Association 2011 Annual Meeting Paper, available at papers .ssrn.com/sol3/papers.cfm?abstract_id=1911642, p. 34.

130 Ibid., p. 17.

has been subject to administrative litigation, that is not the case with expropriation decisions, the reason for which will now be introduced.

Ever since its initial enactment, the ALL stipulates that decisions made by the State Council are immune to judicial review. This means that expropriation authorized by the State Council cannot be questioned in court.[131] In reality, although the power to examine and approve expropriation applications resides legally with the central and provincial governments, the MLR and provincial departments of land are usually put in charge of handling the applications on behalf of the corresponding governments. Therefore, over the years, expropriation approvals issued by the MLR have been challenged in court.[132] The SPC acknowledged in 2006 that the fact that the expropriation authorization documents are signed and sealed by the MLR rather than the State Council has given the false impression that such authorization comes from the MLR and is therefore open to administrative litigation. Instead, it should be seen as the expropriation decision made by the State Council itself, which is judicially unreviewable.[133]

In this case, the received wisdom is correct insofar as it rightly captures the nonjusticiability of this type of expropriation decision, but the reasons suggested are wrong. The nonjusticiability of the State Council's rural land expropriation decisions does not derive from them being abstract administrative acts or administrative decisions made with finality. Instead, it is because they are made by the State Council. Their nonchallengeability is a built-in feature of the Chinese judicial review system.

What about expropriation decisions made by provincial governments? While the ALL does stipulate that provincial government's decisions can generally be reviewed by the intermediate people's courts in the first instance,[134] the court's jurisdiction is subject to a number of exceptions,

[131] Neither can it be subject to administrative reconsideration, according to the 1999 ARL.

[132] Aihua Zou, "The Plight and Solution concerning Remedy for the Expropriated in Land Expropriation: From the Perspective of the Land Expropriation Power of the State Council (被征收人土地征收救济困境及其对策 – 以国务院土地征收决定权为视角)" (2012) 1 *Journal of National Academy of Administration* (国家行政学院学报) 101.

[133] Reply on Whether or Not to Accept the case on Zeng Cheng, Long Ping'an and others suing the PRC Ministry of Land Resources for its Administrative Act on Approval of Land Expropriation (关于曾成、龙平安等六人诉中华人民共和国国土资源部征地批复行政行为是否受理的复函), promulgated by SPC on July 3, 2006, in SPC Case Filing Division (ed.), *Guidance on Case Filing Work* (立案工作指导) (Beijing: Renmin Fayuan Press, 2007), p. 56.

[134] 1989 ALL, art. 14; 2015 ALL, art. 15.

including abstract administrative acts[135] and administrative decisions with finality.[136] As noted, it is widely believed in the existing literature that because the expropriation decisions fall into these two categories, they should be, and usually are, exempted from judicial review. This, however, is a misreading of the law.

To start with, under the current Chinese judicial review system, abstract administrative acts are those administrative decisions "of general binding force."[137] More specifically, they are "issued to address unspecified subjects and can be applied repeatedly."[138] It is then not difficult to see that provincial expropriation decisions are precisely the opposite. First, they are always directed at specified subjects, namely the rural collectives and peasants to be expropriated; second, they can be applied only once. Therefore, provincial expropriation decisions are specific administrative acts that should have been subject to administrative litigation. To consider them as unreviewable abstract administrative acts is legally unfounded.

In contrast, it is not so easy to see through the legal reasoning behind classifying provincial expropriation decisions as administrative decisions made with finality. In Chinese administrative law, to so qualify is dependent on two conditions: the decision is a specific administrative act, and its finality is provided for by statutes enacted by the NPC or the NPCSC. Given the above discussion, the first hurdle is already overcome. The difficulty lies in identifying the statutory basis that grants finality to the provincial decisions to expropriate. On this front, Chinese local courts have commonly invoked Article 30(2) of the 1999 *Administrative Reconsideration Law* (ARL).[139] It reads: an administrative reconsideration decision made by the provincial governments, according to the land expropriation decisions of the State Council or provincial governments,

[135] 2015 ALL, art. 12(2). [136] 2015 ALL, art. 12(4). [137] 2015 ALL, art. 12(2).

[138] Art. 2, Interpretation on Several Questions regarding the Implementation of the PRC (关于执行中华人民共和国行政诉讼法若干问题的解释), promulgated by SPC on April 22, 2015, available at www.court.gov.cn/zixun-xiangqing-14294.html.

[139] *Gao Weiping and Fan Xiaoqi* v. *Anhui People's Government* (高卫萍、范小七不服安徽省人民政府征地行政批复案), Anhui High People's Court (2011), available at www.ahcourt.gov.cn/sitecn/xzjx/44705.html; *Cai Zhicheng* v. *Jiangsu People's Government* (蔡志成诉江苏省人民政府土地行政管理案), Jiangsu High People's Court (2015), available at www.lawxp.com/case/c15239459.html; *Deng Shiquan* v. *Sichuan People's Government* (邓仕全诉四川省人民政府土地行政征收案), Sichuan High People's Court (2016), available at http://wenshu.court.gov.cn/content/content?DocID=34b8479e-f719-4b52-b9dd-bfac7b3ed9fe.

to confirm (*queren*) the ownership and use-rights of land is an administrative decision with finality.

This clause has been interpreted as granting finality de jure to provincial expropriation decisions.[140] From a semantic point of view, however, that reading is flawed. There are two kinds of decisions involved here: one is the administrative reconsideration decisions to confirm land rights, while the other is the expropriation decisions. Being the basis on which rights-confirming administrative reconsideration decisions are made, provincial expropriation decisions are different from and should not to be conflated with those reconsideration decisions. Understood literally, this clause bestows finality only upon the land rights-confirming administrative reconsideration decisions and not their basis, namely the expropriation decisions. If it does mean that both are final, it would have juxtaposed the two and clearly stipulated so. For sure, expropriation decisions do influence land rights – after all, expropriation leads to the loss and reallocation of these rights. However, the SPC has made a clear distinction between land-rights-confirming decisions and expropriation decisions. The former determines the lawful distribution of land rights when there is a dispute concerning what belongs to whom.[141] These two types of decision are distinct from and do not crumble into each other. They are related only to the extent that expropriation decisions can be taken as the grounds for making land-rights-confirming decisions. The fact that the latter has finality does not mean that the former does too.

Alternatively, it has been suggested that finality is granted de facto to provincial expropriation decisions.[142] The reason is that if such expropriation decisions are not final and open to judicial review, they may well be quashed or changed by the courts. If that happens, rights-confirming administrative reconsideration decisions made according to these expropriation decisions will become groundless and must be overturned or altered accordingly. In that case, in order for such reconsideration decisions to be final, their basis – the expropriation decisions – must also be

140 This is the position held by the High People's Courts from Jiangsu and Anhui provinces in the cases quoted in the preceding footnote.

141 Reply to Issues concerning Implementing Paragraph Two of Article 30 of the Administrative Reconsideration Law (关于使用行政复议法第三十条第二款有关问题的批复), promulgated by SPC on September 20, 2005. The full text of this document has never been officially published, though it is often cited in court judgments.

142 Rikai He, "The Confusion and Solution of China's Land Expropriation Compensation and Remedial System (我国征地补偿救济制度的迷误与出路)" (2007) 11 *Legal Research* (法学) 9.

final. This position is untenable for confusing finality with immutability. The former does not entail the latter. If the provincial expropriation decisions are altered by courts, those land rights-confirming reconsideration decisions can still be final in the sense of being immune to administrative litigation. At the same time, however, the provincial governments are obligated to abandon or revise its reconsideration decisions on its own initiative so as to reflect the changes in its legal basis.

In summary, if understood correctly, the existing Chinese law does *not* free provincial expropriation decisions from administrative litigation and the relevant nonjusticiability argument has no legal merit at all. Nevertheless, the reality is that Chinese courts have generally chosen to shy away from exercising their jurisdiction on provincial expropriation decisions, considering them as final and unreviewable. In fact, the SPC itself reiterated this legally unsound position in a 2016 judgment.[143] This is all the more startling given that Article 12(5) of the 2015 ALL explicitly provides that expropriation decisions are open to judicial review. The SPC ruling can only be squared with the current ALL by holding that the article only refers to expropriation of private property on urban land, which is clearly an unwarrantedly narrow reading of the law.

In addition to categorizing expropriation decisions as abstract administrative acts or administrative decisions with finality, some local courts in China have also ruled that these decisions are internal administrative acts that should be exempted from judicial review.[144] Under Chinese administrative law, internal administrative acts are those decisions internal to the government with no direct legal effect upon the citizens outside the government. From a formal point of view, provincial expropriation decisions appear to be merely internal to the government because they are made when the provincial governments approve the expropriation applications submitted by prefectural or county governments. Nevertheless, they clearly have external legal effects on citizens outside the government and should not be classified as internal administrative acts.

In any event, despite having no grounds in effective law, Chinese courts from top to grassroots level have avoided adjudicating on challenges to

[143] *Wang Lianhai et al.* v. *Jilin People's Government* (王连海等与吉林省人民政府土地行政复议行政纠纷案), SPC (2016), available at www.360doc.com/content/16/0826/18/31860415_586129763.shtml.

[144] *Pan Xiang and Cheng Xianfu* v. *Nanjing Lishui District People's Government* (潘祥、程贤富与南京市溧水区人民政府拆迁纠纷案), Jiangsu High People's Court (2014), available at wenshu.court.gov.cn/content/content?DocID=9af13449-a615-4f1d-a365-b4da76705e9e.

provincial expropriation decisions. For that, it is difficult to pinpoint any single cause. They may have done so either involuntarily, under external pressure, or intentionally, hoping to excuse themselves from getting involved in the oftentimes highly contentious expropriation disputes or simply out of a sincere misunderstanding of the law. All these scenarios are supported by empirical evidence. For instance, some local CCP committees reportedly issued internal instructions forbidding local courts from taking on law suits challenging expropriation decisions.[145] It has also been documented that in some localities the people's court simply does not have the nerve to accept cases related to "hot issues" such as land expropriation and illegal demolition of homes.[146] Moreover, even the director of the Administrative Division of the SPC seems to have misunderstood the law and regards expropriation decisions as administrative decisions made with finality by virtue of art. 30(2) of the 1999 ARL.[147]

That said, even if Chinese courts start to interpret the law correctly and to review provincial expropriation decisions, they can hardly overrule such decisions for contravening the constitutional public interest prerequisite. The reason is that administrative litigation in China is limited in the scope of review. According to Article 5 of the 1989 ALL and Article 6 of the 2015 ALL, courts are only empowered to inquire into the legality, not the merits or reasonableness of an administrative act. As mentioned in Chapter 1, Article 42 of the 2007 *Property Law* prescribes that the constitutional requirement of "in accordance with law" in the context of expropriation stands for lawful authority and procedure, which means that the legality of individual expropriation decisions centers on whether or not such decisions are made by competent authorities following prescribed procedures.[148] For example, if a provincial

[145] "Deputy Tribunal Director of Zhengzhou Intermediate Court Replying to the Property Owner who is Expropriated: No Acceptance of Expropriation Case is a Chinese Characteristics (郑州中院副庭长回应被拆迁业主: 拆迁不立案是中国特色)," March 27, 2013, available at news.sina.com.cn/c/2013-03-26/055926638704.shtml.

[146] Kevin J. O'Brien and Lianjiang Li, "Suing the Local State: Administrative Litigation in Rural China" (2004) 51 *The China Journal* 81.

[147] Zhenyu Wang, "Why Land Expropriation Cases give the Courts Headache (征地官司为何令法官头疼)," October 20, 2008, available at www.news.163.com/08/1020/08/4OMF8MIP00012Q9L.html. Rather ironically, this article was published years after the SPC made a clear distinction between expropriation decisions and land-rights-confirming decisions that are final. It shows that such a misunderstanding of the law remains pervasive.

[148] Dongtao Wang, "On the Justiciability and Standards of Review of the Land Expropriation-related Administrative Acts (简析征地类行政行为的可诉性及审查标准)," 7 January 2010, available at syzy.chinacourt.org/public/detail.php?id=4092.

government arrogates the expropriation authorization power that should have been in the hands of the State Council, or violates the statutory expropriation procedures, or deviates from the centrally approved land use plan, it can be held accountable by the courts for unlawful expropriation decisions. Yet none of this relates to the constitutional public interest prerequisite. In fact, any inquiry into the substantive purpose of expropriation and its compliance with a certain conception of public interest will undoubtedly amount to merit review and therefore lie outside the competence of the courts. To be sure, as illustrated by experiences of many other jurisdictions, the line between legality and merit review is a thin one and can sometimes be crossed subtly and covertly. In theory, the Chinese courts may well exhibit some judicial activism and venture to flesh out the public interest clause in individual cases. In practice this is unlikely, given that they are generally reluctant or unable to take on the task of reviewing provincial expropriation decisions. But assume for the sake of argument that they do become willing and able to examine the substantive merit of expropriation decisions under the pretext of legality review – is it possible that the constitutional public interest prerequisite can eventually be judicialized?

In view of the foregoing discussion on the substantive grounds for rural land expropriation decision-making and its foundational continuity, the answer is in the negative. As noted, the spatial plans, on which the centrally/provincially authorized expropriation decisions are based, set out the spatial layout of a particular locality and effectively determine when and where a piece of rural land is to be expropriated. Therefore, to question the purpose of a particular expropriation decision necessarily entails questioning those spatial plans, which are quintessential examples of abstract administrative acts with general binding effects upon unspecified subjects. Under the existing administrative litigation system of China, these plans remain indisputably unreviewable.[149] At most, the courts may examine if an expropriation decision is lawful in being consistent with the spatial plans it is supposed to reflect and implement or whether a spatial plan is lawfully made by competent authorities following legal procedures.[150] This is surely of great importance. Yet in

[149] The SPC confirmed in 2017 that LUMPs are unreviewable by courts. See “Land Utilization Master Plans are Unreviewable (土地利用总体规划不具有可诉性),” June 19, 2017, available at www.gtzyb.com/shiwucuoshi/20170619_105605.shtml.

[150] For relevant discussion on indirect judicial review over the URPs in China, see Chunyan Zheng, “On the Way towards Judicial Review of Urban and Rural Planning: Taking Examples from Judgments related to Urban and Rural Planning Cases (论城乡

no way will it generate any jurisprudence on the constitutional public interest clause.

Nonetheless, one may argue that the court can skillfully bypass reviewing the underlying spatial plans to focus just on what kind of specific purpose a certain expropriation decision is made for. After all, the spatial plans only dictate that a piece of rural land is going to be expropriated. It is up to the initiating prefectural or county government to decide what specific construction project the expropriated land will be used for in each and every individual case.[151] But for the following three reasons, it is practically very difficult, if not impossible, for the court to review the concrete purpose an individual expropriation decision serves. For a start, when an expropriation application is reviewed and approved, the post-expropriation use of land may well be undecided. A telling example is expropriation for land reserve/banking (*tudi chubei*). According to Article 10 of the 2007 *Measures on Land Reserve Administration*, rural land can be expropriated and deposited in the prefectural or county government's land reserves. The prefectural and county governments need to make annual land reserve plans according to the aforementioned spatial plans. Therefore, expropriation for land reserve must also be consistent with such plans.[152] However, no specific construction project needs to be specified in the expropriation application materials. As an institutionalized practice, land banking by Chinese local governments started from Shanghai in the 1990s and diffused across the country later on.[153] To a large extent, this was an intentional choice made by many city and county governments to retain some control over future urban development and exert state regulatory power on how the land is developed.[154]

规划的司法审查路径：以涉及城乡规划案件的司法裁判文书为例)" (2013) 25 *Peking University Law Journal* (中外法学) 803.

151 2004 LAL, art. 44; 1998 LALIR, art. 22. This applies to batched expropriation and does not cover the case of individual expropriation where expropriation decisions are made specifically for provincially/centrally authorized projects of infrastructural development and public works.

152 Art. 7, Measures on Land Reserve Administration (土地储备管理办法), promulgated by MLR, Ministry of Finance and People's Bank of China on November 19, 2007, available at www.mlr.gov.cn/zwgk/flfg/zhgl/201204/t20120413_1083824.htm.

153 Jianbo Lou and Jinping Jin, *Legal Institutions of Land Reserve and Primary Land Development* (土地储备及土地一级开发法律制度) (Beijing: Zhongguo Fazhi Press, 2009), p. 8; Yanlong Zhang, "Institutional Sources of Reform: The Diffusion of Land Banking Systems in China" (2011) 8(3) *Management and Organization Review* 507.

154 Jiang Xu, Anthony Yeh and Fulong Wu, "Land Commodification: New Land Development and Politics in China since the Late 1990s" (2009) 33 (4) *International Journal of Urban and Regional Research* 901.

When this practice was first recognized at the national level, its core function was explicitly stated by the MLR as "strengthening the state's capacity in controlling the land market."[155] As one official from a city land administration bureau put it, expropriation for land reserve changes the situation of "projects waiting for land" to "land waiting for projects."[156] In this way, rural land expropriation can be carried out in the absence of any construction project. Its public interestedness is supposed to be guaranteed by being aimed at enhancing the state's control over the land market. Consequently, there is simply no specific construction project for the courts to review. Nor are the courts able to question the public interestedness of expropriation for land reserve when it is set in law as a legitimate objective for expropriation.[157]

Moreover, even when an expropriation application does involve a particular construction project, it is not a factor to be taken into account by the provincial or central government when reviewing expropriation applications. As already mentioned, the focus of the reviewing authorities is on the compliance of expropriation initiatives with the spatial plans. With respect to the legality of expropriation decisions, the construction project for which the expropriated land is used is an irrelevant consideration. Therefore, even if the courts start to review the expropriation decision, they will not review the post-expropriation land use or pass judgment on its conformity with the public interest.

Last, but by no means least, one should be reminded that decisions to expropriate and decisions on post-expropriation land use are two different administrative acts performed by different government authorities. The public interestedness of decisions on post-expropriation land use is surely up for debate, but there is no way for such decisions to be brought to court by the expropriated in the first place. The reason is that Chinese law requires the plaintiff to be a "victim" of the administrative act in

155 Notice on Tightening Up Administration of State-owned Land Resources (关于加强国有土地资产管理的通知), promulgated by MLR on May 30, 2001, available at www.gov.cn/gongbao/content/2001/content_60846.htm.

156 Xue Leng, "From Projects Waiting for Land to Land Waiting for Projects (从项目等地到地等项目)," March 31, 2014, available at news.qq.com/a/20140331/004932.htm.

157 This of course does not go without opposition. In 2010, a lawyer published an open letter online arguing that some purposes of expropriation for land reserve are against the constitutional public interest prerequisite and that the NPCSC should review the constitutionality of the land reserve system. Yet his effort was to no avail. Zhongzhou He and Juan Wei, "A Lawyer Claiming that Land Reserve System is Predatory and Contradicting the Constitution (律师称土地储备制度与民争利违背宪法)," May 7, 2010, available at news.sina.com.cn/c/sd/2010-05-07/102820223721.shtml.

question.[158] In legal terms, decisions on how and by whom a piece of expropriated land is used are of the state dispensing its own property – the expropriated have no standing whatsoever to challenge such decisions in administrative litigation.

At this juncture, it is worth highlighting a recent development. The Fourth Plenum of the Eighteenth Party Congress announced that policy experiments would be carried out to entrust the people's prosecutorate to act as the advocate for public interest litigation[159], which, according to the explanatory report by President Xi Jinping, will concern, among others, transfer of use-rights of state-owned land.[160] It was openly conceded by Xi that in reality, when the use-rights of state-owned land are transferred, the public interest has oftentimes been undermined or is in danger of being undermined due to the government's unlawful actions or omissions. In these circumstances, ordinary citizens or other social organizations have no direct involved interest and therefore no standing to initiate public interest litigation. Consequently, unlawful administrative acts are actually exempted from effective judicial supervision, which is in detriment to "governing the country according to law."[161] In June 2017, the NPCSC revised the ALL to formally empower the procuratorates to sue on behalf of the public in this regard.[162] This change offers a strong testimony to my analysis above. The central authority is keenly aware where the real problem rests and what should be the solution. As noted, expropriation decisions and post-expropriation disposal of the expropriated land are two separate administrative acts. Whereas the former is to a large extent judicially reviewable, the latter is not reviewable precisely because no one has the standing to challenge it in court. The solution adopted is therefore not broadening the scope of

[158] 1989 ALL, promulgated by CCP art. 11; 2015 ALL, art. 12.

[159] Point 4 (2), Decisions on Important Issues concerning Comprehensively Advancing Ruling the Country according to Law (关于全面推进依法治国若干重大问题的决定), promulgated by CCP Central Committee on October 23, 2014, available at news.xinhuanet.com/politics/2014-10/28/c_1113015330.htm.

[160] Xi Jinping, "Explanatory Report on the Central Committee of Chinese Communist Party's Decision on Important Issues concerning Comprehensively Advancing Ruling the Country according to Law（关于中共中央全面推进依法治国若干重大问题的决定的说明）," October 28, 2014, available at news.xinhuanet.com/politics/2014-10/28/c_1113015372.htm, point 9.

[161] Ibid.

[162] Decision on Revising Civil Procedure Law and (关于修改民诉法和行诉法的决定), promulgated by NPCSC on June 27, 2017, available at www.spp.gov.cn/zdgz/201706/t20170628_194097.shtml. This is the only formal revision of the LAL to date.

administrative litigation. Instead, the people's procuratorates are tasked to step in and bring such matters to court in the first place.

While this is undoubtedly progress, it remains to be seen exactly what this type of public interest litigation will look like.[163] For the time being, however, it is not unreasonable to predict that it will still be very limited since the scope of judicial review remains to concentrate on legality review with rationality review excluded.[164] Arguably, the only legal rule concerning the substantive grounds on which the state transfers its land is that it must be in line with reasonable exploration, use and management of land and shall contribute to urban development and economic growth.[165] Such an abstract prescription obviously provides little guidance for the reviewing courts to determine whether a particular decision of use-rights transfer is lawful or not. To be clear, this does not mean that the court can do nothing when examining the legality of transfer decisions – a fairly extensive body of rules has already been established on the procedures of transferring state-owned land's use-rights, especially on the public tender, auction and listing of use-rights over state-owned land for profitable purposes.[166] Therefore, the reviewing courts can decide if these formal procedural rules are followed when local governments engage in state-owned land-use rights transfers. But what they cannot do is to adjudicate on the question of whether such transfers are in the public interest, which stays undefined thus far.

In summary, contrary to the conventional wisdom, rural land expropriation decisions in China should have been judicially reviewable, at least in part. Those made by provincial governments ought to be justiciable according to the present law if interpreted properly. However, for a variety of reasons, both the national and local courts in China have so

[163] Until this day there has been only one publicized case where a county prosecutorate initiated public interest litigation against a local government's decision to transfer urban land use-rights. But the dispute was about unauthorized occupation of the land rather than the public interestedness of the decision. For details, see "Shanxi Fugu Procuratorates Brought the First Administrative Public Interest Litigation Case concerning Urban Land Use-rights Transfer (陕西府谷检察院提起全省首例国有土地使用权出让领域行政公益诉讼)," July 4, 2016, available at news.xinhuanet.com/legal/2016-07/04/c_129114214.htm.

[164] This holds for the recently amended 2015 ALL (art. 6).

[165] Art. 1, Interim Regulation on the Allocation and Transfer of the Use Right of the State-owned Urban Land.

[166] Rules of Public Tender, Auction and Listing of State-owned Land Use Rights (招标拍卖挂牌出让国有土地使用权规定), promulgated by MLR on April 3, 2002. The most recent version was promulgated by the MLR on September 21, 2007, available at www.mlr.gov.cn/zwgk/zfgw/zfwj/200712/t20071212_96998.htm.

far failed to take on the task. But even if they begin to do so, they can only review the legality of expropriation decisions with respect to their conformity to the spatial plans that are unreviewable abstract administrative acts, not on whether or not expropriation decisions are consistent with any judicially formulated conception of public interest. To make matters worse, it is not easy to challenge the public interestedness of post-expropriation use of land in judicial review, even though the people's procuratorates are now tasked to bring public interest litigation against such decisions. All of this renders meaningful judicialization of the constitutional public interest prerequisite unattainable. The long-standing tradition of unchallengeable expropriation decisions has largely survived until the present day.

To recap, this chapter presents a story of continuity of China's rural land expropriation law in the reform era. It has been demonstrated that insofar as the core features are concerned, the existing Chinese rural land expropriation law is very much a continuation of its own past and there is no fundamental rupture from the historical lineage in which it has originated and evolved over time. This is certainly not to dismiss that there have been notable changes to this body of law, which are also discussed. Rather, the point is that the question of how China's rural land expropriation law takes the shape as it does today can be most appropriately and accurately addressed through revealing its strong yet hitherto neglected path dependence, less so through focusing on the changes, and even less so by comparing it with or measuring it up against the American law of eminent domain. In other words, if the goal is to make sense of the Chinese rural land expropriation law today, continuity of the past significantly outweighs change as the explanatory prism and the key to an internal and sympathetic understanding lies in unpacking how exactly the pre-reform legacy has lived on in the reform period.

On a more substantive note, this chapter reveals that since the early 1980s the presumption of expropriation in nonagricultural use of rural land has not only persisted but has actually been reinforced as a way of realizing top-down state control over rural land use and conversion, which continues to be ever so crucial, in the eyes of the party-state, to the long-established dual objectives of farmland preservation and economic development. Moreover, the socialist principle endures as the normative basis for China's rural land expropriation law, which confirms rather than constrains the takings power of the state regarded as naturally representing the public interest, obligates the peasants to accept expropriation that is more obligatory than transactional and conceptualizes property in rural land as some sort of in-kind welfare and social security. Third, as a result of the previous two points, the decision-making process of rural land expropriation has thus far remained closed within the government hierarchy, and expropriation decisions, especially their public interestedness, are yet to be subject to robust and effective judicial review. The statutory compensation standard is still multiplied agricultural output that purports to maintain the expropriatees' original living standards. Last but not least, as spatial planning replaces economic planning as the new foundation for expropriation decision-making, the pre-reform tradition of rural land expropriation for state-led social transformation has not only been maintained but also reinvigorated.

8

Conclusion

As stated in the opening chapter, the core aim of this book is to offer a contextualized description and immanent critique of China's rural land takings law based on an internal and sympathetic understanding of it. Instead of juxtaposing it with the supposedly more advanced American model of eminent domain law, this is to be achieved through closely examining how it has originated and evolved under distinctive historical conditions over the last century and teasing out the law's own distinctive premises, principles and functions to identify its internal tensions and difficulties. This chapter takes stock and concludes. It first summarizes the insights generated in previous chapters and highlights three salient features of the Chinese law on rural land takings that have been produced by the unique intellectual, political and social conditions. Based on such contextualized description, the second section refutes the dominant Transition Paradigm. The third section takes one step back to ask why the TP, as a moral and political critique against the takings law, emerges in the first place. It will be demonstrated that many of the conditions that have shaped the law have experienced momentous changes over the last three decades. Against this background, the fourth section of this chapter advances an immanent critique of the law by revealing the tensions and difficulties facing its effectiveness, efficiency, fairness and constitutionality. The fifth and final part discusses the law's possible future by examining the draft amendment to the LAL published in May 2017. It is most likely that for the years to come China's rural land takings law will stay within its broad parameters, although marginal and gradual reforms are to be expected.

8.1 Taking Stock

As noted in Chapters 1–3, China's rural land expropriation law has long been under heavy fire for failing to honor the promise entrenched in the 1982 constitutional takings clause, which is generally held to be not so dissimilar to the Fifth Amendment to the US Constitution in both textual and functional terms. Compared with its American counterpart, the Chinese law in this area is widely regarded as defective, and ineffective in limiting the state takings power and protecting land rights. Specifically, the public interest prerequisite faces a triple challenge, the compensation standard is unfairly low and the procedures are a far cry from the requirement of due process. Under this obviously unsatisfactory circumstance, the future of the Chinese law on rural land expropriation is commonly seen to lie in a transition toward the American eminent domain law, the key of which is to make China's own Fifth Amendment tick. Along this line, a series of reform proposals have been put forth over the last decade or so, including, but not limited to, supplying an enumerated list of public interest items, fundamentalization of private property, propertization of property rights, strengthening judicial and legislative scrutiny in expropriation, removing the stringent use control over rural land, making expropriation procedures more participatory and adopting fair market value as the compensation standard. However, despite much popular support, very little substantive progress has so far been made in this field. The lackluster reform efforts are usually attributed to a phenomenon known as land finance, where local governments rely on rural land expropriation and conversion to generate huge fiscal benefits. Their resistance has been held most culpable for stalling the much-needed legal reforms. The hope is that deeper and more systemic reforms will be set in motion once land finance is cleared out of the way. Such conventional wisdom is encapsulated by what I call the Transition Paradigm, which is based on teleological, developmental, temporal and conceptual assumptions about what is wrong with China's existing rural land expropriation law and how it should be remedied.

This book pursues an alternative line of inquiry. By carefully tracking the journey of modern Chinese rural land takings law, it reconstructs the unique historical lineage behind this body of law, which turns out to be not something of a distant and irrelevant past, but a living legacy that has profoundly shaped the present. Chapter 5 documents that since the early twentieth century, both the CCP and the KMT started to view the power of rural land takings not as the last resort to be taken only diffusely and occasionally for specific technical purposes, but as an instrument of first resort to implement state-led social transformation programs from class revolution to economic development. In spite of their crucial difference, the Marxist–Soviet socialist tradition and the theory of socialized property as understood by the nationalists at the time converged in rejecting the idea of natural and absolute private property rights in land and conceptualizing state acquisition as a necessary check of public interest over private interest. Against this distinctive theoretical and intellectual background, the Chinese constitutional framers in 1954 drew on the 1949 East German Constitution to formulate China's original takings clause, which was explored in detail in Chapter 4. It is demonstrated that despite its seemingly restrictive form, the 1954 constitutional takings clause was intended to confirm instead of limit the state takings power. At the same time, as an embodiment of the Chinese revolutionary experiences, the original takings clause included three distinct kinds of takings powers and was normatively underpinned by the socialist principle that holds the state as the undisputable representative of public interest, which was supposed to take precedence over and be in fundamental harmony with private interests.

Chapter 6 shows why Article 10 of the currently effective 1982 Constitution should be seen as a takings clause *sensu lato*, and how it is a continuation of the 1954 takings clause both normatively and teleologically. The first clause on state ownership of urban land is in essence an exercise of the power of nationalization, targeting the privately owned urban land in existence by the time of constitutional enactment in 1982. The second paragraph, on collective ownership of rural and suburban land, defines the subject of expropriation, and the fifth paragraph on rational use of land establishes the guiding principle of expropriation. The fourth clause on prohibition of voluntary land transaction ensures that the state expropriation stipulated in the third clause stays the only way in which collective land can be converted to state-owned land for nonagricultural purposes. These five clauses, in the original design, all find their normative basis in the socialist principle and serve the function of promoting state-led social transformation. Except that the content of such transformative projects was turned from redistributive class struggle to construction and development, the 1982 takings clause is fundamentally an extension of the constitutional takings jurisprudence 30 years before. This new yet unchanged constitutional foundation has subsequently been embodied, as revealed in Chapter 7, by the post-reform rural land expropriation law, which is characterized by profound continuity from its pre-reform roots on multiple levels. Most crucially, three salient features of the law have stayed more or less constant since the early twentieth century up until today.

First and foremost, the presumption of state expropriation in nonagricultural use of rural land has been in existence for more than six decades, initially as a de facto outcome of the division of labor between collectives and state under a command economy before becoming de jure recognized and explicitly entrenched since the opening and reform policy. For all the seismic shifts in political, economic and societal terms, there is an ever-present desire on the part of the Chinese party-state to maintain exclusive control over rural land use and conversion so as to further whatever ends it sees fit, be it preservation of cultivated land or macroeconomic management. Second, from economic planning to spatial planning, between devolution and recentralization of the power of authorization, expropriation decision-making has always been carried out through a review and approval mechanism inside the government hierarchy according to top-down plans. This is the specific way in which state control over rural land use and conversion gets instituted, regulated and disciplined. The fulfillment of the constitutional principle of rational land use is mainly predicated on the extent of rationality in state planning schemes and their strict and effective implementation. Third, this long-lasting tradition of the state's exclusive control over rural land through expropriation in pursuance of top-down planning has been legitimatized by the equally enduring socialist principle, which perpetuates the precedence of the public interest over private interests and the identification of the state as the necessary and undisputable representative of the public interest. Two consequences follow. On the one hand, the opportunity to judicially challenge state expropriation decisions per se is still not available. On the other hand, with expropriation seen as an obligation for private interests to obey the public interest rather than some sort of sacrifice or transaction, for decades the criteria of compensation and resettlement have been anchored upon the original living standards of expropriatees. Therefore, it is fair to conclude that the central role of Chinese law on rural land expropriation has been to facilitate, regulate and justify exercises of the takings power to serve state-led social transformation.

8.2 Doing Away with the Transition Paradigm

In this light, three of the four assumptions of the TP can be readily refuted. First off, the conceptual assumption is falsified by both the theories and the praxes of land takings in modern China that have gone well beyond the conventional notion of compensable acquisition for public works. For one thing, compensationless nationalization was not only carried out extensively but also left an imprint on all four written constitutions of the People's Republic. For another, the scope of land takings has constantly been more expansive than what is typically understood as public works. Second, the temporal assumption with a narrow focus solely on the post-reform period proves to be myopic, as it turns out that much light can be shed on the existing law by looking at what came before the opening and reform policy. Third, it has been shown that China's original and current constitutional takings clauses, in their original configuration, are a world apart from the American Fifth Amendment, normatively and functionally. It is a fault committed under the teleological assumption of conflating the two countries' constitutional takings jurisprudence, which certainly cannot be done without serious distortion of historical facts. The present Chinese rural land expropriation law is therefore a faithful reflection, not an unfortunate betrayal, of what the power-confirming constitutional foundation really entails.

To be clear, none of this is to suggest that the Chinese law on rural land expropriation is perfect and the case for reform is more imagined than real. Evidently, it is not. The upshot of the preceding analysis is to highlight that it is very much a product of its own unique path, which invites us to look beyond the contemporary and the typical and urges us to come to terms with its radical difference from its American counterpart. Nevertheless, one may argue that while all the above findings may be factually correct and there is no contradiction between the law and its constitutional basis, that does not make it morally right or politically legitimate. That the Chinese rural land expropriation law *is not* the American law of eminent domain does not mean that it *should not* be. Quite the contrary – the realization that the two are so different ought to be the reason for renovating the Chinese law in the image of the American model, not the excuse for sticking with the unjust and undesirable status quo. What should be done, then, is to look for measures that will, as it were, close the gap. As noted in Chapter 3, the past decade or so saw very little substantial headway in this respect, which has been commonly blamed on recalcitrance from China's local governments heavily dependent on land finance. Hence, the last surviving component of the TP: the developmental assumption is still valid in the sense that once the obstacle of land finance is eradicated, the Chinese expropriation law will move, gradually but steadily, toward the American model. To test the validity of this last assumption, we need to reflect on the root cause that has thwarted deeper reforms.

To date, most of the popular reform proposals surveyed in Chapter 3 have not come to fruition. To start with, no refined specification of public interest is ever provided to narrow down the expansive scope of expropriation. Neither propertization of property rights nor fundamentalization of private property is taken on board. Legislative scrutiny and judicial review over expropriation laws and individual expropriation decisions remain lacking. Second, the structural challenge that makes the constitutional public interest clause virtually redundant has been to a large extent kept intact, notwithstanding the much applauded recent pilot policy adjustment to marketize for-profit rural construction land. This is because it merely accounts for a tiny portion of China's rural land, leaving more than 90 percent of rural land still under stringent use and conversion limitations that can only be overcome by state expropriation. Third, despite the added procedural requirement that the expropriated be informed of expropriation applications prior to submission, there is still no way for them to participate in the decision-making process.

Last, but not least, the almost universally advocated fair market value standard for expropriation compensation is yet to be embraced. Admittedly, the last ten years have witnessed more substantial reforms in this regard. The statutory 30-times cap of land compensation fees plus resettlement fees has been abolished on the policy level. The multiplied average annual output approach predicated on original use of expropriated land is now replaced by a more consistent, transparent, equitable, broad-based and generous compensation standard. The way in which resettlement is provided changes from one-off cash payment to continuous provision of social welfare or land retention to secure the long-term livelihoods of those expropriated. In the official discourse, the principle of compensation is altered from maintaining to improving the peasants' original living standards. And the central authority has promised that a fair share of the post-expropriation increased land value will go to the expropriatees. However, these reform measures seem wanting compared with the fair market value standard, which is believed to be more objective and measureable in making the condemnees whole.

Should we hold land finance responsible? A counterfactual exercise is illuminating here. Suppose that marketization of state-owned urban land never occurred in 1988 and that the 1994 tax-sharing reform that has left China's local governments cash-strapped never happened – would the Chinese rural land expropriation law still look like it does today? And would expropriation still be practiced on such a large scale and a rapid pace as it has been for decades? The answer to both hypothetical questions is yes. On the one hand, as revealed in this book, the three aforementioned salient features of the law emerged prior to and independent of the conditions that have made land finance possible and necessary since the late 1980s. Even if there is no commodification of urban land, rural land expropriation for state-led social transformation is already a long and enduring theme in modern China, as reflected by related laws and policies. On the other hand, so long as China urbanizes and industrializes at an unprecedented rate as it does in the reform era, massive agricultural to construction land conversion is inevitable. Given that expropriation is the predominant way to do so, short of any fiscal incentive, local governments in China would still have to expropriate extensively. Land finance does not *cause* the pervasiveness of rural land expropriation in China. The two are symptoms of a common root cause.

That being said, I hasten to add that the point here is not to suggest that land finance plays no role in driving China's local governments toward more expropriation. As will be shown in Section 8.4, the opposite is true. However, it does mean that unless the root cause is addressed, dealing with land finance alone will be of very limited help to opening up the space for many of the popular reform proposals.

First of all, as long as the presumption of expropriation in nonagricultural use of rural land persists, any attempt to narrow down the scope of expropriation is doomed. The effect of enhancing land rights through propertization of property rights or fundamentalization of private property will also be superficial at best. More crucially, as has been acutely observed,[1] it effectively renders the fair market value standard impractical in China. As mentioned in Chapter 2, the fair market value standard in American law refers to the value of a property at its highest and best use, regardless of its current actual use. To claim the highest and best use, the owner must establish a reasonable probability that the asserted use could be made in the reasonably near future.[2] One important condition for such reasonableness, however, is that the asserted use is legally permissible.[3] In American eminent domain jurisprudence, therefore, any land value increment generated not by the owner's potential lawful use but by government's own actions has been excluded from the fair market value compensation.[4] Put differently, the fair market value standard

[1] Valerie Jaffee Washburn, "Regular Takings or Regulatory Takings: Land Expropriation in Rural China" (2011) 20 *Pacific Rim Law & Policy Journal* 105.

[2] Yun-chien Chang, "Economic Value or Fair Market Value: What Form of Takings Compensation Is Efficient?" (2012) 20 *Supreme Court Economic Review* 49.

[3] Stephen Sussna, "The Concept of Highest and Best Use Under Takings Theory" (1989) 21 *The Urban Lawyer* 113.

[4] *McGovern* v. *New York, 229 US 363 (1913); United States* v. *Miller*, 307 US 174 (1939); *United States* v. *Cors* 337 US 325 (1949).

denies takees a share of any gains the expropriation of their property generates.[5] Under the abovementioned presumption, the legally permitted highest and best use of rural land in China is none other than its present use. Expropriation surplus is purely a result of state expropriation and subsequent transfer. This means that even if the fair market value standard gets imported from the US to China, it makes no real difference at all. To be sure, China needs not have an exact copy of the fair market value standard as practiced in the US. It can use the term with a different connotation to mean that the expropriated should be compensated with the price that would have been obtained by the expropriatees if they were legally allowed to put their rural land up for transaction. Yet that is still largely unfeasible as liberalization of rural land has just started and the lawful rural land market is too small to generate enough comparable sales for calculating market land prices.[6]

Second, provided that expropriation decisions continue to be formulated via hierarchical review and approval, and remain in essence the expression of top-down planning schemes, strengthening legislative scrutiny over, judicial review of and public participation in expropriation decision-making will be simultaneously unacceptable and inadequate. On the one hand, all of this poses a direct threat to the government's exclusive control over rural land use and conversion, which has been carefully and constantly guarded by the exclusionary mechanism of expropriation decision-making. On the other hand, since expropriation decisions are effectively made according to spatial plans, it does not take us very far to open up just expropriation decisions, but not the spatial plans, to external checks and balances. Lastly, given the lingering impact of the socialist principle, the state's monopoly over the definition of public interest in expropriation is here to stay and expropriation will still be conceptualized as obligation rather than sacrifice or transaction.

5 Katrina Wyman, "The Measure of Just Compensation" (2007) 41(1) *UC Davis Law Review* 255.

6 Valerie Jaffee Washburn suggested a third reason why fair market value standard cannot resolve China's compensation problem. Because fair market value is supposed to be objective, individualized values in land for the owner are excluded. This means that peasants will not be compensated for loss of subjective or sentimental value. As valid as this point may be, it is somewhat irrelevant here. What motivates many to propose the fair market value standard is not that it is perfect but that it is an improvement to the existing compensation standards in Chinese law. This point was well acknowledged in Liantai Liu and Di Zuo, "A Flaw in a Jade Baton in the Fair Market Value Compensation Standard for Eminent Domain Law: the US Law as an Example (征收法上按公平市场价值补偿规则的白圭之玷 – 以美国法为例)" (2013) *Zhejiang Social Sciences* (浙江社会科学) 55.

Compensation and resettlement will still revolve around the original living standards and long-term livelihoods of the condemnees instead of the market value of the land.

To sum up, the above analysis demonstrates that land finance is not the root cause of the existing rural land expropriation law and that the extermination of it is no panacea. Hence falls the developmental assumption, the last vestige of the TP. It is now demonstrably evident that looking at China's rural land expropriation law through a comparative lens and with conceptually and temporally confined perspectives is incapable of telling us either how it has got here or where it is likely to go next. This, then, seems to leave us with a pessimistic conclusion: as the present is very much a product of the past and it is continuity rather than rupture that has been the defining characteristic of China's rural land takings law for nearly a century, chances are that the status quo will be maintained or even perpetuated. But that is emphatically not the point of striving for a contextualized description of the law that pays sufficient attention to the distinctive intellectual, political and social conditions of its formation and evolution. I am not pursuing a deeper understanding of the law in its own logic simply for the sake of being unabashedly unapologetic about its current state of affairs. Explanation is logically separate from justification. Nor am I of the belief that the past is an inescapable trap, since historicism is not historical determinism. As mentioned in the introductory chapter, the aim of the book is to offer, alongside a contextualized description, an immanent critique of the Chinese rural land expropriation law, which is not derived from a critical assessment by the American standards but is based on the law's internal tensions and difficulties. The best place to start, with no sense of irony, is to investigate why the discredited TP ever comes about.

8.3 Making Sense of the Rise of the Transition Paradigm

For all its insufficiencies and inaccuracies, the TP is fundamentally a moral and political critique of China's current system of rural land expropriation, powerful enough to have dominated the thinking on this subject for years. Yet, as has been disclosed by previous analysis, that denounced system and its core elements have been in existence for more than half a century. Why was it only in the last two decades or so that the TP emerged? Surely there had been notable incidents of discontent and objection against rural land expropriation in the pre-reform era, which were briefly touched upon in Section 6.1.1. But systematically evaluating that system through a cross-country comparative and critical prism is definitively a contemporary phenomenon. Why?

Without doubt, the opening up of China, especially the increasing exposure to Western legal discourses, makes such comparative analyses epistemologically possible. But that is trivially true. Short of this intellectual device, for reasons that will be elaborated shortly, some form of condemnation of the system would still happen. Alternatively, it might be pointed out that rural land expropriation occurred on a substantially larger scale in the reform era, when urbanization and industrialization accelerated in China. As mentioned in Chapter 1, 10.58 million acres of rural land were expropriated from 2004 to 2014, increasing from 4.67 million acres between 1978 and 2001. Although there is no pre-reform data available for comparison, it is undeniable that more rural land has been expropriated and more people affected by expropriation over the last three decades. As one landless farmer noted, "Before, the scale of development [and demolitions] was small. It was just a road here and a factory there. [They would say] how much money do you want? Now the development is very wide scale."[7] Due to its sheer magnitude, rural land expropriation features much more prominently in contemporary Chinese social life than ever before. However, this explains only the growing attention to rural land explanation, and not why much of that attention takes a critical stance.

A more substantive explanation can be found in the thesis of rising rights consciousness among the Chinese people, broadly referring to the greater willingness of aggrieved individuals or groups in Chinese society to make claims for redress on the basis of right.[8] This answer nicely captures the prevalence of rights talk in past scholarship in this field, with the proposal for fundamentalization of private property and propertization of property rights being one telling example. And there is an extensive body of empirical research in this regard, with a heavy focus on contentious politics in land takings.[9] Yet, invoking the notion of rights

[7] Christopher Heurlin, *Responsive Authoritarianism in China: Land, Protests, and Policy Making* (New York: Cambridge University Press, 2016), p. 69.

[8] This definition comes from Peter Lorentzen and Suzanne Scoggins, "Understanding China's Rising Rights Consciousness" (2015) 223 *China Quarterly* 639. For a more theoretical discussion, see Michael McCann, *Rights at Work* (Chicago: University of Chicago Press, 1994).

[9] For existing research on rights consciousness of expropriatees, see Zhonghao Qian, Yi Xiao and Futian Qu, "Peasant's Land Rights Consciousness, Willingness in Land Expropriation and Reform of the Expropriation System: an Empirical Study in Yingtan City of Jiangxi Province (农民土地产权认知、土地征用意愿与征地制度改革 – 基于江

consciousness is far from adequate because it does not tell us how in the first place the Chinese peasants start to see their land holdings as property rights and feel that their rights are violated by expropriation. This, I argue, is attributed to a set of critical changes both inside and outside the system of rural land expropriation that have ultimately weakened the "coupling," so to speak, between that system, particularly its three salient features, and the environment in which it is embedded.[10]

To start with, as already shown, the presumption of state expropriation in nonagricultural use of rural land first came into existence in the pre-reform era, as a consequence of China's rigid rural/urban dualistic political–economic system at the time. Under that system, the role of rural collectives was limited to agricultural production and welfare provision for member peasants, whereas nonagricultural construction and development was in the monopolizing hands of state government. The just-mentioned presumption is fundamentally a reflection of such a dual-track regime characterized by an institutionalized division between the urban (industrial) and the rural (agricultural). Into the reform era, that particular political economy started to be phased out in China. For one thing, from the 1980s, rapid rural industrialization took place, exemplified most vividly by the TVE boom discussed in the preceding chapter. For another, concurrent with the decline/privatization of the TVEs from the mid-1990s onwards, private enterprises, including commercial real estate developers, rose to prominence as key participants in the Chinese

西省鹰潭市的实证研究)" (2007) 1 *China Rural Economy* (中国农村经济) 158; Christopher Heurlin, "Ruling the Chinese Countryside: Rights Consciousness, Collective Action and Property Rights," available at www.academia.edu/1971329/Ruling_the_Chinese_Countryside_Rights_Consciousness_Collective_Action_and_Property_Rights; Kai Wang, "Whatever-ism with Chinese Characteristics: China's Nascent Recognition of Private Property Rights and Its Political Ramifications" (2011) 6 *East Asia Law Review* 43; Matthew S. Erie, "Property Rights, Legal Consciousness and the New Media in China: The Hard Case of the 'Toughest Nail-house in History'" (2012) 26(1) *China Information* 35; Eva Pils, "Land Disputes, Rights Assertion and Social Unrest: A Case from Sichuan" (2006) 365 *Columbia Journal of Asian Law* 235; Eva Pils, "'Peasants' Struggle for Land in China," in Yash Ghai and Jill Cottrell (eds.), *Marginalized Communities and Access to Justice* (London: Routledge, 2009); Eva Pils, "Contending Conceptions of Ownership in Urbanizing China," in Hualing Fu and John Gillespie (eds.), *Resolving Land Disputes in East Asia: Exploring the Limits of Law* (Cambridge: Cambridge University Press, 2014); Julia Chuang, "China's Rural Land Politics: Bureaucratic Absorption and the Muting of Rightful Resistance" (2014) 219 *China Quarterly* 649.

10 For the concept of coupling between law and its surrounding environment or context, I draw loosely on the work of Niklas Luhmann. See Niklas Luhmann, *Law as a Social System* (Oxford: Oxford University Press, 2004), chapter 10.

economy.[11] This means that nonagricultural development is no longer monopolized by the state through its affiliated agencies such as government departments and SOEs. For the first time since the late 1950s, nonstate entities become once again the engine for industrialization, and in that process they end up being the primary end-users of expropriated land. Against this backdrop, state expropriation for private uses becomes pervasive and the public interestedness thereof turns increasingly questionable.

Second, it was mentioned previously that in the pre-reform period, state expropriation was already exercised for private enterprises and individuals. But with a blanket ban on land transaction, that was much less of a problem, as land value and any increase thereof were latent in the absence of any price mechanism to reveal them. At that time, land was but the physical material for agricultural or nonagricultural production. Under a command economy, as already noted, it was state economic planning that determined when, how and by whom such material was going to be exploited, as well as the circulation of such materials within the economic system. Absent marketization, the redistributive effect of state economic planning decisions and the concomitant expropriation decisions were neither significant nor exposed. That was completely reversed by the liberalization of the urban land market in the late 1980s, which transformed urban land from a material and a resource to a commodity and an asset. Within just a few years, the worry about repeating national humiliation in land lease to foreign investors was no more, and the market logic was embraced full-heartedly, as attested by the development zone fever and real estate craze of the early 1990s. Land expropriation has since become a potent generator of increased land value. However, when private businesses and commercial developers emerge as the winners out of this land development rush, the grim redistributive effect of rural land expropriation is laid bare in front of the whole world. Although spatial planning has replaced economic planning as the foundation of expropriation decision-making, its economic implications could not be more apparent and glaring: expropriation for private uses is now synonymous with expropriation for private profits, delivering another blow to any public interestedness left therein. One illuminating complaint recorded by the *People's Daily* goes, "It is

[11] For a succinct discussion on the decline of TVEs and rise of private enterprises, see Chenggang Xu and Xiaobo Zhang, "The Evolution of Chinese Entrepreneurial Firms: Township-village Enterprises Revisited," IFPRI Discussion Paper 2009, available at www.ifpri.org/publication/evolution-chinese-entrepreneurial-firms.

unjust that for one *mu* of land we get compensated only in the thousands while commercial developers profit in the millions."[12] Such anger and resentment on the part of many expropriated peasants come from a growing sense of relative deprivation as they see the huge gap between their meager compensation and the exorbitant revenue reaped by private developers.

That sense of relative deprivation was further compounded by the fact that the 1998 LAL abandoned the legal requirement in the 1986 LAL, which asks the expropriation-initiating governments to, besides paying monetary compensation, resettle the expropriated peasants with re-employment opportunities at the TVEs or land-using entities. By the late 1990s, with the general decline of TVEs and a huge wave of lay-offs in the state-owned sector, local governments no longer had as vast a source of employment under their control for expropriation resettlement as they used to. To make matters worse, without government support, expropriated peasants were found to be at a disadvantage in the labor market due to their lack of education and skills.[13] In this scenario, abolishing the legal requirement of employment resettlement in expropriation turned out to be both unavoidable and impactful. It was documented that when resettlement jobs were still available, many peasants actually welcomed expropriation and saw it as an opportunity to incorporate into the urban economy and state-provided social welfare system.[14] But when cash compensation became the norm and post-expropriation employment assistance faded away, long-term social security for the expropriatees took an instant hit. Since the late 1990s, unemployment has been a serious challenge facing expropriated peasants. A 2003 survey by the National Statistic Bureau on 7,187 expropriated peasants in 28 provinces discovered that 20 percent were jobless.[15] A 2009 national survey

[12] Yongping Zhao, "Why the Rush in Land Expropriation, Be More Considerate for the Peasants (征地拆迁何太急，多替农民想一想)," July 15, 2012, available at society.people.com.cn/n/2012/0715/c1008-18518505.html.

[13] Jun Han (ed.), *Inquiry of Rural Land Problem in China* (中国农村土地问题调查) (Shanghai: Yuandong Press, 2009), p. 21.

[14] Haiyun Liu, *Marginalization and Alienation: Study on Landless Peasants* (边缘化与分异：失地农民问题研究) (Beijing: Zhongguo Nongye Press, 2007), p. 82. It was a similar case with urban condemnees prior to the late 1990s as they also welcomed demolition as an opportunity to obtain new housing from the government or working units. See Heurlin, *Responsive Authoritarianism in China*, p. 43.

[15] Feng Mao, "What Should the Government Do for Peasants: A Survey of 2942 Landless Rural Households (政府该为失地农民做什么：对2942户失地农民的调查)' (2004) 1 *The World of Survey and Research* (调研世界) 28.

reported that, on average, 25.92 percent of expropriated peasants were completely out of work.[16] A 2012 *People's Daily* commentary warned that some expropriated peasants had descended into a landless, jobless and hopeless group that was a breeding ground for social instability, as they viewed expropriation as a threat from the government.[17] One landless peasant put it this way: " Since the government has expropriated my land, it should take care of me when I am old; if I cannot feed myself one day, I will go to the government and make a scene."[18]

Third, while the rise of state expropriation for private uses and profits has rendered claims under the constitutional public interest prerequisite less than convincing, it is land finance that sounds the death knell for the presumed identification between the state and the public interest under the socialist principle. Since the turn of this century, the fact that local governments use rural land expropriation and subsequent land transfer to obtain fiscal benefits is increasingly thrust into the public consciousness by extensive media coverage and academic inquiry.[19] The realization that local governments have their own self-interests of a financial nature, which were not so much expressed under a command economy, leads to the perceived bifurcation of the state.[20] The state is no longer seen as a monolithic body but one differentiated between a "benign" central government and the "malign" local governments. The widely known saying that "the center is our benefactor; the province our relative; the county a good person; the township an evil person; and the village our enemy" aptly describes the general perception on this issue. Experience so far suggests that popular protests against rural land expropriation

[16] Hui Wang and Xiao Chen, "Performance Evaluation of Local Governments' Employment Policies for Expropriated Peasants: Based on a Nationally Survey Data (地方政府失地农民就业政策的绩效评估 – 基于大样本调查的实证分析)," in Cifang Wu (ed.), *Global Land Issues in 2014: Key Problems and Cutting Edge* (全球土地2014: 热点与前沿) (Hangzhou: Zhejiang University Press, 2015), p. 194. For a comprehensive list of survey findings on the unemployment of expropriatees, see Shaoyou Chen, *Study on Employment Promotion and Management for Urbanized Expropriatees* (征地农转非人员就业促进及其管理研究) (Beijing: Zhongguo Shangye Press, 2012), pp. 283–91.

[17] Zhao, "Why the Rush in Land Expropriation, Be More Considerate for the Peasants."

[18] Huibo Wang, *Study on Social Exclusion of Landless Peasants* (失地农民社会排斥研究) (Shanghai: Shanghai University Press, 2010), p. 74.

[19] It is no coincidence that at the same time the notion of landless peasants received growing attention. Both happened against the background when the Hu-Wen government promised to establish a people-centered government and to prioritize social equality and justice. See Sally Sargeson, "Villains, Victims and Aspiring Proprietors: Framing 'Land-losing Villagers' in China's Strategies of Accumulation" 21 *Journal of Contemporary China* 763.

[20] Xiaolin Guo, "Land Expropriation and Rural Conflicts" (2001) 166 *China Quarterly* 436.

rarely target the central authority. On the contrary – central mandates such as the constitutional clauses promising to guarantee private property, statutory stipulations, political catchphrases from the central state and top leaders' remarks have often been invoked to buttress the expropriatees' claims of grievance against the local states.[21] The aforementioned developmental assumption that holds local governments' resistance accountable for halting deeper reforms is but another example to show that, typically, it is the local states that get the blame. In the words of one disgruntled condemnee, "The things they say up at the top sound good. 'Harmonious society.' 'Harmonious demolitions and evictions'... Then the police at the lower levels kick you out of your house. How is that harmonious? The central government is good, but the local government is wrong."[22] Empirical research also recorded more poignant complaints about the self-interested behavior of local governments in using rural land expropriation to cover the funding shortage.[23] In this scenario, it does not help when unlawful and unauthorized rural land seizures happen at a substantial scale, which will be discussed shortly. Nor is it any consolation that it has been an endemic practice among local governments to adopt illegal tactics to enforce even lawful expropriation decisions. Most notably, the use of the police force in expropriation has been so widespread that the General Office of State Council, Ministry of Public Security and Central Committee of Discipline and Inspection were prompted to issue consecutive orders of injunction.[24] When releasing scorpions or snakes in your neighborhood and sending mafia (-like)

[21] This is therefore another example of rightful resistance. See Kevin J. O'Brien and Lianjiang Li, *Rightful Resistance in Rural China* (Cambridge: Cambridge University Press, 2006), p. 37. A villager from Sichuan, when arguing with a county official who had just ordered the expropriation of his land, cited Premier Wen Jiabao's remarks about the need to preserve farmland. The official replied, "fine, you go bring him here."

[22] Heurlin, *Responsive Authoritarianism in China*, p. 207.

[23] Hiroki Takeuchi, "Survival Strategies of Township Governments in Rural China: from Predatory Taxation to Land Trade" (2013) 22 (83) *Journal of Contemporary China* 760.

[24] Urgent Notice on Further Tightening Up Management of Expropriation and Demolition and Protecting People's Lawful Rights and Interests (关于进一步严格征地拆迁管理工作切实维护群众合法权益的紧急通知), promulgated by General Office of State Council on May 15, 2010, available at www.china.findlaw.cn/fangdichan/fangwuchaiqian/fagui/208203.html; Opinions on the Tasks of the Public Security System to Establish Clean Party and Government and Fight Corruption in 2011 (2011年公安机关党风廉政建设和反腐败工作意见), promulgated by Ministry of Public Security on March 3, 2011, available at www.mps.gov.cn/n2253534/n2253535/n2253537/c4091668/content.html; Notice on Strengthening Supervision and Inspection and Further Regularizing Expropriation and Demolition (关于加强监督检查进一步规范征地拆迁行为的通知), promulgated by General Office of Central Committee of

crews to tear your house down is the rule of the day,[25] to insist that the expropriating governments always represent the public interest and that expropriation constitutes a presumptive duty for the peasants is anything but persuasive.

In the meantime, because of the commodification of urban land and the resultant financial benefits bestowed upon private users and local governments, the other dimension of the traditional socialist principle – namely, to conceptualize expropriation merely as an obligation owed by the peasants to the state and to view the property in rural land just as a source of welfare and social security – becomes increasingly untenable. The most telling evidence is the pervasiveness of negotiation and bargaining on expropriation compensation and resettlement. As a matter of fact, that was already taking place before the mid-1980s. The 1953 MLRSC (Articles 8 and 13), 1958 MLRSC (Article 14), 1982 RLRSC (Articles 9 and 10) and 1986 LAL (Articles 27 and 28) all stipulated that expropriation compensation and resettlement fees should be paid by land-using entities. Back then, the actual amount of such fees were usually bargained by the land-using entities and the expropriated peasants, and paid directly by the former to the latter.[26] Yet this should not be mistaken for a market mechanism of any sort. Instead, it was in essence the necessary administrative arrangement when there was no uniform agency to manage expropriation affairs prior to the establishment of the land administration bureaus since 1986. Land-using entities from different vertical functional systems had to negotiate with the potential expropriatees on such payments by themselves and separately. But this was not intended to be market negotiation. Article 17 of the 1982 RLRSC explicitly prohibited the expropriated collectives from raising extra demands or conditions with regard to expropriation compensation beyond what was legally provided for. In 1984, the State Council and three ministries imposed a complete ban upon compensation negotiation between the land-using entities and expropriated collectives and required the land-using entities to pay expropriation fees, pursuant to the statutory criteria prescribed in the 1982 law, first to the expropriating

Discipline and Inspection on March 17, 2011, available at www.cnnsr.com.cn/jtym/fgk/2011/20110317000000218220.shtml.

25 Pils, "Contending Conceptions of Ownership in Urbanizing China," pp. 125, 168.

26 Chengyin Tang and Jiyun Yu, "Five Uniforms is the Direction for Land Expropriation System Reform ("五统一"是征地制度改革的方向)," in Chinese Land Society (ed.), *Study on China's Land Use System Reform* (中国土地使用制度改革的研究) (Guangzhou: China Land Society, 1992), p. 46.

governments, which would then make compensation to the expropriated collectives.[27] The main motivation for this order of inhibition, as explained by officials from a provincial land administration bureau, was twofold. The principled reason was that allowing the would-be expropriatees to negotiate directly with land-using entities was considered to be contradicting the nature of rural land expropriation, which should not be bargaining between equal parties but compulsory state decision to acquire land. The practical and more important reason was that in reality free bargaining between land-using entities and collectives had swollen the costs of implementing expropriation decisions as the expropriated generally asked for much more compensation than the statutory standard.[28] Stopping negotiation about compensation was therefore essentially aimed at reinforcing the statutory limit on the amount of compensation.

Yet that prohibition from the top in 1984 was actually indicative of the fact that some sort of market had already kicked in. A 1992 report by the Chinese Academy of Social Sciences conceded that when China began market-oriented reforms of its land use system in the 1980s, "market elements" (*shichang yinsu*) stealthily crept into the process of land allocation, which was manifested in that the actual expropriation compensation had often exceeded government-set standards with a tendency to reflect the supply–demand relationship of land.[29] The reason behind this, as recognized by a city government, was that the peasants' recognition of land as a commodity (*shangpin yishi*) was tremendously strengthened, prompting more and more expropriatees to seek above-the-limit compensation that was reflective not just of their land's original price but

[27] Interim Measures on Reforming the Construction Sector and Administration System of Basic Construction (关于改革建筑业和基本建设管理体制若干问题的暂行规定), promulgated by State Council on September 18, 1984, available at www.chinaacc.com/new/63/73/129/2006/2/hu738243615226002876-0.htm; Interim Measures on Unified Use of Land Expropriation Fees (关于征用土地费实行包干使用暂行办法), promulgated by Ministry of Agriculture, National Planning Commission and Ministry of Construction on December 25, 1984, available at www.pkulaw.cn/fulltext_form.aspx/pay/fulltext_form.aspx?Gid=2240&Db=chl.

[28] Tang and Yu, "Five Uniforms is the Direction for Land Expropriation System Reform," p. 46. It was demonstrated previously that since the 1950s there has always been a set maximum for the statutory compensation standards using the formula of multi-timed average annual output.

[29] Institute of Finance, Trade and Economics Research at Chinese Academy of Social Sciences, *Urban Land Use and Administration in China* (中国城市土地使用与管理) (Beijing: Jingji Kexue Press, 1992), p. 63.

also of its potential value increment.[30] A 2002 MLR research report acknowledged that when paid transfer replaced unpaid allocation as the norm of the primary land market, the peasants were increasingly upset by the price arbitrage between expropriation at low costs and transfer with high premiums.[31] In this situation, it should not be surprising that compensation negotiation returned through the back door. The same MLR report found that the most common way in which compensation and resettlement had been determined on the ground was none other than negotiations between the expropriating governments and the to-be-expropriated rural collectives. The expropriating governments would first formulate a draft compensation and resettlement plan according to the legally set criteria, and then bargain with the rural collectives. In the end, the amount of compensation would usually surpass the statutory maximum.[32] Empirical research by academics from Zhejiang University also corroborated that almost half of the 773 land expropriation cases they surveyed in 12 cities in 2009 involved negotiations about compensation rate, relocation assistance and pension insurance, and that compensation amount agreed after negotiations was more than the legally established standard rates.[33] Moreover, a 2011 opinion survey shows that the expropriatees are equally, if not more concerned with how much say they have on compensation than the absolute amount they are compensated.[34] To be sure, negotiation and bargaining around set compensation criteria is anything but a real voluntary market process. Yet

[30] Editorial Committee of Zhengzhou Local Historical Records (ed.), *Zhengzhou Municipal Record* (郑州市志) (Zhengzhou: Zhongzhou Guji Press, 1998), vol. 3, p. 168.

[31] General Office of MLR, *Investigative Report on Land Resources in 2002* (2002年国土资源调研报告) (Beijing: Zhongguo Dadi Press, 2002), p. 146.

[32] Mingcai Pan (ed.), *Practice and Exploration of Land Expropriation in China* (中国征地工作实务与探索) (Beijing: Zhongguo Dadi Press, 2009), p. 259. The editor was the director in charge of cultivated land preservation under the MLR.

[33] Hui Wang, Pengyu Zhu, Xiao Chen and Sarah Swider, "Land Expropriation in Urbanizing China: An Examination of Negotiations and Compensation" (2017) 38 (3) *Urban Geography* 401. The authors also find that while negotiations are a fairly common practice in land expropriation cases, they are clearly a more established practice in some cities and region. They think that the reason behind this variation is that when local governments offer the lowest compensation possible under the central government's set formulas and as a result, it increases the number of peasants who demand negotiations.

[34] Qinghua Shi, Hongtao Jin and Jianwei Zhuo, "Does Land Expropriation necessarily Lower the Peasants' Income: A Survey of Seven Villages in Shanghai and on the Pitfalls and Reform of Present Expropriation System (征地一定降低农民收入吗：上海七村调查 – 兼论现行征地制度的缺陷与改革)" (2011) 3 *Management World* (管理世界) 77; Xiangqi Liu, Zhao Chen and Yang Zhao, "Procedural Fairness Preferred over Monetary Compensation: the Deciding Factors of Satisfaction of Peasants on Land Expropriation

such practices do show that expropriation has moved closer to a two-party transaction and away from a one-sided obligation.[35]

To summarize, with the series of momentous changes just described, China's rural land expropriation law that took its shape during the pre-reform era and persisted largely intact over the reform period now finds itself in a drastically changed economic, sociopolitical and legal context, where nonagricultural development is no longer monopolized by the state, land value increment gets exposed and expanded through commodification and land finance becomes the bread and butter of the local economy. The long tradition of rural land expropriation for state-led social transformation is now increasingly shadowed by self-seeking incentives and behaviors that are not only endemic but also systemic. This, I argue, is the deep-level source of the moral indignation and popular opposition against the current expropriation law, as epitomized by the TP. Yet, this is not to say that the previous account exhausts all possible causes behind the emergence of the TP. The most notable omission is the constitutional recognition of private property and human rights in 2004, as well as the progressive "propertization" of rural land ownership and use-rights over the past two decades or so. More discussion about that will come in due course. Nor does it mean that measuring the Chinese rural land expropriation law by the benchmark of the American law of eminent domain is the only way to go about critically assessing the former. The next section mounts an immanent critique of the Chinese law on rural land expropriation based on its internal tensions and difficulties. Broadly, the effectiveness, efficiency, fairness and constitutionality of the current system all face serious challenges, some of which are age-old and persistent whereas others are more recent but acute. However, that is not to suggest that the existing system has completely ossified and run out of steam, expecting imminent meltdown or transition. Since the early 2000s, in response to these challenges, legal and policy adjustments and innovations have been rolled out, albeit with different degrees of success. It is these challenges and changes, rather than those popular reform recommendations formulated under the TP,

(程序公正先于货币补偿：农民征地满意度的决定)" (2012) 2 *Management World* (管理世界) 44.

35 The practice of negotiating compensation is also recognized by the government. See Guiding Opinions on Improving Compensation and Resettlement System in Land Expropriation (关于完善征地补偿安置制度的指导意见), promulgated by MLR on November 3, 2004, available at www.mlr.gov.cn/zwgk/flfg/tdglflfg/200506/t20050617_68344.htm.

that represent the dynamism in this field and point to the future direction. After a long twentieth century, China's rural land expropriation law continues to evolve, in its own context and following its own logic.

8.4 An Immanent Critique

8.4.1 Effectiveness: Limits of the Authoritarian Logic

As was shown previously, the PRC has an enduring tradition of exclusive and hierarchical state control over rural land use and conversion through the presumption of expropriation in nonagricultural use of rural land plus an expropriation decision-making mechanism based on top-down planning. As Eva Pils insightfully pointed out, the property and ownership of land is dominated by the party-state's self-perception as custodian of national goals with regard to land, which is what she called the authoritarian foundation to the current property regime.[36] In reality, however, this authoritarian logic of top-down state control over rural land use and conversion has long been circumvented, if not defied, by two dynamisms on the ground: one from within the expropriation system, and the other from without. The former refers to unauthorized expropriation by the government, and the latter means the small property rights (SPR) phenomenon.

SPR in China is a subject worthy of close examination in its own right, and has been so for quite a while.[37] A comprehensive and detailed exploration of this topic is both unnecessary and impractical here. Suffice it to say that, in essence, the SPR phenomenon is an end-run around state expropriation where spontaneous industrialization and urbanization with the attendant development of rural land for nonagricultural purposes are carried out by rural collectives and peasants themselves, effectively in violation of the statutorily established assumption of expropriation in those uses. Hence, the property rights on such land have been dubbed "small," as opposed to "bigger" and stronger entitlements that are legally recognized. A huge informal rural land market grows out of the pandemic SPR practice, especially in the residential housing sector. It has been reported that by 2007 Chinese peasants had built more than 6.6 billion square meters of small property houses, while the total floor

[36] Pils, "Contending Conceptions of Ownership in Urbanizing China," pp. 143, 171.

[37] There is a huge literature on this topic. For a recent book-length treatment in English from a legal perspective, see Shitong Qiao, *Chinese Small Property: The Co-Evolution of Law and Social Norms* (Cambridge: Cambridge University Press, 2017).

space of legal housing sold was merely 0.76 billion square meters.[38] More than 80 million residents are estimated to live in these small property houses.[39] Notably, a whopping 49.27 percent of the buildings in Shenzhen city are small property ones, which have been developed by more than 300,000 peasants, sometimes in cooperation with commercial developers, and rented or sold to over 10 million people, including migrant workers, middle-income workers, white-collar workers, start-up entrepreneurs and real estate speculators.[40] Xi'an and Beijing had 30 percent and 20 percent respectively of their total built-up areas taken up by small property houses.[41]

Apparently, SPR is more than a glitch in the system. It is ubiquitous evasion and defiance of the authoritarian logic that only licenses the state to decide when and where rural land can be used for most nonagricultural purposes. It produces what is now known as "urban villages" (*chengzhongcun*), which are already built up but whose land remains collectively owned without going through expropriation.[42] The underlying motivation for SPR is not difficult to see: when the opportunity of price arbitrage presents itself between a liberalized urban land market and nonliberalized rural land regime, peasants are driven to grab the increased land value by themselves instead of waiting for and accepting expropriation compensation that does not reflect such value increment. Their bypassing of the legalized state monopoly of rural–urban land conversion has received a warm reception particularly among the low-income population when government-supplied affordable housing is too scarce or inaccessible and housing prices on the legal market too high.[43] Empirical research demonstrates that SPR settlements permit poorer household to live at lower costs than is acceptable on the formal market, enabling them to spend more on other welfare-enhancing

[38] "Small Property House Stock Equals Ten Years' Transaction Volume at 6.6 Billion Square Meters (小产权房存量66亿平米相当于十年房产成交量)," November 17, 2008, available at house.people.com.cn/GB/98384/99153/8352580.html.

[39] Runtao Kou, "China's Small Property Houses are Difficult to Clear at 6.6 Billion Square Meters (中国小产权房面积逾66亿平米巨大体量致清理难)," January 13, 2014, available at money.163.com/14/0113/16/9IFVFRD4002534NU.html.

[40] Shitong Qiao, "Planting Houses in Shenzhen: A Real Estate Market without Legal Titles" (2014) 29(2) *Canadian Journal of Law & Society* 255.

[41] Ibid.

[42] For an extensive discussion, see David Wang, *Urban Villages in the New China: Case of Shenzhen* (New York: Palgrave Macmillan, 2016).

[43] Joyce Yanyun Man, "Affordable Housing in China, Land Lines," January 2011, available at www.lincolninst.edu/publications/articles/affordable-housing-china.

expenditures.[44] Some commentators have therefore described the SPR phenomenon as "illegal but rational."[45] Nonetheless, this is precisely what is forbidden in law as the 1998 LAL revoked the permission in the 1991 LALIR that urban residents might use rural land to build residential housing for themselves. Until this day, expropriation remains the only lawful way in which rural land can be utilized to house those who are not members of rural collectives.

What is to be done with the SPR phenomenon? Understandably, the law enforcement strategy is too politically unpopular and practically difficult to be the major response: evicting millions from their illegal housing is virtually adding oil to fire concerning the much-emphasized social stability in China. Alternative and innovative measures have been adopted at the local level, for example in Shenzhen, to deal with the vast SPR regime. Apart from daily and campaign-style legal enforcement to monitor illegal rural land development and demolish illegal buildings, which incurred financial costs, social conflicts and corruption scandals without much success, the Shenzhen government also tried other different policies, ranging from granting formal legal title for free to SPR housing that satisfies certain conditions to charging SPR housing owners a fine before legalizing their property rights.[46] Unsurprisingly, none of these strategies constitutes a one-size-fits-all solution to the SPR problem, which explains why at the national level there has not been any uniform approach other than repeated reminders of the illegality of SPR development.[47] For instance, in 2008 the General Office of State Council reiterated the mandate that unlawful "bypassing expropriation through lease" (*yizu daizheng*) should be strictly prohibited and punished.[48] In 2012, officials from the MLR stressed at a press conference that SPR

[44] Chris Webster, Fulong Wu, Fangzhu Zhang and Chinmoy Sarkar, "Informality, Property Rights, and Poverty in China's 'Favelas'" (2016) 78 *World Development* 461.

[45] Li Sun and Zhi Liu, "Illegal But Rational: Why Small Property Rights Housing Is Big in China, Land Lines," July 2015, available at www.lincolninst.edu/publications/articles/illegal-rational.

[46] Shitong Qiao, "Small Property, Adverse Possession, and Optional Law," in Yun-chien Chang (ed.), *The Law and Economics of Possession* (Cambridge: Cambridge University Press, 2015).

[47] For a list of policy announcements against SPR buildings, see Xiaofang Shen and Fan Tu, "Dealing with 'Small Property Rights' in China's Land Market Development: What Can China Learn from Its Past Reforms and the World Experience," Lincoln Institute of Land Policy Working Paper 8, 2014, available at www.lincolninst.edu/sites/default/files/pubfiles/shen-wp14xs1-full_0.pdf.

[48] Notice on Strictly Implementing Laws and Policies concerning Collectively Owned Rural Construction Land (关于严格执行有关农村集体建设用地法律和政策的通知),

properties would not receive formal rights certification.[49] The aforementioned pilot reform to liberalize existing for-profit rural construction land is by no means an ex post facto legitimation of the huge SPR sector either. Shortly after the reform was pronounced at the Third Plenum of the Eighteenth Party Congress in late 2013, in order to clear any doubts about whether or not the SPR properties would be legalized, the MLR and the Ministry of Housing and Urban-Rural Development jointly issued a notice reiterating the official prohibition on SPR development.[50] Understandably, the reason behind the reluctance to legalize the SPR sector is primarily twofold. On the one hand, it is likely to encourage more unlawful development that will jeopardize the national imperative of cultivated land preservation; on the other hand, it will cause serious disruption to the lawful real estate market when an enormous amount of hitherto illegal properties enter into the legal market.

Besides evasion from the rural collectives and peasants, the authoritarian logic of China's rural land expropriation system is also circumscribed by rampant unauthorized expropriation by local governments. As noted, this has been a persistent challenge ever since the 1950s, giving rise to a variety of countermeasures, from recentralizing the expropriation-approving power to urging practice of thrift in land expropriation, which culminated in the entrenchment of "rational use of land" as a constitutional principle. However, none of these efforts was anywhere near satisfactory, as testified by the establishment of a more sophisticated regulatory system under the 1998 LAL. The hierarchical review and approval mechanism, which had always been the key to expropriation decision-making, then assumed a new level of intensity in terms of top-down control as spatial planning replaced disparate economic planning to become the new foundation for expropriation decision-making. Yet that turned out to be ineffective too. A 2005 MLR survey found that 50 percent of new land under development was expropriated illegally, and that in

promulgated by General Office of State Council on December 30, 2007, available at www.gov.cn/zwgk/2008-01/08/content_852399.htm.

49 Li Ma, "The MLR Will Rectify SPR Properties This Year and Roll Out Pilot Reforms of Social Housing on Collective Land (国土部今年将清理小产权房,试点集体土地建公租房)," February 22, 2012, Available at news.xinhuanet.com/local/2012-02/22/c_122736724.htm.

50 Urgent Notice on Strictly Curbing Illegal Construction and Sale of Small Property Housing (关于坚决遏制违法建设、销售"小产权房"的紧急通知), promulgated by MLR and Ministry of Housing and Urban-Rural Development on November 22, 2013, available at www.mlr.gov.cn/zwgk/zytz/201311/t20131122_1293353.htm.

some places it was above 90 percent.[51] In 2012, the former Premier Wen Jiabao conceded that unsanctioned expropriation of rural land was widespread across the country.[52] Over the years, a wealth of evidence suggested that local governments frequently got around superior oversight either by falsifying application materials or openly breaking the law.[53] That is unsurprising because, as mentioned, they have strong incentives to over-expropriate in light of the expected fiscal, financial and political benefits. Moreover, since the twin goals for the expropriation system – i.e., cultivated land preservation and economic development – are not always in line with each other, many local governments find their hands tied with regard to pursuing local development with limited land use quota assigned from above.[54] In this situation, breaking or bypassing such limitations ends up being a somewhat necessary option.

Since the turn of this century, policy innovations have been adopted to rein in unauthorized expropriation at the local level. The toughest one was a six-month complete moratorium of expropriation approval between April and October in 2004, indicating the perceived ineffectiveness of more light-handed approaches.[55] Meanwhile, the central authorities have endeavored to reassert control by frequently issuing statements[56] and

[51] Guangzhong Cao, Changchun Feng and Ran Tao, "Local 'Land Finance' in China's Urban Expansion: Challenges and Solutions" (2008) 16 (2) *China & World Economy* 19.

[52] Lina Yang, "Premier Stresses Unwavering Reform, Rural Democracy," February 5, 2012, available at news.xinhuanet.com/english/china/2012-02/05/c_131392403.htm.

[53] For a more detailed analysis of land law violation (including but not limited to unlawful expropriation) committed by Chinese local governments, see Reza Hasmath and Jennifer Hsu (eds.), *China in an Era of Transition: Understanding Contemporary State and Society Actors* (New York: Palgrave Macmillan, 2009), pp. 85–88.

[54] Meina Cai, "Land-locked Development: The Local Political Economy of Institutional Change in China," PhD Thesis, University of Wisconsin-Madison (2012), p. 30.

[55] Urgent Notice on Further Regulating Land Market and Strictly Controlling Land Administration (关于深入开展土地市场治理整顿严格土地管理的紧急通知), promulgated by General Office of State Council on April 29, 2004, available at www.moa.gov.cn/zwllm/zcfg/flfg/200601/t20060123_541972.htm.

[56] Point 4, Urgent Notice on Further Tightening the Administration of Expropriation and Demolition and Effectively Protecting Legal Rights and Interests of the People (关于进一步严格征地拆迁管理工作切实维护群众合法权益的紧急通知), promulgated by General Office of State Council on May 15, 2010, available at xxgk.fengxin.gov.cn/fxxgtj/zfxxgk_45007/fgwj_45020/gfxwj_45022/201709/t20170912_393932.html; point 3, Notice on Strengthening Supervision and Investigation and Further Normalizing Practices of Land Expropriation and House Demolition (关于加强监督检查进一步规范征地拆迁行为的通知), promulgated by General Office of Central Party Disciplinary Committee and General Office of Supervision Department on March 17, 2011, available at xxgk.fengxin.gov.cn/fxxgtj/zfxxgk_45007/fgwj_45020/gfxwj_45022/201709/t20170912_393932.html.

launching ad hoc law enforcement campaigns.[57] In a more institutionalized sense, four initiatives have been put into action, all of which are intended to enhance top-down oversight and control.

First of all, the "vertical management" (*chuizhi guanli*) reform was started in 2003.[58] Previously, China's subnational land administration agencies were placed under dual leadership (*shuangchong guanli*). Territorially, they were under the administrative control of local governments. Vertically, they were subordinate to the functional guidance of superior land administration agencies. In comparison, the latter is a much weaker form of control because the local governments have a bigger influence over their land administration departments through the appointment of leadership and provision of funding.[59] This created the problem of local protectionism where local land administration agencies failed to enforce the law against or even colluded with their local governments to trick the approval and review mechanism.[60] The 2003 reform set up a vertical management system for subprovincial land administration authorities to put them under the leadership of upper-level land administration departments, in the hope that they could be freed from local governments' interference.

Second, in 2006 the "state land inspection system" (*guojia tudi ducha xitong*) was introduced to further reduce local protectionism and law-breaking with regard to land administration in general and land expro-

[57] The first large-scale national campaign to stop local governments' illegal land takings took place between 2003 and 2004. See Work Plan of Further Control and Overhaul the Land Market (进一步治理整顿土地市场秩序工作方案), promulgated by MLR on February 26, 2003, available at www.china.com.cn/chinese/PI-c/283302.htm. For an elaborate account of the political-legal campaigns to promote land law compliance, see Benjamin van Rooij, *Regulating Land and Pollution in China, Lawmaking, Compliance, and Enforcement: Theory and Cases* (Leiden: Leiden University Press, 2006), chapter 14. For a more recent campaign, see "China's State Council Orders Special Check into Land Expropriation and House Demolition Practices," May 20, 2011, available at news.xinhuanet.com/english2010/china/2011-05/20/c_13884148.htm.

[58] Notice on Dealing with Issues concerning Sub-provincial Land Administration System Reform (关于做好省级以下国土资源管理体制改革有关问题的通知), promulgated by State Council on April 21, 2004, available at www.china.com.cn/law/flfg/txt/2006-08/08/content_7059549.htm.

[59] Fulong Wu, Jiang Xu and Anthony Gar-On Yeh (eds.), *Urban Development in Post-Reform China: State, Market, and Space* (London: Routledge, 2006), p. 135.

[60] Benjamin Van Rooij, "The Return of the Landlord: Chinese Land Acquisition Conflicts as Illustrated by Peri-Urban Kunming" (2007) 39 (55) *The Journal of Legal Pluralism and Unofficial Law* 232.

priation in particular.[61] Nine regional state land inspection bureaus were set up under the MLR to be entrusted to keep an eye on local governments within their jurisdiction, from which they enjoy institutional independence. One of their key responsibilities is to ensure the lawfulness of the expropriation applications submitted by provincial governments to the State Council or by subprovincial governments to provincial governments.[62] Compared with local land administration departments, these land inspection bureaus are instituted to reinforce the review and approval mechanism, not only due to their independence from local interference, but also because of their strengthened enforcement power. Whereas the local land administration authorities lack the legal authority to act against some of the most serious land law violations committed by local governments,[63] the state land inspection bureaus can directly press compliance and punish noncompliance through gradual escalation of regulatory intervention. For example, local governments may receive written reprimands and corrective action recommendations or face total suspension of expropriation approval.[64] Since 2007, individual officials have been subject to publicized "summoned interviews" (*yuetan*) where they must explain themselves in person at the MLR in Beijing about their irregular or illegal land-related decisions, including those concerning rural land expropriation.[65] In more serious cases, they could face punishment ranging from administrative discipline including demerit, demotion and dismissal to criminal prosecution.[66]

61 Notice on Issues related to Establishing State Land Inspection System (关于建立国家土地督察制度有关问题的通知), promulgated by General Office of State Council on July 13, 2006, available at www.gov.cn/zwgk/2006-07/24/content_343671.htm. Two years before the formal institutionalization, the State Council has announced the initiative in its 2004 Decision on Deepening Reform and Enhancing Land Administration.

62 Point 2, ibid.; arts. 4-7, Supervision Measures of Review and Approval of Agricultural Land Conversion and Land Expropriation (农用地专用和土地征收审批事项督察办法), promulgated by Chief State Land Inspector on October 8, 2008, available at www.hnblr.gov.cn/sitegroup/root/html/ff8080814d40886d014d425fae980030/6981752d6f38451d9ed68f14cd21cdf3.html.

63 Rooij, "The Return of the Landlord: Chinese Land Acquisition Conflicts as Illustrated by Peri-Urban Kunming," 233–34.

64 Chief State Land Inspector, Supervision Measures of Review and Approval of Agricultural Land Conversion and Land Expropriation, arts. 13–14.

65 "Land Ministry Cracks Down on Land Illegalities and Irregularities in Provinces and 100-odd Responsibles are Summoned for an Interview (国土部整治多省市土地违法违规 百余相关责任人被约谈)," June 28, 2003, available at news.xinhuanet.com/politics/2013-06/28/c_116327919.htm.

66 Disciplinary Measures of Activities in Violation of Land Administration Rules (违反土地管理规定行为处分办法), promulgated by Ministry of Human Resources and Social

A third change is to be found in improved monitoring and surveillance techniques. Starting from early 2000, snapshot satellite images of the same area at different time-points have been collected and analyzed by the central and provincial governments to detect unauthorized land expropriation and conversion on the ground, literally. A decade later, in 2010, selective examination was scaled up to full-coverage inspection.[67] Last, but not least, an informant hotline was established in 2009 for the public to report violations of land laws, including unauthorized expropriation, to land authorities from the county level up to the MLR.[68]

Admittedly, the above reforms have had a notable impact: it was reported that between 2006 and 2011, 8,471 officials received disciplinary action and 1,589 officials were held criminally liable for offenses of the land law. Local officials from 35 counties and municipal districts were requested to do summoned interviews.[69] However, the 2016 state land inspection report suggested that illegal rural land expropriation was discovered in 27 of the 31 provinces in the mainland.[70] Apparently, to this day, the effectiveness of top-down oversight regarding rural land expropriation is still limited, mainly for the following reasons.

First, the vertical management reform is lacking in two ways. For one thing, it targets only the subprovincial land administration system and does not affect the central-provincial link. Evidence suggests that provincial governments are in no way immune to unauthorized land

Security, Ministry of Supervision and MLR on May 2, 2008, available at www.mlr.gov.cn/zwgk/zfgw/zfwj/200805/t20080530_104722.htm; "Nine local officials in China punished for illegal land enclosure," May 25, 2011, available at english.people.com.cn/90001/90776/90882/7390106.html.

67 "Minutes of Telephone and Video Conference on Work Arrangements of Enforcement Investigation with Satellite Images by Ministry of Land Resources (国土资源部土地卫片执法检查工作部署电视电话会议实录)," February 8, 2010, available at news.cnfol.com/100208/101,1277,7239755,00.shtml.

68 "Telephone Line 12336 for Reporting Offences related to Land Resource is Opened (12336国土资源违法举报电话开通)," June 25 2009, available at www.mlr.gov.cn/zt/tdr/2009/tpzl/200906/t20090625_122113.htm.

69 "More than Eight Thousand Officials were Disciplined under Land Inspection in Five Years, Leaders from 35 Localities with Illegal Land Uses were Summoned for Interviews (土地督察五年八千多干部被处分 35个违法用地区县负责人被约谈)," November 25, 2011, available at www.legaldaily.com.cn/bm/content/2011-11/25/content_3122561.htm.

70 State Land Inspection Report (国家土地督察公告), promulgated by Office of State Land Inspector on March 25, 2016, available at www.mlr.gov.cn/zwgk/zytz/201603/t20160325_1400164.htm.

expropriation themselves.[71] It remains unclear how provincial land administration agencies can be better placed to carry out central mandates against their provincial masters. For another, the present vertical management reform is somewhat half-baked because although the powers of appointing key cadres in subprovincial land administration departments are now scaled up from local governments to the land authorities at the next level above, local land administration departments remain financially dependent on local governments, which continue to exert considerable influence. A local land bureau official put it this way: "We rely on central (guidance) for work and promotion, but local (government) for rice bowl."[72]

Second, the state land inspection system is also under serious constraints. A 2011 official report evaluating its performance for the first five years acknowledged that state land inspection bureaus generally experienced severe funding and staff shortages.[73] More crucially, the inspection bureaus do not have the power to directly investigate or discipline offending local governments and officials. They can only issue "inspection opinions" (*ducha yijian*) to the authorities in charge, which are sometimes none other than the offenders. Nor is there any institutionalized mechanism to enforce such inspection opinions against local governments.[74]

[71] "1738 Projects by Provincial Governments involves Illegal Land Approval (省级政府1738个项目存在非法批地)", March 21, 2014, available at www.legaldaily.com.cn/index_article/content/2014-03/21/content_5382115.htm?node=5955.

[72] Wu, Xu and Yeh, *Urban Development in Post-Reform China: State, Market, and Space*, p. 138.

[73] "Press Conference on Performance Evaluation of State Land Inspection System in its Fifth Anniversary (国家土地督察制度实施五周年绩效评估新闻发布会)," December 5, 2011, available at www.gjtddc.mlr.gov.cn/hd/zxft/201708/t20170811_1562386.htm.

[74] General Office of State Council, Notice on Issues related to Establishing State Land Inspection System, point 2. An official from the Chengdu land inspection bureau complained that without cooperation of local governments there is no guarantee that the inspection opinions will be implemented. See Yelian Gao, "A Few Thoughts on Land Inspection Bureau's Power of Recommendation (关于土地督察建议权的几点思考)," May 24, 2016, available at www.gjtddc.gov.cn/ztzl/zthd/dcss10/skyj/201605/t20160524_1406303.htm. The draft *Regulation on State Land Inspection* published in 2016 stipulates that if inspection opinions are not carried out by local governments under inspection, the MLR will suspend expropriation approval for that particular locality. See art. 13, *Draft Regulation on State Land Inspection* (国家土地督察条例征求意见稿), promulgated on June 12, 2016, available at zqyj.chinalaw.gov.cn/readmore?listType=1&id=1125&1497841745920. It remains to be seen whether this provision will appear in the finalized legislation and how effective it can be in terms of securing enforcement of inspection opinions.

Third, as technologically advanced as satellite surveillance may be, over the years local governments have reportedly come up with imaginative ways to trick the monitoring eyes from the sky. For instance, it was reported that some of them would go the extent of painting barren hills green or covering roads with potatoes to look like cultivated land if seen from thousands of miles above.[75] Fourth, it was reported that the complaint hotline 12336 registered more than 200,000 calls between 2009 and 2012, almost half of which were reported to the MLR. This is because lower-level land authorities were not generally trusted by the public given their own record of breaking the law. However, even if the public reported directly to the MLR, the overwhelming majority of the cases would still be referred back to local land authorities to deal with simply because the MLR cannot possibly handle such a huge number of reports all by itself.[76] To make matters worse, in some localities the hotline was not functioning at all.[77]

Finally and most importantly, even if local officials are caught and formally disciplined for unauthorized rural land expropriation, they will probably get away with impunity in the end. Numerous reports have shown that officials return to a position at the same level, or even higher, soon after getting demoted or dismissed due to violation of the review and approval system in expropriation decision-making.[78] The reason is likely to be that these officials are regarded as innocent, if not laudable, among their peers inside the government since they are thought to be

[75] Zhifeng Qiao, "Planting Beans on the Highway, Does the Departments of Land Resources Know? (马路种豆,国土部门知道吗?)," July 27, 2014, available at opinion.china.com.cn/opinion_77_105177.html.

[76] Guo Zhang, "The State Land Illegality Reporting Hotline 12336 is "Hot at the Top while Cold at the Bottom" (国土资源违法举报热线12336上热下冷)," February 27, 2012, available at zqb.cyol.com/html/2012-02/27/nw.D110000zgqnb_20120227_4-05.htm.

[77] Notice on Carrying Out Self-check on 12336 Land Resources Legal Violation Complaint Hotline (关于开展12336国土资源违法举报电话自查工作的通知), promulgated by Zhejiang Department of Land Resources on May 17, 2012, available at www.jiaxing.gov.cn/sgtzyj/zcwj_5754/qtwj_5756/201205/t20120518_96063.html. The provincial land administration department found out that the 12336 hotlines in some cities and counties were simply unreachable and that complaint reports were not referred to competent authorities to look into timely.

[78] See e.g. "Investigation of Illegal Land Expropriation in Qingyuan of Guangdong: Responsible Officials Stage a Comeback Afterwards (广东清远违法征地调查: 主事官员事后东山再起)," May 18, 2010, available at news.sina.com.cn/c/sd/2010-05-18/095620294842.shtml; "Media Reports that Many Officials with Records of Land Law Violation are Promoted in Wuhu of Anhui Province (媒体称安徽芜湖多名土地违法官员背处分受重用)," July 7, 2012, available at politics.people.com.cn/n/2012/0717/c1001-18530810.html.

breaking the law for public causes, given that unauthorized expropriation benefits local governments and the economy under land finance.[79]

In summary, the authoritarian logic of China's rural land expropriation system has been critically challenged by both the local governments and the rural collectives and peasants. From the reforms just analyzed, the Chinese central authority is less concerned about the authoritarian logic itself than the evasion and gaming of it. The goal has been to find more innovative ways to detect, deter and discipline violations, however difficult that task may be. There is no sign that the authoritarian logic will be given up due to a lack of effectiveness.

8.4.2 *Efficiency: Limits of the Managerial Logic*

As noted, rural land expropriation decision-making in China is carried out through a hierarchical review and approval mechanism. Its foundation is the spatial planning system characterized by a combination of long-term planning and annual quota allocation, both of which are done in a top-down and command-and-control manner. This managerial logic has its roots in the pre-reform era when economic planning dictated the usage of material resources including land and how it should be converted from collective-owned to state-owned through expropriation for state-led non-agricultural construction. The fact that one set of state planning was substituted by another shows that it has always been considered essential to a balanced approach between conserving arable land and managing economic development, the central purpose of which is to implement the constitutional mandate of rational land use. However, expropriation review and approval according to spatial planning has long been plagued by efficiency problems in both the micro and macro senses.

Inefficiency at the micro level points to the fact that the current expropriation review and approval procedure has been regarded as too protracted and inflexible. As mentioned earlier, the 1998 LAL recentralized the authority to sanction expropriation to the central and provincial governments, a move not so different from what was done in 1962 when expropriation at the grassroots level and on the ground became out of control. But just like the 1960s, the power centralization since the late 1990s proceeded at the expense of efficiency in expropriation

[79] Hongquan Zhang, "What is Wrong with Re-appointing Officials Involved in Forceful Demolition (强拆官员复出有何不可)," December 4, 2011, available at http://news.ifeng.com/opinion/gundong/detail_2011_12/04/11089946_0.shtml.

decision-making, even with all the modern technologies at hands. To be absolutely clear, there is no objective criterion for efficiency in expropriation procedures. It is a relative term that depends on the perspective taken. While for reasons spelled out in Chapter 2 China is very efficient in expropriation with lower administrative costs compared with many other countries – and maybe too efficient, in the eyes of expropriatees – the current hierarchical review and approval mechanism is generally considered to be inefficient by the initiating governments and land-using entities, particularly when batched expropriation is initiated by county governments and goes all the way up to the State Council for authorization. Seven steps are involved here.[80] First, every year the county land administration bureau formulates the county ALUP in light of the yearly land use quotas assigned by superior governments and prepares the batched expropriation application package for that particular year accordingly. Second, the county government approves such materials and submits them to the prefectural government and the prefectural land administration bureau for approval. Third, the prefectural land administration bureau reviews the application materials and makes a decision based on whether or not assigned land use quota limitations are complied with, before requesting further approval from the prefectural government. Fourth, the prefectural government submits the approved application package to the provincial government and its land administration department for review and approval. Fifth, the approving provincial government submits the application materials to the State Council, the MLR and the regional state land inspection bureau. Sixth, the MLR reviews the application and then hands it to the State Council for final approval, after which the MLR replies to the applying provincial government. Seventh, and lastly, the provincial government notifies the initiating county government that its expropriation application has been sanctioned by the central government.

A 2014 MLR report identified the following defects in the above procedure.[81] To begin with, the existing procedure is too lengthy.

[80] Administration Measures on Examination and Application of Construction Land Use (建设用地审查报批管理办法), promulgated by MLR on 2 March 1999, available at www.mlr.gov.cn/zwgk/flfg/gtzybl/200504/t20050426_637326.htm; Notice on Questions concerning Construction Land Review and Approval at the State Council (关于报国务院批准的建设用地审查报批工作有关问题的通知), promulgated by MLR on July 17, 2000, available at www.law-lib.com/law/law_view.asp?id=72283&quot.

[81] Legal evaluation office of MLR, *Land Resources Legal Evaluation Report 2014* (国土资源法律评价报告2014) (Beijing: Fazhi Press, 2014), pp. 59–60. See also Zhiqiang Tian, Siyan Guo and Aihua Peng, "A Study on Reform of the Urban Construction Land

Typically, it takes at least one year for an expropriation application to be reviewed and approved by the State Council, which is responsible for authorizing batched expropriation applications for 106 cities and more than 400 individual expropriation applications. This may look a great deal faster than land takings in other countries, where it could take years if not decades to make a final decision. Yet, against the backdrop of breathtakingly rapid urbanization and industrialization in contemporary China, that is considered too slow and many development projects cannot wait, resorting instead to unauthorized expropriation and construction. Moreover, the present procedure is regarded too rigid. Originally, prefectural governments were allowed to hand their batched expropriation applications directly to the MLR and State Council, and there was no limitation on how many times each city government could make such applications every year. In 2000, a maximum of three times was instituted;[82] four years later, that was increased to five times.[83] From 2007, subprovincial governments can no longer lodge their batched expropriation applications multiple times. Instead, they are required to hand in only one lumped batched expropriation application every year to the provincial government, which will then collect all subprovincial applications and send them in to the central government once every year.[84] Apparently, this adjustment was intended to reduce administrative complexity and cut bureaucratic workload. But consequently, a new problem has emerged. Prior to 2016, the annual land use quotas were assigned by superior governments to subordinate governments in three installments throughout the year. This leaves subordinate governments unable to fully and precisely determine how much land they are allowed to expropriate for the whole year when they formulate

Review and Approval System Based on Land Inspection Practice (基于土地督察实践的城市建设用地审批制度改革思路研究)" (2012) 12 *China Land Sciences* (中国土地科学) 3; General Office of MLR, Investigative Report on Land Resources in 2002, p. 148.

82 MLR, Notice on Questions concerning Construction Land Review and Approval at the State Council, art. 8.

83 Point 2 (8), Opinions on Improving Review and Approval Work of Agricultural Land Conversion and Land Expropriation (关于完善农用地转用和土地征收审查报批工作的意见), promulgated by MLR on November 2, 2004, available at www.xjgtzy.gov.cn/xjgtzy/zcfg/gfxwj/2012/35587.htm.

84 Points 1–2, Notice on Issues concerning the Adjustment of Urban Construction Land Review and Approval Mechanism at the State Council (关于调整报国务院批准城市建设用地审批方式有关问题的通知), promulgated by MLR on December 31, 2006, available at www.mlr.gov.cn/zwgk/zytz/200701/t20070123_79059.htm.

application materials at the beginning of every year.[85] Therefore, in their applications they usually over-report the potential scale of expropriation, in the hope of accommodating as much as possible their needs for rural land expropriation in the coming year. This practice has become so prevalent that the central and provincial governments take the expropriation applications with a pinch of salt. Nevertheless, they have little idea about the extent to which the applications are "ballooned" and are therefore far from accurate in allocating annual land use quotas across localities.

In this circumstance, ever since the start of this century, the MLR has taken reform measures to streamline the review process and enhance the efficiency thereof. First is the standardization and simplification of application materials. For example, in 2012 the MLR issued uniform and simplified templates for the aforementioned one form and four programs and asked provincial land administration departments to offer more training in this regard to subprovincial governments.[86] Second, the MLR has also increasingly digitalized the review and approval process.[87] Last but not least, in 2016 the MLR decided that the annual land use quotas would be assigned in a lump sum and that before the allocation of annual quotas local governments are permitted to plan land use according to 50 percent of the previous year's quota allowance.[88] Understandably, this aims to mitigate the rigidity of hierarchical review and provide more room for flexibility in local land use.

That being said, maintenance of the managerial logic characterized by strict top-down oversight remains paramount to expropriation decision-making. None of the above reform efforts touches on the intrinsic hierarchal and managerial nature of the mechanism. By and large, they amount to no more than technical adjustments on the margin to relax

[85] Ming Yi, "Revised Administration Measures of Land Use Annual Plans becomes effective (土地利用年度计划管理办法修订后施行)," May 23, 2016, available at finance.china.com.cn/roll/20160523/3733572.shtml.

[86] Notice on Issues concerning Further Improving Construction Land Review and Approval Work and Enhancing Efficiency of Review and Approval (关于进一步改进建设用地审查报批工作提高审批效率有关问题的通知), promulgated by MLR on May 5, 2012, available at www.mlr.gov.cn/zwgk/zytz/201205/t20120517_1099674.htm.

[87] Ibid., point 4 (1); point 13, Notice on Improving and Optimizing Preliminary Review and Review of Land Use for Construction Projects (关于改进和优化建设项目用地预审和用地审查的通知), promulgated by MLR on November 30, 2016, available at www.mlr.gov.cn/zwgk/zytz/201612/t20161214_1424197.htm.

[88] Art. 10, Administration Measures of Land Use Annual Plans (土地利用年度计划管理办法), promulgated by MLR on May 12, 2016, available at www.mlr.gov.cn/zwgk/zytz/201605/t20160520_1406065.htm.

bureaucratic restrictions within the broader confines of the existing procedures. As a matter of fact, just like the 1960s, at the same time as adopting efficiency-enhancing measures, it has been stressed that compliance scrutiny should not be lessened but strengthened over both application and implementation of expropriation, using state-of-the-art technology such as satellite surveillance and big data analytics.[89]

In addition to the aforementioned micro-efficiency problem, there is a macro inefficiency associated with China's rural land expropriation decision-making mechanism, particularly its foundation, i.e. the spatial planning system. Strictly speaking, it is less about how expropriation decisions are formulated than about how developable land as a valuable resource gets allocated. And it is now a relatively well-trodden topic in the existing literature on China's land system more generally. Yet, a brief introduction is still warranted here as it demonstrates the pragmatic dilemma facing the constitutional principle of rational land use.

It is generally agreed that China's spatial planning system based on land quota allocation is confronted with three kinds of macro-efficiency challenges.[90] First of all, the maximum quotas for construction land that can be claimed set in the LUMPs are practically unrealistic simply because they cannot accommodate the country's demand for developable land. This has long been the case. In 2007, the deputy minister of land publicly acknowledged that quotas in the previous national LUMP (1997–2010) had already been exceeded.[91] Some cities had used up their shares in 2001.[92] Between 2001 and 2004, the actual amount of construction land claimed in Beijing was 3.2 times more than what was written in the plan.[93]

89 MLR, Notice on Issues concerning Further Improving Construction Land Review and Approval Work and Enhancing Efficiency of Review and Approval, point 4 (3); MLR, Notice on Improving and Optimizing Preliminary Review and Review of Land Use for Construction Projects, point 12.

90 Yuan Xiao, "Making Land Fly: The Institutionalization of China's Land Quota Markets and its Implications for Urbanization, Property Rights, and Intergovernmental Negotiation," PhD Thesis, MIT (2014), pp. 58–59.

91 Yingmei Yu and Chun Lu, "Some Cities Have Used Up Land Use Quotas Until 2010 (部分城市用地指标"爷卖孙粮"已超2010年)," December 13, 2007, available at news.sohu.com/20071213/n254057689.shtml.

92 Fang Chen, "Rampant Land Selling, Representatives and Committee Members Criticizing Unsustainable Approach of Development to Kill the Golden Goose (卖地风猖獗,代表委员抨击"杀鸡取卵"式发展不可取)," March 8, 2004, available at www.legaldaily.com.cn/misc/2004-03/08/content_81306.htm.

93 Dan Li, "Beijing Land Use Quota Breached Multiple Times and Cultivated Land Loss Already Out of Control (北京土地规划指标屡遭突破,耕地流失已经失控)," March 7, 2004, available at finance.people.com.cn/GB/1037/5292289.html.

More recently, with regard to the present national LUMP (2006–2020), as noted earlier, the national target of preserving 1.8 billion *mu* of cultivated land was originally set with the goal of achieving 95 percent self-sufficiency in food supply. That is in tension with supplying sufficient construction land for urbanization and industrialization, which is of lesser priority in the context of quota control. Although that may be precisely the point of spatial planning, in practice it means that quota shortage is almost a built-in feature of the system from day one. Specifically, the total volume of capital investment was 27 trillion RMB in China as of 2010 – more than seven times that of 2001. But for the same time period the conversion quota allowance increased by a mere 4.7 percent.[94] In 2013, the MLR official in charge of land use planning admitted that the gap between quota allowance for construction land and the actual demand was at least 3–4 million *mu* every year.[95] The MLR disclosed in 2014 that some provinces had already exhausted their quotas that should have lasted until 2020.[96]

Second, and relatedly, the distribution of land use quotas among localities is problematic since it is not assigned according to local conditions. This is unsurprising because otherwise hierarchical control would be meaningless. But top-down planning cannot fully reflect the variegated and changing local socioeconomic circumstances, and those with higher demand for developable land do not necessarily get more land conversion quotas.[97] For example, Hangzhou, a rapidly growing city in Zhejiang Province, demanded 31,330 *mu* of construction land for urban expansion, but it had only 3,670 *mu* of construction land quota allocated by the provincial government.[98] It should be noted that this does not mean that these quotas are completely imposed from above regardless of local demand. As a matter of fact, there exists room for bargaining in both total and annual quota allocation. On the one hand, when superior governments review and approve LUMPs formulated and submitted by subordinate governments, the former do take into consideration the

94 Ibid.

95 Min Tang and Hao Chen, "Dilemma of Construction Land: Some Localities Have Used Up Their Quotas for Next Decade (建设用地之困：一些地区指标已透支到下个十年)," 24 June 2013, available at news.sina.com.cn/c/2013-06-24/140027483738.shtml.

96 Jianrong Xi, "MLR: Some Provinces Have Used Construction Land Binding Quotas beyond 2020 (国土部：有些省建设用地已突破2020年控制指标)," April 23, 2014, available at www.chinacourt.org/article/detail/2014/04/id/1281043.shtml.

97 Xiao, "Making Land Fly," p. 58.

98 Cai, "Land-locked Development: the Local Political Economy of Institutional Change in China," p. 30.

demand for developable land reported by the latter in their draft LUMPs in determining the amount of quotas to be allotted.[99] On the other hand, higher-level governments often reserve some quotas as "contingency quotas" for development projects not included in the annual plan.[100] In this situation, as touched upon previously, lower-level governments generally over-report their need for developable land and demand as much as possible,[101] making it extremely hard for the superior governments to make informed and efficient decisions.

Third, the indiscriminate enforcement of land use quotas across localities is also questionable. For instance, as already mentioned, local governments are asked to reclaim the same amount of cultivated land to compensate for what is expropriated and converted so that the fixed amount of cultivated land will not be reduced. But it has been acutely pointed out that some localities have fertile agricultural land, while others have not; some boast relatively abundant land resources, while others are extremely limited. Hence, the implementation costs and opportunity costs of saving agricultural land vary greatly from one locality to another, depending on their geographical endowment and stage of economic development.[102] Such nuanced and complex local variances are not, and indeed cannot be, taken into account in the design of an enforcement strategy for binding land use quotas because it is plainly impractical to do so.

It is against this background that we can better understand why unauthorized and unlawful expropriation by local governments has been so pervasive. Whilst land finance is certainly to blame, the reality is that local governments have been straightjacketed by prevalent quota shortages in supplying sufficient land for development and are therefore sometimes forced to break the quota restrictions.[103] That being said,

[99] Hongbo Zhu, "A Game Theory Analysis of Construction Land Quota Allocation (建设用地指标分配的博弈分析)'(2005) 3 *Land and Resources* (国土资源) 34.

[100] Xiao, "Making Land Fly," p. 66.

[101] In 2011, the MLR revealed that the total demand for developable land reported by 31 provincial governments was 16.16 million *mu* while the annual quota was only 6.7 million *mu*. See Jun Xia, "Planned Construction Land this Year Stands at Nearly Ten Million Mu with Inflated Demand that Needs Improvement (今年用地需求超计划近千万亩需求有水分管理需改进)," April 18, 2014, available at news.163.com/11/0418/04/71T6D6TO00014AED.html.

[102] Xiao, "Making Land Fly," p. 59.

[103] This explains why TVEs and joint ventures initiated by rural collectives have very slim chance to get any construction land quotas in reality, even though they are listed in law as nonagricultural uses of rural land that do not require expropriation. See Section 7.1.2.

alternative options have been adopted to alleviate inflexibility and increase efficiency in the system, though not without introducing new difficulties and problems. First is the adjustment of quotas. In 2016, the MLR cut down the target amount of preserved cultivated land for Beijing, Shanghai and Tianjin because it was found that Beijing and Tianjin had almost reached the 2020 baseline in 2012 and 2009 respectively and that Shanghai had already breached the baseline by 25 percent in 2009.[104] However, since the national target remains the same, the reduced quotas would have to be redistributed to other localities, which is of little help in alleviating the overall deficit of developable land and pervasive rural land expropriation.

Second, in the face of unequal quota distribution and indiscriminate enforcement, some provinces have permitted or encouraged cross-jurisdictional quota trading so that resource allocation distortion can be corrected. The most famous case is Zhejiang. As early as in 2000, intergovernment transfers of cultivated land/PAL quotas and cultivated land conversion quotas were started in that province.[105] The basic structure of these transactions is as follows. Under the transfer of cultivated land/PAL quotas, the responsibility for city A to preserve X amount of cultivated land/PAL is transferred to city B. Consequently, land that used to be cultivated land/PAL in city A can then be converted for construction purposes and city B gets paid by city A for cultivated land/PAL reallocation at a price negotiated by these two cities. The reason that such transactions are efficiency-enhancing is that preservation of X amount of cultivated land/PAL is less costly to city B with a less developed economy and relatively abundant land than to city A with a developed economy but scarce land.[106] Similarly, under the transfer of cultivated land conversion quotas, the more economically developed and less well geographically endowed city A may purchase conversion quotas from the less economically developed and better geographically endowed city B to

104 Kai Ye, "Central Government Adjusts and Reduces Quotas of Cultivated Land Protection for Beijing and Tianjin, though Construction Land can Hardly Expand (中央调减京津沪耕保指标建设用地仍难扩张)," June 28, 2016, available at www.yicai.com/news/5035066.html.

105 Hui Wang and Ran Tao, "Zhejiang Model of Land Development Rights Transferring and Trading: Institutional Origin, Operational Mode and Its Significant Implications (论土地发展权转移与交易的"浙江模式": 制度起源、操作模式及其重要含义)" (2009) 8 *Management World* (管理世界) 39.

106 Cai, "Land-locked Development: The Local Political Economy of Institutional Change in China," pp. 31–34.

supply more construction land for investment.[107] Commentators have praised such intergovernmental collaboration in trading land use quotas as a market-based institutional innovation that strikes a good balance between preservation of agricultural land and economic development. On the one hand, it helps local governments with land scarcity overcome the bottleneck in obtaining the construction land necessary to promote further economic growth. On the other hand, it also helps local governments with land abundance gain revenue and investments. Thus, a Pareto improvement for all localities involved is realized where land use efficiency is improved and regional disparity reduced without compromising the spatial planning system and arable land protection.[108] However, the problem is that rural land expropriation still happens at the same scale, though in a different place. More crucially, it has been observed that practices such as this have now ceased to exist because no city is currently willing to sell the precious land use quotas when quota scarcity is almost universal with faster than ever urbanization.[109]

More recently, a third efficiency-boosting strategy has been adopted to transfer construction land from the countryside to the city, known as "linking the decrease of rural construction land with the increase of urban construction land" (*chengxiang jianshe yongdi zengjian guagou*). It was first recognized by the central government in 2004.[110] In 2006, the MLR approved five provinces to run pilot linking programs. By 2013, the MLR approved a total of 29 provinces to do so.[111] In essence, it is an upgrade variation of the abovementioned dynamic balance policy that requires local governments to reclaim as much agricultural land as they expropriate and convert. Under the linking approach, a city government reclaims and consolidates X amount of rural construction land and turns it back to agricultural land. It thereby creates an extra X amount of agricultural land than its preservation target, which means that it then has an increased X amount of land for urban construction outside the

107 Hui Wang, Ran Tao and Juer Tong, "Trading Land Development Rights Under a Planned Land Use System: The Zhejiang Model" (2009) 17 (1) *China and World Economy* 78.

108 Cai, "Land-locked Development," p. 18; Wang, Tao and Tong, "Trading Land Development Rights Under a Planned Land Use System," 81.

109 Xiao, "Making Land Fly," p. 60.

110 Point 10, Decision on Deepening Reform and Enhancing Land Administration (关于深化改革严格土地管理的决定), promulgated by State Council on October 21, 2004, available at www.mlr.gov.cn/zwgk/flfg/tdglflfg/200601/t20060112_642080.htm.

111 Xiao, "Making Land Fly," p. 72.

annual quota for construction land granted from above.[112] In this way, rural construction land is transformed into urban construction land. Usually the decreased rural construction land is located in a relatively remote location and used for down-and-under TVEs or sparsely occupied rural residences. Peasants who live there are resettled into apartment buildings of higher density that take up a smaller area of land. Such a contraction in rural construction land provides the room for the local government to expand urban construction land of the same size, typically by turning agricultural land into construction land in a prime location such as the urban fringe. Ultimately, the total amount of agricultural land and construction land does not change. What is changed is the location of precious developable land.[113]

It should be pointed out that initially the linking programs were designed with packages of corresponding contraction and expansion areas that are paired up in advance and fall within the same county or city.[114] Yet that proved to be somewhat inflexible and inconvenient. For one thing, it would take years to choose and prepare the contraction and expansion areas, incurring huge investments and complex administrative red tape. For another, finding appropriate and sufficient space for both decrease and increase of construction land in the same locality has not always been possible.[115] In this situation, since 2008, the State Council has authorized Chongqing and Chengdu to try out a pilot policy of transferrable land quota certificates (*dipiao*). Their differences aside,[116] the gist of this policy experiment is that the urban construction land quotas created by consolidating and reclaiming rural construction land will no longer be supplied to predetermined projects in predetermined location within one county or city. Instead, these quotas are put on a government-set market platform where buyers and sellers can trade them across cities and counties.[117]

The benefits of the linking programs and marketization of urban construction land quotas produced therefrom have been well recognized by observers. First, it helps meet the high demand for developable land in cities through densifying underutilized rural construction land and

[112] Art. 2, Administration Measures on Pilot Programs of Linking Contraction of Rural Construction Land with Expansion of Urban Construction Land (城乡建设用地增减挂钩试点管理办法), promulgated by MLR on June 27, 2008, available at www.mlr.gov.cn/xwdt/zytz/200903/t20090302_115435.htm.

[113] Xiao, "Making Land Fly," pp. 71–72.

[114] MLR, Administration Measures on Pilot Programs of Linking Contraction of Rural Construction Land with Expansion of Urban Construction Land, art. 5.

[115] Xiao, "Making Land Fly," pp. 152–53, 155–56. [116] Ibid., pp. 32–33.

[117] Ibid., chapter 5.

transferring the saved development opportunity to the urban periphery.[118] Second, it improves the peasants' position as empirical research does show that peasants who give up their rural construction land to create tradable urban construction land quotas do get higher returns than the compensation they could have obtained if their rural construction land were expropriated.[119] Nevertheless, the linking initiative is by no means without challenges. To start with, from the very beginning the MLR has insisted that the linking should also be placed under quota control.[120] This is understandable because if given a blank check to transfer as much rural construction land as they like, local governments are likely to, and indeed have been, targeting rural construction land that is unsuitable to be reclaimed, in the hope of generating more developable land in the urban areas at the expense of agricultural land protection. In 2010, the Chengdu pilot project was suspended by the MLR, one of the reasons being that it went beyond the linking quota permitted by superior governments.[121] Furthermore, in practice the linking policy may well harm rather than benefit the peasants if distorted and abused, which is exactly the case in some places. Peasants were forcefully "driven upstairs" into apartment buildings against their will so that their residential rural land could be consolidated; or, they were compensated meagerly for turning in their rural construction land and were far from properly resettled afterwards.[122] All of this has been testified by the warnings from both the State Council and the MLR that local governments should never force reclamation and should ensure that the net profit gained from subsequent transfer of newly generated urban construction land goes back to benefit the peasants.[123]

118 Xiao, "Making Land Fly," p. 14.

119 Lixing Li, "Land Titling in China: Chengdu Experiment and its Consequences" (2012) 5 (1) *China Economic Journal* 61.

120 Point 1, Opinions on Regulating the Pilot Programs of Linking Increase of Urban Construction Land and Decrease of Rural Construction Land (关于规范城镇建设用地增加与农村建设用地减少相挂钩试点工作的意见), promulgated by MLR on October 11, 2005, available at http://china.findlaw.cn/fangdichan/fdcfg/nongcunfangchan/96214.html.

121 Yunzhang Jiang, "MLR Suspends Land Ticket Transactions in Chengdu, Opinions Diverge on Rural Land Transfer (国土部浇灭成都地票交易， 农地流转政策意见不一)," January 8, 2011, available at finance.sina.com.cn/roll/20110108/00029221401.shtml.

122 Yina Chen, Song Li and Xuzhong Xu, "Distorted Increase-decrease Linking Programs (增减挂钩变形记)," November 22, 2010, available at www.chinanews.com/estate/2010/11-22/2671576.shtml.

123 Notice on Strictly Regulating Pilot Projects of Linking Increase of Urban Construction Land and Decrease of Rural Construction Land and Diligently Working on Rural Land Reclamation (关于严格规范城乡建设用地增减挂钩试点切实做好农村土地整治工作的通知), promulgated by State Council on December

Last, but not least, linking projects does not curtail expropriation since it is still required in the expansion of urban construction land. What is worse is that private buyers of the tradable quotas in Chongqing are allowed to ask the government to expropriate the land parcel that they are interested in, making expropriation for private uses and profits more evident than ever before.[124]

To sum up, the managerial logic of China's land administration system in general and rural land expropriation system in particular has encountered a great deal of practical difficulties in terms of achieving efficient resource allocation and rational land use, in both the micro and macro senses. Over the last two decades, a plethora of reforms have been implemented to tackle these efficiency problems. Yet, to date, the expropriation decision-making mechanism remains closed and hierarchical and the top-down planning control largely persists. As a matter of fact, it has been explicitly stated by top officials and the MLR since 2013 that the planning-based land use regulatory system is a bottom line not to be crossed by any future reform.[125]

8.4.3 *Fairness: Limits of the Market Logic*

As previously noted, compensation and resettlement benefits for rural land expropriation in China have long been criticized as unfair. While the last decade did witness reforms toward a more consistent, broad-based, generous and sustainable standard, the statutory principle of anchoring compensation and resettlement on the value of land in its original use as well as the expropriatees' original living standards has stayed in place. Enough has been said about how unfair that is when the rural takees are largely excluded from sharing the vast sum of increased land value

27, 2010, available at www.gov.cn/zwgk/2011-04/02/content_1837370.htm. See also Notice on Strictly Regulating Pilot Projects of Linking Increase of Urban Construction Land and Decrease of Rural Construction Land (严格规范城乡建设用地增减挂钩试点工作的通知), promulgated by MLR on December 26, 2011, available at www.mlr.gov.cn/zwgk/zytz/201112/t20111228_1051488.htm.

124 Xiao, "Making Land Fly," pp. 117-19.

125 Hua Feng and Renze Chen, "The Reform of Rural Land System, Baseline that should not be Crossed: An Exclusive Interview with Deputy and Head of the Office of the Central Rural Work Leadership Group Chen Xiwen (农村土地制度改革，底线不能突破：专访中央农村领导小组副组长办公室主任陈锡文)," *People's Daily*, December 5, 2013, p. 2; Qian Li, "Executive Meeting of the Minister: Discussing Issues related to Deepening the Reform of Land System (部长办公会：研究深化土地制度改革有关问题)," August 1, 2014, available at www.mlr.gov.cn/xwdt/jrxw/201408/t20140801_1325541.htm.

generated in the process of expropriation, conversion and transfer. But, additionally, there are two more types of unfairness in the present compensation standard for rural land expropriation and in the way in which actual compensation is decided.

Since 2011, as already mentioned, the compensation standard for withdrawal of urban land and expropriation of the private housing thereon has been changed to be based on the price of comparable real property.[126] Market price is now part of the formula to calculate how much urban residents get compensated for their expropriated properties. On a deeper level, this means that takings of real property in the urban context are now conceptualized as some sort of quasi-transaction where the government is responsible for compensating the condemnees with what they would have received as voluntary market sellers. But such market logic is yet to be embraced in the context of rural land expropriation. The dualism in China's takings law is therefore aggravated, so much so that in March 2011, less than two months after the enactment of the RECHSL, the CCP's Central Committee of Discipline and Inspection and Ministry of Supervision announced that provincial party discipline agencies and supervision departments should urge local governments to refer to (*canzhao*) the spirit of the then newly promulgated RECHSL in demolition of houses on rural collective land before the LAL is formally amended.[127] While this shows that the central authority in China is keenly cognizant of the inequality between compensation standards for expropriating rural and urban properties, the order from the Party and government watchdogs does not, and actually cannot, fully bridge that gap in between, at least not in the formal legal sense until the LAL gets revised. In fact, later in the same year the SPC made it clear that if compensation disputes arise, courts can apply compensation standards for urban housing demolition in the rural context when and only when the following conditions are met: (1) the expropriated rural housing is already located in the planned urban areas; (2) the owner requests that the urban demolition compensation standard be applied; and (3)

[126] For an analysis of how this change came about, see Heurlin, *Responsive Authoritarianism in China*, pp. 155–62.

[127] Point 2, Notice on Strengthening Supervision and Inspection over Further Regularization of Expropriation and Demolition Activities (关于加强监督检查进一步规范征地拆迁行为的通知), promulgated by General Office of Central Committee of Discipline and Inspection and General Office of Ministry of Supervision on March 17, 2011, available at www.zhanjiang.gov.cn/fileserver/statichtml/2016-07/15b8b0e5-c569-4314-9450-6ae20ee5cc08.htm?cid=.

compensation fees for rural land expropriation already paid to the owner should be deducted from the final sum of compensation.[128] Apparently, the gulf between the two unequal compensation regimes remains, which can be called "urban-rural unfairness."

In the meantime, pervasive compensation negotiation and bargaining on the ground have brought about a different kind of unfairness. It has been reported that bargained expropriation compensation can sometimes reach "sky-high price(s)" (*tianjia*), giving rise to a new popular phrase "second generation of demolition" (*chai erdai*).[129] In contemporary Chinese vocabulary, a second generation of someone/something typically has pejorative connotations. For instance, a second-generation government official (*guan erdai*) is someone who relies on nepotism or even cronyism for personal gain. The second generation of demolition describes those expropriatees who become super-rich overnight after receiving a large compensation windfall. While it is difficult to pin down exactly how often sky-high expropriation compensation happens, empirical evidence does suggest that rural expropriatees sometimes secure substantive concessions from the expropriating governments in the form of increased compensation. For example, it has been discovered that expropriated peasants who became nail houses and adopted disruptive tactics such as organized protests were more successful in getting a better deal from the government out of compensation negotiation.[130] This is because apart from repression, local governments under high pressure to maintain social stability resorted to less oppressive means such as handing out side-payments in the name of increased expropriation compensation to appease the protesting expropriatees. They found that compared with repression, which often has negative short-term side effects, the negative side effects of concessions in paying increased

[128] Art. 12, Provisions on issues concerning adjudicating administrative cases involving rural collective land (关于审理涉及农村集体土地行政案件若干问题的规定), promulgated by SPC on August 7, 2011, available at www.court.gov.cn/zixun-xiangqing-3091.html.

[129] Molin Han, "Post-1990s Second-generation Expropriatees in Beijing Becomes Rich: Expropriation is Most Revealing about Human Conditions (北京90后拆二代因房致富：最见人心是拆迁)," January 15, 2017, available at finance.sina.com.cn/china/dfjj/2017-01-15/doc-ifxzqnim4437206.shtml?t=1484453180344; "Second-generation Expropriatees in Xiamen Who Become Super Rich Overnight with Expropriation Compensation Face Different Circumstances (厦门"拆二代"拿拆迁补偿款一夜暴富，境遇各不相同)," March 10, 2014, available at www.mnw.cn/xiamen/news/732003-2.html.

[130] Heurlin, *Responsive Authoritarianism in China*, p. 75.

compensation are only felt in the long run, after officials have been promoted.[131] In localities such as Jiangsu, such concessions became so widespread that local officials lamented that demolition offices increased compensation amounts "again and again, breaking the demolition budgets again and again and resulting in the constant increase in demolition costs, going far beyond the budgets."[132] While we should be cautious about portraying those expropriatees demanding higher compensation as uncooperative and opportunistic negotiators who sacrifice the public interest for personal gain,[133] it is undeniable that a new type of unfairness has emerged when, as the Chinese saying goes, only the crying baby gets the milk.[134] This "intra-rural unfairness" has already contributed to a spiral of disputes as those expropriatees who had already moved out return and join the nail households.[135] In the absence of a developed rural land market with independent and trusted land value appraisal institutions, it is almost inevitable that negotiations about expropriation compensation go unregulated and yield unequal and sometimes inequitable results.

8.4.4 *Constitutionality: Limits of the Comparative Logic*

The fourth and final point of tension in China's rural land expropriation law lies in its constitutionality – or, more precisely, the claimed lack thereof. It has been suggested that the expropriation system is unconstitutional in both the passive and active senses. The claim of passive unconstitutionality points to the fact that the 1988 constitutional amendment stipulates that land use-rights can be transferred according to provisions of the law. It does not specify that *only* urban land use-rights can be transferred. However, as mentioned earlier, since then only urban land use-rights transfer has been permitted and legislated for, and marketization of rural land for nonagricultural purposes has been explicitly prohibited by the 1998 LAL. The criticism hence goes that this is in contradiction with the constitutional prescription because the

131 Ibid., p 78. 132 Ibid., p 77.

133 This is the counter-discourse present in some Chinese media reports, as opposed to the narrative that focuses on victimhood of the expropriatees. See You-tien Hsing, *The Great Urban Transformation: Politics of Land and Property in China* (New York: Oxford University Press, 2010), pp. 77–78; Sargeson, *Villains, Victims and Aspiring Proprietors*, p. 767.

134 The English equivalent is that only the squeaky wheel gets the grease.

135 Heurlin, *Responsive Authoritarianism in China*, p. 77.

legislature has passively failed to honor the legislative task entrusted by the 1988 constitutional amendment.[136]

The problem with this passive unconstitutionality thesis is that although the 1988 constitutional amendment does not specify that only urban land use-rights can be marketized, neither does it say that urban land use-rights and rural land use-rights should be marketized in the same manner. As a matter of fact, marketization of rural land use-rights has long been sanctioned and legislated for, as long as it is not for nonagricultural purposes. For example, in 1993 the CCP Central Committee announced that rural households could transfer their contracted use-rights over rural agricultural land to other parties.[137] The 1998 LAL (Article 15), 2002 *Rural Land Contract Law* (Articles 10, 16, 32–37) and 2007 *Property Law* (Article 128) all have set rules for the circulation of contracted use-rights on rural agricultural land both inside and outside the rural collectives, provided that the transferred rural agricultural land is not used for nonagricultural development. As to rural construction land, transfer of household residential plots among members of the same rural collective has long been recognized in practice by the courts.[138] Since 2014, the CCP Central Committee and the State Council initiated pilot reform programs to allow those rural households who have migrated to cities to return their residential land to the collectives or transfer such land to other members of the same collective in exchange for payment.[139] In the meantime, as already mentioned,

[136] Yuan Xu, "History Retrogresses Here: 1998 Revision of the Land Administration Law (历史在这里倒退: 1998年土地管理法修订)," July 29, 2014, available at money.163.com/14/0729/09/A2AFVROJ00253B0H.html; Xueyang Cheng, "On Constitutional Order of China's Land System: Discussion with Mr. Xuefeng He (也论中国土地制度的宪法秩序：与贺雪峰先生商榷)" (2015) 2 *China Law Commentaries* (中国法律评论) 120; Qiren Zhou, "Road Map for Rural Land Marketization (土地入市的路线图)," August 21, 2014, available at finance.sina.com.cn/zl/china/20140821/102220078261.shtml; Qiren Zhou, "Why is Rural Land and Housing Marketization Indispensable to Urbanization (为什么城市化离不开农地农房入市)," September 11, 2014, available at www.eeo.com.cn/2014/0911/266150.shtml.

[137] Art. 31, Decisions on Several Issues concerning Establishment of Socialist Market Economy(关于建立社会主义市场经济体制若干问题的决定), promulgated by CCP Central Committee on November 14, 1993, available at www.people.com.cn/GB/shizheng/252/5089/5106/20010430/456592.html.

[138] Supreme People's Court's Study Group on Property Law (ed.), *Interpretation and Application of PRC Property Law* (《中华人民共和国物权法》条文理解与适用) (Beijing: Renmin Fayuan Press, 2007), p. 463.

[139] Opinions on Pilot Reform Projects of Rural Land Expropriation, Marketization of For-profit Rural Construction Land and Residential Plot System (关于农村土地征收、集体经营性建设用地入市、宅基地制度改革试点工作的意见), promulgated by General

marketization of for-profit rural construction land has also been practiced, first as a local experiment and then as NPCSC-approved pilot reform since 2015. All of this demonstrates that transfer of rural land use-rights is anything but forbidden, on which plenty of laws and policies have been promulgated over the years. It is for this reason that the 1988 constitutional amendment is not violated in the passive sense, even though the rules on rural land transfer are much more stringent than those concerning urban land transfer.

Nonetheless, that is precisely what is under attack from the standpoint of active unconstitutionality. It has been argued that compared with state ownership of urban land, the collective ownership and peasants' use-rights over rural land have been actively placed under discriminatory treatment because under existing law the conversion and marketization of rural land are severely restrained and expropriation remains the only way through which it can be converted and transferred for most non-agricultural purposes.[140] Admittedly, differentiation is not necessarily discrimination. The former amounts to the latter only when there is no principled justification. The justification for taking the right to convert to nonagricultural use away from the bundle of rights in collective rural land ownership is of course the need to preserve agricultural land, which is generally accepted.[141] But that is no justification for taking away the right to transfer rural construction land that is already put to nonagricultural ends. More crucially, it has been advocated that even for the goal of agricultural land protection, the current expropriation law is still unconstitutional for violating the principle of proportionality in imposing excessive limitations upon property rights over rural land.[142] It is proposed that the same objective may well be achieved with a less intrusive means: while state planning can continue to set the boundaries

Office of CCP Central Committee and General Office of State Council on January 11, 2015. The full text of this document is yet to be made public, but its main content was disclosed by the minister of land resources in an interview. See Libin Wang, "Firmly Grasping the Main Theme of Interrelationship between Peasants and Land: Interview with Jiang Daming on Studying General Secretary Xi Jinping's Important Speech at Xiaogang Village in Anhui (牢牢把握农民与土地关系这条主线 – 就学习习近平总书记安徽小岗村重要讲话专访姜大明)," June 21, 2016, available at finance.sina.com.cn/china/2016-06-21/doc-ifxtfrrf0748890.shtml.

140 Chuanhui Wang, *The Constitutional Protection of Private Property in China: Historical Evolution and Comparative Research* (Cambridge: Cambridge University Press, 2016), p. 303.

141 The famous exception is the economist Mao Yushi. See Chapter 7.

142 Zhongxia Li, "Analysis of the Constitutionality of Transfer of Rural Land (农村土地流转的合宪性分析)" (2015) 4 *China Legal Science* (中国法学) 136.

for the nonagricultural development of rural land, as long as a piece of rural land is designated as developable, that can be done by the rural collectives and peasants themselves without the intervention of state expropriation.[143]

This active unconstitutionality argument sits right at the heart of the proposition that China's existing rural land expropriation represents a broken constitutional promise, especially after the 2004 constitutional amendment solemnly proclaimed that the state respects and protects human rights and that citizens' lawful private property shall not be violated. On a more concrete level, the last three decades did witness the gradual but steady "propertization" of rural land tenure, a process described as "stick-by-stick."[144] For instance, in the late 1970s the household contractual right to use rural land for agricultural production was created; between the 1980s and the 1990s, the legal term of such tenure was extended from 15 to 30 years; since the 1990s, alienability of rural agricultural land has also been permitted to some extent, and liberalization of stock for-profit rural construction land is now underway. All of this makes the remaining restraints over rural land property look out of place and outdated and the existing Chinese rural land property regime the product of an unfinished, partial reform.[145]

It is here that we see most clearly the fundamental tension embedded in China's constitutional jurisprudence on rural land expropriation. As explained, the current rural land expropriation law is a faithful reflection, rather than an unfortunate betrayal, of the long-standing tradition of expropriation for state-led social transformation, embodied in texts none other than the power-confirming takings clauses from the 1954 Constitution to the 1982 Constitution. In the meantime, after many years of gradual recognition of private property, including that related to rural land, the 2004 amendment finally introduced the mandate of respecting and protecting private property rights into the Chinese Constitution, meaning that the constitutional takings clause assumes a new function to constrain the state power of rural land expropriation. It is from this standpoint that the existing expropriation law has been

[143] Cheng, On Constitutional Order of China's Land System: Discussion with Mr. Xuefeng He, 129.

[144] Shitong Qiao, "Evolution of Chinese Property Law: Stick by Stick," in Yun-chien Chang, Wei Shen and Wen-yeu Wang (eds.), *Private Law in China and Taiwan: Legal and Economic Analyses* (New York: Cambridge University Press, 2016).

[145] Shitong Qiao, "The Politics of Chinese Land: Partial Reform, Vested Interests and Small Property" (2016) 29 (1) *Columbia Journal of Asia Law* 70.

held unconstitutional in the active sense for being too interfering with property rights in rural land.

But the central challenge to the active unconstitutionality thesis rests in the fact that China's constitutional takings jurisprudence is also power-confirming. More precisely, it is both power-confirming and power-constraining. Those who subscribe to the active unconstitutionality proposition either ignore the age-old tradition of expropriation for state-led social transformation in conflating the Chinese constitutional takings clause with the American Fifth Amendment, or they dismiss the legitimacy of such a tradition in the belief that it is irreconcilable with the new constitutional imperative of property rights protection and that the former ought to be completely wiped out and replaced by the latter. Neither position is tenable. As demonstrated meticulously in this book, the Chinese rural land takings law has evolved out of and is conditioned by a unique historical lineage that is a world away from the circumstances that brewed the Fifth Amendment. This rather inconvenient fact cannot be wished away, and the ignorance thereof will lead to nothing but incomprehension as to why and how the law we are trying to comprehend is the way it is today. Equally problematic is to hold that the power-confirming tradition is incorrigibly inconsistent with and should be outlived by the power-constraining mandate. There is nothing peculiar about the constitution being at once power-confirming *and* power-constraining. After all, it was James Madison who pronounced in the *Federalist Papers* that "you must first enable the government to control the governed; and in the next place, oblige it to control itself." The key to constitutionality, therefore, is to achieve an appropriate balance between competing constitutional agendas. Unsurprisingly, and arguably legitimately, that balance will not be the same across countries with radically divergent historical backgrounds.

As mentioned, the core of the unconstitutionality criticism is that the presumption of expropriation in nonagricultural use of rural land is unjustified and disproportionate. It may be argued that even though the objective of agricultural land conservation might justify restricting convertibility and alienability of rural agricultural land, such restraints upon rural construction land and the state monopoly over rural–urban land conversion through expropriation are simply the wrong balance and are prejudicial against rural land property rights. But the opposite case can also be made. To begin with, the justification for limiting marketability of nonprofit rural construction land, such as that used for rural residential and public facilities, is that it has long been considered a source of welfare provision and social security to the rural population, not a return-maximizing commodity or investment. When it is no longer playing this role, it becomes alienable under ongoing reforms, which, as mentioned, permit those migrated peasants to return their residential land to the collectives or transfer such land to other members of the same collective in exchange for a payment. The restricted range of marketization, i.e. not allowing peasants to sell residential land to urban residents, is to avoid possible disruption to the urban real estate market, which may pose a serious threat to China's macroeconomic stability. Of course, this line of argument does not cover inalienability of for-profit rural construction land, which, as already noted, is now being relaxed under the recent land reforms. Furthermore, expropriation is certainly by no means the least intrusive way to enforce the public control over nonagricultural development of rural land. For instance, in many other countries, zoning or planning schemes set the limitations on the kind of development activities on land lots, but it is left to private market initiatives to decide exactly when and how a certain land parcel is to be developed. However, as demonstrated, China's spatial planning system is more than just boundary-setting. It is also pace-setting and magnitude-setting in that it grants the power to local governments, subject to hierarchal review, to determine when and how much nonagricultural development happens on rural land, which, as noted, serves as an important instrument for macroeconomic management. Whereas it is relatively easy to ensure that private owners and the market carry out nonagricultural land development within government-set boundaries, there is much less, if any at all, guarantee that they will be dictated by government-set timing and scale. If ever there is such guarantee, it is likely to be realized by way of some sort of forced development or transaction that is no less intrusive than expropriation.

The point of the above analysis is not that the active unconstitutionality thesis is completely unfounded. Insofar as it captures and highlights the now well-entrenched mandate of property rights protection in the Chinese Constitution, it constitutes a valid immanent critique against the present expropriation law. The problem, however, is that it misses out the real crux of the issue – namely, that there exists a fundamental tension between the power-confirming and power-constraining traditions in China's constitutional jurisprudence on rural land takings, which can neither be revealed nor resolved by a comparison with the American jurisprudence about eminent domain. As a result, it is incapable of generating valuable insights into the still ongoing process of searching for a better balance.

8.5 Looking Ahead

On a good day (when I am an optimistic idealist) or a bad day (when I am deeply saddened by tragic takings events), I do wish that China's rural land expropriation law could be like its American counterpart. In the myriad of ways described in the previous section, the current expropriation law is ineffective, inefficient, unfair and arguably unconstitutional. But to say that it is functionally and conceptually equivalent to the Fifth Amendment jurisprudence and that it faces imminent transition to the American model as long as land finance is removed is both inaccurate and unhelpful. This book has demonstrated, convincingly I hope, that the existing rural land expropriation law is neither an anomaly arising out of neglecting the constitution nor a stopgap resulting from partial reform en route to full marketization of land. It is the product of a long and complicated history that originated in the early twentieth century and evolved over an extensive period encompassing times of war, revolution, command economy and opening and reform. It has been deployed to overturn a pre-existing social structure; and it has also been used to develop and manage a new political economy. It exhibits incredibly strong path dependence on both the constitutional and statutory levels; yet it has also been open to adjustments, and is now encountering multiple difficulties and tensions under changed circumstances. It is therefore not a story of constitutional violation, but one of unending constitutional evolution.

Central to this evolution now is the search for a proper balance between the power-confirming and power-constraining/rights-protecting agendas in China's rural land expropriation law, which will not be transplanted from the American law. The best place to peek into the possible future is in the draft amendment to the LAL published by the MLR in late May of 2017.[146] To start with, Articles 43 and 63 that explicitly prohibit development and transfer of rural land for nonagricultural purposes are revoked in the draft amendment. This is in line with the NPCSC-approved reform since 2015 that sanctions the marketization of for-profit rural construction land. But apart from that, the presumption of state expropriation in nonagricultural use of rural land is maintained even though a new provision is now added into the amendment specifying what constitutes the public interest in rural land expropriation. Article 44 stipulates that in the following six scenarios the state may expropriate rural collective land:

146 The full text of the draft law is available at www.gygov.gov.cn/art/2017/5/23/art_11894_1174759.html.

(1) in the need of national defense and diplomacy; (2) in the need of government-organized infrastructural development in energy, transportation and water conservation; (3) in the need of government-organized construction of public facilities in science, education, cultural development, public health, sports, environmental and resource protection, disaster prevention, heritage preservation, social welfare and urban utilities; (4) in the need of government-organized projects of social housing and relocation; (5) in the need of implementation of urban planning by governments in the areas designated as urban construction land according to the land use master plans; and (6) in the need of other kinds of public interest specified by laws and administrative regulations. Apparently, with item (5), so long as it is pursuant to the LUMPs and URPs, rural land expropriation will still be exercised regardless of the specific ends the expropriated land is to be used for.

Second, and relatedly, the expropriation decision-making mechanism is also kept intact. The power to review and approve expropriation applications stays with the central and provincial governments, and there is no substantive change to the spatial planning system as the foundation for expropriation decision-making. Although the procedural requirement that the potential expropriatees shall be notified prior to the submission of expropriation applications is now incorporated into the draft amendment (Article 46), expropriation decision-making remains closed within the administrative hierarchy. Third, according to the draft amendment, the multiplied average annual output approach in determining expropriation compensation is replaced by comprehensive land section price in expropriation (Article 48). However, compensation and resettlement continues to be based on the original use of expropriated land and the principle of maintaining original living standards and long-term livelihood of the expropriated (Article 47).

Overall, the published draft amendment to the LAL is no more than a summary of the reform measures that had already been adopted over the last two decades, documented in detail in Chapter 3. While the draft revision is yet to be finalized, major adjustment is unlikely. In other words, the tradition of expropriation for state-led social transformation is here to stay, and the aforementioned three salient features of China's rural land expropriation law will persist in the foreseeable future. This may come as a disappointment to many, but it should not be a surprise. Unless there is a fundamental rethinking about and repositioning of the role of the state in China's political economy, especially its relationship with land, China's rural land takings law will remain within its current parameters, alongside all the difficulties and tensions in terms of effectiveness, efficiency, fairness and constitutionality.

However, this is not to say that further reform is now entirely out of the question. Signs of change are already in sight. First, the draft amendment of the LAL provides in Article 20 that, when formulating LUMPs, the government should solicit opinions and comments from the public. The 2017 Administration Measures of Land Use Master Plans promulgated by the MLR also makes public participation a necessary step in the making of the LUMPs and asks the local land administration agencies to engage the public by way of notice-and-comment or formal hearings.[147] According to Article 26 of the 2007 URPL, the draft URPs are open for public comment, too. While this does not mean that spatial planning in China is fully democratized, opening up the system to more public input does suggest that the state no longer has the exclusive right to define public interest and rationality in land use. A more participatory and inclusive plan-making process has the potential to make expropriation decisions better reflect public opinions and needs, although to what extent that potential can be realized obviously depends upon how effective and meaningful public participation in spatial planning becomes.

Second, the draft amendment prescribes in Article 47 that the expropriated collectives and peasants shall share a reasonable portion of the expropriation surplus, i.e. the increased land value generated by the expropriation-transfer process. As noted in Chapter 3, this was part of the Third Plenum Decision in 2013, which is presently set to become effective law. Clearly, the Chinese central authority has finally decided that the government should from now on reap less expropriation surplus. This has the potential to make the compensation regime fairer, which may in turn reduce popular protest against and evasion of expropriation. Yet, for this reform initiative to move forward, it is necessary to clear up any lingering doubts concerning its legitimacy. On the one hand, it has been argued that the expropriation surplus is derived from state regulation and general socioeconomic development, not the investment or efforts of collectives and peasants. Therefore, it is an "unearned increase" that the latter do not deserve, and therefore it should not be allocated, even partially, to the latter.[148] This proposition is in essence an extension

147 Arts. 6 and 12, Administration Measures of Land Use Master Plans (土地利用总体规划管理办法), promulgated by MLR on May 8, 2017, available at www.mlr.gov.cn/zwgk/zytz/201705/t20170511_1507370.htm.

148 Xuefeng He, "Must We Reform the Current Rural Land Expropriation System? (现行征地制度必须改革?)" (2014) 4 *Development* (发展) 29.

of the long tradition in modern China of viewing increased land value as undeserved by landowners. On the other hand, giving part of the expropriation surplus to expropriatees will exacerbate the inequality among the rural population because those who live in the vicinity of urban built-up areas will obtain much more compensation due to a larger margin of increased value. Some of them may even become "land rentiers," and hence the eradicated class of landlords will re-emerge in China.[149]

Neither of the above arguments holds. For one thing, the collectives and peasants deserve at least part of the expropriation surplus not because they have somewhat created or are responsible for the increased value, but because they have shouldered a heavier burden than their urban counterparts in obeying the spatial plans. As demonstrated, there is indeed a tradition that insists that the peasants have the obligation to accept state expropriation. But that does not mean that they ought to bear all the costs of doing so on their own, especially when their urban counterparts receive more favorable treatment. Distributing part of the expropriation surplus to the rural expropriatees is not going to render expropriation purely transaction-like, but it does mean that the costs thereof shall be borne more equitably. For another, the worry that one part of the rural population will benefit more than the other in sharing expropriation surplus can easily be solved with a progressive levy upon the windfall. As mentioned in Chapter 3, this is precisely the current policy in relation to the profits created by transfer of for-profit rural construction land.

As to how expropriation surplus sharing should be carried out, there is no clear nationwide guidance for the time being. According to Articles 48, 49 and 51 of the draft amendment to the LAL, it will be up to the local governments to decide how much increased value they are going to share by way of increasing the compensation for rural housing and providing better resettlement arrangements and social security. What we can expect will be more local experiments in this regard. For the years to come, the reforms toward a better balance between the power-confirming and power-constraining traditions in China's rural land takings law will continue. But, as before, it is most likely to be incremental and gradual.

149 Xuefeng He, "Expropriation Compensation should Avoid Helping the Profiteering Class (征地补偿应防止强化食利阶层)," December 27, 2012, available at news.sina.com.cn /pl/2012-12-27/071625904603.shtml.

APPENDIX 1

Constitutional texts	Relevant clauses
1908 Outline of Constitution by Imperial Order	N/A
1911 Nineteen Major Articles of the Constitution	N/A
1912 Provisional Constitution of Republic of China	Article 15: The rights of citizens as provided in the present chapter (including the right of the security of their property provided in Article 6) shall be limited or modified by laws provided such limitation or modification shall be deemed necessary for the promotion of public interest, for the maintenance of public order or on account of extraordinary exigency.[1]
1913 Draft Constitution of Republic of China (Temple of Heaven Draft Constitution)	Article 12: Property ownership of the people of the Republic of China is not to be violated. But its disposal necessitated by public interest should be done according to law.[2]
1914 Constitution of Republic of China	N/A
1923 Constitution of Republic of China (Cao Kun Constitution)	Article 13: Property ownership of the people of the Republic of China is not to be violated. But its disposal necessitated by public interest should be done according to law.[3]

[1] The Chinese translation reads "本章所载人民之权利，有认为增进公益，维持治安或非常紧急必要时，得依法律限制之."

[2] The Chinese translation reads "中华民国人民之财产所有权不受侵犯，但公益上必要之处分，依法律之所定."

[3] The Chinese translation reads "中华民国人民之财产所有权不受侵犯，但公益上必要之处分依法律之所定."

(*cont.*)

Constitutional texts	Relevant clauses
	Article 24: The following affairs are to be conducted by the state according to legislation or by the local governments upon national orders: (7) public use expropriation.[4]
1930 Draft Constitution of Republic of China	Article 10: When each county starts to be autonomous, it shall set the price of all land privately owned within its territory. The landowners report the land price themselves and the local government levies taxes and may purchase the land at any time based on the price. If the land value increases after the price is reported due to political progress and social development, the increment shall be enjoyed by all people in the county instead of falling into the private hands of the original landowners.[5]
	Article 32: People's property ownership is not to be violated, but it may be expropriated with appropriate compensation if public interest demands so.[6]
1931 Constitutional Outline of the Chinese Soviet Republic	VI The Chinese Soviet regime has eliminating the feudal system and thoroughly improving peasants' lives as objectives, it promulgates a Land Law, advocates the confiscation of all land of the landlord class, and its distribution to poor peasants and middle peasants, and has realizing land nationalization as objective.[7]

4 The Chinese translation reads "左列事项由国家立法并执行或令地方执行之: 七 公用征收."

5 The Chinese translation reads "每县开创自治之时，必须先规定全县私有土地之价。其法由地主自报之，地方政府则照价征税，并可随时照价收买。自此次报价之后，若土地因政治之改良、社会之进步而增价者，则其利益当为全县人民所共享，而原主不得私之."

6 The Chinese translation reads "人民财产所有权不受侵犯，但因公益上之必要，得以相当价格征收之."

7 The Chinese translation reads "中国苏维埃政权以消灭封建制度及澈底的改善农民生活为目的，颁布土地法，主张没收一切地主阶级的土地，分配给贫农，中农，并以实现土地国有为目的."

(*cont.*)

Constitutional texts	Relevant clauses
1931 Provisional Constitution of the Political Tutelage Period of the Republic of China	Article 16: People's property cannot be seized or confiscated without legal authorization.[8] Article 17: The exercise of people's property rights is protected by law within the remit that does not harm public interest.[9] Article 18: People's property can be requisitioned or expropriated according to the law and for public interest.[10]
1936 Draft Constitution of Republic of China	Article 17: People's property cannot be requisitioned, expropriated, seized or confiscated without legal authorization.[11] Article 117: The state may levy taxes upon or expropriate land acquired by the people according to the price reported by the owner or appraised by the government.[12] Article 119: A land value increment tax shall be levied on any land whose value has increased not through the application of labor or capital, and the proceeds therefrom shall be used for the people.[13]
1946 Constitution of People's Republic (Chiang Kai-shek constitution)	Article 23: Liberties and rights listed above (including property rights in Article 15), except when necessitated by preventing harm to others' liberty, avoiding exigencies, maintaining social order or promoting public interest, cannot be limited by law.[14]

8 The Chinese translation reads "人民之财产非依法律不得查封或没收."

9 The Chinese translation reads "人民财产所有权之行使，在不妨害公共利益之范围内，受法律之保障."

10 The Chinese translation reads "人民财产因公共利益之必要，得依法律征用或征收之."

11 The Chinese translation reads "人民之财产，非依法律，不得征用、征收、查封，或没收."

12 The Chinese translation reads "国家对于人民取得所有权之土地，得按照土地所有权人申报，或政府估定之地价，依法律征税或征收之."

13 The Chinese translation reads "土地价值非因施以劳力资本而增加者，应以征收土地增值税方法收归人民公共享受."

14 The Chinese translation reads "以上各条列举之自由权利，除为防止妨碍他人自由，避免紧急危难，维持社会秩序，或增进公共利益所必要者外，不得以法律限制之."

(*cont.*)

Constitutional texts	Relevant clauses
	Article 108: The following affairs are to be conducted by the state according to legislation or by the provincial and county governments upon national orders: (14) public use expropriation.[15]
	Article 143: All land within the territorial limits of the Republic of China shall belong to the entire body of citizens. Private ownership of land, acquired by the people in accordance with law, shall be protected and restricted by law. Privately owned land shall pay taxes according to its value and may be purchased by the Government according to its value . . . The State shall levy a land value increment tax on any land whose value has increased not through the application of labor or capital, and the proceeds therefrom shall be used for the people.[16]
1947 Constitution of the People's Republic of Bulgaria	Article 10: Private property and its inheritance, and private economic ownership are recognized and protected by law . . . Nobody can exercise the right of ownership to the detriment of the public interest . . . Private ownership may be limited or expropriated for national or social interest with fair compensation. The state may fully or partially nationalize branches or individual enterprises of industry, commerce, transport and credit. Compensation is determined by the law of nationalization.[17]

[15] The Chinese translation reads "左列事项，由中央立法并执行之或交由省县执行之：十四 公用征收."

[16] The Chinese translation reads "中华民国领土内之土地属于国民全体。人民依法取得之土地所有权，应受法律之保障与限制。私有土地应照价纳税，政府并得照价收买。土地价值非因施以劳力资本而增加者，应由国家征收土地增值税，归人民共享之."

[17] The Chinese translation reads "私有财产及其继承权，以及经济上的私有制，受法律的承认与保护。任何人不得利用私有财产权妨害公共利益。私人财产只有为谋国家或社会的利益，并有公平补偿的条件下始得加以限制或收归国有。国家将某些

(*cont.*)

Constitutional texts	Relevant clauses
1948 Constitution of the Czechoslovak Socialist Republic	Article 9: (1) Private ownership can only be restricted by law. (2) Expropriation is possible only on the basis of the law and with compensation unless the law provides that no compensation is required. (3) No one may abuse the property rights to the detriment of the society.[18]
1948 Constitution of the Democratic People's Republic of Korea	N/A
1949 Constitution of the People's Republic of Hungary	Article 8: (2) Private property and individual initiative may not infringe public interest.[19]
1949 Constitution of the German Democratic Republic	Article 22: Private property is guaranteed by the Constitution. Its scope and its limitations are derived from law and from its obligations toward the society.[20] Article 23: Restrictions on private property and expropriations may be imposed only for the benefit of the general public and on a legal basis. They shall take place against reasonable compensation unless the law provides otherwise. If the amount of compensation is in dispute, recourse to the ordinary courts shall be open insofar as a law does not provide otherwise.[21]

部门或个别工, 商, 运输, 信贷企业的全部或一部收为国有。其补偿办法由国有化法律规定之."

18 The Chinese translation reads "(1) 只有根据法律始得限制私有财产。(2) 只有依据法律始能征用财产，并应予以补偿；但法律规定不予补偿者不在此限。(3) 任何人不得滥用私有财产权为害社会."

19 The Chinese translation reads "私有财产及私人创业不得损害公共利益."

20 The Chinese translation reads "所有权受宪法的保障。其内容及限度服从法律及其对社会所负的责任."

21 The Chinese translation reads "所有权的限制或征收只能在为公共利益时根据法律为之。在法律无相反规定的范围内，得予适当的补偿。对补偿数额的争议，在法律无相反规定的范围内，其诉讼程序于普通法院中进行之."

(*cont.*)

Constitutional texts	Relevant clauses
	Article 24: Property entails obligations. Its use must not run counter to the public interest. Misuse of property by economic ascendancy to the detriment of the public good results in confiscation without compensation and transfer to the people's ownership. Enterprises owned by war criminals and active National Socialists have been expropriated and will be transferred to the people's ownership. The same shall apply to private enterprises offering their services to war policies . . . Privately-owned large estates with acreage of more than one hundred hectares are dissolved and shall be redistributed without compensation.[22] Article 27: Private economic enterprises suitable for socialization may be transferred to public ownership by law under the provisions dealing with expropriation.[23]
1950 Constitution of the People's Republic of Albania	Article 11: Personal property cannot be used to the detriment of the society. Private property may be limited and expropriated by law when the social interest demands it. In what case and how much the proprietor will be compensated will be specified by law. Under the same conditions, certain branches of economy or enterprises may be nationalized by the State if social interests demand it.[24]

22 The Chinese translation reads "所有权负有一定义务。其使用不得违反公共利益。依靠经济上的优势，滥用所有权而损害公共利益时，其财产应予无偿没收，归全民所有。战犯及纳粹积极分子的企业应予没收而成为全民财产。为战争政策服务的私人企业亦同。超过一百公顷的私人土地所有权应予取消，并予无偿分配."

23 The Chinese translation reads "适于公有化的私人经济企业可按适用于征收的规定以法律收归公有."

24 The Chinese translation reads "无论何人不得利用私有财产损害社会。在社会利益需要时，得限制或征用私有财产，但必须根据法律行之。在何种场合并以何种数量补偿物主的财产价值，由法律规定之。在此种条件下，如社会利益需要时，得依法将某些经济部门或企业收归国有."

(*cont.*)

Constitutional texts	Relevant clauses
1952 Constitution of the People's Republic of Poland	Article 74: (3) Confiscation of property can only be done under conditions set by law and with conclusive judgment of the court.[25]
1952 Constitution of People's Republic of Romania	N/A
1940 Constitution of People's Republic of Mongolia	N/A
American constitution	The Fifth Amendment[26]
British constitution[27]	N/A
French constitution	French Constitutional Laws of 1875: N/A French Constitution of 1946: N/A
1919 Constitution of the German Reich (Weimar constitution)	Article 153: Property is guaranteed by the constitution. Laws determine its content and limitation. Expropriation may only be decreed based on valid laws and for the purpose of public welfare. It has to be executed with appropriate compensation, unless specified otherwise by Reich law. Regarding the amount of the compensation, the course of law at general courts has to be kept open in case of a controversy, unless Reich laws specify otherwise. Expropriations by the Reich at the expense of the states, communities or charitable organizations may only be executed if accompanied by appropriate compensation. Property obliges. Its use shall simultaneously be service for the public welfare.[28]

25 The Chinese translation reads "没收财产，只在法律规定的情形下并根据法院的确定判决，始得为之."

26 The Chinese translation reads "不得未经正当法律手续使其丧失生命, 自由或财产。凡私产，非有相当赔偿，不得收为公有."

27 This includes Magna Carta 1215, Habeas Corpus Act 1679, 1689, Parliament Act 1911, Representation of the People Act 1918 and Representation of the People Act 1928.

28 The Chinese translation reads "所有权，受宪法之保障。其内容及限制，以法律规定之。公用征收，仅限于裨益公共福利及有法律根据时，始得行之。公用征收，除联邦法律有特别规定外，应予相当赔偿。赔偿之多寡，如有争执时，除联邦宪法有特别规定外，准其在普通法院提起诉讼。联邦对于各邦自治区及公益团体行使公用征收权时，应给予赔偿。所有权为义务，其使用应同时为公共福利之役务."

(*cont.*)

Constitutional texts	Relevant clauses
	Article 155: The distribution and usage of land is supervised by the state in order to prevent abuse and in order to strive to secure healthy housing to all German families, especially those with many children. War veterans have to be given special consideration in the homestead law to be written. Land, the acquisition of which is necessary to answer the demand for housing, to promote settlement and cultivation of the soil and to elevate agricultural cultivation, may be expropriated . . . The owner of the land is obliged to the community to cultivate and exploit the soil. Any increase in the value of the land that does not result from the investment of labor or capital has to be made utilizable to the community.[29] Article 156: The Reich may transfer economic enterprises suited for nationalization into common property, if the Regulation for expropriation are obeyed and if compensation is paid. It may join in the administration of economic enterprises or syndicates or may order the states or communities to do so, or may otherwise assure its decisive influence.[30]
1874 Swiss Federal Constitution	Article 22: Land ownership is protected. To the extent allowed by their constitutional powers, the Confederation and the Cantons can, by

[29] The Chinese translation reads "土地之分配及利用，应由联邦监督，以防不当之使用，并加以监督，以期德国人均受保障，并有康健之住宅，及德国家庭尤其生齿繁多之家庭，得有家产住宅及业务之所需规定章则时，尤应特别注意参战人员。因应住宅之需要，奖励拓殖开垦或发展农业，土地所有权得征收之。家族内之土地财产应废止之。土地之耕种及开拓，为土地所有者对于社会之义务。土地价值之增加非由投资或人工而来者，其福利应归社会."

[30] The Chinese translation reads "联邦得依据法律，照公用征收之规定，将私人经济企业之适合于社会化者，予以赔偿收归公有。各邦或自治区得参与此类经济企业或组合之管理，或以其他方法，保持其一定之势力."

(*cont.*)

Constitutional texts	Relevant clauses
	legislation and for reasons of public interest, make provision for expropriation and restrictions on ownership. In cases of expropriation and restriction of ownership equivalent to expropriation, fair compensation shall be paid.[31]

31 The Chinese translation reads "土地所有权受保障。联邦和各州为了公共利益，可以在宪法授予的权内通过立法方式征用土地或施加限制。在实行征用或相当于征用的限制时，应付予公正的补偿."

APPENDIX 2

	Amount of cultivated land in 2005		Amount of preserved cultivated land				Amount of preserved PAL	
			2010		2020			
	Hectares (10000)	Mu (10000)	Hectares (10000)	Mu (10000)	Hectares (10000)	Mu (10000)	Hectares (10000)	Mu (10000)
China	12208.27	183124	12120.00	181800	12033.33	180500	10400.00	156000
Beijing	23.34	350	22.60	339	21.47	322	18.67	280
Tianjin	44.55	668	44.20	663	43.73	656	35.67	535
Hebei	641.04	9616	633.33	9500	630.27	9454	554.40	8316
Shanxi	408.16	6122	405.00	6075	400.27	6004	339.20	5088
Inner Mongolia	710.08	10651	705.13	10577	697.73	10466	608.13	9122
Liaoning	409.08	6136	408.00	6120	406.33	6095	354.13	5312
Jilin	553.68	8305	553.00	8295	551.93	8279	483.40	7251
Heilongjiang	1166.95	17504	1163.20	17448	1158.27	17374	1017.60	15264
Shanghai	27.31	410	25.80	387	24.93	374	21.87	328
Jiangsu	480.12	7202	476.20	7143	475.13	7127	421.53	6323
Zhejiang	194.77	2922	191.60	2874	189.07	2836	166.67	2500
Anhui	573.46	8602	571.80	8577	569.33	8540	490.73	7361
Fujian	135.40	2031	132.40	1986	127.33	1910	114.00	1710
Jiangxi	285.90	4289	282.53	4238	281.33	4220	242.73	3641
Shandong	751.89	11278	750.27	11254	747.87	11218	665.33	9980

(*cont.*)

	Amount of cultivated land in 2005		Amount of preserved cultivated land				Amount of preserved PAL	
			2010		2020			
	Hectares (10000)	Mu (10000)	Hectares (10000)	Mu (10000)	Hectares (10000)	Mu (10000)	Hectares (10000)	Mu (10000)
Henan	792.53	11888	791.47	11872	789.80	11847	678.33	10175
Hubei	467.52	7013	465.80	6987	463.13	6947	383.33	5750
Hunan	381.60	5724	378.73	5681	377.00	5655	323.53	4853
Guangdong	295.27	4429	291.40	4371	290.87	4363	255.60	3834
Guangxi	424.71	6371	421.33	6320	420.80	6312	360.27	5404
Hainan	72.76	1091	72.27	1084	71.80	1077	62.33	935
Chongqing	226.27	3394	221.67	3325	217.07	3256	183.33	2750
Sichuan	599.63	8994	594.80	8922	588.80	8832	513.73	7706
Guizhou	450.50	6757	443.80	6657	437.07	6556	361.73	5426
Yunnan	609.44	9142	604.87	9073	598.00	8970	495.40	7431
Tibet	36.08	541	35.73	536	35.27	529	29.20	438
Shaanxi	408.92	6134	399.07	5986	389.13	5837	352.27	5284
Gansu	466.77	7002	465.60	6984	464.60	6969	381.67	5725
Qinghai	54.22	813	54.00	810	53.60	804	43.40	651
Ningxia	109.99	1650	109.47	1642	108.67	1630	88.53	1328
Xinjiang	406.34	6095	404.93	6074	402.73	6041	353.27	5299

INDEX